Posthuman Feminism

For Anneke

Posthuman Feminism

Rosi Braidotti

polity

Copyright © Rosi Braidotti 2022

The right of Rosi Braidotti to be identified as Author of this Work has been asserted in accordance with the UK Copyright, Designs and Patents Act 1988.

First published in 2022 by Polity Press

Polity Press
65 Bridge Street
Cambridge CB2 1UR, UK

Polity Press
101 Station Landing
Suite 300
Medford, MA 02155, USA

All rights reserved. Except for the quotation of short passages for the purpose of criticism and review, no part of this publication may be reproduced, stored in a retrieval system or transmitted, in any form or by any means, electronic, mechanical, photocopying, recording or otherwise, without the prior permission of the publisher.

ISBN-13: 978-1-5095-1807-4
ISBN-13: 978-1-5095-1808-1 (pb)

A catalogue record for this book is available from the British Library.

Typeset in 10 on 12pt Sabon
by Fakenham Prepress Solutions, Fakenham, Norfolk NR21 8NL
Printed and bound by CPI Group (UK) Ltd, Croydon, CR0 4YY

The publisher has used its best endeavours to ensure that the URLs for external websites referred to in this book are correct and active at the time of going to press. However, the publisher has no responsibility for the websites and can make no guarantee that a site will remain live or that the content is or will remain appropriate.

Every effort has been made to trace all copyright holders, but if any have been overlooked the publisher will be pleased to include any necessary credits in any subsequent reprint or edition.

For further information on Polity, visit our website:
politybooks.com

Contents

Acknowledgements		*vi*
Introduction	Feminism by Any Other Name	1
Part I	**Posthuman Feminism as Critique**	**15**
Chapter 1	Feminism Is Not (Only) a Humanism	17
Chapter 2	The Critical Edge of Posthuman Feminism	43
Chapter 3	Decentring Anthropos: Ecofeminism Revisited	68
Part II	**Posthuman Feminism as Creation**	**105**
Chapter 4	New Materialism and Carnal Empiricism	107
Chapter 5	Technobodies: Gene- and Gender-editing	140
Chapter 6	Sexuality Beyond Gender: A Thousand Little Sexes	177
Chapter 7	Wanting Out!	211
Epilogue	'Get a Life!'	236
Notes		*243*
References		*251*
Index		*296*

Acknowledgements

This book would not have been possible without the loyal support of my publisher John Thompson; I truly thank him for his friendship and his enduring commitment to my posthuman project.

I had the honour and pleasure of completing the research for this manuscript at the University of Cambridge, where I was invited as Diane Middlebrook and Carl Djerassi Visiting Professor in Gender Studies in the Autumn term 2019. My sincere thanks to Jude Browne, Lauren Wilcox and Holly Porter for their warm and collegial support during my stay. My heartfelt thanks to Joanna Bush for all her precious professional assistance. In the same period I was honoured to be a visiting fellow at St. John's College, Cambridge. My sincere thanks to my sponsoring fellow, Ulinka Rublack for her friendly advice and mentorship, to the interim President of the College, Steve Edgley, and the deputy master Tim Whitmarsh for their warm welcome.

During the research phase of this book, I also greatly benefited from the discussions with colleagues from several academic institutions I had the honour to visit. My special thanks to Eléonore Lépinard and the Gender Studies Programme at the University of Lausanne in Switzerland, and to Marianne Hirsch of the Institute for Research on Women, Gender and Sexuality at Columbia University in New York.

Acknowledgements

Sections of this book were published in my chapter in the *Oxford Handbook of Feminist Theory* (eds. Lisa Disch and Mary Hawkesworth, 2016) and in *Anthropocene Feminism* (ed. Richard Grusin, 2017). I acknowledge them warmly here. Some earlier drafts were also published in the *Posthuman Glossary* that I co-edited with Maria Hlavajova (2018).

My sincere thanks to Genevieve Lloyd and Donna Haraway for their unflinching support and enlightening criticism. They are precious multi-species travelling companions of my writings. Thanks to Simone Bignall and Matthew Fuller and for their generous insights and theoretical advice.

I am much indebted to Emily Jones for her generous and informed reading of the manuscript and her rigorous comments. Warm thanks also to Beth Lord, Celia Roberts, Djurdja Trajkovic, Maureen McNeil, Christine Daigle, Nina Lykke and Maurita Harney for their comments and support. Thanks also to Premesh Lalu, Sarah Nuttall and J. Halberstam for lively and necessary conversations. Thank you Linda Dement for the stunning image for the cover.

I am grateful to Marlise Mensink and Mischa Peters for their warm friendship. I also wish to thank my personal research assistants Gry Ulstein, Evelien Geerts, Lauren Hoogen Stoevenbeld and especially Onessa Novak for their unfailing logistical and organizational assistance.

Finally, my gratitude to my life partner Anneke Smelik for her intellectual, emotional and moral support, and for the joy of our life together.

Introduction: Feminism by Any Other Name

'Don't agonize, organize!'

Flo Kennedy, 1971[1]

What a time to dare to take on the present, defined as the record of what we are ceasing to be, and the seed of what we are in the process of becoming!

Flashback to 1992: at the physical site of the watershed art exhibition *Post Human* (Deitch, 1992), a giant female figure of an Armani-clad business woman confidently welcomed visitors to the show. This cutting-edge exhibition displayed multiple variations of the new micro-femininities being constructed at that moment in technological culture. The curator Jeffrey Deitch captured the avant-garde spirit of the age by foregrounding the role of technology in blurring the binary boundaries between subjects and objects, humans and non-humans. The exhibition showed that body improvement and the embrace of artificiality were becoming the norm: plastic surgery, dieting, exercises, mind-altering drugs and other practices enhance the humans beyond their dreams. The *Post Human* showed also that art assumed a much more central role as it merged with science, computerization and biotechnology in further re-shaping the human form and perfecting a flair for the artificial. The message was clear: the pleasures of the inorganic have become second nature, producing a deeper intimacy with technological artefacts.

And the contradictions surrounding the female bodies were at the heart of this very first exhibition on the posthuman.

Fast forward to 2013. During her 'Mrs. Carter Show World Tour', American singer Beyoncé flashed the word 'Feminist' in shining letters across the stage and sang her feminist anthem 'Flawless' from the hit album *Lemonade*. Throughout this performance, Beyoncé repeated, like a mantra, the following definition, taken from the work of Chimamanda Ngozi Adichie: 'Feminist: a person who believes in the social, political and economic equality of the sexes.' Simple and to the point, who could quarrel with that?

Well, some actually did. Celebated black feminist bell hooks, for instance, voiced critcism of celebrity media culture and of the explicitly sexualized nature of Beyoncé's performances (hooks, 2016). This stirred quite a controversy (Gay, 2014c; Plate, 2019). But what is striking is that a mega-star like Beyoncé is actually entering the feminist debate at all. She is defending the equality-minded feminist agenda and interrogating her own politics of locations as a black woman, a sexed female and a passionate professional. And she is not alone. Media mogul Oprah Winfrey is also up there while other feminist celebrities today include Hillary Clinton, Emma Watson, Michelle Obama, Ellen de Generis, Caitlyn Jenner, Laverne Cox, Lady Gaga and many more (Hamad and Taylor, 2015). There is no aspect of contemporary popular culture where feminists, emancipation-minded, anti-racist and LGBTQ+ people have not made their mark. What was blasphemy thirty years ago is banality today, livestreaming from our home screens.

In this book I unravel the deep imbrications between the two 'isms' that are so dear to my heart: feminism and posthumanism. The claim of this book is that mainstream posthuman scholarship has neglected feminist theory, while in fact feminist theory is one of the precursors of the posthuman turn. *Posthuman Feminism* aims to fill that missing link and argues that they are two sides of the same coin. This intellectual endeavour is urgent because we live in times of what I have called the posthuman convergence in the two predecessors to this book, *The Posthuman* (Braidotti, 2013) and *Posthuman Knowledge* (Braidotti, 2019). The present book builds on and expands from the two previous volumes, exploring the consequences for feminism of thinking through and with posthuman theory. In keeping with my approach, I refer to the posthuman as both a marker of present conditions and as a navigational tool. In both cases the term aims to assist in reaching a more adequate understanding of the challenges confronting us in today's world and in steering a course across them. More specifically, I want to detect and assess emergent trends in contemporary feminist theory and practice.

Feminism is by now an established social movement, greatly diversified across multiple constituencies and locations. It is therefore not easy to give a comprehensive definition, other than pointing to a broad range of feminist positions. The spectrum includes the quest for equality between men and women, the recognition of multiple genders, the abolition of gender identities altogether, the intersectional connections across gender, race and class, and more. Feminism is the struggle to empower those who live along multiple axes of inequality. It involves empowering the dispossessed and impoverished, not only women, but also LGBTQ+ people, people of colour, Black and Indigenous peoples. In that sense, feminism is not just an egalitarian movement for the mainstream, but also a transformative decolonial and radical struggle to affirm positively the differences among marginalized people(s). These differences of material location express different life experiences and also multiple ways of knowing. The radical spark of the feminist project for me lies in its subversive politics. It means creating the alternative visions of 'the human' generated by people who were historically excluded from, or only partially included into, that category. It means creating other possible worlds. This transformative edge assumes that no emancipatory process, however partial, is ever completely subsumed or incorporated into the dominant socio-economic life conditions, to which it is attached by critical opposition. Margins of intervention remain available, albeit as virtual potential. The trick is how to activate them.

By posthuman convergence I mean to indicate the present historical condition of the Anthropocene – not a utopian future – that is marked by three momentous and interconnecting changes. First, at the social level we witness increasing structural injustices through the unequal distribution of wealth, prosperity and access to technology. Second, at the environmental level we are confronted with the devastation of species and a decaying planet, struck by climate crisis and new epidemics. And third, at the technological level, the status and condition of the human is being redefined by the life sciences and genomics, neural sciences and robotics, nanotechnologies, the new information technologies and the digital interconnections they afford us.

The COVID-19 pandemic that is raging as I am writing is emblematic of the posthuman convergence. It is a human-made disaster aggravated by undue interference in the ecological balance and the lives of multiple species. The pandemic foregrounds the importance of human/non-human interaction and its destructive, as well as generative, potential. Paradoxically, the contagion has resulted in an increased use of technology and digital mediation, as well as enhanced hopes for vaccines and bio-medical solutions. It has thus intensified the humans' reliance on the very high-tech economy of cognitive capitalism that caused the problems in the first place.

Living with these internally contradictory developments is part of our historical deal. Thinking adequately about them is an urgent task for feminist thought, all the more so because the posthuman turn is marked by fundamental disruptions of received understandings of what it means to be human. The blatant inequalities exposed by the COVID-19 pandemic such as the disproportionate loss of lives among women, LGBTQ+ and ethnic minorities and socially underprivileged people, brings home a reality that feminist, postcolonial and race thinkers had already voiced: that the 'human' is neither universal nor neutral but shot through with power relations organizing access to privileges and entitlements (Hammonds, 2020).

Advanced capitalism is at the core of the disruptions that characterize the posthuman convergence, its advanced technologies barely concealing the brutality of the social injustices it enforces. The combined pressures of these power mechanisms are simultaneously uniting humanity in the threat of extinction and dividing it by controlling access to the resources needed to meet the challenge. The economically dispossessed and impoverished are missing out on the advantages and profits of advanced capitalism and are in fact the most exposed to the lethal effects of ecological depletion and global pandemics. The posthuman convergence thus makes for polarized socio-economic divergences, as well as manic-depressive swings of moods and emotions. Excitement and exhilaration in view of the advanced technologies and automation that drive the 'Fourth Industrial Age' (Schwab, 2015), alternate with exasperation and fear at the thought of the damages inflicted by the 'Sixth Extinction', the potential mass extinction of both human and non-human inhabitants of this planet (Kolbert, 2014). The affective economy of the posthuman convergence is characterized by suffering interchanging with hope, fear unfolding into resilience, and anxiety flipping into action.

A pandemic on the scale of COVID-19 brings home to the Western world an ancient truth, carried by Indigenous philosophies and cosmologies: that 'we' are all in this planetary condition together whether we are humans or others. It is high time for this heterogeneous and collective 'we' to move beyond the Eurocentric as well as humanistic habits that have formatted it, and to dislodge the philosophical anthropocentrism they entail and enforce.

This shift of perspective underscores the need for posthuman feminist theory. In this book I will address questions such as: how do emancipatory political movements position themselves within the posthuman convergence? How do these already complex intersections between advanced technology and accelerating environmental crisis affect the feminist agenda for intersectional social justice, transnational environmental justice, and women's and LGBTQ+ people's rights?

In a concomitance of events that marks the extraordinary period we are going through, the voices, experiences and perspectives of multiple others are bursting all around us. The power of viral formations has become manifest in the pandemic, stressing the agency of non-human forces and the overall importance of Gaia as a living, symbiotic planet (Lovelock and Margulis, 1974). At the same time a global revolt against endemic – and indeed viral – racism took off in the fateful year 2020, led by the 'Black Lives Matter' movement. The feminist mass mobilization epitomized by the #NiUnaMenos and #MeToo movements continues to fight globally. As these multiple crises unfold, the politics of sexualized, racialized, naturalized minorities – the 'others' – are moving centre stage, pushing dominant 'man' (or Anthropos) off-centre.

Posthuman feminism is thus a critical intervention in some of the most controversial and urgent contemporary debates about the ongoing transformations of the human. The feminist agenda of the posthuman convergence is the analysis of the intersection of powerful structural socio-economic forces, led by technological development, in combination with equally powerful environmental challenges, centred on the climate crisis. These multiple factors join forces in dislocating the centrality of humans and require new definitions and practices of what being human may mean.

Posthuman feminism revives the radical tradition by offering an updated analysis of advanced capitalism – not only its sophisticated technologies but also its brutal environmental deterioration. In this book I argue that posthuman feminism offers a more adequate analysis of contemporary relations of power, because it has relinquished the liberal vision of the autonomous individual as well as the socialist ideal of a privileged revolutionary subject. Whereas liberal feminism is perfectly attuned to capitalism and socialist feminism dialectically opposed to it, posthuman feminism attempts a more nuanced position while keeping a critical distance from both. Building on the radical insights of ecofeminism, feminist studies of technoscience, LGBTQ+ theories, Black, decolonial and Indigenous feminisms, posthuman feminists stretch in multiple, rhizomic and tentacular directions. A posthuman feminist framework encourages a different notion of political subjectivity as a heterogeneous assemblage of embodied and embedded humans.

The posthuman turn is about the becoming-otherwise-human of feminist and critical theory. The converse is equally true: those who do not fully occupy the position of human subjects, in the fullness of the rights and entitlements that notion entails, have a unique vantage point about what counts as the unit of reference for a re-definition of the human. My argument will remain what it has been all along in my work on critical posthuman theory: the posthuman turn can result in a renewal of subjectivities and practices by situating feminist analyses productively in the present.

It may be difficult for people who have never been considered socially and politically fully human to adopt an affirmative relation to the posthuman predicament. Women, LGBTQ+ people, the colonized, Indigenous peoples, people of colour and a multitude of non-Europeans who historically have had to fight for the basic right to be considered and treated as human, have at best an ambivalent relationship to the humanity they were and continue to be denied admission to. But my point is that this dominant, exclusionary notion of the human is precisely what is challenged by the posthuman convergence. While multiple new scenarios are circulating about the transformation of the humans, it is crucial that the voices of the marginals should be heard. The insights and critical knowledge of those who are considered less than human is urgently needed in the debates on the posthuman, both for their own sake and for the common good. The vital and more democratic project is to combine social justice and bottom-up, community-based experiments with transforming the ways in which we are becoming (post) human. These processes imply dense webs of interaction with and through the new technological universe, but also demand awareness of their environmental groundings and responsibilities.

My argument cuts both ways: first, feminist theory and practice are a major factor in defining the contemporary posthuman predicament. Some strands of feminist theory – not always the more dominant ones – are generative hubs that have inspired critical posthuman insights. I want to urge contemporary feminist theory to engage more actively with the public debates on the posthuman convergence and with mainstream posthuman scholarship. I will highlight throughout the book the original contributions of feminism to the making of distinctly posthuman ways of understanding the world and redefining politics.

Second, mainstream posthuman scholarship must make an effort to move beyond its self-referential insular tendencies and engage openly with feminist theories, including the minoritarian strands that may not be as central to the canonical Anglo-American tradition. Posthuman critical theories cannot continue to indulge in their masculinist and Eurocentric solipsism. It would be mutually beneficial if feminist theory and posthuman theory would exchange and dialogue more systematically.

Feminists working on the posthuman convergence have to confront another fundamental tension: 'we' feminists may well be confronting the threats and challenges of the third millennium, together, but 'we' are not One or the same. We are differently positioned in terms of the very historical conditions of power, entitlement and access that define us: not only are we not the same as Man, but 'we' feminists have never been a homogeneous, unitary notion among ourselves: we are otherwise others. This book does not take the feminist community for granted as a pre-constituted and institutionalized entity; instead, I formulate the 'we' as: 'we'-are-not-one-and-the-same-but-we-differ.

The context points to the necessity of rethinking subjectivity as a web of interconnections, acknowledging that 'we' – all living entities – share the same planetary home, though we differ in terms of locations and access to environmental, social and legal entitlements, technologies, safety, prosperity and good health services. The materially embedded differences in location that separate us do not detract from our shared intimacy with the world, our terrestrial *milieu*. 'We' are in *this* together. This leads me to the sentence I developed in *Posthuman Knowledge* (2019), and that will recur throughout this book as well: '"we"-who-are-not-one-and-the-same-but-are-in-*this*-together'.

Posthuman feminists aspire to nurture and implement the ongoing process of unfolding alternative and transformative paths of becoming. We need to work together to reconstruct our shared understanding of possible posthuman futures that will include solidarity, care and compassion. We need to do so while rejecting universal and fixed notions of who 'we' are, respecting differences of locations and power. The politics of immanent locations allows for a non-oppositional mode of critique and enables affirmative engagement.

To those who fear that emphasizing the 'post' in the posthuman may result in short-circuiting the process of emancipation of the devalorized others who were not considered fully human to begin with, I reply that I share their concern. But I would add that it is becoming painfully clear that those who are marked negatively as the dehumanized and marginalized 'others' are currently missing out on the profits and advantages of the fourth industrial revolution, while being excessively exposed to the ravages of climate change and pandemics. Mindful that 50 per cent of carbon emissions are produced by the wealthiest 10 per cent of the population, one can only concur with Greta Thunberg that 'the people who have contributed the least to the crisis are the ones who are going to be affected the most' (2019: 24). This is the cruel imbalance that posthuman feminism wants to address. In other words, the posthuman condition is neither post-power nor post-injustice. The emphasis on 'post' in the posthuman rather implies a move forward, beyond traditional understandings of the human, so that the analyses of contemporary power and knowledge become an essential part of the feminist posthuman project.

A Posthuman Feminist Agenda

Posthuman Feminism is an intergenerational and transversal exercise in constructing a discursive community that cares for the state of the world and wants to intervene productively in it. Intergenerational, because the book reconnects to different feminist genealogies, archives and counter-memories across space and time and does not stay within the contemporary or dominant theories. By transversal, I mean a relational way of thinking by cross-referencing through categories and disciplines. It desegregates the domains of knowledge production, by creating connections and cultivating resonances among positions that may at first sight appear incompatible. Intergenerational and transversal thinking helps create the collective 'we' that makes for a chain of solidarity between the 'others', while respecting the different perspectives and lived realities of each. Intergenerational and transversal subjects are allied but differentiated, and all other differences notwithstanding, they affirm that 'we' are in this together, but we are not one and the same.

The book inscribes the feminist subject in a social context framed by multiple mediations in the posthuman convergence we live in. I propose that feminism is a relational ethics that assumes one gives enough of a damn about the world to look at the broader picture and try to minimize the fractures. Affirmative relational ethics is the value that can support the task of telling the difference between profit-minded, entropic flows of self-interest and generous, empowering flows of solidarity. This is where the collective praxis of constructing social horizons of hope and affirmation becomes essential.

To address these complex questions, I will present the building blocks of posthuman feminism and analyse the distinctive features of its agenda. The book has two parts: the first offering a critique of humanism and anthropocentrism and the second outlining the creative theoretical and practical aspects of the posthuman feminist agenda. Throughout the book I will highlight the contributions of different strands of feminism as forerunners of posthuman ideas and methods across several generations of feminist scholars and multiple fields of research and activism. This means I will offer large amounts of explanatory material, a critical selection of key texts and a rich bibliography to honour and preserve the memory of the diverse genealogies of feminism.

Part I, 'Posthuman Feminism as Critique', starts with the chapter 'Feminism Is Not (Only) a Humanism', in which I outline the feminist critiques of humanism as an exclusive practice that supports structural inequalities and forms of social and symbolic disqualification. Humanism upholds an implicit and partial definition of the human, while claiming to provide a universal and neutral representation of all humans. This dominant idea of the human is based on an assumption of superiority by a subject that is male, white, Eurocentric, practising compulsory heterosexuality and reproduction, able-bodied, urbanized, speaking a standard language. This subject is the hierarchical 'Man of Reason' (Lloyd, 1984) that feminists, LGBTQ+ people, anti-racists, Black, Indigenous, postcolonial and ecological activists have been criticizing for decades. At the same time humanism historically supported a political programme of emancipation that benefited some of the sexualized and racialized minorities. The chapter carefully traces the contradictions and the limitations of the humanist legacy as well as its lasting appeal.

In chapter 2, 'The Critical Edge of Posthuman Feminism', I look at contemporary elaborations of different schools of feminism, notably the liberal and the socialist traditions. Situating them in the posthuman convergence, I analyse neoliberal and neo-socialist feminisms in terms of their respective relationships to humanism, power and politics. I single out their interaction with the mutations of advanced capitalism, in terms of technological developments on the one hand, and investment in living systems on the other. Adaptable in its pursuit of profit, contemporary capitalism perpetuates old inequalities while inventing some new ones. The capitalization of living matter through technological intervention is embraced by transhumanists as a way of enhancing the human, but meets with sceptical receptions by posthuman feminists. It calls for more complex frames of analysis of the interaction between capital, science, technology and social justice.

In chapter 3, 'Decentring Anthropos: Ecofeminism Revisited', I argue that human exceptionalism needs to be challenged from within by decentring anthropocentrism. It is not only the case that not all humans are the same to begin with, but also that the entire category of humans is distinct from all, and assumed to be superior to other, species. The naturalized others are excluded categorically from the realm of subjectivity and rights. Appeals to 'nature' can be discriminatory as they create structural distinctions and inequalities among different categories of beings, always favouring the humans. Posthuman feminism is innovative because it extends the analyses of sexualized and racialized hierarchies to the naturalized differences of non-human entities. It calls for the recognition of species equality and a more collaborative sense of interdependence between humans and animals, plants, the earth and the planet as a whole. The chapter examines in detail ecofeminism and Indigenous feminisms as the precursors of the post-anthropocentric turn in feminist theory and as a crucial building block of the posthuman turn.

Part II, 'Posthuman Feminism as Creation' brings together the creative writings of theorists, artists and practitioners of posthuman feminism.

In chapter 4, 'New Materialism and Carnal Empiricism', I argue that while a specific form of situated materialism is central to feminist theory, it has been slightly overshadowed by an emphasis on social-constructivist methods. New-materialist feminism is a precursor of the posthuman turn because it stresses the embodied, embedded and sexuate roots of all material entities, humans included. The strength and relevance of new-materialist feminist thought is to defy binary oppositions by thinking through embodiment, multiplicity and differences. Posthuman feminism challenges the opposition of nature versus culture and argues for a 'natureculture' continuum to enable a better understanding of the mutual interdependence of human and non-human others. Many appeal to a critical Spinozist perspective to strengthen this claim. I analyse these approaches as a strategic form of re-naturalization. In the context of the climate change crisis, posthuman feminism shows the extent to which women, LGBTQ+ people and Indigenous people are exposed to risks and hazards. It also proposes new relational practices and ethical values to strengthen cross-cultures and cross-species collaboration.

In chapter 5, 'Technobodies: Gene- and Gender-editing', I claim that mainstream posthuman scholarship has marginalized or even obliterated the material bodies of all entities, humans included, through an emphasis on technological mediation and enhancement. But, as feminist new materialism confirms, bodies matter – even though nowadays bodies have mutated into complex relational nodes. Human bodies are in a continuum with the non-human on two fronts. The first is animal life (*zoe*) in its diversity, aware of their grounding on an endangered planet (*geo*). The second is the sharp awareness of being fully immersed in technological mediation (*techno*). Hence the assemblage of what I call '*zoe*/geo/technobodies'. I see this approach as a critical form of de-naturalization. Bodies are neither natural nor cultural but in constant process between them, as a heterogeneous assemblage of complex relational components. The corporeal empiricism at work in posthuman feminism is the source of counter-knowledges, methods and values. The chapter examines in detail feminist technoscience studies and disability studies as the precursor of the post-anthropocentric turn in feminist theory and as a key building block of the posthuman turn.

In chapter 6, 'Sexuality Beyond Gender: A Thousand Little Sexes', I examine the implications of the new-materialist, posthumanist and post-anthropocentric approach for the analyses of contemporary formations of sexuality. I argue that posthuman feminism implies a redefinition of sexuality as an elemental and cross-species force that precedes and exceeds the inscriptions of a binary gender system. I will examine the implications of this position for a reappraisal of the elemental pleasures of materialist posthuman flesh – the powers of Eros – beyond gender dualism. Reference to Indigenous cosmological systems will illuminate the generative power of sexuality and its profound relational ethics. A feminist genealogy of transgressive sexual radicals contextualizes contemporary queer and trans sexualities. The chapter examines the work of feminist literary and visual artists, including Virginia Woolf as the precursor of a molecular sensibility in posthuman feminism.

In chapter 7, 'Wanting Out!', I address the creative, imaginative and speculative strands of posthuman feminism. Arguing for the importance of the radical imagination to the feminist posthuman project, I look at different examples of this specific style, ranging from figurative thinking in academic feminist scholarship, to science fiction, fantasy novels, utopian texts of a political or fantastic nature, through Afrofuturism and black space-travel narratives. The speculative genre voices the transversal alliance of sexualized, racialized, naturalized others against the dominion of Man/Anthropos. It combines dystopian and utopian elements in envisaging alternative feminist futures. The chapter ends with a feminist assessment of the economics and politics of the contemporary race for new materials in far-away regions and in outer space.

Finally, in the short Epilogue, 'Get a Life', I concentrate on the ethical implications of the feminist posthuman agenda in a world damaged by the tensions and contradictions of the posthuman convergence. I argue that the radical feminist imagination can be a source of inspiration for new scenarios of endurance and reconstruction. This is all the more relevant for a world haunted by a lethal pandemic and the need to reconstruct communities in highly divisive and painful times. An affirmative posthuman ethics entails the composition of communities sharing the same imaginings and values. It involves imagining a collective subject as the 'we' who are not one and the same, though we are in *this* posthuman predicament together.

Posthuman Feminism aims to be a navigational tool as well as a conceptual toolbox: it offers a series of roadmaps into and out of the posthuman convergence. This is a book that longs to be active outside the written page. It wishes to be out there with the other entities that are trying to negotiate an affirmative path amidst the speed and the paralysis, the boom and bust, of the posthuman convergence.

The book connects to and works across different temporalities. Crucial to feminist politics is the memory of oppression – of the injury and pain of exclusion and injustice. That kind of memory is made of repetitions of often traumatic events and ideas that we do not so much remember but rather refuse to forget. Activist time is made of zigzagging detours that bring productive repetitions to bear on the ethical orientations and the political praxis of the present. Feminists today are struggling through the contemporary posthuman turn with concern, but also with curiosity, wondering what's in it for them. What is the posthuman future of those who were never fully human? And what is the time measure of the posthuman feminist cause? Now, forever, and all at once is the time of feminism.

For feminist activists it is always the year zero, even after thousands of years of oppression and struggle for liberation across many feminist plateaus of movements and counter-movements. What is at stake in feminism is human freedom. This is the process of liberation as the ongoing eventualization of many virtual pasts, of many radical ideas that never quite made it, but never quite died either. Feminism is an affirmative gesture, a leap of faith in what humans may still be capable of. The positive becoming of posthuman feminism expresses a trust in the future, which allows not so much a flash-back nor a flash-forward, but a 'back-cast'; casting paths of becoming from the future back to the now. The agenda of feminism is truly present, but still unfulfilled, and truly past, though highly relevant to a present that is trying to become an actual, sustainable future. Inexhaustible and always about to self-combust back into life, feminism, by any other name, endures.

Part I
Posthuman Feminism as Critique

Chapter 1
Feminism Is Not (Only) a Humanism

> He he he he and he and he and and he and he and he and and as and as he and as he and he.
> He is and as he is, and as he is and he is,
> he is and as he
>
> Gertrude Stein, *If I told him*, 1923

The main tenet of posthuman feminism is that the notion of humanism needs to be reviewed and assessed critically but not thrown away entirely. The posthuman predicament assumes the relative success of equality-minded feminism. This chapter lays the groundwork by first briefly explaining the masculinist roots of Eurocentric humanism as well as its philosophical critiques. It will then proceed by giving a genealogy of the historical ties that bind Western feminism to humanism. Humanism is the backbone of the women's emancipation project carried out in three major bodies of thought proclaiming universal human rights: classical liberalism; socialist humanism; and Black, anti-colonialist, anti-racist and Indigenous voices. The chapter ends with an evaluation of how LGBTQ+ theories and practices are positioned in the aftermath of humanism. They pursue a similar project of emancipation with claims to equality and struggles for recognition and justice, but they radically move away from the normative idea of the human built into humanism, 'queering' it into *in*humanism.

The Man of Reason as the Image of Humanism

Humanism has helped construct liberal democracies by upholding the separation of Church from State and instigating fundamental freedom under the rule of law. From the Enlightenment, humanism took its emancipatory belief in the universal powers of scientific reason and faith in technological progress, as well as adjacent values such as secular tolerance and equality for all. As such, humanism supports the Western project of modernity, including its industrial, imperialist and bellicose inclinations (Davies, 1997).

The main version of humanism that plays out in the posthuman convergence is a retake on the European renaissance ideal of the human as 'the measure of all things' or the 'Man of Reason' (Lloyd, 1984). This European humanist ideal positions the universalizing powers of a sovereign notion of reason as the basic unit of reference to define what counts as human. This hegemonic idea of 'Man' as coinciding with universal reason also claims exclusive rights to self-regulating rational judgement, moral self-improvement and enlightened governance for European subjects. That image was represented visually by Leonardo in the famous sketch of the Vetruvian body as the perfectly proportioned, healthy, male and white model, which became the golden mean for classical aesthetics and architecture (Braidotti, 2013). The human thus defined is not so much a species as a marker of European culture and society and for the scientific and technological activities it privileges.

The humanist values and their rationalist underpinnings apply both to individuals and to groups operating within scientific and moral criteria of human perfectibility. They thus act as the motor of human evolution coinciding with the teleological progress of human civilization (intrinsically assumed to be European) through science and technology. The 'Man' of classical humanism was positioned at the pinnacle of an evolutionary scale, which classified different classes of beings lower down the hierarchical ranks and files. They are the 'others' defined as the negative opposites of the dominant human norm.[1] The point here is that difference, being 'other than' or 'different from' 'Man', is actually negatively perceived as 'worth less than'

'Man'. This epistemic and symbolic exclusion is no abstraction: it translates into ruthless violence for the real-life people who happen to coincide with categories of negative difference. They are the women and LGBTQ+ people (sexualized others), Black and Indigenous people (racialized others) and the animals, plants and earth entities (naturalized others). Their social and symbolic existence was denied, leaving them disposable and unprotected. They are multiple and disqualified, whereas 'Man' is One and fully entitled.

The power of 'Man' as a hegemonic civilizational model was instrumental to the project of Western modernity and the colonial ideology of European expansion. 'White Man's burden' as a tool of imperialist and patriarchal governance assumed that Europe is not just a geo-political location, but rather a universal attribute of human consciousness that can transfer its quality to any suitable subjects, provided they comply with the required discipline. Europe as superior universal consciousness posits the power of reason as its distinctive characteristic and humanistic universalism as its particularity. It encloses an allegedly universal notion of reason within 'the snowy masculinist precincts of European philosophy' and its relentless pursuit of gaining material access to real-life others (Weheliye, 2014: 47).

Controlled by white, European, heterosexual, property-owning, male, legal citizens, mainstream humanistic culture upholds dominant memory and selects who gets to write official history. It functions as a centralized databank that edits out and de-selects the existence, activities, practices as well as the alternative or subjugated memories of the multiple sexualized and racialized minorities (Wynter, 2015). Think, for instance, of the extent to which European mythologies, National Art Galleries, Science and Natural History museums are filled with signs and traces of the subjugation of women, Black and Indigenous people, animal and earth others (Ang, 2019). Their representations are overdetermined and depicted as necessarily absent, excluded from the centre stage. These multitudes of others are as plentiful as they are nameless: so many Indigenous people, Orientalized women, exotic birds, captive Africans, devious mermaids and scary monsters of all denominations abound, but there is only ever one 'Man'. In the *Odyssey*, the archetypical figure of Odysseus goes by the name of 'Nobody', representing all men and as such becoming the negative of 'everybody'.[2] Man, thus defined is the zero degree of otherness or deviation from the human standard he embodies and projects to normative heights. Like a blank that can be endlessly refilled, he who-shall-not-be-named is entitled to call all others by his name. The mythologized Man in the figure of Odysseus is the face of Anthropos in Western culture.

Disenchantment with the Humanist Figure of 'Man'

There is a strong European philosophical genealogy of critical reassessment of humanism in modernity, starting with the controversial case of Nietzsche, and moving beyond. As early as 1933, Freud and Einstein pointed out in their correspondence – published as the pamphlet *Why War?* – that the relationship between humans and science was broken. Technologically driven modern warfare was revealing the depth of the collective death drive (*Thanatos*) and humans' fatal attraction for self-destruction. The post-war generation of Continental philosophers expressed their disenchantment with the unfulfilled promises of the humanist belief in science-driven progress and false announcements of equality-for-all. They proposed a critical break from the exclusionary version of humanism that positions Eurocentric 'Man' as the alleged universal measure of human progress.

In the 1950s, anti-colonialist psychiatrist Franz Fanon exposed the depth of irrational and traumatizing violence that drove European domination of the colonized dispossessed others. Jean-Paul Sartre stated plainly that Europe had betrayed the humanist ideal in the colonies and the concentration camps of the Second World War and exposed the complicity of humanism with both fascism and colonialism. In keeping with postcolonial thought, Sartre endorsed a possible renewal of this concept through non-Western humanisms, notably in his preface to Fanon's *Wretched of the Earth* (1963 [1961]). In the 1961 meditation *Has Man a Future?*, Bertrand Russell excoriated the hypocrisy of the scientific community regarding the irrationality of nuclear weapons and assessed future technological options for humanity rather negatively. The role of science in enabling nuclear doom – rather than enlightened human progress – weighed heavily upon that generation.

Beauvoir's feminist humanism (1973 [1949]) was multi-layered but at some level quite familiar, in that her vision emphasized women's equality that has since become mainstream. Equality is defined with reference to the rights and entitlements enjoyed by men, and the feminist project consisted for Beauvoir in balancing the power relations between the two sexes.[3] Emphasizing citizenship rights, but also the symbolic representation of women as capable of transcendence, and hence of higher levels of consciousness, Beauvoir targeted the patriarchal arguments for the alleged inferiority of women and tore them to pieces. She argued that patriarchal culture is not dominant because it is superior rationally, epistemically or morally. It is rather the case that, being dominant, it has appropriated the rational, epistemic and moral means to build its hegemonic hold over the social and symbolic structures, including knowledge production, science and technology. Another significant level of Beauvoir's humanism concerned her socialist creed: she followed Marxist humanism in arguing that the full potential of all humans, and especially of women, has been thwarted by capitalism. Only a full-scale socialist revolution can liberate women, and men, by transforming society radically. Beauvoir never questioned the validity or power of the model of the human built into the feminist emancipatory and socialist politics, but wanted to open it up to the excluded.

Critiques of the tradition of humanism grew in the 1970s when the second wave of feminism arose, the Black anti-racist movement took off, the decolonialization movement unfolded, gay liberation started, radical ecology blossomed, and youth rebellions multiplied. Those radical social movements of the 1970s, in the context of the Cold War, challenged both the unfulfilled promises of Western democracies and the never-achieved utopias of the Marxist revolutionary programme (Judt, 2005). Their aims and constituencies often overlapped, with many socialist feminists doubling up as ecofeminists and peace activists.[4] Gilles Deleuze and Felix Guattari (1977) assessed historical and contemporary forms of European fascism[5] as the sign of the definitive failure of humanism. Michel Serres (2016) added to this list of grievances the technologically driven Hiroshima and Nagasaki genocides by the US military. He attacked the contemporary 'thanatocracy' and its uses of science to destroy humanity and its planetary home. Derrida (1984) also commented on the nuclear end-time and pointed out that flawed humanism and anthropocentric exceptionalism threaten the well-being and survival of all species, including our own.

Both the horrors of the Second World War and the nuclear era in the Cold War that followed had turned upside down the Enlightenment promise of liberating mankind through scientific rationality. Foucault (1970) drew his own conclusions from these critical insights in his famous thesis about the death of 'Man'. He argued that the historical project of humanism, a pillar of European modernity and of its rationalist, technological development, was reaching the end of its historical cycle and was destined soon to be over. That particular 'Man' is dead and his zombified replicants are quite scary. What was left over from European humanism is a glorious tradition of texts and a mixed history of world events. They need to be reassessed critically in terms of the systemic patterns of sexualized, racialized and naturalized exclusions which they endorsed, operationalized and hence made thinkable. This passing of 'Man' was not merely a negative comment, as the end of a specific – and for Foucault relatively recent – vision of the human. It was meant also as an affirmative inauguration of new processes of knowledge and insights about life, living systems and what constitutes the human in all of its complexities and multiplicities.

Let it be noted, however, that the announcement of the death of that Man of Reason may have been exaggerated and that he may still be quite capable of multiple after-lives. The NASA-led explorations of outer space, for instance, adopted the Vitruvian Renaissance representation of that human as the badge for their missions. That image was therefore sewed onto the astronauts' suits and has been flying on the flag that was planted on the surface of the Moon on 20 July 1969. As we shall see later, the project of human enhancement and intergalactic expansion is not necessarily incompatible with humanism.

The vicissitudes of philosophical critiques of humanism followed their own itinerary (Soper, 1986), intersecting productively, but not always necessarily coinciding with discussions about the status of the human in feminist, anti-racist, decolonial and Indigenous theories. There are several variations on the theme of humanism at stake within the feminist traditions, which are often oblivious to the lament about the crisis and decline of 'Man'.

Feminist Liberal Humanism: Gender Equality

The status of the human is central to feminist, anti-racist, decolonial and Indigenous thought, basically foregrounding the highly contested question: how inclusive and representative is the idea of the human implicit in the allegedly universal humanist idea of 'Man'? Can I, as a woman, Black, Indigenous, LGBTQ+ person, claim access to that humanist idea and ideal? Why were the sexualized and racialized others excluded in the first place? And how can I get included in so far as my exclusion was justified in terms of my alleged deficiencies and shortcomings in relation to the white, masculine ideal? If my exclusion is instrumental to the definition of that privileged subject position and I am the constitutive outside of 'Man', how can I ever hope to be included? If the excluded, disqualified and deselected others want to be included, the dominant image of 'Man' must change from within. Equality is not about sameness. And to be different-from does not have to mean to be worth less-than.

Feminist and anti-racist critiques of the idea of a common undifferentiated humanity and the claim to humanist universalism, were raised from the eighteenth century onwards, for instance by Olympe de Gouges (1791) on behalf of women, and by Toussaint Louverture (2011) on behalf of enslaved and colonized people. They both reacted against the flagrant violation of the very human rights asserted in the French Universal Declaration of 1789. They criticized respectively the exclusion of women from civic and political rights and the inhumane violence of slavery and colonial dispossession. All claims to universalism lose credibility when confronted by such abuses of power. Both de Gouges and Louverture paid a heavy price for their daring: Olympe was promptly dispatched to the guillotine while Toussaint was deposed by the French imperial army. So much for universal brotherhood – and of sisterhood nothing more shall be said for a few centuries (Morgan, 1970).

The humanist motif that women's liberation is human liberation, and that women's and LGBTQ+ people's rights are human rights, is an empowering humanist mantra with an instant emotional and intellectual appeal. The same message, 'women's rights are human rights', was proclaimed by Hillary Clinton at the United Nations 'Fourth World Conference on Women: Action for Equality, Development and Peace' in Beijing, China, in 1995, and was reiterated during her unsuccessful presidential campaign. They are echoed on a planetary scale by multitudes of women and LGBTQ+ people, dehumanized people of colour and colonized others, whose humanity was historically not granted. And yet they carried on and built their worlds. From Mary Wollstonecraft's *A Vindication of the Rights of Women*, to Sojourner Truth's 'ain't I a woman too?', from the Riot Girls to Pussy Riot, via the Guerrilla Girls and the cyberfeminists, the Xeno feminists, the Gaia ecofeminist activists, and multiple others, the humanist aspiration to dignity and inclusion proves inspirational.

Liberal feminists trust the liberating powers of the capitalist market economy to achieve these aims, but are also driven by a social conscience and a sense of responsibility, as one of its historical figures, Betty Friedan, argued in 1963. Feminist politics, in this view, is about organization and procedural tactics to correct a flexible social and economic system that is open to improvements. An underlying optimism supports the political gradualism of the liberal branch of the feminist movement: egalitarian changes will come and equality will eventually be achieved if women and men work towards this goal. Patriarchal power is not a structural notion for liberal feminism, the focus being the unfair distribution of power positions and relations between individualized men and women. The emphasis falls entirely on individualism and personal empowerment.

Many twentieth-century feminists took a more radical stand and were sceptical of the lofty liberal humanist ideals, as they were unequally implemented in world history. This resulted in the systemic exclusion of those who did not conform to that dominant norm. The injustice of these violent exclusions led the disqualified others to question the norm and reject the discriminatory practices, on the basis of their lived experience. They called humanism to account over and over again. Their rebellions voiced the concrete demands and the political urgency of specific empirical referents such as women, LGBTQ+ people, Black, decolonial and Indigenous subjects. But their critique also contained blueprints for the improvement of the human condition as a whole. They produced counter-notions of the human and of humanity, in non-masculinist, non-anthropocentric, non-heteronormative and non-Eurocentric terms. In other words, they acted as feminist, cross-species, gender non-conforming, polysexual and planetary subjects.

Feminist critiques of patriarchal posturing were formulated, in the wake of Beauvoir, by key philosophers like Alison Jaggar (1983), Genevieve Lloyd (1984), Jean Grimshaw (1986), Sandra Harding (1986, 1991), Hill Collins (1991), Jaggar and Young (1998) and many others. The allegedly abstract ideal of 'Man' as a symbol of classical humanity was brought down to earth and revealed as very much a male of the species. As the French poststructuralist feminists claimed: it is a he (Irigaray, 1985a [1974]; Cixous, 1986). Or rather, as we read in the epigraph to this chapter in Gertrude Stein's merciless words: 'He he he he and he and he and and he and he ...'. The triumph of this abstract masculinity (Hartsock, 1987) entails the erasure of the feminine, especially as embodied by women (Irigaray, 1985b [1977]) and LGBTQ+ people. More recent feminist criticism of the limitations of European humanism aims at delinking the human subject from the universalistic posture and debunking his narcissistic delusions of grandeur (Braidotti, 1991, 1994). As late as 2007, MacKinnon raised the question 'are women human?'. Although MacKinnon's definition of women was criticized for implying almost exclusively white, middle-class females (Harris, 1990) and upholding a unitary category of women (Braidotti, 1991, 1994; Butler, 1990, 1997), it remains a highly relevant question. Feminist phenomenologists were especially vocal in rejecting universalism (Sobchack, 2004; Young, 2004) by emphasizing the carnal nature of thought, and racialized theory in the flesh (Moraga and Anzaldua, 1981), and hence the embedded and embodied structure of subjectivity (Braidotti, 2011a, 2011b).

This particular vision of the human as male and white is, moreover, assumed to be European, a full citizen of a recognized polity, head of a heterosexual family and legally responsible for its children (Deleuze and Guattari, 1977, 1987; Braidotti, 1994). And finally, 'he' is also able-bodied and handsome, according to the Renaissance parameters of Vitruvian symmetry and aesthetic perfection (Braidotti 2013), as critical disability studies point out (Shildrick, 2002, 2012; Goodley et al., 2018; Murray, 2020). Feminists refuse to reduce feminism to homologation or integration into this Eurocentric masculine standard of sameness and offer more situated and hence more accurate analyses of the power relations upheld by the humanist paradigm.

Feminism, in its first, second and multiple successive waves, has achieved relative success in terms of equality. Viewed from basic emancipatory expectations, feminism has worked wonders in some quarters and has laboured to ensure that *some* women acquire full citizenship status. The basic requirements of a feminist programme of social emancipation, formulated in the 1970s in terms of equal pay, equal educational opportunities, socially funded child-care, access to contraception and abortion, have been partially accepted, if not fully achieved. The pursuit of equality can be documented with hard data.

Sociometrics provide examples worth reading. Salary equality has not been achieved even in advanced liberal democracies, despite a quantitative increase in the presence of women in the labour market. The disparity rates remain high: the average gender pay gap in the EU is 16.2 per cent, while the gender overall earnings gap in the EU is a staggering 39.6 per cent.[6] Worldwide, the average gender pay gap is reported to be 15.6 per cent based on standard measurements and 18.8 per cent based on factor-weighed measurements by the International Labour Organization.[7] At this rate, as Laurie Anderson wittily suggested in one of her memorable albums, it will be the year 3642 before women actually achieve salary parity.[8]

Across the EU today,[9] 26.8 per cent of ministers and 27.7 per cent of members of parliament are women, and world-wide on average, 18 per cent of ministers and 24 per cent of parliamentarians are women.[10] At the time of writing, the presidents of the International Monetary Fund and the European Central Bank are women (respectively Kristalina Georgieva and Christine Lagarde), as is the President of the European Union (Ursula von der Leyen). From Germany to Nepal and Serbia to New Zealand, quite a few countries now have women presidents or prime ministers (respectively Angela Merkel, Bidya Devi Bhandari, Ana Brnabić and Jacinda Ardern), some of whom are quite media-savvy and Instagram-able. The young prime minister of Finland, Sanna Marin, is the happily heterosexual daughter of a lesbian couple. With Nancy Pelosi as Speaker in the American Congress, and Kamala Harris, the first woman of colour to serve as Vice-President of the United States, things have never looked better for women in politics.

Women nowadays can be financially autonomous and own property, although they still own less than 10 per cent of the world's wealth.[11] Just as importantly, girls and women in most regions have secured access to higher education, although the problem of female illiteracy in the world remains serious, as Nobel laureate Malala Yousafzai's work shows. Many women have fulfilled Virginia Woolf's (1980 [1930]) dream of joining the academic procession of the learned men and thus gaining admission to the formal professions, as well as to scientific research and scholarship.

Academic feminism and the feminist revolution in education and academic research are successful ongoing experiments. However, as Howie sharply put it: 'the amount of extraordinary work already published in the field of feminist theory is a blessing and a curse' (2010: xi), as theory does not always connect to practice. Academic feminist scholarship has indeed produced extensive commentaries on the major topics and texts in the Humanities and Social Sciences, from companions and encyclopaedias, to the *Handbook of Critical Menstruation Studies* (Bobel et al., 2020). Despite intersectional efforts, however, the issue of diversity is still central to feminism and the few feminist professors of colour in the mostly white women's and gender studies curricula experience isolation and extra burdens of responsibility (Wekker, 2016). Greater efforts are needed to diversify gender studies and to respect multiple axes of oppression, in keeping with demands voiced by contemporary movements to change the university and to decolonize the curriculum. Moreover, the success of academic feminism has been contained mostly within the faculties of the Humanities and Social Sciences. Women's, feminist, gender and queer studies courses are practically absent in the Life Sciences and generally slow in Science, Technology, Engineering and Mathematics (STEM) education.

But the data also tell another, more cautionary, tale. The social category of 'women', which was statistically absent from most social and economic data research in the post-Second World War years in keeping with traditional patterns of patriarchal exclusion of gendered subjects, has now been made very visible. Emancipation can therefore be assessed by the extent to which women have achieved the status of fully quantified statistical units. Their individual complaints, pain, secrets and silences have been reformatted into manageable scientific information, which is a powerful tactic in data-driven cognitive capitalism (Moulier-Boutang, 2012). Gender metrics and statistics are a welcome index of progress, which indicates that 'women' are now a majoritarian category integrated into the economic and social structure of advanced economies (Braidotti, 2002). The hegemony of gender as a feminist notion can be seen 'as a sign of the hegemonization and denaturalization of the gender apparatus, as well as its consolidation across a spectrum of social and political contexts' (Repo, 2016: 126).

This is definitely a step forward, but, on closer scrutiny, the newly acquired quantified visibility turned out to be a sideways move, mostly confined to Europe and North America, that created as many problems as it solved. Firstly, metrics tell a partial tale and even the documented extent of the political and professional success of women is incomplete at best. The relative degrees of equality in fact are not evenly spread across all social classes and ethnicities and a sole statistical focus on gender plays to the detriment of other intersectional variables (Chow, 2010). This restricts the field of relevance and applicability of feminist politics.

Secondly, gender mainstreaming comes with a hefty price tag. It is indeed the case that since the 1980s, analyses of gender have become a widespread practice in leading institutions such as the World Bank and the European Union, which is the main source of the figures I am presenting in this chapter. Gender has become an accepted instrument to assess the discrepancies in power and privilege in relation to social progress and capital accumulation. The objective of gender equality in most liberal democracies is not to reform or remove gender roles but 'to break down their stringency in order to allow individuals to make allegedly better, more rational choices for the benefit of the species and the economy' (Repo, 2016: 154).

Equality narrowly defined as balancing the ratio between the two sexes, however necessary as a starting point for the implementation of a feminist agenda, is not sufficient on its own. Even assuming that women – or rather, *some* women – have become more equal, who are they actually equal to? (Braidotti, 1994; Irigaray, 1994 [1987]). Which vision of the human have they become the equal of, similar to, or even the same as? What's the human for feminism? Clearly the outreach and wider implications of the feminist agenda mobilize not only the whole of society, but also shared assumptions about our species. This is why I think that feminism is indeed the mother of all questions (Solnit, 2017); that it is for everyone (hooks, 2000), and although not everyone actually is a feminist, maybe they should be (Adichie, 2014).

But the generous fecundity of the assertion that feminism is for everybody is tricky. For one thing, the fact that the more radical or transformative aspects of the feminist political agenda are still in progress means that everyone can activate them. The tendency of liberal economies to blur the boundaries of binary gender oppositions also means that women – even in their great variety – do not own feminism. It is undeniable that today 'Men, nonbinary and genderqueer people are proud to call themselves feminists and use feminist thought in their work' (D'Ignazio and Klein, 2020: 14). With mainstreaming comes transversal diversification.

The contradictions of neoliberal feminism expose the limitations of the project of equality-minded emancipation but also its enduring appeal. It is worth stressing that I recognize the necessity of continuing to pursue this project, limitations notwithstanding. In this respect, I disagree with Grosz's assertion that recognition is not worth fighting for (Grosz, 2002). I would rather say that recognition alone is not sufficient, but it is necessary and a very good place to start from. What matters, however, is to keep on moving and not get stuck in the Master's gaze, even in his tolerant mode (Brown, 2006).

Assuming that feminism is in its essence a transformative project, not just a reparative one, and without wishing to dismiss the often-encouraging statistics, I am worried by in-built drawbacks of equality-minded feminism, be it in their liberal, socialist or anti-racist versions. Demographic, quantitative and economic analyses of gender equality are not neutral. They are based on an implicit notion of the social subject as a liberal individualistic self. This vision assumes adherence to the dominant parameters of subjectivity, such as belonging to the dominant ethnicity, being a legal citizen, practising heterosexuality, speaking a standard language, being able-bodied and healthy and engaged in waged labour. This is hardly an inclusive understanding of what it means to be human today, even in advanced economies and democratic regimes, let alone elsewhere. All these factors police access to entitlements and advantages. They underplay the multiple systemic structures of oppression and exclusion by patriarchal, capitalist and colonial powers and how they affect the social status of marginalized others. These structures can no longer be contained within the parameters of emancipation platforms that were drawn up at a different historical stage of capitalism. Feminists today cannot speak solely in terms of access to labour, child-care or a bank account – though these issues are still unsolved. We need to broaden that range and scale of social and economic activities and assess our participation in the advancement of cognitive capitalism. This requires a change of scale and a more complex sense of time. The framework of the posthuman convergence is an urgent and necessary way of updating this political platform for feminist practices, as I will further argue in the next chapter.

Feminist Socialist Humanism: Class Equality

The flagrant contradictions of liberal feminism can leave one aghast. Like a character in Sally Rooney's *Normal People* (2018), one stops and wonders at the incongruous behaviour of those most responsible for the economic and social injustices of our times. Never was so much owned by so few to the detriment of so many. In January 2019 the world's twenty-six richest people owned as much as the poorest 50 per cent. The World's Inequality Report co-authored by economist Piketty shows that between 1980 and 2016, the poorest 50 per cent of humanity received 12 per cent in every dollar of global income growth. By contrast, the top 1 per cent, got 27 cents of every dollar. No wonder that the widespread acceptance and mainstreaming of liberal feminism triggered a strong reaction on the Left of the political spectrum, making socialist feminism more relevant than ever.

Although socialist humanism shares with liberalism the belief in 'Man' as the universal emblem for all humans, it bases its political faith in structural revolutionary changes. Socialist humanism rests its revolutionary faith on the teleological idea of history that Marxism borrowed from Hegel and argues that the fulfilment of humanity's full potential is contingent on the elimination of capitalism. Contemporary socialist feminism has inherited a close historical relationship to the political Left, but cooperation is also fraught with difficulties. People may forget, in this regard, that the second feminist wave was indeed marked by 'a structural critique of capitalism's androcentrism, its systemic analysis of male domination and its gender-sensitive revisions of democracy and justice' (Fraser, 2013: 1). But it was also triggered in reaction to the sexism and bullying of the Left-wing men who had automatically elected themselves leaders of the 1960s political and cultural revolution. As Ellen Willis put it 'The women's liberation movement was created by women activists fed up with their subordinate position in radical organizations. Their first goal was to take on an equal active part in the radical movement instead of being relegated to secretarial and other service chores' (2000 [1970]: 513). The Left confused the human with the male proletariat.

Confined to the classical role of handmaids – albeit of a radical community – serving food and drinks and providing sex-on-demand, 1970s feminists took a stand against Left-wing patriarchal domination and split from it. This is how feminist separatism was born and feminism turned into a revolutionary movement of its own. This foundational moment was captured by Helke Sander in the classic feminist film *The Subjective Factor* (1980). Using a combination of fictional and newsreel footage, the iconic filmmaker documents the sexism of Leftist male leaders and traces the origins of feminist communes. Although much has changed since the 1970s, the Marxist Left has yet to fully overcome its masculinist tradition.

Historically, the socialist feminist agenda focused on liberating women's sexuality and reproductive labour within patriarchal capitalism. Arguing that the origins of women's exploitation lay in the usurpation of their reproductive capacities and the appropriation of their offspring, they placed these issues at the core of their political programme. As early as 1966, British feminist Juliet Mitchell was writing on the radical force of the feminist revolution and its impact on the political Left. Combining her Marxist background with psychoanalytic theory, Mitchell produced path-breaking analyses of both the material and the psychic foundations of female sexuality (1973). Sheila Rowbotham (1973) stressed the materialist roots of the women's revolution and the dual structure of their oppression, as the underpaid reproductive workers of the world. Postcolonial ecofeminists Mies and Shiva (1993) added the impact of colonial exploitation of both women and natural resources as key factors in primitive capitalist accumulation. By intersecting this socio-economic dimension with the analysis of persistent patriarchal and racist violence against the women, in both capitalist and colonial regimes, they moved beyond the parameters of classical Marxist analysis.

Socialist feminists reject liberal capitalist ideology because it erodes 'the core of human essence everywhere by destroying women and nature with an unsustainable growth model' (Mies, 2014 [1986]: 2). But they also take Marxist socialism to task for adopting a gender-neutral definition of 'workers', thereby concealing the active complicity between patriarchy and capitalism. Capitalism could not function without the ongoing exploitation of women's reproductive labour, the unpaid work by farmers and colonized people, and the extraction of natural resources. To really support the liberation of women, a socialist agenda needs to be supplemented by the analysis of the sexual division of labour. Conversely, 'the feminist movement cannot ignore the issues of class, the exploitative international division of labour and imperialism' (Mies, 2014 [1986]: 1).

In her commentary on Mies' work, Silvia Federici (2014) criticizes especially the process of 'housewifization' of women, their unpaid domestic work and the emotional work of care, and revives the Italian activist tradition of wages for housework (Della Costa and James, 1972). Federici shares Mies' contention that capitalism accelerated the destruction of the planet's natural wealth and the demise of the people who live closest to it. In relation to the current technological revolution, Federici argues that the real heroes of our times are not the male computer programmers, but the millions of women who are paid less than $1 a day as the labourers of the digital revolution.

Socialist feminists today are also the most consistent critics of capitalism and its liberal apologists. For socialists, mainstream feminism has become a useful 'handmaiden of capitalism' (Fraser, 2009) and complicit with its liberal economics (Eisenstein, 2005). All-too-familiar patterns of social and economic inequality, social exclusion and symbolic disqualification on the grounds of class, race, ethnicity, religion, age and body abilities persist unchanged and are even becoming exacerbated. Fraser argues that liberal feminism, despite its claims, actively enforces capitalist injustices by forcing women into part-time work and flexible practices of low-waged services. This has resulted in increased precarization and racialization of the workforce and, in the long term, more poverty and inequalities.

Moreover, liberal feminism has become hyper-individualistic and prone to the commodification of everyday life through the ideology of well-being, health and fitness. Liberals sabotage state intervention and welfare support and replace them with a more entrepreneurial approach, which legitimizes the expansion of a market economy. Fraser calls for a return to feminist solidarity and a redistributive sense of justice. She also campaigns for economic equality, not only in terms of waged work, but also of unpaid care work.

Critical questions were raised, however, about Fraser's selective account of feminism (Funk, 2013). Moreover, socialist-minded feminists do not fall neatly into party lines. Many contemporary socialist movements are led by citizen activists and journalists (Baker and Blaagaard, 2016), as, for instance, is the case with the French 'gilets jaunes' (yellow vests) movement. It was started by Priscillia Ludosky in protest at rising fuel prices and the impact on people living and working outside the public transport networks of urban areas. Yet, the movement transformed into a broader social organization in defence of workers' rights, tax reform in favour of the working class, and general political resistance to the government.

Socialist feminist energies run high in the second decade of the new millennium and are not confined within any specific political formations. Other important contemporary movements that are socially minded and quite radical are the successful #MeToo movement that was started in 2006 by Tarana Burke, a Black feminist educator and activist. The 'Black Lives Matter' movement was founded by three activists with a strong feminist profile: Alicia Garza and Patrisse Cullors have a background in gender and queer studies, and Opal Tometi in immigration and anti-racism studies.

Patriarchal power is a prominent notion for socialist feminism, the focus being on the systemic economic and social injustices and the unfair distribution of income and power between men and women across the class system. A basic optimism supports the revolutionary politics of the socialist feminist movement: egalitarian changes will come, and equality will eventually be achieved, if women and men work together to bring about a socialist system first.

For socialist feminists, authentic humanity has been perverted by capitalist greed and 'Man' cannot fully come into his own in the oppressive and unjust capitalist patriarchal system. The point of socialism is precisely to liberate and deploy the human potential that was previously harnessed to the profit economy, and thus repressed. The inferior social conditions of women and other minorities will be automatically adjusted once the new socialist system is in place. Feminists are socialist co-workers and travelling companions in the struggle to precipitate the end of the capitalist system, which is taken as the main source of their oppression. In this view, feminism is a revolutionary movement to the extent that it works alongside a larger socialist revolution, in a form of double militancy and a fight against double oppression.

Feminist Black Humanism: Race Equality

Gender, class and race are never too far apart from each other in the intersectional mode pioneered by feminist race theory (Harding, 1993; Crenshaw et al., 1995; Brah, 1996). Black feminist critical theories have a distinguished tradition of rethinking the human, building on African anticolonial activism and theory. Some of the most vocal criticism of European humanism has been produced by Black, Indigenous and decolonial feminist theorists. They have historically advanced pertinent contestations of the dominant powers of 'Man' as the marker for Eurocentric, white, masculinist supremacy.

The Black feminists hold European humanism accountable for its false claim to universalism, assessing it against the real-life history of colonialism and slavery. Black feminism takes critical distance from that humanist ideal by exposing the racialized ontology that privileges whiteness as the human ideal emanating from the transcendental mind of European philosophers (Silva, 2007). The Eurocentric humanist model is criticized because it entails the imposition of hegemonic whiteness and hence implements the racialization of the categories of the excluded (hooks, 1981, 1990, 1992; Ware, 1992; Tuana, 1992; Alcoff, 2006, 2015). They argue consequently that we need to rescue humanism from the contradictory and violent mess into which Western culture plunged it, as evidenced by the legacies of colonialism, slavery and imperialism. As Gayatri Spivak writes, 'There is an affinity between the imperialist subject and the subject of humanism' (1987: 202). And this imperialist and exclusive form of humanism needs to be historicized and held to account.

Race theorists also point out the proximity between European humanism, as the foundation for the Enlightenment rule of scientific reason and democratic rule, and practices of violent domination, enslavement and instrumental use of terror. Reason and horror need not be, and historically have not been, mutually exclusive within the European colonial mindset and patriarchal system of values. This is what Sylvia Wynter defines as the paradox of the complementarity of European modernity and colonialism. This produces 'the Janus-faced effects of large-scale human emancipation yoked to the no less large-scale human degradation and immiseration' (Wynter, 2003: 270). Acknowledging that reason and barbarism are not self-contradictory, nor are humanism and genocide, may horrify the 'clarity fetishists' (Spivak, 1989: 206) of Western rationalism, but remains true. By extension, the claim to universality by Western scientific rationality is challenged (Spivak, 1999) as an expression of aggressive Western culture and of white supremacy (hooks, 1990).

Post- and decolonial feminist thinkers developed trenchant analyses of the physical and epistemic violence involved in reducing the sexualized, racialized and naturalized 'others' to inferior ontological status (Spivak, 1985, 1999). In her classic 'Under Western Eyes', Chandra Talpade Mohanty (1991) extended postcolonial feminist criticism to bear on Western feminist scholarship, exposing the binary constructions of first world and third world women within that community. The European colour-blindness and disregard of diversity has been revealed as everyday racism (Essed, 1991). Decolonial feminism developed from South and Native American feminists, such as Gloria Anzaldúa's Chicana feminism (1987). They foregrounded the decolonial figuration of mestiza consciousness as an empowering alternative to dominant subject positions (Lugones, 2010).

In spite of these powerful critiques of humanism, postcolonial and race theory have not given up entirely on humanism, as Franz Fanon (1963 [1961]) and Aimé Césaire (2000 [1955]) teach us. For instance, Paul Gilroy (2000, 2016) thinks it is crucial to rescue humanism from its treacherous European perpetuators, looking to other cultural sources of hope and inspiration. He argues: 'We might consider how to cultivate the capacity to act morally and justly not just in the face of otherness – imploring or hostile – but in response to the xenophobia and violence that threatens to engulf, purify, or erase it' (Gilroy, 2004: 75). A vernacular form of multiculturalist and planetary cosmopolitanism is Gilroy's response to exclusionary ethnocentric humanism.

Drawing inspiration from a variety of non-European sources, such as African Ubuntu (Mandela, 1994), Black, decolonial and Indigenous feminists rescue the humanist project by inscribing it into transformative politics with a strong spiritual undertone (hooks, 1990; Hill Collins, 1991). Buddhist, Marxist and other schools of ecofeminism and environmental activism produce their own brand of humanist defence of the human, combining the critique of the epistemic and physical violence of modernity with that of European colonialism (Shiva, 1997). These non-Western forms of radical humanism allow us to look at the 'human' from a more inclusive and diverse angle. They suggest new recompositions of humanity after Eurocentrism. This leads to a critical form of humanism referring to non-Western sources and looking at the human from a more inclusive and diverse angle (Narayan, 1989).

Black, decolonial and Indigenous feminists adopted a cautious approach to the generative potential of other traditions of humanism. Or, as the Combahee River Collective argued decades ago (1979), for those who have been systematically excluded from humanity, to be recognized as human, levelly human, is enough. They take humanism as an unfulfilled project, betrayed by Eurocentric violence and aim to develop its anti-racist and inclusive potential. They are committed to explore new understandings of humanity after colonialism and to draw from non-Western sources the inspiration to fully realize the potential of the humanist project.

This is the line defended by Sylvia Wynter, in a strong claim to a specific Black ontology (2015) that draws from a radical anticolonial tradition to argue that 'the human' is always, somewhere, 'a colonial figure'. For decolonial scholarship, especially when inflected by queer theory, race is the primary mover in ontological formations of the human and not just a problematic side-effect of it (Jackson, 2018; Winnubst, 2018). The production of the figure of 'the human' is located within the violent colonial history of racialization, as a central tool of European power. Wynter analyses the human accordingly as a colonial figure that is always *becoming* something else and whose presence implies a principle of deselection of Black people. Wynter makes an exclusive ontological claim for the primacy of race as a constitutive element of the human, alongside the politics of gender and processes of genderization. Maria Lugones (2007, 2010) analyses the colonial gender system and argues that any discussion of the human implies a racialized ontology implemented by colonialism. She argues that in the framework of empire, race functions as the defining factor in the construction of all other intersectional differences, notably class, sexuality and gender. Lugones joins forces with feminist race theory (Davis, 1981; Crenshaw, 1991) to draw attention to the specific and systematic violence visited upon women of colour. She criticizes the bias of feminist theory, which tends to reflect the bio-politics of white, middle-class women, ignoring women of Black and working-class backgrounds (Repo, 2016).

By extension, the racialized ontology of 'Man' in Western philosophy is assessed by Black feminists as non-representative of humanity. Wynter urges to correct this through a revision of humanism in relation to concepts of Blackness. She makes a useful distinction between the humanist 'Man of Reason' – whom she defines as 'Man 1' – and the nineteenth-century version – 'Man 2' – of post-Darwinian science. She argues that neither version of 'Man' does justice to the dehumanized others; only a full recognition of the racialized character of all ontologies can provide an adequate analysis of the human. For Wynter, 'the human has not yet come'. She calls for the need for a third event (after Man 1 and Man 2), in which the deselected people join forces to recognize what they actually are. This involves contesting the workings of capital and developing a new kind of politics emerging from those who have been 'de-selected' (2003).

I describe this position of Black neo-humanism as 'strategic anthropocentrism',[12] echoing the 1980s definition of 'strategic essentialism' by Gayatri Spivak (1985). The strategy consists in setting up a provisional morality – the belief in the absolute priority of certain categories (gender, race, class), which entails taking the calculated risk of making them more robust and stable than they may be in reality. This strategic statement expresses epistemic faith in the real-life experiences of the racialized (and sexualized and naturalized) subjects – the marginalized 'others'. The politics of locations and their perspectivist method mean that, though there are significant points of encounter between a posthuman feminist position that targets Eurocentrism and racism from within and a decolonial perspective, there are divergences as well between the respective positions. Both deal with how to take ethical and political accountability for structural exclusions. Practising embodied and embedded perspectives allows for immanent points of encounter without appropriation.

Looking back at the mixed legacy of European humanism, notably its historical connection to empire, colonialism and enslavement, Audre Lorde put it with characteristic visionary force: 'Our survival means learning to use difference for something other than destruction. So does yours' (Lorde in Rodriguez, 2020).

Queer and Trans Inhumanism: Equality and Diversity

LGBTQ+ theories and practices are positioned in the aftermath of humanism in that they pursue the political project of emancipation with claims to equality and struggles for recognition and justice. These claims rest on a sense of radical alienation from the heteronormative idea of the human built into European humanism. Many queer and trans feminists express a deeper bond to other species, notably animals, or rather 'transanimals' (Hayward and Weinstein, 2015). They feel not only excluded from, but also deviant, abnormal and monstrous in relation to the dominant definition of the human. Socially coded as 'unnatural' in their rejection of compulsory heterosexuality and reproductive normativity, queer and trans theorists deploy an extreme form of dis-identification from the Vitruvian humanist image of 'Man'. Queer and trans theorists join forces with disability studies scholars in critiquing the discriminatory aspects of that idealized depiction of human normality.

Queer and trans feminisms work on the intersectional resonances between sexuality, gender, race, colonialism and the full range of the non-humans. They prefer the category of '*in*humanism' to indicate their liminal and marginal position in relation to the hegemonic figure of 'Man'. But 'inhuman' also refers to the violence and the various forms of de-humanization inflicted upon LGBTQ+ people, in social, environmental and symbolic terms (Muñoz, 2015). Strongly allied to the dehumanized and non-human others, LGBTQ+ theories stress the parallels between the treatment of sexualized and racialized others, their increased vulnerability and mortality.

What also binds them is the shared desire to escape from the power of heteronormativity scaled on an abstract notion of 'Man' and a binary gender system either by equalizing rights and entitlements and thus fight back against the exclusions, or by devising altogether new visions of what humans could become. That points to the posthuman moment, which includes the production of alternative ways of knowing, new epistemologies and new ways of relating to and understanding the contemporary world. Susan Stryker sums it up clearly: '(In) human thus cuts both ways, toward remaking what human has meant and might yet come to be, as well as toward what should be turned away from, abandoned in the name of a better ethics' (2015: 228).

Rejecting the naturalization of the normative model of the human, LGBTQ+ theorists want to be rescued from a human condition that spells contempt and disqualification for them. As Emi Koyama (2001) put it: '*transfeminism* views any method of assessing sex to be socially and politically constructed and advocates a social arrangement where one is free to assign his or her own sex (or non-sex, for that matter)'. Transfeminists consequently explore multiple possibilities for constructing alternative bodies, relying on technological interventions – be it bio-chemical, technological or surgical – to achieve their mutations (Preciado, 2013a). This ethics of self-transformation is in fact a collective, relational political project. Through such intense mediation, LGBTQ+ theorists escape the humanist model, while getting re-grounded and re-materialized as enhanced or alternative embodied subjects. This double pull – towards de- and re-materialization – is a constant process that deigns posthuman subjectivity. While this is an energizing and affirmative practice, the sheer reliance on technological mediation and the pursuit of a project of perfecting embodied selves through science and technology, brings queer and trans theories paradoxically closer to the Enlightenment project. Scientific reason and technoscience become the means to achieve a political revolution and to get out of the injustices of a social order based on an idea of human nature indexed on the qualities of the 'Man of Reason', which discriminates and excludes the sexualized and racialized sub-humans.

Queer and trans in-humanness indicate these fraught trajectories: to ascribe to the humanist creed of emancipation and full equality for all, while also being painfully aware that the lofty ideal could never do justice to the complexity, impurity and generative force of their anomalous vitality. LGBTQ+ people want in, although the desire to get out of the patriarchal heteronormative colonial and ableist world remains overwhelming.

Conclusion

Liberal, socialist, Black, anti-colonialist, Indigenous, queer and trans – these feminist variations and critiques of humanism have been important in promoting equality and recognition of the marginalized, excluded and oppressed. In so far as humanism upholds basic democratic rules and fundamental freedoms, it is an integral part of the system in which feminists and other activists have positioned their ongoing struggles for inclusion and equality. The humanist project of emancipation has encouraged the equality of the minorities and motivated forms of activism among women, LGBTQ+, Black, Indigenous and colonized peoples. In this book I therefore assume the relative success of the historical legacy of humanism as supporting equal rights for all. As I wrote in the introduction to this chapter, humanism should not be discarded easily, because some humanistic premises about equality and emancipation are relevant and necessary. Moreover, they have become integral elements of the legal and political systems of advanced democracies, thus the emancipatory potential of the posthuman condition needs to be assessed cautiously (Cudworth and Hobden, 2017). It is a measure of the value and strength of humanism that I am able to write such criticism and have it published, without fearing negative institutional retaliation, beyond the by now predictable mutterings against postmodern relativism in some quarters. It is a fact that one can criticize humanism in the name of humanism and that this gift of freedom does create an insolvable double bind (Said, 2004).

The appeal of humanism is perfectly justified in the light of the long history of injustices and exclusions endured by women and LGBTQ+ people, Black, Indigenous and colonized peoples. As the chosen targets of patriarchal violence, feminicide, homo- and trans-phobia, colonial expropriations and mass killings, they have borne a disproportionate percentage of human suffering. They, or rather, we, are not all human in the same way, and some categories of humans are definitely more mortal than others. Therefore, it is politically impossible not to support the ongoing efforts to extend human rights across all categories in a more equitable manner. At the same time, it has also become urgent to question the alleged self-evidence of the idea of the human at work in the very humanist concept of universal human rights. I think that such an idea needs to be treated with critical care. In a brilliant contribution to the feminist volume *Posthuman Bodies* (Halberstam and Livingston, 1995), significantly called 'The end of the world of white men', the novelist Kathy Acker settles her score with the culture of violent exclusions enforced by patriarchy. In a self-ironical twist, she concludes: 'If you scratch hard, you find that I'm a humanist in some weird way. Well, humanist, you know what I mean' (Acker, 1991: 17).

From the posthuman perspective, humanism needs to be reviewed, historicized and assessed critically. Because it is so built into our system, we need to dis-identify with it. It is necessary to cultivate the ability and willingness to practise collective dis-identification and critical distance from, or even disloyalty to (Rich, 1978) the humanistic paradigm. Feminism today cannot only be a revised or updated version of humanism, but needs to look farther and make an extra effort to rise to the contemporary challenges of the posthuman convergence. My emphasis on the need for critical thought is motivated by the analysis of the material and historical conditions of the posthuman convergence.

The intersection of advanced technological enhancements of the human and impending environmental depletion of species, tears apart traditional understandings and practices of the human. What used to be the measure of all things, the human body, is now an obsolete piece of machinery by comparison with the speed and liveliness of the new technologies. Nature, far from being an endless reservoir of resources, is impoverished to the point of extinction. Technology, far from being the promise of radiant futures for humanity, is a threat to its very survival.

In order to be worthy of the urgency and complexity of our times, feminism needs to keep engaged with these paradoxes and contradictions. What is at stake for posthuman feminism is how to produce other ways of thinking about the basic units of reference to define the human, what thinking means, how knowledge is produced, and to develop new forms of ethical engagement. In the next chapter I will develop a posthuman critique of humanism and of its feminist variations and inflections, by showing that we need to keep connected to humanism, but also need to move ahead and beyond.

Chapter 2
The Critical Edge of Posthuman Feminism

A wild patience has taken me this far.

Adrienne Rich, 1981

The overview and assessment of feminist traditions critical of humanism that were presented in the previous chapter indicate that the feminist movement has produced dominant subjects functional in the management of *potestas*, the dominant and restrictive face of power. But it has also engendered transformative subjects, driven by *potentia*, the transformative and subversive face of power. In both cases feminism combines critique with creativity, politics with the imagination, and material cartographies of the present with speculative anticipations of the future. In the posthuman convergence today, the feminist strands can also be coded in terms of different modes of relation to power in their 'neo' appearances. A majoritarian corporate branch – *neoliberal* feminism – is by now subsumed into the political economy of advanced capitalism, which its *neo*-socialist counterpart opposes dialectically.

From a posthuman perspective, neoliberal and neo-socialist feminisms share some specular similarities and striking resemblances despite their manifest differences. Both variants are aligned on dominant humanist ideas of 'Man' as the motor of human history and evolution. This positions women firmly as the second sex and feminist emancipation as the project that seeks equality, by adjusting or overthrowing power relations within this dominant paradigm. Moreover, they are both anthropocentric, though in different ways: neoliberal feminists because they tend to naturalize capitalism and universalize liberal individualist exceptionalism,[1] and neo-socialist feminists because they do not grant political agency to environmental non-human factors and translate them back into socio-economic inequalities indexed almost exclusively on the needs of humans. Thus, an active environmental awareness is dimmed in the neoliberal frame by universalizing the individual and in the neo-socialist mindset by an entrenched bias in favour of the socio-cultural pole of the nature–culture divide.

Of course, their strategies differ: the neoliberal's unshakeable belief in the self-regulating force of the capitalist market economy is echoed by the neo-socialist's equally passionate conviction that the capitalist system is destined to break down because of its deep contradictions. While they are both single-minded about identifying capitalism as the defining feature of the current socio-economic model of the state, they react to it antithetically. Where the liberal feminists rush to embrace it, the socialist ones labour to eliminate it.

In a posthuman feminist perspective, however, both variants of feminism fail to tackle the specific features of contemporary, cognitive and technology-driven capitalism. The opportunistic boundary-breaking nature of capitalism is a crucial feature if we want to understand its power. All the more so as a residual form of humanism has returned with a vengeance through the influential transhumanist movement. I will discuss transhumanism critically in the last part of this chapter. But first I will tackle aspects of advanced capitalism that humanist forms of feminism fail to address, such as the neo-colonial order of migration, innovative technologies and biopolitics of life as capital. As capitalism has mutated into an information-processing system, to miss or underestimate that mutation is a cartographic and political error of great consequence for the future of feminist humanisms. In this chapter I argue that posthuman feminism offers firstly a relevant critique of neoliberal and neo-socialist versions of feminism today, and secondly a more adequate reading of the fractures and paradoxes of the posthuman convergence. It is therefore both urgent and necessary.

The Contradictions of Neoliberalist Feminism

Political contradictions
Although it claims to build on the legacy of its distinguished classical liberal predecessors, neoliberal feminism is quite a distinct and more pernicious phenomenon. Liberal feminists have a distinguished political pedigree, which neoliberalism takes quite some liberty with (Brown, 2015; Rottenberg, 2018). Classical liberalism bases its political faith in emancipation on a utilitarian view of humanity as a collection of individuals bound by common interests and ambitions. Neoliberal feminists are 'wealth supremacists' (Reich, 2021: 3) who identify human nature with capitalism. By extension, an egalitarian evolution under the aegis of capital market economies is for them not only desirable, but also possible without disrupting the existing market economy and its democracies.

Neoliberalism accomplishes a wilful reduction of the social ideal of equality into a hyper-individualistic form of personal empowerment. It replaces a political process with the instant gratification of financial success, self-pampering and conspicuous consumption. These are the ambivalent outcomes of mainstream integration, accompanied by selective adjustments to the system (Fraser, 2013). Neoliberal feminists are less concerned about solidarity and thrive on the glorification of economic success and the opportunities afforded by the fourth industrial revolution.

In so far as it aligns the emancipation of women within the frame of the market economy, neoliberal feminism has entered a 'dangerous liaison with advanced capitalism' (Eisenstein, 2005: 511). To give an example, the ethos of capitalist individualistic self-empowerment is supported by many female CEOs, also known as 'She-EO',[2] 'girlboss',[3] 'fempreneur',[4] 'mompreneur' or 'momtrepreneur',[5] who have come into their own over recent decades. Overwhelmingly successful on multiple scores and seemingly perfect in their performance (McRobbie, 2015), neoliberals make everyone else feel like a bad feminist (Gay, 2014a). The emblematic figure here is Sheryl Sandberg of Facebook, whose neoliberal manifesto *Lean In* became an instant bestseller in 2013. Mindful of the difference between militant feminists and 'Professional Feminists', Roxane Gay (2014b: x) was quick in picking up the absurdity of Sandberg's highly privileged perspective. Something that reads like a corporate fairy tale can only trigger 'delectation and irritation' in normal, average feminists (Gay, 2014a: 321). As Rottenberg sharply asked (2018), how reliable is a feminist manifesto drafted by the Chief Operating Officer of tech giant Facebook? Not only does it run the risk of turning into an imperialist assertion of the cultural and political superiority of American culture, but it also over-individualizes the practice of empowerment, losing sight of minimal requirements of feminist solidarity. Neoliberal feminists ignore or forge one of the founding values of feminism, namely that 'Feminism is the political theory and practice to free *all* women: women of color, working-class women, poor women, physically challenged women, lesbians, old women, as well as white economically privileged heterosexual women. Anything less than this is not feminism, but merely female self-aggrandizement' (Smith, 1998: 96).

Corporate feminism is also successful in public institutions, best exemplified nowadays by the first woman to chair the IMF and now the European Central Bank, Christine Lagarde. Committed to gender equality, and the professional advancement of women, as well as to fighting poverty and social inequalities, Lagarde famously declared that had Lehman Brothers been called and functioned as 'Lehman Sisters', the 2008 financial crisis would not have happened. More critical feminists may add that, sisterhood or brotherhood notwithstanding, we would all be better off without such a hegemonic financial sector, but such radicalism cannot be expected of neoliberal feminists. Their political agenda remains the fight against institutional sexism for an equal share of the spoils of an essentially exploitative system.

Not all neoliberal feminists, however, have a sense of public service. Gwyneth Paltrow, for instance, turned the idea of a happy work–life balance into the ultimate luxury commodity. Her company – Goop – is devoted to wellness, inner balance, health and fitness. Spuriously transgressive, it sells allegedly 'vagina and orgasm' scented candles. Playing to perfection the orientalist appeal of the wellness industry, Goop promises a healing mind–body harmony which is lacking in the West (Stacey, 2000). The neo-colonialism of this line of business is not lost on green activist Greta Thunberg who is unforgiving in her comments: 'celebrities, film and pop stars who have stood up against all injustices will not stand up for our environment and for climate justice because that would infringe on their right to fly around the world visiting their favourite restaurants, beaches and yoga retreats' (2019: 43). The financial success of the global wellness enterprises is central to liberal feminism, which rests on a global emulation of the luxurious lifestyle and shameless consumerism of celebrities and Internet-backed influencers. It has the added disadvantage of exposing the *lack* of wellness in the general population of common mortals. Burn-out, anxiety, exhaustion, obesity, binge-drinking and self-harming practices are rising in large sectors of the population in advanced economies and especially among women, LGBTQ+ people and ethnic minorities.

Sleep is a significant concern for the wellness industry and the 'sleep economy' is a profitable proposition. Marketing high-tech mattresses, high-performance pyjamas and technological sleep-tracking devices, it is estimated at around US$432 billion (Mahdawi, 2020). Remedies against insomnia and bad sleep plunge directly into the psycho-pharmaceutic industry, which is one of the pillars of advanced capitalism (De Sutter, 2018). Gender, labour and class relations are crucial in structuring access to adequate sleep (Fuller, 2018). Paltrow seems to ignore the basic fact that sleep is a class prerogative and that well-off people, and men, have always slept longer and better than economically disadvantaged ones.

The opportunistic commercial pursuit of wellness by the 'happiness industry' (Segal, 2017) reinforces the shallow ideology of capitalism as the coercive 'promise of happiness' (Ahmed, 2010). Lauren Berlant calls this ideology 'cruel optimism' (2011): a constant pressure to succeed in every single aspect of life, including health, happiness, wellness and fitness. Promoted as a social imperative across members of the public, regardless of their actual social situation, it is doomed to fail and cause even greater misery. This neoliberal ideology conceals the concrete socio-economic causes of the ill health, mental fatigue and other problems encountered by large sections of the population. These are due to the consequences of economic austerity regimes; the reduced purchasing power of waged labour and the brutal cuts in social services and welfare introduced by neoliberal economics in the last twenty years (Finlayson, 2019).

Barbara Ehrenreich (2009) stresses the devious ways in which the happiness industry also conceals the lack of adequate health care and insurance in the United States. Even worse, it shifts the responsibility for well-being from social institutions and the state, to the single individual. Women – the privileged target of the happiness industry – are also the primary victims of the lack of health care. Rates of female physical and mental illnesses, such as depression, are alarming. The happiness industry accomplishes a slight of hand: it sells individual remedies against the collective adversity and anxiety induced by the socio-economic conditions of our times (Spicer, 2019). This simultaneously eliminates any collective elements and over-individualizes the issues at stake.

This uncritical support of the *status quo* shows up dramatically in politics, where at least some neoliberal feminists are prone to turn to the right-wing and even become civilizational warriors in the name of women's rights. This crusaders' zeal emphasizes the commitment of Western culture to emancipation and equality set in opposition to the allegedly backwards discriminatory practices of other cultures, notably Islam. In a remarkable reversal of past habits, many Right-wing and populist movements in the West have come out in favour of women's and gay rights, provided they meet set standards of national cultural identity. They paradoxically stress this emancipated position while perpetuating the populists' nationalism and inclination to sexism, misogyny, homo- and trans-phobia, as well as virulent racism.

This is the case, for example, in France, where the National Front, under the influence of its former deputy leader and gay activist Florian Philippot, took a firm stand against the ancestral homophobia of Jean-Marie and Marine Le Pen's party. It happened even earlier in the Netherlands, where Right-wing parties embraced the LGBTQ+ people's cause as a sign of liberation from supposedly Muslim conservatism (Duyvendak, 1996; Mepschen and Duyvendak, 2012). The most recent phenomenon occurred in Germany, where Alice Weidel, an out lesbian, became the leader of the Parliamentary group of the Far-Right Party 'Alternative for Germany'. The gay (the term 'lesbian' is deliberately avoided) Serbian Prime Minister Ana Brnabić also operates within the rank and file of conservative patriotic nativism.[6] At the same time, those Islamophobic political movements are doing nothing to fight growing anti-Semitism across the EU region; in fact, some of them are quite embroiled in an anti-Semitic stance.

These hyper-nationalist and racist political organizations make opportunistic use of LGBTQ+ people's and feminist issues, using them as an example of alleged Western superiority over the Global South in general and Islam in particular. This tactic, practised regularly by neoliberal governments, is also known as 'femonationalism' (Farris, 2017), 'pinkwashing', 'sexual nationalism', 'homonationalism' and 'queer nationalism' (Puar, 2007). It is an attempt to enlist the transformative project of feminist and LGBTQ+ people's rights to xenophobic civilizational campaigns.

This spurious neoliberal feminist pride can even be complicit with Western militarism, in quite a devious manner. At the time of the Afghan war, notorious anti-feminists like President George W. Bush and his wife Laura, together with Tony Blair, proclaimed their support for the Afghan women as a reason to invade their country. As feminist legal scholar Emily Jones points out (Bertotti et al., 2020), this tendentious argument was also quite central to justifying the illegal use of force by the United States and allies in 2001 in Afghanistan (Cloud, 2004) and, to a lesser extent, in 2003 in Iraq (Al-Ali and Pratt, 2009). In this respect, liberal feminism is perfectly allied with Western patriarchal interests and practices, as Hillary Clinton's support for the invasion of Afghanistan and later Iraq, and her work as State Secretary, clearly demonstrated.

This 'embedded feminism', as it became known (Hunt, 2006), co-opted feminist and women's rights to legitimize armed intervention by the West. Critical feminist scholars denounced this operation as a double defeat. Firstly, it created hierarchical divisions among the women, betraying feminist solidarity (Ferguson, 2005; Perugini and Gordon, 2015). Secondly, it violated human rights and further endangered world peace (Denike, 2008; Otto and Heathcote, 2014). It does remain a fundamental tenet of postcolonial feminism, however, that all differences among women are flattened by the imperial gaze of the colonizers who occupy their lands, cultures and bodies (Mohanty, 1991). The white patriarchs gleefully proclaim the necessity to wage war because they allegedly want to save brown women from brown men (Spivak, 1985).

By becoming mainstream, neoliberal feminism has shifted from a radical and even revolutionary movement to a dominant or majoritarian mode of governance, including serious parliamentary legal and military uses of power (Halley et al., 2019).[7] This aggressive and punitive position has been described by critics (Engle, 2019) as a move from a liberal rule of law to 'carceral feminism' (Bernstein, 2012). Yesterday's radicals are today's governors.

Reproductive contradictions

Let us reflect for a moment about what happens when a feminist project of equality comes partially true. Firstly, as we saw in the previous chapter, visibility is gained. Gender has acquired legitimacy in neoliberal governmentality and has become a formidable normative tool for policy making on demographics, public health, population growth and decline. Socio-metrics, however, far from being neutral analytical tools, are instruments of political power: they control, monitor and quantify, but also discipline and punish as Foucault revealed (1977). Gender as a mainstream instrument of analysis to measure discrepancies in power and privilege between the sexes is functional to neoliberal economics, in so far as it allows biopower to penetrate every aspect of social, sexual and personal life.

Secondly, equality, narrowly defined within the gender binary, strengthens possessive individualism (MacPherson, 1962). The subject of neoliberalism is an autonomous entrepreneur of the self (Lemke, 2001), bound to a morality of responsible self-management of its human capital, to produce the utmost results, profits and surplus value. For Repo, neoliberalism is 'an expansive political rationality that generalizes the logic of the market to the entirety of the social body' (2016: 114). The workers or labourers are turned into astute managers of their physical and genetic abilities and those acquired through education and social opportunities. For women, this adds extra pressure to the management of their fertility as reproductive capital.

The issue of reproduction is, as ever, capital. The process of emancipation worldwide has complicated the demographic issue further by demonstrating that – contrary to earlier expectations – increased wealth results in actual decrease in childbirths. This unexpected result led to higher investments in the fewer children, making the downsizing of families a key consideration of cost–benefit analyses of economic profitability. The sexual conduct of contemporary reproductive subjects is of the greatest importance in ensuring rational choices that benefit the market economy as well as individual fulfilment by the same standards. This is the system that neoliberal or 'choice' feminism fervently upholds, foregrounding in an individualistic manner the role of women as co-producers of wealth and capital value.

But when it comes to measuring rates of human reproduction, the dominant template of the human that is built into statistical analyses and policy making on gender deploys all of its contradictions. It prioritizes the fertility of white middle-class women as factors of productive prosperity for developed society (Repo, 2016). Other demographic data, from the South of the world for instance, is often presented as a social problem, as in over-population or uncontrolled population growth. Access to the social capital of parenthood is therefore strictly limited. As the Xenofeminists put it: 'the wealthy, white "yummy mummy" might be applauded for her contribution to the future of the nation state, but teenage mothers, black and Latina parents, trans* and genderqueer subjects, immigrants, refugees, and benefit claimants receive no such treatment' (Hester, 2018: 52). The exclusion of the lived experience of these 'others' exposes the problematic nature of gender metrics, which are as seductive in their promise of objective data as they are limited in making such data representative and inclusive (Merry, 2016).

Mainstream motherhood becomes a major investment for neoliberal economics, devoting ample technological resources to the task and demanding returns on capital. The profit motive overrides all other concerns. Working with Indigenous populations and focusing on the women's role in the Arctic region, Rauna Kuokkanen makes a crucial observation: 'Neoliberal discourses of self-reliance, responsibility and individual capacity-building restructure Indigenous self-determination into a limited decision-making authority within the confines of the global capitalist economy' (2019: 19). Reproduction and fertility are key issues in the neoliberal governance of human capital, gender and individually gendered subjects. If women are to become successful self-entrepreneurs within this system, reproductive biopolitics requires them to make some serious managerial readjustments. The reproduction of human capital implemented in neoliberal reproductive politics is subjected to the dominant social codes and values. It implements individualized gender roles that rest on a patriarchal idea of binary sexual difference and compulsory heterosexuality.

Technology matters here. The boundaries between reproductive humans and technologies have become far more porous, intimate and interactive than they used to be. The political economy and the management of human reproduction benefits from the parallel rise of the Life Sciences and of a neoliberal economy that approaches 'life as surplus' (Cooper, 2008). Instead of individualizing and psychologizing the issues, posthuman feminism invites seeing the repositioning of both women's reproductive bodies and biotechnologies at the core of the neoliberal governance of economic production, energy consumption, reproduction and population growth. Neoliberalism displays 'a particular kind of biopolitical deployment of gender as an apparatus of population control', which is also racialized and Eurocentric in its applications (Repo, 2016: 145). Thus, the deployment of gender as a tool of neoliberal reproductive politics is built on the silencing of the more radical and critical feminist sources of analysis. I will return to this in chapter 5.

Reproductive technologies play a central role in the emancipation of neoliberal feminists, who individualize the responsibility for reproduction, by inventing a new ideology of 'happy work–family balance' (Rottenberg, 2018: 14). This 'happy' ideology relies on a number of factors for its success. Firstly, it is capital intensive in that it requires investments in the fitness, health and wellness industries to achieve that much coveted level of happiness and individual balance. It also calls for intense biotechnological and medical intervention to assist reproduction, notably frozen egg implants and IVF, all commercially available.[8] And last but not least, it relies on the assistance of paid domestic female help. The latter entails the creation of new subcategories of reproductive workers, mostly migrant women and women of colour, who take over the tasks of care, welfare and child-rearing. The present-day 'global care chains' position migrant workers as central to the project of taking on the care work that middle-class women in the Northern hemisphere give up in order to participate in the labour force. The emancipation project of liberal feminism thus depends on the exclusion of migrant and sexual minorities from the same rights enjoyed by white middle-class women (Ehrenreich and Hochschild, 2002; Gottfried, 2007; Peterson 2007; Eisenstein,

2009). In commercial surrogacy, also carried out mostly by migrant women, even the task of gestation is outsourced commercially (Lewis, 2019).

This neoliberal sleight of hand does not solve the patriarchal division of labour between the sexes. It achieves a relative redistribution of family and work responsibilities that allows privileged women to enter elite economic positions, while supporting an international division of labour that is compatible with patriarchal family values and the capitalist market economy. As Rottenberg put it, neoliberal feminism 'reinscribes white and class privilege and heteronormativity, while ... representing itself as post-racial and LGBTQ friendly' (2018: 20). To call this liberation merely adds insult to injury.

The 'indirect supplementation of rich women in the North by poor women from the South' is at the core of the racialized economy of advanced capitalism (Bhattacharyya, 2018: 48). These sexualized and racialized modes of production inevitably raise the issue of labour and class relations. What is a critical feminist to make of a hegemonic model of equality that is ethnically indexed and biased in favour of white, professional heterosexual women? Can such a model be equated with emancipation? Or is it just a reconfiguration of a racialized and sexualized class division of labour that upholds capitalist inequalities and reasserts traditional gender roles? The neoliberal feminist rides this hyper-individualistic wave and is willing to accept that the price for her individual freedom is a new system of class-stratified and racialized labour relations that put other women in charge of domestic and caring tasks. The wages thus paid exonerate neoliberal feminists from further solidarity or social criticism.

Just how superficial the social transformations actually are and the shallowness of the cultural and political changes they enact was exposed by the COVID-19 pandemic. During the long periods of lockdown at home, the female workforce and women in general reverted to traditional roles as caretakers of the young and the elderly and as primarily responsible for household tasks. The scholarly output of female academics collapsed, whereas that of male academics actually increased. In other words, the underlying patriarchal cultural infrastructure and the traditional divisions of labour were still in place and ready to be reactivated. Meanwhile, in the surrogacy clinics scattered on the margins of the Western world, carrying mothers were waiting for the purchasing parents to pick up their deliveries, which were delayed by the global lockdown (Grytsenko, 2020).

It is important to note that the cartography of advanced capitalism provided by posthuman feminism engages with exactly the same historical conditions that fuel neoliberalism. These are the productive as well as problematic aspects of ubiquitous technological mediation; the depth and scale of environmental devastation; the socio-economic inequalities; and the misogynist, sexist, homo- and trans-phobic character of populist rage. If some of the diagnosis matches, the political response could not be more different. Posthuman feminism pursues a radical critique not only of liberal individualism, but also, as I will show in the next section, the cruel delusions of cognitive capitalism.

Neo-socialist Feminism and the Mutations of Capitalism

Socialist feminism opposes step-by-step the aims and political agenda of neoliberal feminism and ends up being a reverse image of it. From a posthuman feminist perspective, socialist feminism relies on a slightly outdated reading of capitalism, or rather focuses on familiar negative aspects of this new economy. This is a limited and limiting approach, which still has the advantage of foregrounding issues of labour relations and economic disparities, but fails to understand the extent of the technological apparatus and how it reshapes the new economy. As Donna Haraway puts it: 'the tendency of the political "left" ... to collapse molecular genetics, biotechnology, profit, and exploitation into one undifferentiated mass is at least as much of a mistake as the mirror-image reduction by the "right" of biological – or informational – complexity to the gene and its avatars, including the dollar' (1997: 62).

Neo-socialist feminists, not unlike LGBTQ+, Indigenous, decolonial and anti-racist scholars, have focused on the fractures and injustices of the capitalist system. They have argued forcefully that since the first industrial revolution, human lives have been organized according to sexualized, racialized and naturalized hierarchies that made many of them disposable, exploitable and dispensable. They were sacrificed at the altar of Western modernity. These injustices continue, and even get exacerbated, but in a system that has mutated into a non-linear, post-industrial, global circulation of often immaterial capital.

The fourth industrial revolution is driven by advanced technologies and automation. More specifically, it marks the convergence between previously distinct branches of technology, notably bio-genetics, neural sciences, information technologies and AI, nanotechnologies and the Internet of Things. It has come to indicate the relative marginalization of human intervention in this smart technological universe run by machine-to-machine communication. Previously inanimate objects, now technologically enhanced, become data-collecting and retrieving devices, or 'smart' things.

In a posthuman feminist perspective, the post-industrial economy of today is driven by cognitive capitalism and the neoliberal economic system that supports it. It continues to draw profits from raw materials and is thus 'fossil capital' (Malm, 2016). It also continues the inhumane exploitation of labour and perpetuates patterns of sexualized and racialized oppression. In addition, however, it also profits from the production of de-materialized items, such as information, data, bits and bytes of codes that transfer massive amounts of material across the global economy. It has therefore evolved into 'platform capitalism' (Srnicek, 2016). The financial system runs on advanced computational networks, alongside other marketable forms of information and ever-smarter platforms. It has therefore become 'cognitive capitalism' (Moulier-Boutang, 2012). Among the tradeable financial commodities there is credit, which engenders ever-growing debts (Lazzarato, 2012). This system also doubles as a massive, militarized 'surveillance capitalism' apparatus (Zuboff, 2019), notably in immigration and border control.

Capitalism proved far more flexible and adaptable towards the proliferation of differences than the Marxist Left expected. It has gone post-binary, schizoid and slightly delirious in its aspirations to break the boundaries of everything that lives (Cooper, 2008). The differences that used to be pitched as dualistic dialectical opposites – racialized, sexualized and naturalized – are now delinked from their oppositional attachment to a single unit or standard, like 'Man'. They have become rhizomatic, multi-dimensional and scattered in an unpredictable and often imperceptible manner. When it comes to items of consumption, they have been inserted into a global flow of distributed, marketable and disposable commodities.

A significant proportion of capitalism today, however, is immaterial in that it rests on the flow of data and informational capital. Contemporary capital has perfected the capitalization of knowledge about living systems, also known as 'cognitive' capitalism (Moulier-Boutang, 2012). Years before this hype, Donna Haraway (1985) had already labelled it 'the informatics of domination'. This type of knowledge is drawn from technoscientific practices extracting the informational power of living systems, both organic and inorganic. How to profit from the generational power and self-organizational vitality of matter is the name of the capitalist game today. This is the political economy of 'biocapital' (Rajan, 2006), that produces the 'politics of Life itself' (Rose, 2007), or 'Life as surplus' (Cooper, 2008). In her work on the Visible Human Project,[9] Catherine Waldby (2000) introduced the related term 'biovalue' to designate the extraction of surplus value from biological matter by contemporary technoscience and its capitalist enablers.

As Bhattacharyya (2018) suggests, for an economy based on the politics of life, those who stand as targets of necro-politics do not qualify as labour reserves: they may not be mobile enough, not be qualified or – as the South Korean film maker Bong Joon-ho points out in the remarkable 2019 film *Parasite* – they may just not smell right. The suppression of human labour, that is to say of disposable bodies, is a qualitative change: 'to be rendered surplus is not to be paid less, it is to be left dying or for dead' (Bhattacharyya, 2018: 20). It operates by de-skilling, exploiting and eliminating various sources of waged labour. The dehumanizing tendency built into capitalism is accelerating in the posthuman convergence, as an ongoing form of dispossession.

From the posthuman perspective, therefore, the sacrificial logic is far from over because entire populations are handed over to risk analyses through genetic screening, used as clinical labour, exploited by the neoliberal austerity measures, and exposed to the ravages of climate change, the violence of forced migration, expulsion and dispossession (Sassen, 2014). The 'wrath of capital', as Parr rightly names it (2013) upholds discriminatory distinctions between valuable and disposable bodies and dehumanized and devalorized subjects. At the height of the second feminist wave, in 1971, D'Amico spoke up on behalf of these marginalized subjects (D'Amico 2000 [1971]: 52): 'We are the invisible women, the faceless women, the nameless women ... We are the poor and working class white women of America, and we are cruelly and systematically ignored. All our lives we have been told, sometimes subtly, sometimes not so subtly, that we are not worth very much.' Nowadays as ever, women, LGBTQ+ people, undocumented migrants, asylum seekers, people of colour, the pauperized and the unemployed constitute the bulk of these sacrificial bodies that are the new proletariat of the digital and bio-capital era.

The sense of emergency arising from the posthuman convergence introduces new patterns of discrimination upon older modes of oppression. It exposes the inner power structures of advanced capitalism and the sexualized, racialized and naturalized political economies of exploitable labour and dispensable bodies that support it. Importantly, it combines this analysis with a sense of urgency arising from the spectre of the Sixth Extinction, the ecological crisis and climate change. Environmental scarcity clashes with technological abundance within the fast flows of capital, triggering a short-circuiting of planetary dimensions.

Cognitive bio-capitalism is an internally fractured system that combines high degrees of technological mediation with deep social and economic inequalities. It manages to combine the free circulation of data and capital with a neo-colonial order of migration, control of borders and movement which, like all colonial contact zones, is fraught with violence and struggle (Mezzadra and Neilson, 2013; Tofighian, 2020). The flow of capital controls the space-time of human mobility and migration through disciplinary regimes and highly selective mechanisms of technological surveillance and control (Braidotti, 2011b; Zuboff, 2019). Advanced capitalism functions as the great organizer of the mobility of commodified products.

Human mobility, migration and border-crossings are intensely sexualized and racialized activities. Racialized capitalism functions by systematic practices of coercive mobility (Braidotti, 2011b), expulsion (Sassen, 2014) and expropriation (Fraser, 2016). Unregistered migrants, asylum seekers, homeless and paperless people compose the bulk of the population subjected to controlled mobility. The paradoxical automated landscapes of contemporary global cities reflect these social partitions, with hyper-modern, wired infrastructure (Sassen, 1994, 2002, 2005) and glossy architectural facades standing alongside post-industrial slums and postcolonial wastelands (Harvey, 2006; Bhattacharyya, 2018). Advanced capitalism produces economic polarizations and a schizoid affective economy that alternates between exhilaration and exasperation, and expectation and exhaustion. It shows the staggering ability to accommodate programmes of human enhancement with a cynical acceptance of the need to sacrifice entire sectors of the labour market, neglect large parts of the world population, and exploit most non-human species. All kinds of non-human organisms fit into this logic of technologically mediated intervention for the sake of consumption, alongside various specimens of humanity. The genetic propensities of entire populations are patterned and stored for the sake of further research and capitalization. The commodification of the informational capital of all species relies on what Vandana Shiva calls 'bio-piracy' (Shiva, 1997); Eisenstein opts for 'global obscenities' (1998).

Feminist technoscience scholar Sarah Franklin offers an illuminating example in her analysis of contemporary stem cell research. The first cloned transgenic animal, Dolly the sheep, is the product of a 'realignment of the biological, cultural, political and economic relations that connect humans, animals, technologies, markets and knowledges' (2007: 2). Dolly the sheep provides valuable insights into the working of cognitive capitalism and how it constructs life forms for the sake of commercialization. Biology is accordingly denatured and modified. Not a clone in the strict sense of the term, Dolly's cells were reworked and transferred dozens of times, in a mixture of sexual and asexual forms of reproduction. This mixture of science and business is in itself not new, but it increases in speed and scale, de-naturalizing and commercializing biological matter more than ever before. Feminist anthropologist Marilyn Strathern first identified this practice in 1992 as 'entreprised-up biology' (1992: 212), where cellular reconstruction is explicitly connected to bio-commerce and bio-capital. The capital is the regenerative potential of cells themselves, especially stem cells, which can be cultivated and engineered into a number of life-science products. Cognitive capitalism harnesses and capitalizes upon living material. Reproduction is inevitably caught within a technological exploration and exploitation of the potency of life.

What counts as 'life' is not only the embodied and embedded realities of bound individuals, but also the specific properties, propensities and inclinations of matter itself: genes, cells, codes, algorithms, stocked in databanks that can be stored, sold and exchanged. Knowledge is mediated and the true capital is the generative power of matter itself. This intense degree of technological intervention produces a de-materialization of the lived experience of empirical humans, but also their re-materialization as retrievable and sellable data on a global scale. The posthuman turn is at work right there, in this schizoid double pull between the de-materialization of production – given that what is produced are data and information – coupled with the re-materialization of exploitative, embodied labour conditions. As the case of Dolly proves, biology gets technologized as much as technology gets biologized. Advanced capitalism is thus a research-driven knowledge economy bent on profit.

Trans-feminist theorist Paul Preciado stresses not only the mediated materiality of technoscience and bio-engineering, but explores its subversive potential in terms of gender identities. Biogenetic technologies invented by advanced capitalism can be appropriated to construct radically different bodies. Acknowledging that bodies are malleable and transformable, Preciado puts it as follows: 'the success of contemporary technoscience consists in in transforming our depression into Prozac©, our masculinity into testosterone, our erection into Viagra©, our fertility/sterility into the Pill, our AIDS into Tritherapy, without knowing which comes first: if depression or Prozac©; if Viagra© or an erection; if testosterone or masculinity; if the Pill or maternity; if Tritherapy or AIDS' (2013b: 269). For this branch of posthuman feminism, bio-technosciences and queer and trans subjects are actually joining forces to re-design biological structures and defy determinism. They are bio-hacking the future.

Much as I share an enthusiasm for technoscience, I want to introduce a note of caution here against a complete de-naturalization of bodies. It is paradoxical, to say the least, that a system built on bio-power displaces the human the better to exploit its genetic material. The same system that profits from life itself neglects the humans crushed by the structural injustices of our social and economic systems, including structural indebtedness (George, 1976, 1988, 2015). Socialist feminists are right in reminding us that many marginalized and disposable people are denied access to these technological advances and their economic profits.

Posthuman feminist scholars take a materialist, but not necessarily socialist, approach to the analysis of the embodied and waged aspects of post-industrial labour. In keeping with the politics of locations, they focus on the embedded and embodied materialized relations of work and production and take critical distance from any claim that the global economy is virtual and de-materialized. In addition to issues of wage inequalities, the context of cognitive capitalism imposes a new agenda, which includes what Cooper and Waldby call 'clinical labour' (2014: 4). That idea refers to the provision of reproductive and bio-medical services related to technologically assisted reproduction and other forms of bio-medical care. Within the posthuman convergence, these technoscientific practices are often presented as delinked from real-life embodied subjects and focus instead on specific activities such as surrogacy, the exchange, donation or sale of organs, tissues and cells. Similarly, the unmistakably material, carnal nature of this labour contradicts any claim by the new economy to be 'de-materialized'. A posthuman feminist perspective foregrounds the bodily contribution of sexualized and racialized subjects to the new economy in terms of their biological labour and their genetic capital. This also means that feminists cannot restrict the analyses of contemporary capitalism to the mere claim of technological liberation, or the fear about de-materialization of labour, anymore that we can separate the fourth industrial revolution from the Sixth Extinction. We need to approach this with more dexterity as a convergence, which means focusing on the intersection of these phenomena.

The current economy is not only about technological mediation, or exclusively about gene-editing and stem-cell engineering, or only about the exploitation of labour, or just about climate change and the spectre of species extinction. It is about *all* these factors *at the same time*. The fact that the human mind may crack under the strain of thinking through so many painful complexities is that mind's problem. The imperative to think about and within that complexity remains, and posthuman feminism is keen to rise to that challenge.

The Transhumanist Delusion

The urgency of keeping up with recent technological, social and ecological developments is also shown by the extent to which classical humanist ideas and anthropocentric habits are returning in the school of transhumanism. While the transhumanist movement is one of the most dominant trends within mainstream posthumanism, I will argue why this school is problematic and controversial from a *feminist* posthuman perspective.

Transhumanism proposes to overcome the current format of the human through technologically mediated enhancement techniques. Transhumanism believes in the fusion of human consciousness with computational networks. The aim is to achieve human enhancement via brain–computer interface and it is proposed that cerebral and neural expansion is a way of fulfilling the potential of rational human evolution. The fusion of human brainpower and biology with technologies, in a phenomenon called Singularity, is presented as the fulfilment of the humanist project of perfecting humanity through scientific reason and technological advancement (Kurzweil, 2006). Human enhancement, far from making humans obsolete, is seen as an evolutionary leap forward of human abilities. However, transhumanism revives humanism insidiously through active interaction with the fluid but brutal workings of cognitive capitalism. Politically, the transhumanists defend liberal individualism and contribute to it. The transhumanists remain indebted to the Enlightenment project of social and political emancipation, through the moral deployment of the universal values attached to rationalist scientific progress (Bostrom, 2014).

While preaching moral universalism, the transhumanists pursue self-interest and implement the profit motives of advanced capitalism. In so doing they stipulate the dominant formula of transhumanist ethos: it is analytically post-anthropocentric, in that it confirms the decentring of the human by technology, but normatively, it reinstates the individual as holder of neo-humanistic ethical values, and politically it is aligned with economic neoliberalism. The combination of analytic posthumanism and normative neo-humanism, under the aegis of capital, makes transhumanism the mainstream model of posthumanism.

However, from a feminist perspective this is problematic because it entails an explicit template for human evolution, which perpetuates and even exacerbates the patterns of discrimination, exclusion, disqualification (Braidotti, 2013) and de-selection (Wynter, 2015). Posthuman feminism works through the intersectional critical lenses of gender, race, class, sexual orientation, ability, age, among others, acknowledging the differences in power and status among humans and between humans and non-human species. Posthuman scholars stress the relational bond and symbiotic continuum to the non-human world (Wolfe, 2010; Haraway, 2017). The transhumanists, on the contrary, dwell within the humanistic tradition (More, 2013), and embrace it for the sake of human enhancement, as indicated by their symbol 'H+' as an abbreviation for 'Humanity Plus'. Science and technology are the means to reach this goal, which is set somewhere in the near future, with some humans becoming posthuman faster than others (Bostrom, 2014). You may remember that I argue instead that the posthuman convergence as the site of convulsive transformations of the human is already here. Contrary to the equivocations of the transhumanists that both support and undermine the 'Man' of humanism, posthuman feminism can be seen as a paradigm shift towards posthumanist, post-anthropocentric and post-dualistic ways of thinking and being.

The feminist engagement with the transhumanist project as a problematic response to the posthuman convergence dates back decades. It ties in with the postmodern discussion and its feminist repercussions.[10] Hard-core postmodernists like Baudrillard (1988) and the Krokers (1987, 2014) took a euphoric stance on the changing status of the human and espoused early AI experiments with human–machine symbiosis (Minsky, 1985). They neglected the more sober accounts of this technologically driven mutation, offered, for instance, by Jean-François Lyotard (1984 [1979]; 1989 [1988]). From the 1980s onwards, a generation of cyberpunk writers, notably William Gibson (1984) made the switch from the postmodern flair for the artificial to the posthuman synthetic. In no time they confined the enfleshed human body to the rubbish heap of history, and synthetic biology and information technologies carried the day. Bruce Sterling, who wrote a passionate cyberpunk *Hacker Crackdown* manifesto (1992), initiated a current of speculative posthumanism in 2012. Surveying this early posthumanist landscape, Katherine Hayles summarized it as follows: 'Humans can either go gently into that good night, joining the dinosaurs as a species that once ruled the earth but is now obsolete, or hang on for a while longer by becoming machines themselves' (1999: 283). These male-centred and body-denying positions of hyper-humanism were targeted by many feminists from the 1990s and formed the core of my critique in *Metamorphoses* (2002). Cyberfeminists, as we shall see in a later chapter, paved the way for this criticism. Writers and activists like Kathy Acker (1990), Faith Wilding and the Critical Art Ensemble (1998), Pat Cadigan (1991), VNS Matrix (1991, 1994), and the Old Boys Network (1998) led the charge. They were technophilic, but not naïve, and took a more critical and original stance about technological enhancement (Plant, 1997). After all, the feminist tradition had by then already produced one of the most visionary pioneering texts on the mutations of the human: Donna Haraway's 'A Manifesto for Cyborgs' in 1985 (subtitled as a socialist-feminist manifesto). These agenda-setting interventions position feminism as both one of the originators of the posthuman turn and a vehement critic of its exclusionary aspects.

The rallying point for feminists is the acknowledgement that the human is changing in ways that put an end to 500 years of European humanism, as Hassan predicted in 1977. The concern shared by cyberfeminists, as by posthuman feminists, is that this mutation may entail a replication of the old patterns of patriarchal, capitalist and colonial exclusions. As we have seen in transhumanism, the danger is indeed that it perpetuates the denial of the embodied and embedded structure of all the subjects, and the more vulnerable forms of embodiment of the oppressed. On the contrary, cyberfeminists embraced the new technologies but with a difference (Braidotti, 1996), which means grounding and embodying the posthuman subject. That is also Francesca Ferrando's tactic (2013, 2018). She makes a useful distinction between posthumanism and transhumanism by stressing the non-dualistic and intersectional strength of posthumanism. Ferrando radicalizes transhumanism by hacking it, that is to say delinking the project of human enhancement from the humanist ideal of perfection.

This creative interpretation of the posthuman predicament is not new, but in fact a recurrent feature of feminist thinking. Feminism produced the very early posthumanist texts, such as *Posthuman Bodies* (Halberstam and Livingston, 1995). Feminists also focused on the technologies of sexed and gendered bodies (Bukatman, 1993; Stone, 1995; Turkle, 1995; Balsamo, 1996; Plant, 1997). All these theoretical interventions trust the embodied intelligence of humans as a species that has perfected its own complexity over a long evolutionary history, which cannot be reduced to, or incorporated into, the machinic apparatus. In so doing, they oppose the transhumanist project.

In her important intervention, Hayles (1999) takes on the dominant idea of the transhuman as an extension of the Cartesian illusion of a mind–body dichotomy, where the mind stands for informational patterns that get privileged over material instantiation. This means that all matters related to the body and biology, including affects and emotions, are accidental and not fundamental. They can accordingly be manipulated at will. This illusion is built into an evolutionary programme whereby human consciousness and cognition, the core of the humanist definition of 'Man', can be enhanced by integration into machinic systems. The result is a fusion of human and technology, whereby one cannot distinguish bodily existence from computer simulation, cybernetic from biological organisms. Hayles argues that this approach expresses an enduring attachment to the liberal humanist vision of the individual, endowed with more-than-human technological powers.

More recently, working from an Indigenous perspective, Danowski and Viveiros de Castro (2017) also single out the complicity between Eurocentric humanism and advanced technology, as expressed both in the Silicon Valley ideology and the Oxford school of transhumanism. They are critical of the transhumanists' definition of the posthuman condition as moving analytically beyond the human, but normatively remaining more humanistic than ever. How such a contradictory position can have any credibility is a wonder for critical posthumanists, who see transhumanism as one of the major reasons for the current demise of the human.

Danowski and Viveiros de Castro also remark that transhumanists preach a recodification of old Nature by the rules of the techno-capitalist machine, but present it as a mere matter of managing resources, including human capital and environmental governance. The technological reductivism of the transhumanists is the exact opposite of environmentalism, which – as we shall see in the next chapter – predicates a materially embodied and embedded ontological egalitarianism across the species. By comparison with the digital sophistication of transhumanism, environmentalism often gets dismissed as naïve. Viveiros de Castro (2014) emphasizes that, in so far as it connects to Indigenous and more specifically Amerindian cosmologies, which are diametrically opposite to the western Singularity, an environmentally grounded approach is charged with primitivism. This world view posits a common belonging to a sense of 'humanity' that is shared with all living entities. All that lives partakes of the same soul and expresses it through the specific perspective that each entity embodies. Radical perspectivism is the key term, at once relational and site-specific or grounded. This relational ontology pitches anthropomorphism against anthropocentrism, in that it positions humans in their own specificity as species alongside other species, thereby undoing their claim to exceptionalism. This advanced perspectivist philosophy is also known as 'multinaturalism' (Viveiros de Castro, 2014). It exposes the transhumanist delusion in all its exclusionary force.

Posthumanism feminism is wary of, but also embedded in, this scenario, 'interrogating it for its triumphalist rupture from the animal, its complicity with the class politics of big capital and its fantasmatic investment in patriarchy' (Banerji and Paranjape, 2016: 2). By questioning the global practices and narratives of the transhumanist transformations of the human, posthuman feminism voices the perspectives of the margins and the global peripheries of the contemporary world.

What is problematic for critical posthuman feminists is the transhumanist illusion of grafting the posthuman onto a liberal humanist view of the self and subjecting it to technological enhancement and economic profit. The demarcation line is that critical posthumanists abandon the liberal individual rendition of the human subject, whereas the transhumanists not only preserve it, but want to enhance it technologically into hyper-techno-individualism. Posthuman feminism is instead in favour of heterogeneous assemblages that embed the contemporary subject in an expansive web of vital but also gratuitous relations between humans and non-humans. That is enhancement enough.

Conclusion

Posthuman feminism is an intervention upon the legacy of neoliberal and socialist feminisms as well as on the transhumanist delusion. A posthuman turn is needed as a corrective and alternative to the intersecting critiques of power. I see feminism as repositioning the mixed legacy of humanism in a profoundly different historical context from that which generated it. Feminism today needs to be a transformative, not just an egalitarian movement. I concur with Iris van der Tuin that 'feminism is the struggle against sexism, homophobia, transphobia and other intersecting forms of structural power imbalances based on naturalizations of inequality' (van der Tuin, 2015: xiii). As such, not only is it more necessary than ever, but I also think activists should keep some critical distance from the very institutions they have gained the right to enter, occupy and sometimes even run. How can one still cultivate the world-changing passions of feminism, while ensuring the gradual success of its reforms? Where are the radical forces today?

The feminist posthuman answer is multi-layered. In addition to criticizing the social injustices implied in the neoliberal position, and thus striking an alliance with the traditional socialist feminist politics, it also deepens the analysis of advanced capitalism and its concomitant technoscience and bio-genetic technologies. Posthuman feminism revives the radical tradition by offering an updated analysis of cognitive capitalism, based on the study of its advanced technologies, while situating these advances within the ecological crisis and environmental deterioration. As I argue in this book, posthuman feminism has a more adequate analysis of contemporary transversal relations of power, having relinquished the liberal notion of the autonomous individual as well as the socialist ideal of one privileged revolutionary historical subject.

The criticism of the limitations of classical humanism is the premise to the collective construction of acts of resistance, as well as the creation of alternative scenarios. My call is for a democratic participation of all in the discussion about what we are capable of becoming in this posthuman convergence; what the dangers of exclusion and discrimination might be; and how we can develop an ethics worthy of the complexities we are facing. Our ability to do so is directly proportional to our ability and willingness to learn from the failed promises and internal fractures of Eurocentric humanism and develop more inclusive practices (Armstrong and Montag, 2009). A posthuman relational ethics respects our species and cultures, while differentiating and recognizing the worth of the human community. It is a material but differential feminist ethics, that embraces a decolonial and anti-racist stand in assessing humanism from the perspective of those it excluded and tormented. It importantly also embraces the non- and the in-human entities as constitutive components of human subjectivity.

Transcendentalist claims to exceptionalism (such as found in transhumanism) are cut down to size through an emphasis on immanence and the recognition of our mutual interdependence. 'We' are definitely in this posthuman convergence together – in the injustices, the staggering technological developments, the epidemics and other environmental devastations, alongside promises of technological evolution. Our social imaginary is fraught with planetary anxieties and increasing contradictions. In such a context, rejecting human exceptionalism is a way of embracing the immanence of a life that we do not own. Life is not restricted to hegemonic 'Man', but includes his multiple, disposable and despised others. A posthuman approach avoids the recreation of a pan-humanity that would dialectically absorb these others into a new superintelligence project. It rather calls for differential, materially embedded accounts of the respective prices 'we' are prepared to pay for being and staying alive here and now.

Chapter 3
Decentring Anthropos: Ecofeminism Revisited

> All century trash floated round the gyre
> of the Pacific (…).
> Worst of all in the warm clutter
> were the shopping bags of every shade,
> plaited by the waves' regular hand
> or domed, translucent as a bloom of medusae,
> ripped membranes flickering like something precious.
> Sarah Westcott, 2016

In this chapter I will unravel the relation between posthuman feminism and post-anthropocentrism through the lens of ecofeminism and Indigenous thought. Anthropos, 'Man', as a species, gets decentred in the posthuman convergence. The anthropocentric socio-political order is challenged by the combined accelerations of the posthuman convergence: faster technologies, faster climate change patterns, faster growth, faster decline, fast priority lanes for living but also for dying. Exposing anthropocentric arrogance and the violent exploitation of non-human others is a core value for posthuman feminism, which joins forces with, but also goes beyond, the critique of humanism. As Stacy Alaimo puts it eloquently: 'Who is the "anthro" of the Anthropocene? In its ostensible universality, does the prefix suggest a subject position that anyone could inhabit?' (2017: 89).

Decentring Anthropos: Ecofeminism Revisited

Neither 'Man' as the universal humanistic measure of all things, nor Anthropos as the emblem of an exceptional species, can claim an exclusive and central position in contemporary, technologically mediated societies and their automated modes of production. Nor does this sovereign subject have the power to stop the climate changes triggered by reckless overdevelopment. More often than not, this human subject is part of the problems of the posthuman convergence, not of their solution. My argument in this chapter is that feminist theory, and more particularly the ecofeminists, indigenous feminists and LGBTQ+ theorists, are the pioneers of post-anthropocentric practices and consequently also the precursors of posthuman thought. It is not my aim in this book to survey feminist theory as a whole,[1] but rather to select the strands that lead to a posthuman perspective.

Coined in 1974 by French feminist Françoise d'Eaubonne (and translated into English only 20 years later), 'ecofeminism' brings into focus the environmental consciousness inspired by Rachel Carson's seminal text *Silent Spring* (1962). The term 'has come to refer to a variety of so-called "woman–nature connections" – historical, empirical, conceptual, religious, literary, political, ethical, epistemological, methodological, and theoretical' (Warren, 1994: 1).

Ecofeminists foresee the posthuman turn in several interlinked ways. Firstly, by embracing the natural pole of the foundational nature–culture distinction, allowing for collaborative modes of relation to the non-humans. This move starts with the reappraisal of the organic animals, plants and the entire planet, but in the course of time it grows to encompass also inorganic entities such as technological artefacts, networks, codes and algorithms. This is a strategic but also an ethical choice that is rich in implications.

Secondly, ecofeminists extend the critique of humanist reason to the ecological dimension, adding to the charges of sexism and racism an undue sense of entitlement to use and abuse all other species: 'species-ism'. This critique of 'species-ism' results in more complex analyses of the social and epistemological violence involved in the systemic exclusions and disqualifications of the devalorized others. It also calls for more ethical responsibility and for new forms of ethical care for the non-humans.

Thirdly, post-anthropocentric ecofeminist thought connects productively with Indigenous and decolonial feminists, who have inherited and developed distinctive traditions of nature–cultural relations and care for the land. They are of great relevance to the current conjuncture, specifically in exposing the links between empire, colonial dispossession and the devastation of the environment.

Ecofeminists think transversally as well as intersectionally across axes such as sexism, heteronormativity, racism, colonialism and ableism (Adams and Gruen, 2014). They highlight the common structures that connect the exploitation of women, LGBTQ+ people, Indigenous and (post)colonial people to that of other species. Patriarchy, capitalism, racism, colonialism, anthropocentrism and technoscience are intertwined phenomena exerting their power through institutionalized practices and power relations. The critique of 'species-ism' makes for strikingly original perspectives. It also helps to understand that 'we' are in this posthuman convergence together, and that we therefore need transversal connections across different perspectives and locations.

Is Culture to Nature as Man to Woman/Native/Others?

A fair assessment of the contribution of ecofeminism to the posthuman predicament must start by stressing its criticism of the dominant distinction nature–culture and the social-constructivist method in feminist theory. In so far as the feminist tradition of emancipation reduces appeals to 'natural differences' to justifications of inequality, nature becomes a corrupt and mistrusted category. A critical form of anti-naturalism is constitutive of feminist practice, as is a preference for social-constructivist methods that allow for historical interventions and reject the biological realm as a form of determinism.

Feminists are painfully aware of the dangers involved in being assigned to nature. Nature is the cover for a hierarchical naturalization of inequalities, which circulates within the socio-cultural system of patriarchy as a pretext for discrimination. Appeals to nature and to a naturalized world order are a tactic that the patriarchal, capitalist, neo-colonial system uses to lend legitimacy to the social structures it has created. It allows for an uneven distribution of power, for the benefit of those who most approximate the dominant ideal of 'Man'. Patriarchy can be described as the regime that turned biology into destiny by naturalizing the differences between the sexes and the races, so that the sexualized and racialized 'others' can be classified and organized in a hierarchical system that dehumanizes them. The nature–culture divide translates into real-life discriminations, the concrete loss of social, legal, economic and symbolic rights by people who differ from the dominant norm of 'Man'. Consequently, feminists from the seventeenth century on focus on dislodging nature from its biological essentialist premises and expose it as a socio-historical construction, namely a political apparatus of exclusion. As we saw in the previous chapter, equality-based feminists rejected the allegations that the inferiority of women, LGBTQ+ people, racialized and ethnic minorities was somehow 'natural'.

Moreover, this dualistic opposition nature–culture implies a negative understanding of nature itself, as a chaotic and violent state of disorder, which can only be regulated by the political power of the state to protect its citizens. Political liberalism since the eighteenth century has aligned nature with servitude, violence and brutality and defended an anthropocentric and political order based on the rule of law. Social contract theory distinguished human life (*bios*) from the non-human (*zoe*) and presents the *polis*, the political space of social and legal mediation, as a necessary measure to counteract the anarchical and destructive forces of nature. Human progress – measured in terms of cultural and scientific development – is defined by the distance it establishes from the natural order and those who inhabit it. Working with Indigenous philosophies, Bignall and Rigney make this point admirably: 'modern European political theories of social contract have conceived "nature" as a pre-social baseline from which human culture advances through increments of "civilization" and "Enlightenment"' (2019: 166). Sexualized people (women and LGBTQ+), racialized people (Black, Indigenous and native), and the naturalized earth as a whole, are excluded from the social and cast on the side of abject nature. In colonialism, moreover, this natural order is expropriated by eliminating, both physically and symbolically, the presence of Indigenous cultures, cosmologies and legal systems.

The nature–culture divide is consequently foundational for feminism. It rests on the firm social-constructivist assumption that nature is a term that naturalizes and thus justifies inequalities. The proper object and site of politics is the social sphere. Simone de Beauvoir's 1949 statement that one is not born, but one becomes a woman – as the second sex of 'Man' – is emblematic in this respect. This statement is positive because by exposing the social construction of what our culture calls 'human nature', it enables feminists to organize against its oppressive aspects. It de-naturalizes, or rather de-essentializes nature, making it historically variable and hence subjected to changes through human activity. This distinction then provides the template to define gender roles and differences as mere social constructions, as mechanisms of power without biological grounding. On the negative side, however, this is also a restricting move in that it institutionalizes a dichotomous opposition between nature and culture and instils a dualistic mode of thinking into feminism. It also denigrates the biological grounding of subjectivity itself.

In 1974, social anthropologist Ortner, in an effort to identify the cultural logic behind the universal oppression of women, built a further argument on the basis of the nature–culture distinction, namely, the notion that women are to nature as men are to culture. This equation provided the analytical frame to explain women's inferior social roles, depreciated economic values and less symbolic worth than men. Culture – always assumed to be the culture of men – refers to the products of human consciousness, notably systems of thought, meaning and knowledge, including technology.

Women are positioned as pre-social, as having more direct affinity with nature, mostly because of their reproductive role in assuring the continuation of the species. The procreative function defines female physiology and women's social role in child-rearing, which in turn shapes their social psychological profile with a focus on care and nurturing, emotions, rather than reason. Positioned as closer to nature and to living beings, women also act as intermediary spiritual figures in traditional practices of healing and mourning, birthing and dying. Throughout this political economy, binary oppositions act as instruments of power and governance: they divide and conquer.

In her influential essay 'Traffic in women', Gayle Rubin (1975) develops the social-constructivist equation further into a feminist version of Levi-Strauss's anthropological analysis of the sexed division of labour. This results in a public sphere controlled by men, while women get confined to the private (Elshtain, 1981), that is to say a domestic world of love and rituals (Smith-Rosenberg, 1975). The exchange of women, as Freud had already suggested in *Totem and Taboo* (2001 [1913]), has far-reaching social and symbolic consequences in monotheistic societies. The circulation of women among men constitutes the social order: in marriage as wives and mothers, but also in the margins as sex objects and prostitutes. It also constructs and upholds an intimate but mediated bond among the men, which transits through the bodies of women. The social contract, by extension, is a sexual contract (Pateman, 1988), objectifying women as items of exchange to appease and connect the men. Women are confined to the private sphere as sexualized merchandise, destined for circulation in a male-run public sphere of market commodity exchanges (Irigaray, 1985b [1977]).

Rubin pushes the analysis of how sexuality constructs the social field even further. She argues that the naturalization of women's reproductive roles and their constitutive function in the making of a socio-symbolic world order also has the side-effect of naturalizing heterosexuality. Compulsory heterosexuality in patriarchy results in the reduction of homosexuality and LGBTQ+ sexualities to the realm of the unnatural and the abhorrent. Sterile and 'against nature', all non-reproductive sexualities become morally reproachable, demographically useless and politically undesirable (Edelman, 2004). This amounts to major constraints for non-heterosexual subjects and discriminates fiercely against LGBTQ+ people's sexualities.

The control of women is constitutive not only of the patriarchal family structure and its kinship system, but also of the social nexus as a whole. Patriarchal power gets institutionalized through masculine control of the symbolic functions of cultural systems, namely religion, instruction and war. Women and LGBTQ+ people are excluded from this model of active citizenship and public function well into the twentieth century. Active male homosexuality is banned from the social and political space of the polity and penalized heavily. By institutionalizing men's bond to one another and interposing the bodies of women as their physical connectors, patriarchy strikes a double blow. It simultaneously recognizes a sublimated form of male homoeroticism at the heart of the social contract of the *polis* while repressing it. This means that men's recognition of their shared entitlements, their admiration and love for one another is symbolized and rewarded, but also repressed and penalized. European culture since classical Greek times has filled the public space of the Western world with statues of men, representations of male achievements and buildings that institutionalize male pleasures and desires. Patriarchal culture has confused the human with the heterosexual male.

Feminism thus produced a sharp political analysis of how the coercive heterosexual model is imposed upon all subjects, not only the women. It also replicates the binary gender system as the dominant process of subject formation. By identifying women with nature, men with culture, and heterosexuality with human normality, the patriarchal socio-cultural system imposes a number of instrumental reductions. These proved to be formidable tools of power, which the feminists exposed and re-purposed.

The Ecofeminist Critique of Anthropos

Ecofeminists are the exception to the dominant twentieth-century social-constructivist paradigm, in that they are critical of the separation of nature from culture and the hierarchical binary distinctions that were built upon it. This is where ecofeminism strikes a fundamental chord, by showing how artificial the nature–culture distinction is. They also reveal this divide to be Eurocentric, knowing that most cultures on earth do not rest on such binary oppositions. But ecofeminists go further by contesting the inferior status and the negative connotations attributed to the natural order itself. Some even endorse a tactical embrace of the closeness of women to nature and turn it into a magnifying lens with both a critical and a creative focus. On the critical side, ecofeminists highlight the injustices of patriarchal, capitalist, colonial and anthropocentric power systems. On the creative side, they show the advantages of this proximity because a re-naturalized approach affords new perspectives and margins of political action as well as new ethical frameworks. On both scores ecofeminists spell their position about patriarchy loud and clear: 'We won't play nature to your culture!' (Kruger, 1983).

Ecofeminism argues further that the nexus 'woman–nature' becomes a model of political governance, as well as an index of hierarchy and inferiority. It complicates women's relationship to society, politics, economics and technology, which are masculinized by default. Proximity to nature has negative connotations for all the 'others' of Anthropos. Processes of sexualization and racialization dehumanize women and LGBTQ+ people, but also Black and Indigenous people, bringing them closer to animals and other non-humans. Femaleness, blackness, sexual deviancy, disability and animality are markers of primitivism and are cast on the outside of white masculine civilization. From Antiquity doubts were cast as to whether women had any intelligence at all, and Linnaeus's classification of species in the eighteenth century confirmed that non-Europeans and Africans fell on the wrong side of humanity. The naturalized others of Anthropos – the life-systems of animals, plants and earth entities – are even excluded *a priori* from these anthropomorphic hierarchies.

The hierarchical distinctions between the natural and the social support a capitalist and colonial system of power that institutionalizes discriminatory social structures. It allows for the division between a social realm of production and economic profits on the one hand, and exploitable 'natural' resources and raw materials on the other. The former has rights and agency, the latter has none and is accessible and disposable. Nature is conceptualized within a Cartesian grid, reduced accordingly to an endless supplier of resources for commercial exploitation by colonialist capitalism. Colonized, Black and Indigenous people – who are considered to be close(r) to the earth and nature – are defined in pejorative terms, in a systemic animalization of Indigeneity (Byrd, 2011) and of Blackness (Jackson, 2020). Their social status is tied to the colonial extraction economy and its long-lasting aftermath (Weheliye, 2014; Wynter, 2015; Yusoff, 2018). Non-humans have also been subjected to processes of racialization in what is known as 'bio-colonialism', with the introduction of foreign botanical and animal species replacing Indigenous agricultural practices (Frawley and McCalman, 2014). Bio-racism is common in nationalist and xenophobic discourses against foreign or non-autochthonous species – insects, plants and weeds included – invading the homeland.

The nature–culture split and the anthropocentric privilege it sustains is therefore instrumental not only to patriarchy, but also to the workings of capitalism and its exploitative colonialist economy. By being located on the margins of the cultural order and its capitalist economic exchange system, the dehumanized others bear the brunt of capitalist, masculinist and colonial violence and dispossession. As Bhattacharyya put it (2018: 8) 'capitalism cannot function if we are all allowed to become fully human. Dehumanization seems to be an unavoidable outcome of the process of capitalist development.'

Ecofeminism is quite explicit in its criticism of this system. It singles out the role played by scientific rationality and the privileges it grants to the technological apparatus and to extraction economies. Mies and Shiva (1993) develop a feminist critique of capitalist exploitation of both 'natural' resources and of women's reproductive labour. Both Mies (2014 [1986]) and Federici (2004) have argued that primitive accumulation of capital was made possible by the joint effect of the subjugation of women, the slave trade and the exploitation of the earth's resources. This racist system deprives native and Indigenous populations of the right to be fully human. It proceeds by annexing, expropriating and confiscating their homelands the better to exploit their resources. Biased in favour of men, this colonialist enslavement system dispossesses the women, reduces their generative powers and life-producing abilities to unpaid reproductive labour and persecutes LGBTQ+ people.

The ecofeminist analyses of the structural power relations built into what goes by the name of nature – and the nature–culture divide – have therefore far-reaching political but also methodological implications. Ecofeminists are the pioneers of the transversal extension of feminist ethics and politics to a natural world that was perceived as contiguous with the subjugated condition of women, Black, Indigenous, animals and earth others. Their transversal method thus complicates and enriches the analysis of patriarchal domination (King, 1989; Gaard, 1993; Braidotti et al., 1994). Ecofeminism urges a rethinking of the process of naturalization itself, to question the simplistic reductions and binary oppositions by which social constructivism conceals the dynamic material interdependence that is the strength of all living entities. Ecofeminism is critical of the dismissal of this relational force that binds all living systems. In this respect, ecofeminists strike a minoritarian note that proves inspirational for posthuman feminism.

Posthuman feminists build on these insights to explore the consequences of the fact that nowadays 'nature is unhumanized and mankind is artificialized' (Ansell Pearson, 1997a: 101). Ecofeminism paves the way for a posthuman turn through a methodological intervention by promoting a strategic re-naturalization of the human. This allows for new-materialist perspectives and transversal alliances of human and non-human entities. By rejecting the reduction of nature to a socially constructed, discriminatory and hierarchical indexation system, ecofeminism points to the political and theoretical necessity of a critical and an anti-essentialist re-naturalization of the feminist project. Moreover, this 'ecologically informed intersectionality', as Tuana calls it (2019: 3), includes non-human agents and entities into feminist thinking and practice. The feminist struggle thus connects transversally with other liberation movements, notably Indigenous, decolonial, ecological and animal liberation. Instead of approaching women's, Indigenous and non-humans' proximity to the earth as a problem, ecofeminists turn it into a resource and critical part of the proposed solution.

Feminist Critiques of Ecological Reason

The ecofeminist critique has highlighted the transversal and intersectional links between the sexualized, racialized and naturalized others. By exposing the multi-layered and overlapping variables that compose the socio-economic system, ecofeminists reveal the porous boundaries between them. Power flows across these multiple plateaus of oppression. This kind of transversality will prove crucial to the posthuman turn, as we shall see in the next few chapters.

Ecofeminism combines the critique of anthropocentrism and species-ism in the name of ecological justice, with feminist social justice claims and the critique of racism, imperialism and ethnocentrism. These axes of exclusion point to a 'sex–race–species' system of domination, which demands a political response beyond the application of universal humanistic rights to all non-human entities and molecular compositions. By setting up such equivalences between parallel systems of domination of human and non-human entities, ecofeminism connects the liberation of women to that of nature and naturalized others, and vice versa (Shiva, 1988; Warren, 1994). Ecofeminism focuses on 'the ways that sexism, heteronormativity, racism, colonialism, ableism, speciesism, and environmental degradation all participate in an interlocking logic of domination' (Neimanis, 2015: 1).

Ecofeminists have pursued a consistent line of enquiry against species hierarchy as being analogous to sexism or racism in privileging humans, males and whites over all others. Moral philosopher Mary Midgley rejects anthropocentrism as the regime of 'anthropolatry', that is to say as a deficit of rationality and a distortion of our thinking: 'The kind of anthropolatry that would always set immediate human interests above those of other life-forms is surely no longer defensible' (1996: 106). She criticizes this attitude as an inflated ideal of individual autonomy and independence by an entitled male subject, who displays a fundamental lack of moral relational force and sympathy.

The critique of scientific rationality is therefore built into the ecofeminist case. Midgley holds the culture of scientific research accountable for the hegemony it has granted to scientism, turning scientific practice into a religious dogma (thereby fulfilling Freud's prediction in *Future of an Illusion*, published in 1927). An example of this kind of intransigence is the scientific dogmatism of geneticist Richard Dawkins, notably his apology of masculine selfishness as the key to human evolution (1989). Anthropocentrism encourages egotistic narrowness: 'It could also be called exclusive humanism, as opposed to the hospitable, friendly, inclusive kind' (Midgley, 1996: 105). Ecofeminism favours the latter and encourages us to think beyond human exceptionalism and accept that we are not self-contained and self-sufficient, either as a species or as individuals, but live naturally 'in deep mutual dependence' (1996: 9–10).

Ecofeminism celebrates diversity and notably re-appraises the hidden knowledge and values of those dismissed as being too close to the natural. It re-values the epistemic, rational and moral values of the marginalized others. It produces a critique of reason that asserts the importance of human/non-human interdependence and promotes a collaborative disposition towards all species. By making a compelling case for mutual interconnectedness, ecofeminism emphasizes the ecological idea that 'we' are all in *this* together, although we differ. These insights are key to the making of a notion of posthuman subjects as heterogeneous alliances.

Ecofeminist philosopher Val Plumwood (1993) produces a classic critique of ecological reason, which consists of the rejection of the patriarchal desire for mastery over nature while reappraising women's moral resources in the care of the world. Plumwood supplements the feminist criticism of the instrumental rationalism of masculine techno-culture, with an endorsement of Indigenous systems of thought and ethical values. Lorraine Code argues further that ecofeminism is not simply thinking *about* ecology or *about* the environment: 'It is a re-visioned mode of engagement with knowledge, subjectivity, politics, ethics, science, citizenship, and agency that pervades and reconfigures theory and practice' (2006: 5). Essentially, ecofeminism is a critique of the *ethos* of domination, scientist reductionism, instrumental and utilitarian political theories. It dismisses the dislocated and disembodied vision of the thinker as the knower-as-spectator. Ecofeminism combines feminist empiricism, postcolonial and critical race theories, and non-deterministic naturalism as epistemological models.

Ecofeminism, inspired by social psychologist Carol Gilligan's idea of a feminist 'ethics of care' (1983), takes a slightly different route and celebrates feminine values of love and care as an alternative source of moral value. Ecofeminist care ethics builds on the moral role women play as the traditional caretakers of vulnerable humans and extends it to the natural environment, radicalizing it in the process. As Donovan and Adams put it: 'as with feminism in general, care theory resists hierarchical dominative dualisms, which establish the powerful (humans, men, whites) over the subordinate (animals, women, and people of color)' (2007: 2). I would also add that, from the Victorian angels in the house and the colonized workers in all fields, through to the – mostly black, Asian and migrant – professionals in the nursing and health care sectors today, women just do the work of care. Enloe (2020) reports that women comprise 85 per cent of all nurses and midwives worldwide. They are the planetary 'angels in the ecosystems' (Plumwood, 1993: 9). Incidentally, a painfully high proportion of these health workers made up the casualties of the COVID-19 pandemic of 2020–21.

Because care is not merely a moral virtue but also a political one, the task of caring pertains to the public realm and thus helps to construct responsible citizenship in a participatory democracy (Tronto, 1995). In the same vein, ecofeminists have grown a geo-political and transnational dimension, exposing the links between militarization, violence and environmental degradation (King, 1989). In all these instances, masculinist culture is called to accountability for the toxic environmental sphere it has created and its fundamental disregard of the well-being as well as the rights of others.

The structural equivalences between the sexualized and racialized others of 'Man' and the naturalized or earth others are activated by ecofeminists in a more radical direction. Women's role as the managers and caretakers of the well-being of others is effectively extended to include non-human recipients. In the posthuman convergence, ecofeminism has expanded the relational ethical approach in ways that transcend women-identified feminine values, moving beyond gender identity issues. Ecofeminist care ethics today emphasizes mutual trans-species interdependence and inscribes relationality at the ontological core of ethical subjectivity (Puig de la Bellacasa, 2017). The trend in ecofeminism is a move towards more fluid forms of interrelation across species and organisms and in-between them. A recently launched 'Care Manifesto' (The Care Collective, 2020) pleads for universal care as a political principle that needs to be made operative at every level and scale of contemporary societies. Helen Hester (2019) proposes a combination of sapience and care, reason and responsibility, as key to posthuman xenofeminist ethics.

From Animal Rights to *Zoe*

Focus on the well-being of non-humans has resulted in new objects of study and subjects of critical discourse. Animals get top priority, but the agenda of post-anthropological feminism encompasses all kinds of unusual, naturalized 'others'.

The status and plight of animals has historically taken centre stage in the ecofeminist debate. It is the centrepiece of the critical analysis of species-ism and the violent dichotomies that structure the Western mindset. Eco-philosopher Plumwood (2002) was a path-breaking thinker in animal ethics, as were Carol Adams (2018 [1994]) and Josephine Donovan (1990), who produced some of the most comprehensive analyses in this field (Adams and Donovan, 1995; Donovan and Adams, 2007). Adams' analysis of the sexual politics of meat is especially relevant for posthuman feminist politics, as it proposes a position between animal rights, feminist politics and philosophy of rights (Adams, 1990; Donovan and Adams, 1996).

The ecofeminist critique of species hierarchy leads inevitably to the study of food production and to the plight of animals in the agro-business and biotechnological sectors. This unfolds into a socio-economic critique of industrial meat production, the ruthless economic exploitation of animals and plants, and the risks this economy entails for infections, epidemics and public health. Ultimately, it blows the cover on the unsustainable structure of Western eating habits. According to Greenpeace in 2019, with 60 per cent of arable land in Europe used for grazing, one fifth of the EU budget was devoted to livestock farming, for total costs ranging between £28 billion and £32 billion. Europeans eat more than twice the amount of meat than health authorities recommend, and twice the global average. Greening the European economy would require a 77 per cent reduction in meat consumption (Greenpeace, 2019). Cows are central to this aspect of the environmentalism debate and food production. As International Booker Prize winner Marieke Lucas Rijneveld remarked in relation to the Dutch livestock industry: 'no one stood a chance against the cows anyway; they were always more important. Even when they didn't require any attention, even when their fat clumsy bodies were lying sated in the stalls, they still managed to take priority' (2020: 11). Also, I wish to add, in terms of financial support. The emphasis on respect for diversity and on building collaborative networks across species is central to feminist environmental ethics. Whereas morality as well as moral philosophy is about rules and protocols of behaviour based on established norms, ethics is about power and forces. The distinction is not merely academic, because it impacts on the kind of issues that get attention and end up on the agenda. Ethics brings into focus power relations (in the dual sense of *potestas* and *potentia*) and foregrounds issues of subjectivity and accountability. Morality, on the other hand, is intrinsically normative and disciplinary.

Lori Gruen (1994) proposes a situated, materially embedded and accountable ecofeminist ethics, based on values of mutuality and compassion, as ways of bridging the differences between humans and non-humans. Gruen describes her approach as epistemological humility, which requires a balancing act between reason and emotion. More recently, Gruen (2015) expanded these insights into an ethics of compassion especially when confronted by the painful decay of our planet. Gruen's emphasis on affective entanglements, feeling with and gaining insight into animals is a plea for expanding the human relational capacity. A form of *zoe*-related empathy becomes constitutive of ecofeminism and through it of posthuman feminism.

This position is explicitly set up against the formal discourses and practices of the law, with its rationalistic basis and normative moral structure. Arguments based on reason and law, partaking of the humanistic legacy of emancipation, are highly influential and played a major role in shaping the field of environmental ethics. This is, for instance, the case in granting universal (human) rights to non-humans, which started with animals (Singer, 1975) and was extended to other living species (Nussbaum, 2006). Taking critical distance from the residual humanism, as well as the anthropocentrism of these well-meaning positions, ecofeminists pointed out the limitations of the legalistic case made by mainstream ecological thinking. The emphasis on the logic of rights actually upholds the distinction between humans and non-humans. It also results in neglecting both the role of feelings, empathy and compassion and more complex forms of ethical relationality towards the non-humans (de Waal, 1996; Braidotti, 2002; Weil, 2010; Sands, 2019).

Ecofeminism has thus historically acted as a corrective to the economic rationalism and the juridical and moral normativity that marked ecological thinking in the 1970s. The universalist logic of rights in traditional humanism had already been called into question by other feminist thinkers on two interconnected grounds. The first charge was racist Eurocentric universalism (Smith, 1978; Moraga and Anzaldua, 1981; Hill Collins, 1991) and the second was the uncritical imitation of masculine prerogatives (Irigaray, 1985b [1977]). The logic of animal rights, however necessary, is not sufficient to address as complex an issue as contemporary human–animal interaction in the frame of environmental destruction. Such an anthropocentric approach may even backfire by extending the status of humans to non-human entities, at a time when the human has been decentred under the joint pressure of multiple forces (Braidotti, 2006). However benevolent, such a move reasserts an anthropocentric hierarchy between the species and paradoxically confirms the binary distinction human/animal by extending the prerogatives of one category – the human – to others. Imputing human entitlements to non-humans by applying to them the liberal notion of individualism may turn out to be a poisoned chalice.

Animal rights activists nowadays cover a broad range of issues like vivisection and the use of animals in laboratories and medical testing (Birke et al., 2004; Holmberg, 2011), but also hunting and cross-species companionship (Haraway, 2003). In some ways, ecofeminist scholarship split into different branches according to which biological entity they prioritize. Animals are a major concern, but by no means the only one. The agenda itemizes also plants and the vegetable world; water, fish and marine organisms; the geological earth including insects, soil and dust; seeds, cells, microbes and all the naturalized others. Empathy with animals has also evolved into political vegetarianism and radical vegan activism (MacCormack, 2014), which nowadays includes active abolitionism not only of human exceptionalism, but of the very category of the human. The ecofeminist political agenda includes transnational environmental justice, but also reaches out to the Green political movement, the anti-toxics movement, the women's spirituality movement, the animal liberation movement, and anti-war and peace movements (Sturgeon, 1997).

What makes ecofeminism relevant to posthumanism is its radical decentring of Anthropos. These post-anthropocentric aspects of ecofeminism become important building blocks of posthuman feminism in that they open the possibility of a large range of non-human objects and subjects of enquiry. No privilege is granted to an allegedly pure bio-dimension, replaced instead by a biocultural continuum. Moreover, the traditional distinction between human life (*bios*) and non-human life (*zoe*) is erased and a multitude of *zoe*-related entities become relevant to and involved in defining posthuman subjects today.

Posthuman feminism thus builds on the post-anthropocentric mode of this line of ecofeminism, which adds the non-human to the critique of the bio-centred world of 'Man' and its exclusion of the dehumanized humans (Rabinow, 2003; Esposito, 2008). In earlier work I have proposed serious consideration for *zoe*, the non-human life in its great diversity (Braidotti, 2006). *Zoe*-centred egalitarianism is the alternative political ecology to universalist human rights (Braidotti, 2013). This approach gives priority to the existence, experience and welfare of non-human biological entities in a grounded and differential manner. It also affects our self-understanding as the human species. Instead of the moral universalism of human or animal rights, the posthuman ethics of *zoe*-centred egalitarianism emerges as a more adequate response to the challenges of the posthuman convergence. It shifts the emphasis away from the logic of rights and universal moral values to the multi-layered complexity of posthuman relations of care and solidarity. Accepting proximity, but also the absence of equivalences between species, posthuman ecofeminism introduces more subtle distinctions between categories and domains. It draws productive parallels between the species, while preserving the distinct capacities, propensities and predispositions of humans. Posthuman feminism opts for relational ethics that points to the mutual dependence of all entities: 'we' are, after all, in *this* together.

Against Environmental Racism

Ecofeminism inspired the field of 'green postcolonialism' (Huggan and Tiffin, 2007) and 'postcolonial ecocriticism' (Huggan and Tiffin, 2010). Building on the premises of postcolonial historical research on 'green imperialism' (Grove, 1995), green ecocriticism focuses on colonization as the missing link between anthropocentrism and Eurocentrism. It paves the way for a transversal link across key critical discourses by actively reaching out to scholars from different academic disciplines as well as cultures (Huggan, 2004; Mertens and Ulstein, 2020). The ecofeminist imprint pushes these analyses into the non-human world of animals and plants, beyond the anthropocentrism of legal theory on human rights, social justice issues and bio-ethics.

The agenda of postcolonial ecocriticism includes the study of how imperialism altered and damaged ecosystems across the globe, through 'invasion ecologies' (Elton, 2000 [1958]) and 'ecological imperialism' (Crosby, 1986). The consequences of bio-colonization – the forceful introduction of foreign plants and animal species across the colonized territories – is another aspect of the climate crisis that comes back to haunt the world in the posthuman convergence. As Frawley and McCalman argue, this natural diaspora results 'in the crippling of the new country's ecological heath and balance' (2014: 4). Bio-colonization entails the appropriation of Indigenous land, with the ensuing enslavement of the First Nation people as well as the incorporation and erasure of Indigenous perspectives on environmental practices and land management, and the coercive introduction of Western agricultural methods and technical equipment.

The effects of environmental racism do not stop with historical colonialism. As Shiva (1997) argues, Western biotechnological supremacy enforced by development programmes has escalated into the genetic commodification of Indigenous plants, seeds and species through the legal practice of patents, in a form of corporate theft, or 'biopiracy'. Significantly, Shiva is equally critical of the biotechnological practices of the Indian state's economic policies and their devastating consequences on both cultural and biological diversity. Monocultures that were born from the colonial plantation economy continue through the homogenization of global neoliberalism. The global spread of monocultures such as the eucalyptus tree across tourist resorts and residential areas all over the world is a pertinent example.

Another aspect of environmental racism is the environmentally discriminatory treatment of sexualized, racialized and marginal subjects and economically disadvantaged people. Examples are the indiscriminate land-mining activities of the extraction economies across ancestral Indigenous lands and the transfer of both organic and technological toxic waste to the same countries where the minerals are extracted from. The effects of the accumulation of toxins in impoverished, marginalized and racialized subjects is especially high among women and LGBTQ+ people (Chen, 2012). It gives rise to 'toxic embodiment' as a key feminist environmental, social and affective issue (Cielemęcka and Åsberg, 2019). Also relevant in this respect is the racial and social segregation of efforts at setting up a 'Green New Deal' and a clean economy (Klein, 2019). The financial and technological means of addressing the consequences of climate change are concentrated in the overdeveloped parts of the world. Discussions of climate justice need to pay attention to the intersections between race, gender and the environmental movement. Failing to develop an ecologically informed intersectionality runs the risk of falling into what Nancy Tuana calls 'climate apartheid' (2019) and thus perpetuating racism and the invisibility of Black and Indigenous women.

Postcolonial theory meeting ecofeminism has proved to be a source of inspiration for the critical Environmental Humanities as a new and transdisciplinary area of research (Rose et al., 2012; Neimanis et al., 2015). This field covers transnational environmental justice, postcolonial environmental ethics and Indigenous land rights. It focuses on how the disenfranchised and impoverished populations of the world are encountering climate change and the posthuman convergence. Considering the excessive price that Black, decolonial and First Nation people are paying within the fractures of this posthuman conjuncture, it is urgent to learn from their experience of devastating changes and their tradition of resilience. It is crucial to build bridges across the different perspectives and locations, because 'we' are in *this* challenging convergence together, though we are not one and the same.

Post-secular Plateaus

Ecofeminism approaches the earth as Gaia, a self-organizing living organism based on symbiotic connections, cemented by ceaseless microbial activity (Lovelock and Margulis, 1974). This approach tips the balance of ecofeminist thought in a distinctly post-secular direction (Braidotti, 2008), including celebrations of the sacred Mother Earth as the mystical feminine principle (Griffin, 1978; Starhawk, 1979). Ecofeminist spirituality, both in Christian (Merchant, 1980) and in other traditions (Shiva, 1988, 2012; Maathai, 2010), joins forces with a situated cosmopolitics (Stengers, 2011). It emphasizes the sacredness of life and the integrity of all living organisms and aims at healing the earth from patriarchal violence, instrumental rationality, and capitalist and colonial eco-cide. Pope Francis recently took an analogous position, from within Christianity (2015).

I do concur with Gaard (2011) and Neimanis (2015) that this aspect of ecofeminism contributed to the negative image of this movement, in the eyes of the social-constructivist feminist mainstream, as a naïve and essentialist mode of relation to Earth Mothers and green goddesses. The post-secular approach has also complicated the reception of ecofeminism in at least two important areas. The first is scientific research and the second is left-wing politics. Any form of spirituality is suspicious in academic circles where standards are set by scientific criteria of objectivity and secular reason. The separation of affects and spirituality from rationality is a key feature of academic reason, still indexed on scientific humanism. A post-secular turn has been debated in critical feminism (Harding, 2001; Mahmood, 2005), while fields such as religious studies made brilliant excursions into feminist materialist thinking (Meyer, 2012). But mainstream academic feminism upholds the dichotomy of spirituality-versus-science, while being critical of coercive secularism (Scott, 2007). In her comments on the contemporary witch and spiritual leader, Starhawk, Gaard corrects this misperception: 'Starhawk has persistently engaged with issues of globalization and economic and ecological justice, from the 1980s antinuclear protests through the anti-globalization movements of the 1990s and beyond' (2011: 39). The millions of followers Starhawk has gathered over the years testify to the broad range of issues covered by her vision. Spirituality is not a single-issue movement. In an ironical acknowledgement of this important dimension, Donna Haraway described her techno-ecofeminist stance also as the expression of her failed secularism (2006).

But the post-secular approach has other problems, for instance in relation to gender. For some, ecofeminism tended to slip too easily into a glorified celebration of the eternal feminine and in so doing reinforced the very dichotomies it purported to unmake. Starting from the gender binary, they then engender other oppositions such as nature–culture, emotion–reason, religion–politics and spirituality–science. Feminist and LGBTQ+ theorists criticized the heteronormative, maternalist assumption that dominated the early ecofeminist discussions of spirituality, care and nurturing (Gaard, 1997). As the notion of 'woman-identified-women' (Radicalesbians, 1971; Walker, 1983) lost favour in lesbian theory, even subversive practices like lesbian motherhood (Rich, 1976) were found somewhat wanting. The feminization of values was met with suspicion as a residual form of colonization of human diversity by a dualistic gender system.

Queer ecofeminists (Mortimer-Sandilands and Erickson, 2010; Gaard, 1997) find that previous ecofeminists did not question compulsory heterosexuality and rather left heterosexism unchallenged as the dominant paradigm: 'From a queer ecofeminist perspective, then, we can examine the ways queers are feminized, animalized, eroticized, and naturalized in a culture that devalues women, animals, nature, and sexuality. We can also examine how persons of color are feminized, animalized, eroticized, and naturalized. Finally, we can explore how nature is feminized, eroticized, even queered' (Gaard, 1997: 119). The transversal connections across the different kinds of sexualized, racialized and naturalized others get priority, bringing Indigenous and Western posthumanist feminisms together while cautioning against any simplistic reduction of the two to a basic equivalence. Their sheer multiplicity undoes the restriction of any binary system.

By extension this also means that the unnatural position to which LGBTQ+ people are reduced in patriarchal culture can be turned into a resource, in that it supports the possibility of an egalitarian and generative alliance with non-humans, including monstrous and deviant others. As Susan Stryker put it: 'The enemy of my nature is a Nature that is home to Man, but not to me' (2020: xviii). This position inaugurates a 'transecology' (Gaard, 2020), as a way of relinquishing anthropocentric privilege and introducing diversity of genders and gendered identities into ecofeminism. Embracing one's hybrid un-naturalness is an affirmative way of dealing with the negative connotations associated with deviant and non-conforming sexualities. Many LGBTQ+ theorists, however, prefer to abandon nature altogether and appeal to technology as an instrument of liberation, as we will see in chapter 5. What matters for my argument here is to see how in the posthuman convergence the boundaries between the environmental and the technological dissolve and become porous. The popularity of the social-constructivist method led many queer and trans feminists to privilege technology over nature, but the pending ecological crisis is forcing everybody to reconsider their environmental footprint. Strong affects are at play. Technofeminists may well disagree with ecofeminists in that they'd much rather be cyborgs than goddesses, following Haraway's famous quip (1985). In the posthuman juncture, however, binary thinking (either/or) is not particularly helpful. The challenge is to deal with both the technological revolution and the climate crisis: two internally contradictory phenomena. Ecofeminism, Indigenous feminism, technoscience and LGBTQ+

theories all contribute in different ways to the making of a post/in/non-human turn in feminist theory. Transversal connections are the motor of posthuman feminism. To conclude the point about spirituality: as a posthuman feminist I acknowledge residual elements of a spiritual dimension as integral to the critical practice and central to affirmative ethics (Braidotti, 2008).

Let me turn now to the second problematic area of reception of both the nature–culture continuum and its spiritual connotations, namely the relationship to left-wing politics. There is a real disagreement between ecofeminists and socialist feminists – and more broadly between environmentalism and Marxism – literally on the 'matter' of oppression and on how political change can be activated. Instead of prioritizing violent dialectical confrontation as the trigger for systemic change and activating antagonism, posthuman ecofeminists propose a collective process of transformative becoming. This means that the devalorized others of 'Man' are also – and by virtue of their marginalization – endowed with qualities and values, competences and knowledge that transcend the misery of their oppression. Alienation can be generative. They are never completely saturated by the dominant codes of here and now and their negativity. Firstly, because all subjects are in process and perpetual motion, being immanent to the vitality of matter. Secondly, because they possess degrees of endurance and imagination beyond what the capitalist and colonial order has reduced them to. Or rather, they exist in excess of the negativity of their imposed social condition and embody virtual possibilities of engendering 'otherwise other' modes of subjectivity, community and knowledge (Braidotti, 2019). Post-anthropocentric politics challenges the dialectics of negativity of Marxist politics.

Ecofeminism, like other branches of the feminist movement, has suffered from a fraught relationship with the political Left: socialist and environmental politics historically do not mix well. In the last century ecological issues in general were dismissed as conservative and even reactionary by leading left-wing intellectuals like Michel Foucault and Edward Said. This negative attitude is partly justified by the nationalistic origins of nature conservation programmes, like national parks, since the nineteenth century and by their connection to colonial expropriation of Indigenous land (Taylor, 2016). Stacy Alaimo comments on this aspect of the environmental scepticism on the part of the Left: 'the environmental movements of the early twentieth century, devoted to conserving "natural resources" or to preserving aesthetic natures, were not just unconcerned by the plight of the poor or otherwise disenfranchised, but actively took up positions that articulated "conservation" with a white, middle-to-upper class' (2010: 29).

The negative relationship between Red and Green politics[2] has affected the representations and the status of ecofeminism, which resulted in underplaying its role as precursor and inspiration for contemporary Anthropocene studies and politics. Posthuman scholarship nowadays neither acknowledges nor appreciates ecofeminists for their fair worth, while still capitalizing on their intellectual labour (Fraiman, 2012). This is a repressive tactic that Gaard describes as: 'keep the focus, lose the name' (2011: 41). The field of mainstream posthuman research on the Anthropocene at present tends to engage in 'mansplaining' (Solnit, 2014) the environmental crisis in an intellectual model that remains predominantly masculine, white, middle-class, urban, anthropocentric and Eurocentric. I am constantly surprised at the devotion with which mainstream posthuman scholars refer to their patriarchal father figures. The object ontologists' re-discovery of Bruno Latour's work on the Anthropocene is a perfect example of this approach[3] (Harman, 2009), or take Derrida's critique of anthropocentrism, in the essay on the cat confronting his nudity (2002). Similar enthusiasm surrounds John Gray's disquisition on canine humanism and his suitably cynical dismantling of human arrogance (2002). But surely the debate on posthuman values cannot be confined to Derrida's cats and Gray's straw dogs. We also need Haraway's companion-species, chickens included. And we cannot do without Margulis' bacterial neighbours, Franklin's multi-tasking sheep, Alaimo's clever jellyfish and Tsing's millennial mushrooms. That is to name but a few of the alternative figurations for non-human and distributed posthuman subjectivity invented by ecofeminists. It is important, therefore, to reposition ecofeminism as an original and reliable scientific source and a provider of political strategies and policies, as well as original knowledge and methods. A movement that pioneered so many radical ideas, politics and values – and managed to annoy so many mainstream scholars – must be doing something right.

Indigenous Critique of Anthropos

Ecofeminism interpellates colonialism and colonial racism directly, starting from the perspective of the naturalized others. As Indigenous people are spread over 90 different countries in the world, one cannot generalize about their epistemological and ethical approach. I will rather rely on the published material of Indigenous scholars and shared insights in order to carefully construct points of common interest and contact. Val Plumwood argues that nature is a politicized category, which 'continues to function to justify oppression in both the human and the nonhuman spheres' (1994: 77). In the specific case of Australian colonialism, it has led to the reduction of the land to the notion of *Terra Nullius*, legally classified as unoccupied by the colonialist settlers. This allowed the colonizers to annex the land and obliterate the existence, as well as the resistance, of the original inhabitants (Huggins, 2001). The claim of depopulation deprived the Indigenous people of both their land and their humanity and allowed for the conquest and the genocide to become legal. For the surviving native population, colonial violence meant a transformation into a category of humans without land and without a world: 'castaways, refugees, precarious lodgers in a world in which they no longer belonged, because it could not belong to them' (Danowski and Viveiros de Castro, 2017: 106).

Gibson et al. (2015) address the feminist agenda in dialogue with Plumwood, spelling out clearly the specific features of an Aboriginal approach to feminist environmental politics, and, through it, to the climate crisis. Indigenous feminists uphold and proclaim holistic principles beyond all binaries and reassert the importance of relinquishing the position of anthropocentric mastery and listening instead to the world, the land, the territory. They emphasize the need for both citizens and scholars to change quite radically in their interaction and to become curious, experimental, open, adaptive, imaginative, responsive and responsible.

The theoretical point of encounter between ecofeminism and Indigenous thought is the refusal to separate humanity as an exceptional category from the living environment in which it is positioned and by which it is co-produced (Ingold, 2000; Descola, 2009). This point of intersection accelerates in the posthuman convergence, with the addition of insights from technoscience and the life sciences. A more expansive understanding of the human is introduced that includes a range of new knowledge: from the role of the ecological environment, to the myriads of bacteria that constitute our bodies; the human is a complex and heterogeneous multi-species collectivity. Enforcing any categorical or ontological separations would be a denial of interdependence and relational coexistence. It would also reiterate the violent mark of colonialism upon the lands and the people it dispossessed (Moreton-Robinson, 2003, 2009; TallBear, 2013; Whyte, 2013; Viveiros de Castro, 2014).

From a feminist posthuman perspective, ancient Indigenous epistemologies constitute a philosophical form of perspectivism. They posit a 'multinatural' continuum across all species, all of which partake of a common idea of distributed humanity, also the non-humans (TallBear, 2015). Indigenous relational philosophies target dualism as the specific pathology of Western philosophy. As Rose (2004) points put, these dualities are in fact hierarchies, consolidating the One, a sovereign subject with the right to autonomy, while denying all dependency on others, who get designated as an absence. The sexualized, racialized and naturalized others suffer an ontological erasure that reduces them to nothingness (Irigaray, 1985b; Moten, 2003; Stryker, 2015; Wynter, 2015).

What Plumwood called an 'ecological crisis of reason' (2002) prompts a radical feminist critique linking patriarchy, colonization, racism, modernity, technological development and environmental devastation. For thinkers like Rose (2004, 2015), it inaugurates a systemic decolonial strategy, which consists in instilling a cross-cultural and multi-species relational ethics, and breaks loose from the violence of monological thinking. In a posthuman feminist frame it increases our relational capacity to connect, accept dependency and act affirmatively. The key motif of posthuman feminism is to cultivate affirmative resilience by accepting to go beyond humanism, but also to stress the humans' post-anthropocentric interdependence on the entire living environment.

Rose (2017) proposes a situated, embodied ethics of care and builds on ecofeminism by stressing the links between colonial genocide and environmental ecocide, the war against natives, women and that against nature as part of the same fundamental violence. This position builds on, but also moves beyond, the critiques of humanism advanced by postcolonial and race theory in earlier poststructuralist inspired analyses of gender and race (Young 1990, 1995; Stoller, 1995) and deconstructive postcolonial scholarship (Spivak, 1985, 1987, 1990, 1999; Bhabha, 1994). Postcolonial literary and cultural theory (Nixon, 2011) also pushes boundaries, by combining textual analysis with materially embedded concern for transnational environmental justice movements.

The fear of extinction and panic, triggered by mainstream discussions of climate change, the Anthropocene and species extinction, have struck a sceptical chord in Black, decolonial and especially in Indigenous feminism. The ancient guardians of the earth and First Nation people have already experienced the devastation of their lands and cultures through the violence of colonization (B. Clarke, 2008; Todd, 2015, 2016; Whyte, 2016, 2017). As Danowski and Viveiros de Castro poignantly put it: 'Indigenous people have something to teach us when it comes to apocalypses, losses of world, demographic catastrophes, and ends of History ... for the native people of the Americas, the end of the world already happened – five centuries ago. To be exact, it began on October 12, 1492' (2017: 105). They consequently call for a more balanced account of the posthuman convergence and especially of the climate change emergency, one that allows for decolonial perspectives and anti-racist approaches.

Defining the contemporary market economy with Deleuze and Guattari as 'Integrated World Capitalism', Danowski and Viveiros de Castro (2017) connect it to a devastating list of environmental damages that accompany it. They analyse the current environmental crisis as affecting adversely the dominant classes, ethnicities and genders. The most entitled subjects seem to be suffering the most from the awareness of their own limitations. From a decolonial perspective, these fits of 'white panic' (Danowski and Viveiros de Castro, 2017) signal the revisitation of colonial violence upon those most responsible for it. The Anthropocene is an intrusion of nature into the dominant, Western, Christian, capitalist civilizational matrix. From a philosophical angle, Viveiros de Castro (2014, 2015) also singles out the similarities and resonances between Indigenous perspectivism, ecofeminism and the materialist philosophical perspectivism of Leibnitz and Deleuze. This is important for posthuman feminism, because it provides common theoretical grounds in a vital new materialism that is non-binary and transversal. All the perspectivist philosophers argue that 'there are souls everywhere' and that entities and organisms differ in their capacity of perception and cognition. They embody different degrees of intensity. Indigenous cosmologies in particular emphasize that all living entities are considered as being endowed with a soul, with specific faculties and forces. Of course, they differ, but these differences are not situated in a divide between human/non-human species, but within each of them (Viveiros de Castro, 1998, 2014).

In other words, each entity is differential and relational. There are no species hierarchies in terms of assigned anthropological traits and abilities, but rather a more distributed idea of living beings, all of which are considered human. What makes perspectivism relevant to posthuman feminism is the crucial idea of ontological relationality. Every being is relational and exists not in-itself, but being-as and being-with others. In the beginning is the relation and the relation is heterogeneous by definition.

Ontological relationality provides the robust and dynamic foundations for posthuman subjectivity as something removed from both humanism and anthropocentrism, yet connected to an infinity of other instances and entities. It combines the rejection of individualism with a positive reappraisal of the productive and empathic relations between humans and non-humans. They stress the extent to which their interrelation is internal to and constitutive of the identity of each category. Similarly, for Barad (2003, 2007) a relation is intra-active and performative; for me it is materially embedded and differential. A relation is a transformative bond that defines – by hybridizing – the 'nature' of each component. This relational ontology challenges the parameters of liberal individualism that is implicit in universalist animal rights, and foregrounds instead the relational ethics and cross-species interdependence. The relation is the middle ground, or the 'milieu' of new modes of human/non-human interaction. It is a politics and poetics of relations (Glissant, 1997) that calls into question human/non-human interaction within a decolonial framework.

But relations are not intrinsically positive; on the contrary, negativity is almost the norm. Viveiros de Castro points out that the European invasion of the Americas and the destruction of the Amerindians through the combination of guns, viruses and Biblical texts accomplished an eco-colonial genocide. The fact that so many of the First Nation people not only survived, but created new worlds, within or parallel to that of their invaders, is an achievement and a lesson for all the contemporary posthuman subjects who fear the consequences of the Anthropocene. Indigenous resilience is an asset in the collective construction of vital margins of assertion of alternatives. It is the implementation of virtual possibilities through the praxis of processing pain, loss and negativity. Women are central to this endeavour as the ones primarily responsible for species reproduction. From a decolonial perspective, the climate change emergency and the general condition of the Anthropocene expose both the limitations and the responsibilities of European humanism and its techno-industrial culture. The same Eurocentric violence and capitalist greed that was at work in the dispossession of Indigenous people and the dispersion of their cultures also brought about the environmental crisis (Bignall et al., 2016).

The dialogues between Indigenous thinkers and European and feminist postcolonial scholars are not widespread yet, but growing. Bignall and Rigney (2019) provide one of earliest intercultural collaborations of Indigenous and non-Indigenous scholars. They bring Western posthumanist philosophical perspectives in relation with Indigenous transformations of colonial polities, with collaborative work in posthuman postcolonial philosophy. Simone Bignall (2010) draws from Deleuze's reading of Spinoza a submerged potential for a non-imperialist ethics of association. Bignall's contribution to postcolonial philosophy is valued specifically as a materialist intervention, because it counters the assumption that postcolonial studies is about discourse and discursive operations of power. She points instead to the material basis of colonial oppression in stolen land, slavery and the societal effects of policy.

Within a shared interest in perspectivism and materialism, Deleuze's philosophy has proved helpful in creating connections. Deleuzian postcolonial theory (Bignall and Patton, 2010; Burns and Kaiser, 2012; Braidotti and Bignall, 2019) shows how capitalism and colonialism turn the smooth space of the indigenous earth into the striated space of Western privatized stolen property of the earth. That entails the analysis of how the open, unmarked land is turned into exploitable territories. Other Continental philosophers who reference Deleuze's work have addressed the issue of race theory and racial formations (Saldanha and Adams, 2013), colonial possession of the land, and include ground-breaking scholars who developed collaborations between Indigenous and non-Indigenous perspectives (Benterrak et al., 1983; Morrissey and Healy, 2018).

Academic disciplines like feminist geography and geopolitics are rich in cross-fertilizations. Juanita Sundberg (2013) is a non-Indigenous geographer whose work brings posthumanism into contact with Indigenous perspectives. More recently, the fast-rising field of the Critical Posthumanities, notably the Environmental Humanities, have supported a lot of Indigenous and non-Indigenous collaborations. These include studies by prominent people like Petina Pert (Pert et al., 2020) Sue Jackson (Jackson et al., 2020) and Margaret Somerville (2020), who work collaboratively with Indigenous communities.

Fields such as critical anthropology and ethnography have a long tradition of collaborative scholarship with Indigenous knowledge holders (Rose, 2004, for example). This is 'critical scholarship' because it takes Indigenous people as participants in the research, rather than as objects of anthropological enquiry, as in the colonial methods used by imperial anthropology as a discipline of control. Working within and on Arctic Indigenous philosophies, Rauna Kuokkanen positions feminism at the intersection of Indigenous peoples' struggle for decolonization and self-determination, and more specific issues of gender equality and justice (2019). Studying the specificity of Indigenous knowledge production systems (2017), Kuokkanen calls into question both the Eurocentrism and white bias of the university as an institution (2007) and the need to decolonize feminism as a whole (2015).

To place different orders of knowledge and different traditions of subject formation in dialogue with each other does not mean creating false equivalences or overarching meta-theories. It rather aims at amplifying possible resonances between them, for instance, in relation to different ways of understanding survival and the composition of a 'missing people' – women and LGBTQ+ people and Indigenous people included. It creates collaborative links across differently situated knowledge practices of immanence and accountability.

The Posthuman Acceleration

The decentring of Anthropos as species exceptionalism and the rejection of anthropocentrism as a habit of thought are crucial for posthuman feminism. By instituting a *zoe*-centred transversal link of interdependence across species, posthuman feminist thought gets ready to address the shift of perspective that has helped shape the posthuman agenda. The first shift marks the end of the nature–culture divide and of the many binary oppositions that structure the Western social, scientific and symbolic order. Most cultures on earth do not separate so drastically between nature and culture, mind and body, humans and animals. The second shift is the challenge to sexual difference, gender binaries and gendered division of labour, which favours compulsory heterosexuality and heterosexual reproduction. This has direct consequences for the status of women and LGBTQ+ people the world over.

To cope with contemporary accelerations, posthuman feminism combines ecological awareness and appreciation of technology with a commitment to social justice and the viewpoint of the excluded, the subaltern, the dehumanized, sexualized, racialized and naturalized others. Ecofeminists, Indigenous and Black feminists had already shown how patriarchal regimes are operational in colonialist and capitalist modes of appropriation of natural resources. They add species supremacy to the analysis of that system of power. This produces a more precise critique of anthropocentrism and of other power relations, through transversal links to other critical discourses, notably postcolonial and race theories. These generative assemblages bring into full force new research themes, diversifying the study of non-human entities, from upper primates and genes, to the earth, water, dust and plastic. Conceptually, posthuman feminism promotes a cross-species way of thinking that includes the *zoe*-geo-techno-mediated relations to the multiple ecologies composing the posthuman convergence.

Video artist, researcher and essayist Ursula Biemann[4] provides a relevant example of materialist feminist artworks, through targeted fieldwork in geo-politically significant and often remote locations. Her method is a visual ethnography that connects the micropolitics on the ground with a meta-discursive theoretical level, combining creativity with critical reflexion. Starting with documenting the serial murders of women on the Mexican border and the gendered dimension of migration, Biemann then performed a spatial turn. She focused on the clandestine migration networks and patterns of asylum seekers trying to cross the Mediterranean.[5] She studied the human, ecological and political effects of the oil pipelines from the fields in the Caucasian, investigating climate change and the ecologies of oil and water.[6] In other words, Biemann took a distinct turn first towards non-human elemental agents of change – notably geo-techno apparatus. Having encountered Indigenous epistemologies, she focused on natural resources and their situated materiality to assess the combined effects of climate change and colonialism.[7] Her recent fieldwork takes place in the Arctic region and the Amazon.[8] She is currently collaborating with the Inga people of South America to set up an Indigenous university in the rainforests of Colombia. The core values of that project are perspectivism, relationality and ethics of care for humans and non-humans alike.

One of the qualitative shifts introduced by ecofeminism occurs in terms of ethics. Ecofeminists and Indigenous feminists have developed a range of more egalitarian, affective caring and just modes of ethical relation to non-human entities: animals, plants, the earth as a whole. Ethically, it calls for an environmental relational ethics that grants full agency to the non-humans. Politically, it promotes transnational environmental justice against the unsustainable growth models of global capital.

On all these scores, ecofeminists and Indigenous feminists have contributed some of the most original insights into the posthuman convergence, independently of mainstream, corporate and philosophical anti/trans/in/posthumanisms. In this regard, they are the originators of posthuman perspectives and insights, and have played a pioneering role in exploring the materialist and ecological roots of processes normally flattened onto a social-constructivist model. Ecofeminists and Indigenous feminists have acted as a corrective to the well-meaning but hasty moral universalism of animal rights movements. They proposed alternative environmental ethics by turning the proximity to the earth into a source of inspiration. The bond to the land is the connection between ecofeminism and Indigenous cosmologies and value systems, which is of great relevance to Anthropocene scholarship. The climate change crisis forces a reappraisal of many ecofeminist agenda points, notably vegetarianism, food production and coercive consumption.

The posthuman convergence acts as an accelerator of all these factors and insights, which had been built up patiently over decades of feminist practice. The double challenge of climate change and advanced technologies revives and intensifies the ecofeminist insights. For one thing, the ancestral bond 'woman–nature' comes to the foreground once again, as women and girls still constitute the bulk of the agricultural workers of the earth in charge of the collection of firewood and water (Harcourt, 2016). These tasks expose them to physical hardship and hazards, which grow ever worse as a result of climate change, as droughts, or floods make basic resources like wood and water even scarcer. There is therefore a direct correlation between thinning environmental and economic resources and the increasing poverty of women, as well as higher risks for their health and well-being. As poverty increases, so does violence against women and the risks of forced marriages and sex trafficking. This increases the urgency of a political process of emancipation that links climate action to women's empowerment. As Mary Robinson, chair of The Elders,[9] put it recently: 'Tackling climate change and environmental degradation without the full inclusion of women will not succeed: gender equality is a prerequisite to the collective effort needed to address the climate emergency'.[10]

Fortunately, things are moving fast and environmentalism as a social movement has attracted strong female leadership, from Vandana Shiva to Greta Thunberg. A new community project called 'Climate Reframe' was initiated by the people behind Mary Robinson's feminist climate podcast Mothers of Invention with Aisha Younis and Suzanne Dhaliwal to build a community of experts.[11] The project aims to amplify the voice of Black, Brown, Asian, People of Colour and UK-based Indigenous Peoples who are climate experts, campaigners and advocates living and working in the UK. Considering the low representation of BAME climate experts in public debates and policy-making circles, 'Climate Reframe' wants to make it easier for media, funders, conferences and campaigns to find them and include their expertise and perspectives.

The Indigenous communities are taking the lead in this process the world over, as for instance in the community-based project 'Violence on the Land, Violence on our Bodies: Building an Indigenous Response to Environmental Violence' (VLVB).[12] Based in Alberta, Canada, this organization addresses the interlocking ways in which violence against Indigenous women is connected to violence against Indigenous cultures and against the land itself (Konsmo and Pacheco, 2016). Resting on the Indigenous cosmologies that respect the wholeness of the earth, they stress the need for sovereign autonomy and self-determination as a first step towards the expression of both environmental care and justice, as well as gender equality. The political edge of this message is clear: it is impossible to discuss environmental politics, policies and ideals of justice without taking into account Indigenous women's social and symbolic systems within an imperial history of violent dispossession and exploitation. Ecocide, femicide and genocide work in tandem in Black and Indigenous histories.

Posthuman feminism moves towards a decolonial multispecies feminist ecology, marking a critical shift of focus away from the dichotomous thinking of feminist social- constructivist theories. Stacy Alaimo's description of this defining moment is telling: 'As a poststructuralist feminist myself, I sought the destabilization of any set definitions of "woman", but as an environmentalist I feared that the critique of essentialism sometimes mirrored humanist trajectories of transcendence from corporeality, biology, animality and "nature"' (2018: 47). Posthuman feminism challenges the constructivist tradition of anti-naturalism and prompts a critical re-naturalization and a reappraisal of grounded foundations. This cannot fail to affect also the critical theories that rest upon constructivist premises. As Chakrabarty (2009) warned, some basic tenets of critical thought are dislocated by the deep time and non-linear temporalities introduced by climate change. Critical re-naturalization is a strategic move that aims at empowering critical theory, notably feminism, to cope with contemporary Life Sciences and smart technologies. They also enable feminists to address the capitalization of life and living systems by advanced capitalism, while addressing the climate change catastrophe.

By extension, in the posthuman convergence, the social-constructivist gender paradigm that started with Ortner and Rubin is no longer adequate to the specific contradictions of the times. Not only can the distinction nature–culture no longer be held, as Indigenous philosophers convincingly argue, but it cannot support the binary gender system that came to be indexed upon it, let alone the reductive equation of women to nature and men to culture. What is deficient is not only the binary structure of these oppositions, though the rejection of the nature–culture dualism is important (Tuana, 1989, 2008). The complexity is also internal to ideas such as nature, biology and earth-matter, that appear too monolithic and require a more diversified angle of approach including multiple discourses and categories: scientific, historical, socio-economic and political.

Posthuman feminism cannot be mono-paradigmatic. Multiple cartographies are needed to account with greater accuracy and precision for the multi-dimensional impact of the posthuman predicament. They must include not only socio-economic factors but also the environment, the natural world, the extractable resources and the people living alongside them. A methodological form of re-naturalization emerges as the preferred posthuman ecofeminist method. This is an internally diversified process of accounting for the earth, and the naturalized others, now when they emerge as political agents in their own right. This means exercising ethical and epistemological care for the non-human entities and agents, not only in geological terrestrial terms, but also through a multiplicity of elements: hydrological, geological, meteorological, economic, health, social and other factors. But because the nature–culture continuum allows for a better understanding of technological mediation, as a process of grounded relations, the strategic re-naturalization paradoxically accomplishes a relative de-naturalization. It produces a complex ecology of mediated practices, because the environment is technologized, just as technology is grounded and ecologized. Technology has become second nature, but the environmental toll of technological development is enormous. Old nature pays a heavy price. For instance, cryptocurrency Bitcoin consumes 121.36 terawatt (TWh) hours of electricity per year, which is more than each of the whole of Argentina (121 TWh) and the Netherlands (108.8 TWh). Bitcoin-mining computers produce the same amounts of CO_2 emissions as Las Vegas (22 megatons) per year (Young, 2021). Transhumanist billionaire Elon Musk, who is a pioneer of alternative car energy and a Bitcoin currency enthusiast, is an emblem of such posthuman paradoxes and contradictions.

The posthuman acceleration is a magnifying glass that brings to the fore often implicit conceptual and methodological complications. They are due to the utterly banal and yet underplayed insight of ecofeminism, namely that, as embodied and embedded entities, we are all inhabitants of the earth and hence part of nature (Lloyd, 1994). The earth is not one element among others, but rather that which brings them all together in a form of radical immanence: living matter (Braidotti, 2006, 2013).

As Michel Serres, an environmental philosopher of science put it: 'In fact, the Earth speaks to us in terms of forces, bonds, and interactions, and that's enough to make a contract' (1995: 39). Serres pleads for serious re-naturalization in the form of drawing up a new natural contract to replace the old social contract, based on reason and law. The natural contract stipulates symbiosis and reciprocity in our relationship to a world Europeans have treated with mastery and violent appropriation. A new natural contract would bind humans to a different relationship to their planetary host. Serres considers the human species as a parasite – a virus – that fails to honour the host organism – in our case the earth – and, by depleting it, seals its own death warrant. Thus, in the end, ecofeminism and Indigenous feminism are fully vindicated as both an analytic and an ethical frame to make sense of and atone for the damages we are inflicting on the earth. We either embrace symbiotic interdependence or face death. No insight could be more relevant to the posthuman predicament.

Conclusion: But 'We' Are in *this* Together

As I have shown in this chapter, posthuman feminism emerges at the confluence of different strands of feminist thought and interacts with them all productively. It is not just the sum of their parts but a qualitative leap in a new direction. A convergence is not a synthesis and need not work in a linear manner. The posthuman convergence is a zigzagging pattern of conjunctions and crossovers (and/and) rather than a geometric grid of drastic selections (either/or). My code word to describe this approach is transversality; it is about making affective connections across the ecological, the social, the technological and other domains. Here I want to come back to the spiritual dimension as integral to the critical practice of posthuman feminism, but rather discuss it further in its ethical implications. A sense of interconnection between human and non-human others produces and supports a fundamental openness and generosity towards them. There is a kind of ontological pacifism at play in this recognition that 'we' (humans and non-humans) are in *this* environment together. This awareness is for me the motor of the ethics of affirmation as political praxis. It is the transformative moment that turns the negative charge – for instance the experience of exclusion – into a collective force capable of activating a potential. This transformative practice is not a magical trick that happens in a metamorphic flash, nor is it a miracle, but rather a humble praxis of collectively driven change.

This is the affirmative force of posthuman feminism that combines sharp critique with intense compassion and care for a damaged and suffering world. It is a case of posthuman feminist *pietas* on a planetary scale. It has produced critical and creative forms of re-naturalization of those who, being socialized as the devalorized others of 'Man', have not had the historical opportunity to express the forces, qualities and values that constitute them. Posthuman feminism constructs a new vision of the political and epistemic subject as a heterogeneous assemblage: 'we' is an inextricable mix of humans and non-humans.

The Covid-19 virus manifests these entangled, rhizomatic connections and highlights both their lethal force and their affirmative potential. Adamson and Hartman (2020), working within the Environmental Humanities, apply the term 'syndemic' (coined by medical anthropologist Merrill Singer in the 1990s) to describe the combined and cumulative effects of the pandemic. They list among the synergetic factors of the epidemic the social effects of poverty and increased food insecurities, malnutrition and other health crises affecting specific people, classes, ethnicities and age groups. A chain reaction is thus triggered that is central to the social-economic and environmental effects of the pandemic. Of course, these risk factors, connected to social conditions, lifestyle choices and addictions, make entire social groups more exposed to risks and vulnerable to diseases. Many so-called 'natural' disasters and diseases are human-induced. The distinctions between environmental, social and affective aspects of an emergency like COVID-19 or climate change pale into insignificance. What comes to the fore is how they join forces to certain strata of the population with more systematic violence than others. And how inseparable they make each individual body – embodied and embedded subjects – from all others.

These complex entanglements also contain an important affirmative ethical nucleus. The inextricability of social, technological and environmental factors reveals the fact that 'we' are in *this* together although we are not one and the same. At a broader level, it highlights the mutual capacity to affect and be affected by others, which is constitutive of a new-materialist relational vision of subjectivity. As such it is capable of triggering unplanned transformative changes in the ways we live and work together. Confronted by such injustices, and the mirroring pandemics of the virus and of racism and xenophobia, contemporary posthuman feminists need to work towards a posthuman ethics of accountability, transversal solidarity and cross-species care, transnational environmental justice, and a democratic distribution of healthcare provisions. This requires a post-anthropocentric and posthuman shift as well as the recognition of mutuality and multi-species interdependence (Cohn and Lynch, 2018).

An adequate response to a crisis on the scale of COVID-19 calls for community-based experiments to see how and how fast we can transform the way we live and die. That means facing up to the social and environmental inequalities and the collective responsibility towards exposed or vulnerable populations. It is a praxis that promotes action and critical self-knowledge, by working through negativity and pain. This proactive activism manifests living beings' shared ability to actualize and potentiate different possibilities and generate multiple and yet unexplored interconnections. Where Anthropos used to rule as sovereign, let heterogeneous alliances emerge. This is a way of affirming the immanence of life as jointly articulated in a common world. Not some transcendental and abstract notion of Life with capital letters, but rather the more patient task of constructing one's life, alongside so many others: just *a* life.

Part II
Posthuman Feminism as Creation

Chapter 4
New Materialism and Carnal Empiricism

Thinking is the stuff of the world.

Stacy Alaimo (2014: 13)

In Gitanes cigarette smoke-filled classrooms at Vincennes university, I inhaled new-materialist thinking with every breath I took as a graduate student of Foucault, Irigaray and Deleuze in Paris in the 1970s. The embodied and embedded form of materialism developed by the philosophers of that generation was the perfect antidote to the historical materialism of the Marxists and the hysterical materialism of Lacanian psychoanalysis. I drew a deep sigh of relief because those schools of thought were so dominant in that period – indicted by Deleuze and Guattari as intimidating 'bureaucracies of thought'. New materialism provided an infusion of oxygen for critical thinking. Philosophy tends to be insular and self-referential, removed from the real world and often forgets what fresh air (Irigaray, 1999 [1983]) and healthy breathing (Deleuze, 2003) actually feel like. Most students of my age were breathless with anticipation at the discovery of this renewed current of materialist thought. I have always been and will always be a new-materialist feminist.

In this chapter I examine how posthuman feminism expands and redefines materialism and how it bears on the complexity of the posthuman convergence. I will select the specific strands of feminist new materialism that are most relevant to the posthuman convergence and outline their basic tenets. In so doing I will reconnect them to the feminist genealogies and the work of previous generations of materialist thinkers. Poststructuralism includes both the linguistic and the materialist strands, but in the Anglo-American feminist tradition, the former became dominant. However, materialism has a brilliant feminist heritage. I concur with Coole and Frost (2010) that the contemporary instantiation instead of 'new', should be labelled 'renewed' materialism, in that it revisits older and more established traditions. And yet it also transforms them significantly through 'new ways of thinking about matter and processes of materialization' (Coole and Frost, 2010: 2). A significant number of recent books explicitly signal a change of theoretical direction towards new materialism (Braidotti, 2002; Grosz, 2004; Fraser et al., 2006; Alaimo and Hekman, 2008; Bennett, 2010; Howie, 2010; Dolphijn and van der Tuin, 2012; Barrett and Bolt, 2013; Pitts-Taylor, 2016).

Materialism, I argue, is the most relevant philosophical foundation for posthuman feminism. What is new about the new materialism today, when compared with the earlier versions, is the more comprehensive understanding of matter itself, which entails a closer relationship to scientific culture. I agree with Huffer (2016) that the current new-materialist wave is carried by a younger generation of feminist philosophers, who turned for inspiration to the natural sciences. Posthuman feminism looks seriously in the direction of the Life Sciences. In so doing, it addresses the categorical distinction between the two cultures of the Humanities and the Sciences and redefines it in the direction of the 'three cultures', by including the natural sciences and technoscience (Kagan, 2009). This places a new burden of responsibility on posthuman feminists to advance their double critique of humanism and anthropocentrism towards a fuller analysis of the status of the human today. Moreover, by challenging dominant transhumanist practices and ideals, posthuman feminism pursues these lines of enquiry not only in the critical margins, but also at the centre of institutional academic discourses and public opinion (Braidotti 2013, 2019).

Contemporary feminist materialism rests on the premise of a naturecultural continuum that is technologically mediated. This transversal approach bridges the gap between the binary oppositions of nature/culture and technology/matter. My aim is to continue showing the diversity of the feminist traditions of thought and avoid mono-paradigmatic thinking, while steering a clear course for posthuman feminism. I propose new materialism as a plane of encounter between several scholarly and activist communities coming from different theoretical traditions. This will take me from the primacy granted to the body, to the politics of location, through the reappraisal of Spinozist materialism and Margulis' symbiotic thought, and Indigenous thought, to a more expanded definition of materialism that includes non-human elements as well as technology. By the end we have moved from feminist embodied materialism to a heterogeneous ecology embracing the organic and non-organic. New materialism underlines the multiple interconnections that make up the posthuman convergence, while also sustaining the intersectional axes that define posthuman feminism.

The Materialist Turn

Historically, the renewed emphasis on matter can be seen as a reaction to postmodernism and deconstruction. It marks a change of orientation from the linguistic turn, with its emphasis on language, representation and the power of the phallic master signifier and the process of subject-formation (Coward and Ellis, 2016 [1977]). Inspired by Lacanian psychoanalysis and Saussure's semiotics, linguistic deconstruction interrogates language as the vector of a metaphysically grounded system that functions by binary distinctions. In this framework, the origin for humans is not a biological location but rather an un-natural sense of originary technicity (Derrida, 2002, 2006). The *tekhne* in question is the prosthetic power of language (Wills, 2016) to suspend any self-evidence and throw human subjects onto the opacity and complexity of representation. In other words, as Kirby (2008) suggests, maybe culture was just nature all along. New-materialist techno-feminist Luciana Parisi describes it as follows: 'The model of representation reduces all differences – biological, physical, social, economic, technical – to the universal order of linguistic signification constituted by binary oppositions where one term negates the existence of the other' (2004: 284). The linguistic theory of deconstruction became dominant in North American Humanities, especially in feminist and queer theories (Cusset, 2008; Redfield, 2016). Consequently, the materialist branch of poststructuralist feminism faded into the background (van der Tuin and Dolphijn, 2010). When materialism re-emerges at the turn of the millennium, coinciding with the posthuman convergence, it changes the focus, the agenda and the critical approach.

French philosophy has a century-old tradition of 'enchanted materialism' (De Fontenay, 2001 [1981]). A non-deterministic notion of materialism runs from Diderot to La Mettrie, via Sade through Bergson, and critical re-visitations of Nietzsche. It has paved the way for a methodological naturalism as joyful transformative knowledge.[1] This tradition greatly influenced the anti-humanist philosophers of new materialism, such as Michel Foucault, Michel Serres and Gilles Deleuze. For example, philosopher of science Georges Canguilhem, working on the material vital foundations of living matter, was Foucault's and Deleuze's professor. And Gaston Bachelard, philosopher of materialist scientific epistemologies, supervised the doctoral work of both Deleuze and Serres. This corporeal materialism, also known as 'the line of immanence', is specific to French epistemology and philosophy of science. Its 'affirmative naturalism' (Ansell Pearson, 2014), however marginal in Anglo-American feminist theory, is compatible with discussions of sexuality and sexual difference, all the way through to feminist figures like Luce Irigaray, Hélène Cixous and Virginie Despentes.

A new-materialist approach does not entail the dismissal of the importance of language, signification or meaning-making, but criticizes the limitations of the linguistic turn. When confronted by the thick and painful materiality of the current environmental crisis on the one hand and the divisive social implications of the new technologies on the other, posthuman feminists argue that a new materialism is urgently needed. There are several different ways in which posthuman feminism can be said to be new-materialist. Materialism is about being embodied and embedded, as I have argued throughout my work (Braidotti, 2002, 2019). It is a philosophy of immanence as well as of realism in that it assumes that matter is vital, intelligent and self-organizing. Matter cannot be reduced to a social construction, but should be understood to exist independently of human representation, as 'matter-realism' (Fraser et al., 2006). And last but not least, it includes a structural relationship to non-human entities.[2]

Whereas the linguistic turn gives priority to the laws of language and semiotic representation, the materialist turn looks towards the vitality of matter, and its self-organizing capacity. This is in keeping with the physics of matter itself, as Carlo Rovelli put it: 'the world is a continuous, restless swarming of things; a continuous coming to light and disappearance of ephemeral entities. A set of vibrations, as in the switched-on hippy world of the 1960s. A world of happenings, not of things' (2014: 31). Moreover, the 'minuscule moving wavelets' (2014: 30) of matter are never stable, but rather 'vibrate and fluctuate between existence and non-existence' (2014: 30). The vitality of matter today has been extended to the technological apparatus, which is 'live', smart and self-correcting. This is what I mean by vital materialism. It is an enlarged and dynamic materialism that cannot be easily accommodated within binary and polarizing oppositions of matter/mind and nature/culture. On the contrary, posthuman feminism is materialist in a differential manner. It moves away from dualistic thinking while avoiding holistic organicism. Posthuman feminism rejects an undifferentiated system that would form flat equivalences across all species, all technologies and all organisms under one common signifier. This means that posthuman feminism is materialist in an egalitarian manner: it acknowledges cross-species interconnections, respects differences in locations, and prioritizes a relational ethics of mutual dependence and care. The transversal character of new materialism allows for materiality to emerge as the common denominator across the human, non-human and dehumanized entities of all species.

By being materially grounded, posthuman feminism enables more precise analyses of power. Exploring both discursive and material practices, it exposes the normative power of a humanist and anthropocentric ideal of 'Man' as I showed in the previous chapters. It also analyses adequately the role they play in constructing sexualized and radicalized hierarchies of dehumanized others and of non-anthropomorphic others. A posthuman materialist approach thus moves beyond identity and makes it imperative to look at the broader picture. It focuses on the complex workings of the system of human exceptionalism within neoliberal, biogenetic and cognitive capitalism. New materialism reveals more specifically how the market economy capitalizes on the genetic propensities and vital potencies of matter itself. This is important for women and LGBTQ+ people, whose bodies are already problematized in patriarchal systems.

New materialism involves relational collaboration with the material eco-systems and its non-human entities, but also inscribes it in a framework of technological mediation. It reflects the two-pronged framework of the posthuman convergence, namely the co-occurrence of technological development (the fourth industrial revolution) and environmental depletion (the Sixth Extinction). Posthuman feminism intervenes strategically upon both, relying on material foundations as their unifying factor. Accordingly, matter is *re*-materialized by becoming embedded and embodied in the ravages of environmental depletion, climate change and global pandemics. At the same time, matter is also *de*-materialized, through advanced bio-genetic intervention, data collection and information technologies. This is only an apparent dematerialization, however, which can best be described as a material abstraction into another kind of matter: numbers, storage, cables, codes, etc.

This double pull towards re-materialization and de-materialization is constitutive of posthuman feminism. It is an internal vacillation or swing that need not be resolved but must be acknowledged and operationalized. As I argue in this book, what happens in the posthuman turn is an epistemic acceleration. Posthuman feminism embraces the tensions of new materialism and repurposes them in a dynamic manner, by alternatively re- and de-naturalizing strategically all naturecultural matter. It thus produces a process ontology of cross-species relations that includes the inorganic and the technological apparatus. In order to accommodate these complexities, posthuman feminism builds on and brings together different feminist materialist traditions, for instance by introducing ecofeminist insights. Mindful of the fact that for feminism the fundamental matter is the body itself, this produces an expansion of the notion of corporeal matter to include non-anthropomorphic and non-human bodies. It results in new developments, which I will explore in this and the next chapters.

Bodily Materialism and Carnal Empiricism

The body may well be the fundamental matter in feminist theory. Yet, it is never one unitary entity. For new-materialist feminism, the body is not merely a biological given, or a social construction, but rather an ontological site of becoming. Posthuman feminists return to material bodies, and their materiality includes mediated representations. The focus is on real-life, embodied and embedded, relational and affective women and LGBTQ+ people, with their pleasures and pain and respective implications in mechanisms of power. Posthuman feminism also adopts intersectional axes of analysis such as race, ethnicity, age, able-bodiedness and class. The new-materialist approach stresses that bodies, even anthropomorphic ones, are never only human, although they are bound and specified as such. Bodies are posthuman in that they are heterogeneous genetic and bacterial assemblages modulated by social and technological infrastructures. In this respect, materialism is the robust epistemology that makes posthuman feminism into a reconstructive, rather than deconstructive, philosophy of heterogeneous living systems.

From a new-materialist perspective the embodied subject is flesh activated by wavelets of desire, the effect of unfolding genetic codes, and formatted by social relations. The enfleshed subject is both brute materiality and signified sociality, but above all, bodies are relational and affective. This means they are capable of incorporating external influences and unfolding outward their own affects (Massumi, 2002; Clough and Halley, 2007; Protevi, 2009). A new-materialist body is a time machine as well as a spatial object. It is a mobile entity in space and time, because it is enfleshed memory capable of lasting through discontinuous variations of intensity while remaining faithful to its core. That core is the ontological desire to persevere in one's existence, which requires a relational approach to ethics. This forms the basis for an ethics of affirmation, whereby the pursuit of freedom is shared collectively by kindred spirits. What is affirmed is desire, freedom and becoming.

Living matter – including embodied human flesh – is intelligent and self-organizing, but it is so precisely because it is not disconnected from the rest of organic life and connects to the animal and the earth (Braidotti, 2002; Grosz, 2004). We think with the entire body. We have to acknowledge the embodiment of the brain and the embrainment of the body (Marks, 1998). The human mind and the world it inhabits are inextricably entangled in a myriad of ways. This relational materialism entails a form of philosophical realism that asserts the existence of entities in the world independently of the existence of the human mind (DeLanda, 2006, 2016). Of course, the human mind has the ability to perceive and visualize the world but the concepts and mental representations of the world we form in our minds do not have the power to change the qualities of the entities thus perceived. This non-representational apprehension of the world is the core of the environmental, geological, meteorological and elemental approach of new-materialist feminism: there is no such thing as unmarked or inert matter awaiting socio-cultural coding by a symbolic system dominated by Man/Anthropos. Natural and pre-linguistic signs convey information between embodied and embedded entities across all species. New materialism argues for 'the essential complementarity of the biogenetic and socio-cultural dimensions of human existence' (Ingold, 2000: 2). This is a distributed sense of neural agency that connects human cognition to the external environment and its multiple ecologies.

In this respect, vital materialist feminism strikes quite an alliance with extended mind theories (A. Clarke, 1997, 2008; Clarke and Chalmers, 1998) and distributed cognition models inspired by Spinoza (Deleuze, 1988a [1970]; 1990 [1968]; Damasio, 2003).[3] Posthuman feminism pushes this connection further and argues that thinking and the capacity to produce knowledge are not the exclusive prerogatives of humans. They are rather distributed across all living matter and replicated throughout self-organizing technological networks.

Working with a 'nomadic ontology', Gruber (2019) re-thinks neurobiology and the idea of a distributed relational brain that stresses flows, affects and desires. Arguing against the imperial narrative of the master brain as a fetishistic representation of the human, Gruber dissolves neural functions across networks of multiple organisms, cells and socio-environmental factors and finds even Clarke's notion of 'extended cognition' lacking in flexibility. On the one hand, it complexifies neuro-reductionism, but it still attributes a self-guided and guiding function to the brain. Moreover, it perpetuates a mechanistic approach to neural functions through the language of 'platforms', 'systems' and 'machinery'. Gruber defends instead a materialist process ontology with a more collaborative approach, beyond dualism. Against neuro-normativity backed by a social psychology that supports the status quo and medicalizes differences of gender, class, age and culture, a materialist feminist approach calls for a neural science that values diversity and questions dominant norms.

As I argued elsewhere (Braidotti, 2019), there is a qualitative difference between accepting the structural interdependence among species and actually treating the non-humans as cognitive partners and knowledge collaborators. The posthuman predicament is encouraging us to move precisely in this direction. Situated in the age of computational networks, transecology and post-biology on the one hand and climate change and planetary depletion on the other, posthuman subjects need to learn to think differently.

This is not to say that the mind is isolated from the social context and impervious to its power relations. On the contrary, it is immersed into both the social and the environmental forces that sustain it. Human minds as embrained and embodied heterogeneous relational structures are embedded in these dynamic and autopoietic elements as their multiple ecologies of belonging. In a new-materialist approach, the existence of matter is given as part of a process of human interdependence on non-human environmental factors. It is all in the relation. In the beginning, there is always differential and material heterogenesis, that is to say the relational principle of ontological difference defined as differing within a commonly shared matter.

Feminism is a new materialism in that it mobilizes the knowledge about the embodied, embedded and sexed roots of subjectivity of women and LBGTQ+ people and enlists them as unexplored resources to support the project of alternative subject formations (Braidotti, 1991, 2013). It mobilizes the premises for bodily empiricism to produce more accurate analyses of the power these marginal subjects endure (*potestas*), but also the power that they wield (*potentia*). Posthuman feminism can be understood in terms of bodily materialism (as a theory) or carnal empiricism (as a method).

Exploring the sophisticated workings of carnal awareness (Sobchack, 2004), and the 'sensible transcendental' structure (Irigaray, 1993 [1984]) of human subjectivity, new-materialist theory has pioneered an original form of relational embodied empiricism and highlighted its role in producing knowledge. Carnal empiricism in the feminist tradition respects the phenomenology of experience, while avoiding exclusive identity-indexed or biologically deterministic reductive claims. Immanence, complexity and heterogeneity are the premise for ethical and political accountability.

The other interesting point about carnal empiricism is that it produces for feminism the cartographic method of the politics of locations. This is a politically infused and theoretically framed map of power relations. Critical cartographies are the collectively composed tools by which marginalized subjects of knowledge can both speak truth to power and document what they already know, through the experience of marginalization and exclusion. Cartographies are crowd-sourced exercises in assessing both the documents (discursive production) and the monuments (material structures) that construct our present conditions. A feminist critical cartography is a way of negotiating an adequate understanding of the negative conditions of the present in a critical and creative manner. Accounting for these multiple locations involves collective exercises in assessing the present. This process of extracting knowledge from the experience and the pain of exclusion is a way of reworking collectively the negative elements and proposing alternatives that fit the needs and the aspirations of the marginal subjects.

Politics of Locations

The feminist politics of locations has a significant genealogy, starting with activist techniques of consciousness-raising in the 1970s.[4] It has undergone a series of formulations that has shaped it collectively over several decades. Adrienne Rich (1984, 2001) coins the term as a testimonial to the deep wisdom generated on the margins. The term received a thorough scientific re-examination as feminist epistemology entered the academic realm, supporting the experience-based method known as 'standpoint theory' (Harding, 1986; Hartsock, 1987). This is a materialist approach that is situated and accountable. It is intersectional in its practical application and epistemologically driven in that it grants privilege to the experience and knowledge produced by oppressed groups. Being free of vested interests, marginal subjects practising the politics of location achieve greater objectivity than subjects situated in and adopting the methods at the centre of social systems. The marginal and oppressed groups have a more direct experience of the pain of exclusion, and hence a more lucid perception of how power works concretely. The 'pedagogy of the oppressed', as Paulo Freire argues (2005 [1970]), is better placed to speak truth to power and therefore offers higher degrees of objectivity. Generated by feminist materialist, black and intersectional theories (Smith, 1978; Moraga and Anzaldua, 1981; Carby, 1982), the method is expanded to claim alternative ways of doing scientific research. It also includes the analysis of the racialized economy of science (Hill Collins, 1991; Harding, 1998) and its in-built racism (Ware, 1992; Alcoff and Porter, 1993).

The ways in which knowledge is extracted by feminists from the empirical accounts of lived experience is both historically variable and methodologically consistent. Feminist thinkers engage in a critical and creative manner with the scientific knowledge and dominant ideas of their time. Throughout the 1980s, feminist 'standpoint' theory stressed women's embodiment, experience and the collective nature of feminist knowledge production (Harding, 1991, 1993; Hill Collins, 1991). The method of the politics of location inaugurated a new epistemological perspective that expanded the embodied kind of materialism and allowed for feminist philosophical enquiries into the exclusionary and discriminatory nature of philosophical and scientific reason (Lloyd, 1984; Grimshaw, 1986; Bordo, 1987, 1993; Tuana, 1992).

The reception of poststructuralist feminism in the United States in the 1990s resulted in an intense debate between standpoint theory and postmodernism,[5] which I have discussed elsewhere (Braidotti, 2011a). Important for the genealogy here is that the materialist methods of the politics of locations and standpoint theory consolidated into the epistemological consensus about the situated character of feminist knowledge (Haraway, 1988). The concept of situated knowledge is a consistent materialist line that acknowledges social-cultural codes in the construction of subjectivity, but also emphasizes the primacy of material locations and situated perspectives.

The carnal empiricism that results from the feminist politics of locations as both a method and a political strategy, however, is also the starting point for feminist reflections on how these minority subjects co-construct the status of humanity as a whole. Posthuman feminism focuses on this specific angle and extracts from the lived experiences of the marginals the possibility for a jointly articulated political praxis that affects the current transformations of the status of the human.

One of the medium-term methodological consequences of this method in the posthuman convergence is a shift to interdisciplinarity and transdisciplinarity as the preferred feminist posthuman approach (Birke et al., 2004; Åsberg and Lykke, 2010; Buikema et al., 2011; King, 2011; Åsberg, 2013). Feminist and LGBTQ+ theories move further away from the academic disciplines. Catharine Stimpson refers to these developments as 'the nomadic humanities' (2016).

The most significant change in a posthuman approach to the method of the politics of locations is the rejection of dualistic premises and binary oppositions. This results in the development of post-foundational qualitative inquiry methods (St. Pierre et al., 2016; Ulmer, 2017) and post-constructivist methods (Lykke, 2018). Moreover, these methodologies have a significant impact on teaching methods. Explorations of new materialist feminist posthuman pedagogies are opening new perspectives for Humanities education (Bozalek et al., 2018; Lenz Taguchi, 2018; Geerts, 2019; Geerts and Carstens, 2019; Ringrose et al., 2019).

These methodological challenges and innovations offer accountable cartographies of the multiple webs of power and relational connections that structure the formation of a subject of knowledge as a heterogeneous assemblage of human and non-human components. These cartographies are sustained by a politics that aims at recomposing political and epistemological subjects. This praxis is supported by an affirmative ethics that acknowledges the shared desire of all entities to persevere in their collaborative interdependence and to increase it for the common good. That ethical good is also enhanced through carnality and pleasure. In this empowered sense, it redefines a collective increase in the relational ability to take in and take on more of the world. In this respect, feminist new materialism indexes the epistemological dimension on a fundamentally ethical project.

Critical Feminist Spinozism

A different branch of feminist materialism emerges within continental philosophy by reappraising a thinker who had not been very influential in the previous feminist waves: the Dutch-Jewish philosopher Baruch Spinoza. Yet, a major feminist figure, George Eliot, the pen name of Mary Ann Evans, already completed the first English translation of Spinoza's *Ethics* as early as 1865.[6]

Spinoza's central idea is that we, humans and non-humans, are all part of a common matter or nature. For him, there is no mind–body dualism, but rather a continuum. He postulates a parallelism between mind and matter in a way that is a great source of inspiration for the current revival of feminist materialism. Spinozist philosophy produces a careful re-naturalization of subjectivity that challenges the reductive reading of reason. It also refuses to see the political sphere as being dualistically opposed to matter. What vital materialism proposes instead is a parallelism between mind and body as well as nature and society.

This deep anti-Cartesianism is well suited to the feminist project within the posthuman convergence. For Spinoza, the immanent, naturalistic world view demands an adequate understanding of one's life conditions, through a process of gradual clarification of the ethical forces at play in one's relationship to the said conditions and their affective charges. Adequate understanding is rational, in the sense of not being superstitious, fanatical or caught in the delusions of unchecked passions.

The task of reaching an adequate understanding of the conditions that weigh upon us is collaborative and relational. It is driven by 'common notions' that connect us to kindred spirits and link the force of the imagination to the power of reason. The process therefore entails better knowledge of ethology, the physics of bodies as well as the validity of ideas. Spinoza applies these basic notions to a political analysis that opposes despotism, authoritarianism and mob politics, electing democracy as the only system capable of supporting free subjects' quest for adequate knowledge and joyful passions. Spinoza takes critical distance from liberal philosophers such as Locke and Hobbes and contests the contractualist model of the social contract (which is, after all, a sexual contract biased against women and LGBTQ+ people) with a more radical idea of democracy from below.

Many new-materialist feminists came to Spinoza through Deleuze and other French philosophers of the 1970s, who turned to a different political ontology from Marxism after the political disappointments of the May 1968 insurrection. Duffy (2010) argues that Spinoza played a crucial role in Althusser's project of freeing Marxism from Hegelian idealism and that a recourse to Spinoza enabled a radical critique of historicism.[7] Spinoza, like Darwin, is one of the thinkers that until recently was missing from the feminist critical philosophy tradition, which has been largely dominated by Marx, Freud, and to a lesser extent Nietzsche.

The contemporary feminist new-Spinozist genealogy in English is centred in Australia, where an original and enduring tradition of critical materialism has developed. They produced the first translations of the works of Deleuze and also those of Guattari (Morris and Patton, 1979) at the time when American publishers were mostly translating Derrida and Kristeva. Australian feminist philosophy stands to new materialism as the United States stands to the linguistic turn.[8] The philosopher Genevieve Lloyd, one of the most significant Spinoza scholars of the second half of the twentieth century, however, points out that Spinoza is not Deleuze, nor can he be hastily considered a vitalist thinker. While recognizing that each entity and body has its specific capacities and pleasures, Spinoza privileges rational understanding and scientific enquiry and is no animal rights activist and certainly no rhizomic thinker. Yet, Simone Bignall draws from Deleuze's reading of Spinoza a submerged potential for a non-imperial ethics of association to inform a postcolonial and pluralist politics of mutuality and a critical engagement with Australian Aboriginal epistemologies (Bignall and Patton, 2010; Bignall et al., 2016; Braidotti and Bignall, 2019).

New-materialist Spinozist feminists argue that we are all part of nature (Lloyd, 1994, 1996), not in a manner that opposes it to the social but more like a continuum between the two spheres. This assumption allows them to build on 'vital politics' premised on that continuum (Olkowski, 1999; Braidotti, 2002; Bennett, 2010; Sharp and Taylor, 2016). As a consequence, there is no nature–culture divide at the core of our living systems: all living entities are variations on a common matter. Materialism is not an idealized internalization of the outside world through grids of cultural representations. As I argued before, there is no such thing as an inert outside-of-the-human – be it body, stone, earthworm or code – whose existence depends on the activities and perceptions of the human mind, although matter does get filtered by a linguistic grid and internalized by humans as a psychic representation. This dualistic grid ends up reinstating the same premises it questions.

What I take from critical Spinozism is a specific theory of materialism that avoids dichotomies, by endowing matter with a dynamic principle of relational self-organization. This is what I mean by vital process ontology. Spinoza argues for the parallelism of different dimensions: real objects that exist independently of the human mind (realism) and the mental representations of these objects (idealism). What matters is their parallel and contiguous existence. Matter – and all living entities, humans included – are composed of the same elementary particles in perpetual motion, following the same laws of physics. Matter and thought are different but equal attributes and expressions of the same substance. As theoretical physicist Rovelli put it: 'I am, as Spinoza maintained, my body and what happens in my brain and heart, with their immense and, for me, inextricable complexity' (2014: 73). Body and mind are not set in a binary opposition, nor is there a causal connection between them. It is more a matter of productive resonances between them.

The impact of Spinoza is radical, both in his critique of the liberal notion of individual autonomy in favour of an environmentally integrated form of trans-individuality, and his non-unitary vision of the subject as a heterogeneous assemblage. Lloyd (1996) qualifies the statement that we are all part of nature, by pointing out that our relationship to the natural continuum is affected by the historical social context in which we live. Nature is immersed in history and social structures and vice versa, without dualistic oppositions – it is natureculture. What gets foregrounded is the constitutive trans-individuality of all entities, human beings included, thereby rejecting the transcendental power of consciousness as the distinctive human trait (Deleuze, 1988a [1970]; Balibar, 1994).

This critique is helpful in decentring human exceptionalism. Defining affirmative ethics as the establishment of mutually empowering relationships based on cooperation and the combination of the specific powers of each entity, aims at increasing each entity's individual capacity to preserve themselves against adverse forces. Entities and individuals grow thanks to a collaborative community. The capacity to resist and fight back emerges from the same relational capacities that can also potentially cause harm and discomfort: all we have is others, and relationship to others is constitutive of ourselves. What binds us together over and above contractual interests and the limiting constraints of humanism, is a common propensity to persevere in our existence and increase our relational capacities. An ethics of affirmative collaboration is our common factor.

Freedom is posited within a re-naturalized framework, whereby the natural laws also affect our individual capacity to act and make decisions. The emphasis on freedom as non-reactive activity driven by the ethics of joy is another source of inspiration for posthuman feminism. Affirmation is the force that endures and sustains, whereas sad passions bring about impotence and disaggregation. Affirmative ethics is the affect that binds together the heterogeneous components of the complex subject assemblages.

Contemporary re-readings of Spinoza's naturalist philosophy of mind–body parallelism and his insistence that all matter is dynamic in the sense of being capable of affecting and being affected, has proved inspirational for feminist new materialism. There are also strong Spinozist undercurrents in ecofeminism and deep ecology. On all these scores, critical Spinozism has become an inspiring source for posthuman feminism.

Symbiotic Matter

Another major source of inspiration for posthuman materialism and the idea of ecological interdependence is the concept of symbiotic life and the genetic research of Lynn Margulis (Margulis and Sagan, 1995). Margulis defends from the early 1970s a symbiotic idea of life. It is based on the notion that bacteria join together to create emergent properties and become the complex cells that then form all other organisms. The initially controversial idea of 'symbiogenesis' is by now scientifically accepted to explain the ability of different organisms to join forces and recombine to produce new organisms. For Margulis, this cooperative effort is how genetic change is generated. By extension, she argues that the driving force of evolution is the productive relationships between organisms of different phyla or kingdoms. Instead of mechanistic views of random mutation, their interaction explains genetic variations, notably the transfer of nuclear information by bacteria cells.

The idea that a bound organism – including humans – is an assemblage of microbial colonies of dynamic bacteria decentralizes the notion of the human individual as some exceptional entity. Margulis' approach resonates with Deleuze and Guattari's notion that life is a net of interconnected collaborative systems of symbiotic communities, which are genetically quite distinct from one another.[9] They are heterogeneous, multi-species and thus hybrid, but work together in nested sets organized from the simple to the complex. They interact to the extent of modifying their life cycles. They compose heterogeneous biological communities, which are site-specific, embodied, embedded and interactive. This radical idea has deep ethical and political implications, in that these entities are defined by their respective degrees of intensities or life. This model is non-linear and non-vertical; in other words, rhizomic.

In contrast to the 'genetic parochialism and planetary small-mindedness' of the Darwinian tree of life, as Bruce Clarke succinctly put it (2020: 174), Margulis argues for the topology of the collaborative web. She defends an eco-centric system of mutual specification and environmental interdependence. This idea rests on another major notion, namely that the central point of reference for living systems is not the gene, but the cell. The DNA is part of the cell, but functions just as a storage unit. Life is cell-driven, and cells are self-transforming systems, in an 'autopoietic' mode. Here, Margulis builds on the pioneering work of Barbara McClintock (Fox Keller, 1984) on jumping genes and transpositions, to show that the cells control the DNA through its metabolic system. This saltatory and non-linear definition of evolution as a set of transpositions grants a larger role to the environment than Darwinism ever allowed.

Margulis' work resonates with philosophical materialism in critiquing genetic determinism, which set her on a collision course against the genetic establishment of her times. This was dominated by the Darwinist school of evolution, epitomized by Richard Dawkins' idea of the selfish gene (1989). Margulis disagreed with the violent and aggressive approach to genetics, which she also took as the *zeitgeist* of her times in that it reflected competitive capitalist values. Feminist scientists as different as

Lynn Margulis, Val Plumwood, Mary Midgley and Hilary Rose have taken issue with this vision of 'the stable macho molecule of the 1962 Watson–Crick prize story' (Rose, 2001: 61). Nature is not composed of competing individuals, but rather by interdependent self-organizing communities; 'thought collectives' that are capable of making choices. 'We think, therefore I am'!

From the idea of symbiotic matter, materialist feminism makes a case with and on behalf of the non-humans, be it animals, plants or the earth. Haraway summarizes Margulis' radical evolutionary theory as follows: 'Her first and most intense loves were the bacteria and archaea of Terra and all their bumptious doings. The core of Margulis's view of life was that new kinds of cells, tissues, organs, and species evolve primarily through the long-lasting intimacy of strangers' (Haraway, 2017: M26). The mutual imbrication of living matter, cells and the environment, including the social context and its cultural codes, makes the socialized structure of scientific thought evident. This opens an epi-genetic dimension that places the living organisms in a position to instruct their genes. Information flows from the environment into the genome through bio-chemical processes. Squier (2018) refers to the term epigenetic landscapes to describe the role of the environment in guiding cell development and differentiation beyond the DNA genetic code. She stresses the nonlinear relations at play in epigenetics. This means that there is no genetic determinism at work, but that the environment is a living, self-organizing system where nothing is pre-determined and where all living organisms are sentient. Life is matter that chooses on the basis of sensory information and has the power to transform the organism by transferring that information. Thinking is indeed the stuff of the world, as the epigraph to this chapter runs.

This led Margulis to develop, in 1974 together with James Lovelock, the 'Gaia Hypothesis', arguing that the earth is a self-regulating physiological system made by collaborative bacterial communities. They foreground the self-organizing or autopoietic activity of the planet and oppose the narrow-minded self-interest of the human inhabitants. The atmosphere is the great connector in our planet, and it is regulated by the organisms that live in it. Because all kinds of bacteria produce gases, they run Gaia by controlling its atmosphere. This implies the notion that the biosphere is 'an active adaptive control system able to maintain the Earth in homeostasis' (Lovelock and Margulis, 1974: 2). Bruce Clarke summarizes as follows the shift of paradigm introduced by Margulis: 'Gaia theory is thoroughly ecosystemic in its interpenetration of life with its planetary and cosmic environments. The planetary mesh of the microbes networks the coevolution of life altogether with the parts of the Earth reached by living processes and the solar radiation in our neighborhood of the cosmos' (2020: 10). This creative form of autopoietic evolution is a process ontology that defines the vitality of matter as an ecology of differentiation within systemic interdependence. It reaches across to a multiplicity of humans but also transversally to the entire living environment. It also points to the devastating implications of environmental pollution as a factor in climate change. In what she describes as a 'generative friction', rather than an opposition to Margulis' notion of the autopoietic structure of matter, Haraway argues that, considering the mutual imbrication of biology, technology and ecology today, autopoiesis should be replaced by 'sympoiesis' (2017: 61). It is not just a matter of self-producing and self-organizing systems, but the emphasis falls on the relational and collaborative nature of all living systems. Symbiosis defends the dynamic organization of all living beings as an emergent form of 'animal multi-cellularity' (Haraway, 2017: 64). Becoming-with bacteria and all other living entities is what staying alive is all about. This multi-species ethical interconnection is also the lesson of indigenous cosmologies and life philosophies (Rose, 2004). *Zoe*-centred egalitarianism is, for me, the materialist core of post-anthropocentrism and hence of posthuman feminism.

Elemental Feminist Materialism

At the intersection of feminist materialism with ecofeminism, some crucial new ideas emerged that inspired posthuman feminism. They concern ecological interdependence and cross-species collaboration beyond human exceptionalism. Elemental new-materialist feminists have long stopped believing that the proper study of mankind is 'Man' or Anthropos. No pure object of study exists for posthuman feminists: they study forests, fungi, bacteria, dust and bio-hydro-solar-techno powers, rubbish and high art (Braidotti and Hlavajova, 2018). Living matter is materially embedded and embodied, but it flows, transversally across multi-relational entities. All the interesting events happen in transit: transversality is life. Life is a complex system of non-human elements, as in animal and vegetable (*zoe*), earthed and planetary relations (*geo*), while it is also technologically mediated (*techno*). Posthuman new materialism proposes a general ecology of interdependence, a terrestrial kind of materialism, that is capable of combining a planetary with an earthy or grounded dimension.

Heterogeneous assemblages expose the primacy of matter and material substances, in a manner best described as 'elemental'. The classical elements of earth, air, water and fire had already inspired quite a philosophical reflection on the materiality of the cosmic and planetary forces, for example the Epicurean and Stoic traditions, which influenced the French school of non-deterministic materialism.[10]

An elemental approach was pursued in the feminist tradition by Luce Irigaray in the first phase of her work: the trilogy on air, about Heidegger (Irigaray, 1999 [1983]), water, about Nietzsche (Irigaray, 1991 [1980]) and the essay 'The "mechanics" of fluids' (Irigaray, 1985b [1977]). She lays the foundations for a materially embodied philosophy of the feminine as not-One; as a figure of complexity who is 'otherwise other' than the second sex of 'Man'. These materialist aspects of Irigaray's philosophy make her notion of the virtual feminine into a precursor of feminist carnal materialism in both a conceptual and a visceral manner (Braidotti, 1994; Grosz, 1994b; Lorraine, 1999). Irigaray's carnal materialism has been recognized and expanded by contemporary feminist scholars in less anthropocentric and non-binary directions (Stone, 2006, 2015; Jenkins, 2017; Stark, 2017). This is the aspect of Irigaray's work that resonates the most with new-materialist and Deleuzian feminists (Colebrook, 2000; Olkowski, 1999; MacCormack, 2010).

Posthuman feminism brings back the elements to their non-anthropomorphic strata, through a series of relational assemblages with non-human others. The vital approach to living matter displaces the boundary between *bios*, the portion of life that has traditionally been reserved for Anthropos, and *zoe*, the wider scope of animal and non-human life. The dynamic, self-organizing structure of non-human life as *zoe* stands for generative vitality (Braidotti, 2006, 2011b). It is the transversal force that cuts across and reconnects previously segregated species, categories and domains.

The posthuman acceleration alters the classical natural elements – fire, earth, air and water – and transforms them into post-natural objects of interaction. Studying these posthuman permutations, Genosko (2018) comments on their altered molecular structures and how the elements mutate under the multiple pressures of climate change and technological development. Thus, the atmosphere, or air, is transformed into greenhouse gases. The geosphere follows suit, with the earth turning into minerals and mines, then dust and particles. The biosphere is all over the place, as fire combusts into ashes, smoke and gas. And the hydrosphere sees water getting redistributed through multiple networks and vectors.

New-materialist feminists focus on different elements, but mostly on water and earth. Fire and its devastating effects take central stage in Yusoff (2018), and also in Protevi (2013, 2018), but does not get much more attention. Air and the atmosphere, as we just saw, was covered by Margulis and returns in mainstream posthuman scholarship as atmospheric pollution. Allen (2020) argues that within geography, there is an emerging line of 'aerography' (Jackson and Fannin, 2011) and new literature on atmospheres (Anderson, 2009). Breathing has become a hot political issue, not only because of climate change, but also due to the COVID-19 epidemic that causes respiratory diseases. Moreover, 'I can't breathe' also became the rallying cry for Black Lives Matter protests against the suffocating effects of racism after the murder of George Floyd in Minneapolis in 2020 (Mbembe, 2021). Resistance against increasing social hatred of women and LGBTQ+ people and the devastating effects of the COVID-19 pandemic also generated an atmospheric political economy of breathing freely (Chen, 2020).

Stacy Alaimo shows a distinct preference for water and marine biology, working through oceans, jelly-fish and seas (2010, 2016) to produce what she wittily calls 'a gelatinous posthumanism' (Alaimo, 2013). Astrida Neimanis coined the term 'hydro-feminism' (2017) and planetary 'bodies of water' (2018: 55) to define the sea-bed change propelled by this field. She relates the porosity and liquid nature of femaleness to the generative power of the watery material, with due reference to the placenta as the gestational milieu. Feminist new-materialist scholars working on water also include Hayward, who studies star-fish (2008, 2012) and Schrader who works on algae and slime (2012). The hydrosphere sees water getting redistributed through multiple networks and vectors intersecting with infrastructure and medical biotechnology. Roberts (2008), for instance, follows the course of hormones circulation through and outside the human bodies into the general environment in water systems and leakages. This spread caused a problematic increase of endocrine-disrupting chemicals that affect the food chain of fish, animals and humans. The effects of the fluid ecologies of *zoe*-geo-techno-spreading hormones are global as well as local. Human bodies are also made of carbon, air and minerals, but water is the dominant element and one that configures the interconnectedness of living matter with admirable simplicity.

The earth – land, territory, ground, soil and dust – features prominently in elemental feminist new materialism, not only as a geological entity but also as a planetary one: the earth is our common home. Work on the earth in a Deleuzian perspective is relevant here, in terms of materially embedded becoming (Braidotti, 2002; Grosz, 2004). What is distinctive of elemental materialism in the posthuman frame is that attention to the elements is not a single issue but becomes a transversal, relational one. This means that we are looking at crossovers through the politics of strata (Clark, 2008, 2016) and the geopolitics of the physical world (Bonta and Protevi, 2004; Protevi, 2013; Genosko, 2018). Feminist materialists reach across transnational politics and planetary emergencies, from bushfires to the plastic ocean and beyond.

Geo-centred perspectives are critiques of bio-centric visions of subjectivity and as such relevant for posthuman feminism. It is a basic tenet of posthuman feminism that the Foucault-inspired biopolitical and biopower analyses now have to be replaced by elemental ones, which means that the political subject must also include the potency and the vitality of life itself. For Povinelli (2016), this is 'geontology', centred on the life of the inorganic. She makes a useful distinction between three stances on geontology and the very idea of *geo*: as a living planetary organism (*Gaia*); as the part of the planet defined as inorganic; and matter as the opposite of the social and bio-political governance. Even the old biosecurity has now become geo-security and meteo-security, because of the effects of climate change. The legacy of ecofeminism is foundational here in so far as it grants political agency to matter and material entities beyond the anthropocentric definition of politics and sociality as being inherently and exclusively human.

As we have seen in the previous chapter, Indigenous and decolonial populations had been thinking about the need to think-with and take care of the land, the country, the earth. In the continuum 'naturecultures', the elements are active forces: bodies are soil and dust, but also water, fluids, oxygen. Yusoff (2018) develops critical race studies of rocks, minerals, dust and mines. She focuses on the geo-graphical, geo-logical and imperialist dimensions of the posthuman predicament, which she reads through the lenses of the 'geotrauma of the Anthropocene' (2018: 59). Defining geology as 'a technology of matter' (2018: 14), she strongly argues for a focus on the role that the extraction economies introduced by Western colonialism play in the making of the current juncture. Yusoff posits environmental racism as central to the Western world view and the political economies enforced by advanced capitalism. Unsurprisingly, Yusoff considers the panic generated by the Anthropocene as 'a white man's overburden' (2018: 28).

A focus on elemental materialism illuminates the extent to which matter can turn into a hermeneutical key for work in the Humanities and cultural criticism. Arguing for the materially grounded and hence elemental nature of contemporary culture is a basic tenet of posthuman knowledge. The transversal emphasis on cross-connections is also central to both the mainstream and the feminist Posthumanities (Åsberg and Braidotti, 2018; Braidotti, 2019). Materialist and elemental ecocriticism (Cohen and Duckert, 2018), for instance, merges with technology studies, while the environmental roots of digital media become more manifest. These intersections use terms like 'cloud' to designate information hubs and the 'swarms' of artificial intelligence bytes (Hu, 2015; Peters, 2015). Feminist new materialism moves beyond the metaphorical dimension of such denominations. A substantial materialist approach deals with language, literature, art, maths and ideas by focusing on the 'natural' elements.

Cultural studies of science and technology and media studies make quite a crossover into the elements, by paying attention to rocks, dust, waste and minerals (Fuller, 2005, 2008; Gabrys, 2011, 2016, 2020; Parikka, 2015a, 2015b). This shift towards a materialist technoculture (Fuller, 2004) and a general media ecology (Horl, 2017) moves beyond the continuum 'nature-cultures' to embrace a materialist cultural geology that focuses also on 'medianatures' (Parikka, 2015a). The method of 'geological materialism' reworks the linguistic, semiotic and representational approach to media by focusing on the hardware. Parikka foregrounds instead the thick materiality of these technologies, and the concrete social realities, including labour relations, that make media possible in the first place. This transdisciplinary approach centres on the earth's geological formations, the geophysical resources and the geo-political locations of minerals. This allows for a critique of the power relations involved in advanced capitalism, which is in fact a brutal extraction economy based on the deregulation of mines and mining companies that operate with impunity the world over. Moreover, because mining takes place mostly on Indigenous and First Nations people's lands with complete neglect of their rights, it revives and exacerbates the colonial legacy (Rose, 2004; Yusoff, 2018). Recent studies look specifically into the issue of post and decolonial computing (Irani et al., 2012; Benjamin, 2019; Chun, 2021).

In a crossover into computational technologies, Jennifer Gabrys (2011) presents a 'natural history' of electronics in her study of digital waste disposal techniques and practices. Adopting a new-materialist approach, she stresses the geological and mineral formations that compose the infrastructure and basic components of the deceptively abstract notion of information technologies. Gabrys contests the idea that technologies are somehow 'immaterial' by exposing the grounded practices of electronic waste disposal. By studying how electronic rubbish is broken down, disassembled and stored, from containers to landfills, museums and archives, Gabrys discusses the labour relations involved in electronic rubbish disposal and exposes the racialized, digital proletariat taking care of this dangerous work. An expert in sensing technologies, Gabrys (2016) also explores citizens' alternative use of technologies to measure climate change and other contested issues. Gabrys' most recent work (2020) analyses the extent to which environmental management is relying on new digital technologies to monitor the progress of 'natural' forests. Cleverly called 'the Internet of trees', the phenomenon of smart forests results in woods becoming technologized sites of data production, which can also be put to the task of mitigating environmental change and foster well-being.

New materialist emphasis on elemental bodies as transversal assemblages results in what Neimanis (2018) defines as a 'feminist posthuman phenomenology', in which human bodies are interlinked with plants, animals, the earth, weather systems, technology and other kinds of matter. The synergy between feminist new materialism and critical studies of the natural elements produces the multiple convergences and crossovers that structure the posthuman juncture. The expanded definition of matter as a non-human elemental force (*zoe*) allows for the inclusion of the earth (*geo*), and for technological artefacts and mediation (*techno*) as elements in the transversal networks that compose posthuman subjectivity. This is a situation whereby *zoe* embraces *geo* and *techno* as interrelated dimensions. We are such stuff as *zoe*/geo/techno-bound matter is made of.

Racialized Feminist Materialism

Feminists are well placed to know that vital materialism – and the life philosophies based on it – are not only sexualized, but also racialized and naturalized. The intersectional materialist effort to overcome the binary oppositions and the emphasis on cross-species interdependence raises the same concerns as the strategic reappraisal of nature by ecofeminists: namely, the fear of biological determinism and its discriminatory effects. I concur with Jones (2010: 5) that: 'One cannot understand twentieth-century vitalism separately from its implications in racial and anti-Semitic discourses and that we cannot understand some of the dominant models of emancipation within black thought except through recourse to the vitalist tradition.' Many critical theorists have stressed the impact of the racialized ontologies that were developed through colonialism and historical European fascism (Stoller, 1995, 2002; Braidotti, 2002, 2011; Jones, 2010).

In order to come to terms with the challenges of the posthuman predicament, feminists are formulating a critical philosophy of life that accounts also for the exclusions and the genocides. Living in the bio-capitalist age of 'life as surplus' (Cooper, 2008), they engage with the bio-political management of the living and the dying and set up an effective opposition to the commercialization of life and the manipulation of cognitive systems for the sake of profit. Closer links are being established between critical race theory and science and technology studies. Adequate philosophies of life are developed by feminist and anti-racist thinkers to counteract the pervasive effects of cognitive capitalism. Considering the extent of the silencing of slavery and colonialism, one cannot overstress the importance of introducing more colonial scholarship into philosophies of life, also in the feminist tradition. These transversal connections take seriously the racialized roots of materialism and bring them to bear on the posthuman convergence.

This emphasis on multiplicity is enlisted to the task of exploring the complexity of multi-dimensional relations across and beyond the classical dualistic oppositions. Nancy Tuana's work on materialism (2008) as 'viscous porosity' or thick interaction between nature and culture, humans and non-humans and other categories is emblematic in this respect. By arguing that 'our flesh and the flesh of the world we are of and in, are porous' (2008: 198), she calls for a re-materialization of the social and a re-socialization of the natural. Tuana also stresses the need to recognize the racialization of this interactive philosophy of natureculture, sociology, biology and geology.

Yusoff (2018) stresses the link between the geological substratum of colonial economies and slavery and racism. She exposes the racial categorization implicit in definitions of the human and warns against any suggestion that the current posthuman convergence may automatically solve the unequal power relations and the patterns of dispossession that have marked Western expansion. Preferring the term 'inhuman' to describe the continuing patterns of racialized oppression, Yusoff's project aims to 'think with the inhuman as an analytic with which to scrutinize the traffic between relations of race and material economy and to think race as a material economy that itself emerges through the libidinal economy of geology (as the desire for gold, mineralogy, and metallurgy)' (2018: 7). In a form of 'inframaterialism', Yusoff posits the racialized ontology of Blackness and the political economy of slavery and colonialism as the missing link between the allegedly inorganic matter of the soil, geology and the organic matter of biology. Capitalist production works through extraction of natural resources and exploitation of Black labour.

Working within a non-Western ontology, Danowski and Viveiros de Castro confirm the new-materialist insight and argue from the angle of Indigenous epistemologies that 'Humankind is con-substantial to the world, or rather, objectively, 'co-relational' with the world, relational as the world' (2017: 75). If the point of origin is given as ontological relationality, then the social-constructivist method that consists in undoing, de-constructing or reversing the binaries shows its limitations. In this respect, Danowski and Viveiros de Castro astutely point out that it is not sufficient to undo the human/animal opposition by stating that humans are fundamentally animals, because this reduction reinstates the anthropocentric hierarchy on different grounds. Reversals miss the point of how relationality works: the porous boundaries, the flows and incessant exchange of information at all levels between the humans and their multiple non-human environments. Paraphrasing Deleuze's work on immanent perspectivism, Viveiros de Castro argues that 'Amazonian multinaturalism affirms not so much a variety of natures as the naturalness of variation – as nature' (2014: 74). Material process ontology is thus central to non-Western systems of thought. Another name for such vital energy is resilience, which is the ability to survive ontologically, as well as individually, as Indigenous thinkers teach us. It is the affirmation of 'we' as a people; an interconnected ensemble that is stronger than the necropolitical edge of biopower and the excesses of sovereign capital. The bio-political critique is insufficient to deal with posthuman ways of living, dying and negotiating the steps in-between.

This inseparable connection between diverse Indigenous world views and the natural world makes for the method of 'Indigenous expressivism', whereby one speaks as country (Bignall et al., 2016). Within the Aboriginal tradition, Rose (2004: 153) points out that the notion of land or country is a method as well as the matrix for Australian Aboriginals' world view and their relationship to space and time. Country is a multi-dimensional concept that includes people, rocks, birds, animals and the weather. Embedding human subjects into their environment, Indigenous philosophies posit environmental, social and personal sustainability as a continuum. To destroy the land or the country is to destroy yourself. Each country is morally equivalent to all other countries, because there is ultimately only one earth. Rose argues: 'Country is a conscious entity. Place is one kind of embodiment of being, and the encounters of living things are recorded there. Signs are memories, they may become obscured, but not, perhaps, lost' (2004: 163). The land as the living record of these multiple encounters is full of concrete traces and vivid signatures of human lives as tracks. The intimate participation in the well-being of the land is a moral form of engagement of past in present, which Rose juxtaposes to Western Nature Resource Management. An Indigenous earth philosophy is illuminating: 'Against domination it asserts relationality, against control it asserts mutuality, against hyper separation it asserts connectivity, and against claims that rely on an imagined future it asserts engaged responsiveness in the present' (2004: 213).

As already explained in the previous chapter, Indigenous philosophies refer to this approach as 'perspectivism' (Rose, 2004; Viveiros de Castro, 2014). The central tenet of Indigenous peoples' cosmologies is the impossibility of separating humans from non-humans and the attribution of subjectivity, active agency and humanity to them all. Kim TallBear (2015) argues that even organic matter such as stones, meteorological phenomena like thunder, or stars are known within Indigenous ontologies to be sentient and knowing persons.

This is another, far more ancient, form of vital new materialism, that intersects with Western philosophical attempts to rethink the unity of matter without deterministic hierarchies. Indigenous approaches moreover foreground the critique of settler colonialism and its violent management of less-than-human and non-human others.

Heterogeneous Assemblages

Building on new materialism, ecofeminism and elementalism, a new generation of posthuman feminists radicalizes the mutual implication of the material, environmental and technological to such a degree that it is impossible to tell them apart. A step beyond hybridity, in the posthuman acceleration we enter the world of heterogeneous assemblages. Transversality becomes the operative word: beyond the humanist paradigm there is a recomposition of the human along posthuman axes of multi-scalar relational interconnections to non-human others. Interspecies relationality moves centre stage (Livingston and Puar, 2011).

Birke and Holmberg (2018) offer the term 'intercorporeality' to describe the multiple ways in which embodied entities of different species can be conceptualized as a collaborative affective continuum. Stacy Alaimo, a posthuman ecofeminist, for instance, builds on human/non-human interconnection as a radical relational ontology (2008). She coins the 'trans-corporeal' ecofeminist subject: 'Trans-corporeality is a mode of posthumanism that begins from the unacknowledged site of human corporeality, insisting that what we are as bodies and minds is inextricably interlinked with the circulating substances, materialities and forces of the wider world' (2018: 49). Trans-corporeality is both posthuman and environmentalist, entailing new models of ethics and politics that connect across vast expanses of actors. It also argues for material posthuman agency for all kinds of subjects across the full spectrum of living organisms. This posthuman relational subject acknowledges the transversal micro-political connections and constitutive affective bonds across all entities.

Queer new materialism is of the non-human kind. It combines the Environmental Humanities with LGBTQ+ studies, disability studies and brings them to bear on the assessment of contemporary human–animal discussions and the rights of those who are excluded from 'the elite status of human' (Hayward and Weinstein, 2015: 206). This approach generates new theoretical figurations of posthuman becoming. For instance, Hayward and Weinstein (2015) define it as 'queer trans-animalities', Mel Chen (2012) as 'animacies' and Eva Hayward (2008) 'trans-speciated selves'. The symbiotic relationship between humans and bacteria communities, pioneered by Margulis and Sagan (1995, 1997) and Tsing (2015), is reworked into a new paradigm of bacteria as queer and trans-sexual entities (Parisi, 2004; Hird, 2009). The scale of these posthuman feminist interventions moves in the direction of the molecular and cellular (Roy, 2018). They aim accordingly at recombining human subjects into 'irreducible transanimalic assemblages' (Hayward and Weinstein, 2015: 206). But all species are encompassed in the heterogeneous sweep. Critical plant studies and emergent ecologies come to the foreground (Kirksey, 2015), as multi-species ethnography takes off across an open sequence of organisms (van Dooren et al., 2016).

Alaimo sums up these developments about inter-species dependence in a more conceptual direction: 'the trans-corporeal recognition that humans are part of the flux of the material world – and not transcendent, rational, securely enclosed commanders – strikes a blow to human(ist) exceptionalism and feminist new humanism' (2018: 51). Arguing – in line with radical ecofeminism – that thinking is the stuff of the world and all beings are sentient, Alaimo (2014) favours a distributed model of consciousness and subjectivity. By taking place in the world, the activity of thinking is made accountable to multiple constituencies, not only the academic community.

Alaimo defines these heterogeneous assemblages as a form of exposure, not only in the negative sense of vulnerability and their expectations of wounds to come. Being exposed also refers affirmatively to a new ethical understanding of all matter as being dynamic and relational. This environmental posthumanism stresses the notion of 'exposure', to express our constitutive ability to affect and to be affected by others. It expresses the intensity of humans' relation to a common nature and shared naturecultures. Alaimo (2016) foregrounds the distinctive advantages and pleasures, as well as the challenges of trans-corporeal entanglements, proposing a materialist ethics. This stresses the crucial importance of affirmation, the subjects' capacity to generate together alternative affirmative values and relations.

Vital materialism is all the more relevant today, where knowledge is being produced across a broad range of social, corporate, activist, artistic and mediated locations, as well as in professional scientific, technological academic settings. The new fields of posthuman feminist knowledge production embrace both the 'natural-ness' of anthropomorphic entities called humans (re-naturalization) and the ubiquity of technological mediation (de-naturalization). In the posthuman acceleration, re-naturalization and de-naturalization are intermeshed. This is not just a blurring of boundaries in the postmodernist mode, but an active reconstruction of trans-species, trans-corporeal and trans-versal heterogeneous assemblages. This takes materialism to a new height, in that the self-organizing vitality of matter pertains both to the organic and the technological, the human and the non-human. The heterogeneous assemblages foreground the intelligence and agency of multiple non-human species as well as the technological apparatus.

Conclusion

I have argued in this chapter that new materialism is foundational for posthuman feminism. It offers a dynamic and immanent frame to steer a course between the risks of biological essentialism and technological determinism. Feminist new materialism goes hand in hand with the rejection of dualism and instrumental rationality. A new-materialist approach supports a middle ground composed by alliances between human and non-human agents. I have described these alliances as heterogeneous assemblages. To be materialist means to be situated along differential locations: we are grounded, but we differ. What keeps the human and non-human connected is affect, or in my words, ontological relationality. This is the capacity to affect others and be affected in mutual interdependence. This is where the ethics come in, which is for me always an ethics of affirmation. The interrelation is shaped by an ethics that starts with the recognition of the vital importance of the transversal connections to multiple others. This ethics pursues an affirmative path of relations in order to increase the mutual and respective ability of materializing the unrealized or virtual potential of what 'we' are capable of becoming.

New materialism entails several consequences for posthuman feminism that I want to draw out. Firstly, methodologically it produces a post-naturalist but also post-constructivist form of embodied and embedded empiricism, which is operationalized in a variety of ways. If there is one common factor in posthuman feminist scholarship, it is the notion of embodied subjects as complex assemblages that cut across multiple categories. There are no unitary subjects in posthuman feminism; no self-referential entities locked up in their own truth. The subject at work in these assemblages is transversal, heterogeneous, molecular and collaborative. Moreover, this multiple subject is rooted in embodied and embedded experiences, and flowing in a multi-layered intersectional manner. The subject of posthuman feminism does not correspond to the unitary idea of 'Man' that regulates access to the category of the human. It is post-anthropocentric in the sense of elemental materialism, because it includes several non-human agents and factors.

Another methodological innovation is the change of the object of enquiry. The scholarship in the Humanities becomes *zoe*-oriented: studying animals, insects, plants, seeds, cells, viruses, etc. They are also geo-related through studying earth elements like the soil, minerals, seas, air, atmosphere – the environment as a whole. And they intensify the studies of technological mediation with focus not only on media but also on algorithms, codes, software, platforms, networks, etc. (Fuller, 2017). That is why I call the object of study *zoe*/geo/techno-mediated matter.

Next, a materialist and vital philosophy offers clear political advantages in that it provides a more adequate understanding of the fluid and complex workings of power in advanced capitalism and hence can devise more suitable forms of resistance (Patton, 2000; Macherey, 2011 [1977]; Repo, 2016). By understanding living matter as *zoe*-driven, geo-centred, and techno-mediated, it allows for a critical posthuman politics of life. This is an enlargement of politics by encompassing matter as a dynamic co-agent in the making of posthuman feminist materialism. The issue at stake is how to rethink life as an immanent force, to understand how matter is co-constructed and shaped by multiple effects of power as both *potestas* and *potentia*. In cognitive capitalism, power is defined as the scientific and economic control of living systems, their genetic codes and possible applications, as well as the smart nature of algorithmic codes and data-storage capacities.

As a final reflection on new materialism in relation to posthuman feminism, I want to draw attention to a mutation of the politics of location. For humans, life will always be anthropomorphic, characterized by the qualities, faculties and potentials of the modes of embodiment specific to our species. Human beings cannot help but be anthropomorphic and although they are diverse, varied and differentiated, they do share some basic material parameters: morphological, cellular, neural and hormonal. Posthuman feminism embraces anthropomorphic specificity in order to take distance from the arrogance of anthropocentrism and human exceptionalism, in the same ethical mode as it embraces the grounded contingency of just *a* life. The acknowledgement of the immanence and limitations of just *a* life inoculates against the intoxicating metaphysics of life itself. Paradoxically, it is by embracing resiliently the specificity of the anthropomorphic frame and the limits and possibilities it entails, that humans can connect to non-human others. The shared imaginary and the collaborative efforts of the less-than-human and dehumanized others, who were not allowed to be fully human to begin with, have sizeable margins to negotiate the transformative power of their differences. Accepting to be *zoe*-geo-techno-matter is a way of opening up to possible alliances, which in turn promotes alternative ways of becoming posthuman.

Chapter 5
Technobodies: Gene- and Gender-editing

> If nature is unjust, change nature!
> Laboria Cubonics, *The Xenofeminist Manifesto*, 2018

In a stunning live-art and video work called 'Creating the Spectacle!', British disabled artist Sue Austin features the world's first underwater wheelchair performance.[1] She floats or rather flies along mid-water, freeing abilities left virtual until then, in a display of joy and freedom of movement as one would in zero gravity. Produced through her company 'Freewheeling' as part of the London 2012 Festival during the Olympic and Paralympic Games, that artwork has received over 150 million views since.

A disabled artist dancing underwater in a wheelchair pushes the boundaries of what bodies can do and moves advocacy for the disabled to an altogether new dimension. It is emblematic of posthuman bodies in so many ways. Firstly, by interacting in a creative manner with a technological artifact; secondly by embracing the natural environment, the water world. Thirdly, by challenging expectations and set patterns of perception of bodies through the juxtaposition of a wheelchair with the fluid underwater environment. And last but not least, Austin shows the virtual possibilities of what bodies can do, not in order to be repaired or fixed, but by experimenting with specific forms of embodiment.

All feminist politics is body politics. But, to paraphrase Deleuze (1988a: 127), a body can be anything: animal, or vegetable; it can be a body of sounds, a linguistic corpus, a mind or an idea; it can be a social body, a line of code, a DNA sequence, or a collectivity. They are all modulations on the same, vital, matter. We saw in the previous chapter that materialist feminism is a precursor of the posthuman turn, because it redefined the body as a materially embedded heterogeneous assembly and not only as a socially constructed entity.

In this chapter I will concentrate on the implications of the posthuman theoretical framework for the feminist understandings of the body. Noting the primary importance feminism attributes to the bodily or corporeal locations, I explore both the continuities and discontinuities in feminist body politics within the posthuman convergence. I show how feminism finds a critical middle way between a reductive re-naturalization of the body akin to biological determinism on the one hand, and extreme de-naturalization of the body complicit with capital-driven technologies on the other. I will do so by tracing the genealogical hub of feminist studies of technoscience that has been so crucial to this field. As we will see, most feminist technoscience studies push towards a critical de-naturalization, while ecofeminism and feminist materialism rather propose a strategic re-naturalization. But that opposition is not substantive and in the posthuman context the two approaches often come together. The task of reconstructing a posthuman subject that is rooted, but also flows, implies a challenge that is crucial for feminism, namely the quest for alternative visions of subjectivities, sexualities and reproductive systems. I will show how cyberfeminism is one of the precursors of posthuman feminism. Then I move on to the field of trans feminism and disability studies as the current deployments of technobodies. As reproduction is one of the key issues of posthuman feminism, I finish with reflections on queer kinship and placenta politics.

Posthuman Bodies Are Back with a Vengeance

Posthuman feminism accepts its historical location within the posthuman convergence and draws the consequences of this particular moment. As we have seen in earlier chapters, posthuman feminism makes it a priority to honour the disenfranchised, dehumanized and excluded bodies, defying the dominant version of the human as Man/Anthropos. The transformative force of posthuman feminism turns feminist subjects and bodies into the site of multiple experiments with alternative modes and figurations of becoming posthuman. This position requires a loss of innocence about the 'natural-ness' of bodies, involving a high degree of dis-identification from set habits of thought (Muñoz, 1999). The posthuman technological artifact is 'autopoietic' (Maturana and Varela, 1972; Guattari, 1995), in that it is self-organizing, like biological organisms. The idea of intelligent and self-organizing matter refers to the vitality of bodies that are neither inert nor passive (Ansell Pearson, 1997b). It is also 'sympoietic' (Haraway, 2016, 2017) in combining biology, technology and ecology.

This vital definition of matter has significant implications for the materialist method of feminist situated knowledges and the politics of location. What happens indeed when the traditional notion of the body as a bound and specified entity explodes into a web of human and non-human components? What happens when the skin is no longer the firm boundary of the body, but rather reveals its true nature as a porous membrane that is open onto the outside world? What if the body, in addition to perceiving, storing and retrieving flows of information and sensorial data by itself, can also be accelerated through technological enhancement? These materially grounded questions reconstruct bodies along multiple and potentially contradictory lines of de- and re-territorialization. Posthuman bodies being *zoe*/geo/techno-mediated are caught within a range of de-materialization techniques that turn them into providers and retrievers of data and information, integrated into the electronic circuit. But they also contribute to re-materialization of bodies within extensive multi-species webs of environmental and social relations. This engenders the simultaneous exposure and disappearance of what used to be 'the' body into multiple networks of techno-mediated, bio-genetic and computational practices.

The famous feminist slogan 'our bodies, ourselves' acquires an ironic twist in this process of posthuman transition. The embodied feminist self, far from being the unitary point of epistemological verification of lived experiences, turns into a crowd of human and non-human housemates. By implication, this means that the bodily markers for the organization and distribution of sexual differences and gender roles also shift. Contemporary technoscience has come a long way from the crude system that used to mark differences on the basis of visually verifiable anatomical and physiological variations between the sexes, the races and the species, although society still discriminates along those lines. It has moved from bio-power (Foucault, 1977a) to the informatics of domination (Haraway, 1985, 1992, 2003).

Posthuman *zoe*-power is now located in micro instances of vital materiality, like the cells of living organisms and the genetic codes of entire species. Significantly, it is left to the minorities to provide an accountable location for embodied subjects within the posthuman convergence and its *zoe*/geo/techno-mediated potentialities. Women, LGBTQ+ people, anti-racist and other alternative forces, with their historically 'leaky bodies' (Grosz, 1994b; Shildrick, 1997) are ideally placed to reassert the powers, prerogatives and pleasures of the posthuman flesh. They deal with the speed of technologization of bodies and reproduction, while coping with the perpetuation of traditional gender roles and the institution of the patriarchal family that enforces normative rules about reproductive practices and their offspring.

In the previous chapters, we have seen that the convergence of materialism, technofeminism and ecofeminism lies at the core of posthuman feminism. This means that technobodies are environmentally grounded, socially accountable and affectively related. Conversely, the vitality of the technological artefacts is re-grounded in the material roots and environmental resources that compose them. Under the pressure of the material conditions of advanced capitalism and its speedy deterritorializations of the posthuman convergence, the modernist vision of the relationship between bodies and technology, which was dualistic and confrontational, is coming apart. This oppositional relationship between bodies and machines has been reorganized by cognitive capitalism's predatory incursions into living matter on the one hand and environmental devastation on the other. Posthuman feminism adds technology into the materialist re-reading of the environment as a symbiotic system of cross-species collaborative egalitarianism. The strategic re-naturalization effort is matched by a critical de-naturalization twist. Or rather, technological mediation is added as the second nature within a dynamic block of naturecultural interrelations.

Posthuman feminism bridges the split between the biosciences on the one hand and the computational technosciences on the other. The former focus on reproduction, reproductive health and sexuality, the latter on networks and platforms. Their intersection opens a full range of strategies of re-naturalization or de-naturalization of the posthuman body. Posthuman feminism takes for granted the mixture of deterritorialized effects of the posthuman convergence and understands that matter is de-materialized and re-materialized at once or in quick succession. It enjoys a fluid interaction between the different degrees of re-naturalized and de-materialized compositions.

Posthuman bodies are re-naturalized by reconnecting to their ecological foundations and environmental grounding. They are also de-materialized through practices of data encryption, storage and retrieval of information. In addition, bodies are pinned down by the accelerating speed of cognitive capitalism, exposed to violence, discrimination and inequalities. The simultaneous re-naturalization of the environment and its de-naturalization via technological mediation, call for an extra effort of the feminist political imagination in a world that is ruined and wounded, and for our 'compromised times' as Shotwell (2016) so well describes it.

Posthuman bodies are simultaneously exploded into relational sites of multiple interrelations and reasserted as locations of powers, pleasures and values specific to the anthropomorphic beings known as humans. On both scores, it can be said that posthuman bodies are back with a vengeance, but they are neither natural nor artificial. Moreover, they do not come back to the same space they inhabited before the posthuman convergence. This is due to the fact that technological mediation has blurred the boundaries and scrambled the locations. If the technological artifact is now our second nature, we need a new paradigm to deal with the complexity. That is where posthuman feminism can help, by rethinking the specific features, values and pleasures of the assemblages of the techno-living, dynamic and 'smart' inorganic networks. Posthuman feminism is especially committed to devise an ethics of interaction with and care for the environment that supports the growing intimacy with a techno-world that feels like home. Mapping these complex power relations is a crucial task for posthuman feminism. But it does not exhaust its purpose. The force of feminist politics lies in its transformative passion, which encourages experiments with what embodied and embedded subjects are capable of becoming.

Cyberfeminists and Other Bad Girls

Experiments with feminist technobodies have been ongoing in cyberfeminism since the 1980s, as a positive reaction to the rise of the Internet and new media culture.[2] The legendary Australian art collective known as VNS Matrix published *The Cyberfeminist Manifesto for the Twenty-first Century* (1991). Together with artist Linda Dement (2017), they constitute the first wave of cyberfeminist activists (Miss M., 1996; Barratt, 2016), who constructed with feminist scholars the founding theories of feminist techno-cultures (Haraway, 1985; Plant, 1997, 2000).

Arguing forcefully that 'cyberfeminism is one of many feminisms, and feminism has not gone away', this movement joined forces with radical feminism in the critique of patriarchal violence and the exploration of alterative sexualities and virtual genders. It also fought alongside the political opposition against the rise of neoliberal economics and the transformation of advanced capitalism through the destruction of its industrial base. It worked in tandem with the punk cultural revolution of those times, which propelled the 'Riot Grrrl' and the women's punk bands to the centre of popular musical culture (Bikini Kill, 1991). In all these respects, cyberfeminism is in some ways the predecessor of critical posthuman feminism in that it includes an intimate and productive relationship to the technological universe, which breaks from a tradition of either utopian hope for, or deep suspicion of, technology.

As early as the 1990s, by the time 'Bikini Kill' burst onto the scene and punk and rock women's bands like 'The Slits' and 'The Raincoats' wove feminism into their rhythms, the polemical edge of feminist critical thinking addressed the masculinism of popular culture. The confrontational spirit between commercialized pop culture and politicized punk culture was anticipated in 1983 by Cindy Lauper's anthem of bad girls the world over, the hit song 'Girls just wanna have fun'. That slogan was recently amended by signs spotted at the 2017 Women's March in Washington, which stated 'Girls just wanna have fun(damental human rights)' (Lewis, 2020: 100). This is in keeping with cyberfeminist and feminist punks' culture of rejecting gender normativity and doing their utmost to imitate the sluts, dropouts and other bad girls.

Kathy Acker is the quintessential cyberfeminist bad girl and one of the most significant punk feminists, a major intellectual activist and a precursor of the posthuman turn (1990, 1997). Acker was a student of the Marxist philosopher Herbert Marcuse at the University of Brandeis before she became a cutting-edge experimental artist. She was inspired by literary avantgardes while fully immersed in the commercialized pop culture kitsch that the punk revolution rebelled against. A passionate reader of Deleuze and Guattari, and a good friend of the latter, she credited them with providing the fundamental concepts and tools that shaped her own work. Kathy Acker learned how to affect her readers at the molecular level.

Acker fought on several fronts at once: in writing, music, performances, body-building and in the extreme stylization of her own sex and love life. From her short and punchy essays to the more elaborate collages and impersonations of other authors' work, through to her novels, the lyrics of her songs, the poems, the mock-porn, the opera librettos and catalogues of exhibitions, Kathy Acker's texts deploy difference as a positive force. I have described them as endowed with a relentless, tough, daemonic beat that mesmerizes the readers but never violates their trust (Braidotti, 1994, 2011a). She accomplished one of the most rigorous attacks on unitary identities and gender binaries of her generation. With her punk band 'The Mekons', Acker recorded the queer punk, gender non-conforming *Pussy, King of the Pirates* and *Pussy* albums, both of them with lyrics extracted from her book-length publications. It is no coincidence that Acker chose the figuration of the pirate as her artistic persona; the seafaring pirate but also the counterfeit criminal.

Cyberfeminism loves the transformative potential of technologically mediated bodies. All cyberfeminists want out of the techno-capitalist system and the degraded desire it instils and rewards. It is a radical movement that asserts a high degree of critical dis-identification from heteronormative patriarchal capitalist technological values. Practising a series of creative de-territorializations, cyberfeminists like Acker (1991, 1995) produce one of the most incisive dissections of patriarchal violence of her generation of feminists: she zooms into the nexus of sexuality, power and male violence and pulls it to pieces. It is a heart-breaking and yet edifying experience to read her account of the bruises, the wounds and the losses little girls and women accumulate under patriarchal rule. The indecency, insolence and sadistic pleasure men find in pursuing the humiliation of women and girls haunts Acker's work. She captures it and vomits it back at them. She may be profane, but they are impure; she is truly obscene because they are insane, and she is totally enraged at their demented sense of entitlement. Kathy Acker is the punk ethical force that passes a moral judgement on the sexual violence of those who tormented her. In a brilliant contribution to the feminist volume *Posthuman Bodies* (Halberstam and Livingston, 1995), significantly called 'The end of the world of white men', Acker settles her score with the culture of rape that patriarchy has so successfully installed. Exposed and vulnerable, Kathy Acker died at the age of fifty from a breast cancer that could not be cured, but also for the lack of resources and benefits that health coverage in the United States provides.

It is a well-known fact that feminists take pride in being 'nasty women'.[3] In some ways they cannot avoid it, because as analysts of patriarchal violence, they are often blamed for the ills and injustices they disclose (Chemaly, 2019). As Lewis (2020) rightly argues, feminism has always celebrated the undutiful, bad girls who defy patriarchal norms and expectations. From the role of 'angel in the house' that Virginia Woolf warns women against, to other forms of subjugation in the public sphere by coercive niceness and serviceability, in a heteronormative patriarchal world, women are oppressed by tougher moral rules than men. Double standards favouring men and protecting their interests, entitlements and indulgences are common practice also in professional life, in the entertainment, film and culture sectors. Feminists across the ages, from the women in Aristophanes' Greek play *Lysistrata* to the contemporary #MeToo movement, have protested this systemic injustice. Being nasty or difficult women can be seen as a feminist statement, in so far as feminism is not a branch of the service industry, but a political movement geared to overturn the patriarchal regime of power. It is supposed to be provocative, transgressive and, at times, downright rude. In Sarah Ahmed's terms (2004) a feminist can and should be a political killjoy, for perfectly legitimate and constructive reasons. Contemporary patriarchal rage against nasty women can also be seen as a defensive reaction to the relative success of confrontational, rebellious, sarcastic women in media, journalism and popular culture. These 'difficult' public women foreground the struggles involved in being good enough feminists today and pursue the transformations of the bad girls' image that started with cyberpunk and cyberfeminism. And they do so with great flair, capturing perfectly the spirit of their times.

For example, in the early 2000s, the Russian punk group Pussy Riot stormed into Moscow's main cathedral to perform a punk act, praying to the Virgin Mary to deliver them from Putin's rule. Three of them, Nadya Tolokonnikova, Maria Alyokhina and Yekaterina Samutsevich, were arrested and sentenced to two years in prison on the charge of blasphemy. They defied clerical and political power by voicing their dissent, survived two years in jail, and achieved global stardom upon their release. This courage bordering on recklessness is one of the sources of the provocative and defiant tone of feminists the world over. 'And I am not afraid of you', Alyokhina shouted to the Russian judges who sentenced them to jail (Gessen, 2014: 216).

Cyberfeminism takes a firm stand against techno-totalitarianism, unceremoniously labelled by the VNS Matrix collective (1991) as 'big daddy mainframe'. The battles of cyberfeminism pave the road for the posthuman turn. If you take a radical contemporary movement such as Xenofeminism, it is already fully immersed in mediated techno-culture and well placed to assess it, building on the legacy of previous generations. The Xenofeminists are synthesizing 'cyberfeminism, posthumanism, accelerationism, neorationalism, materialist feminism and so on in an attempt to forge a project suited to contemporary political conditions' (Hester, 2018: 1). In this respect, they are situated polemically within the posthuman convergence. They do deal explicitly with the complexity and contradictions of power relations in a global, technologically mediated world (Jones, 2018a, 2019). More recently, digital feminism has moved towards the search for alternative algorithmic codes and practices, addressing the problem from within (D'Ignazio and Klein, 2020).

Critical of the project of Western modernity, while situating themselves within it, cyberfeminists de-link scientific and technological developments from any teleological transhumanist vision of progress and emancipation, focusing instead on the fractures and failed promises of that project. Stressing the scrambled temporalities of technological futures, they foreground the alienated subjects that fall out of utopian visions: women, blacks, queer, other species. Gender abolitionists and anti-naturalists, they also claim to be new-materialist and ground their feminist and emancipatory practice on large-scale social changes based on human and non-human relations and intersectional bonds, proposing a web of intertwined, cross-species connections and multiple temporalities.

Gaga Feminism

Whereas cyberfeminists were concerned about the pitfalls of media culture, contemporary media stars show that success and political resistance can go hand in hand and that technology assists in striking a balance. J. Halberstam's original work on posthuman mediated bodies (Halberstam and Livingston, 1995) is of great significance in this respect, in that it rejects the very separation of fleshy, embodied subjects from their mediated image and representation. There is no pure or authentic feminism independent of the media culture that supports it: what was the artificial has become our second nature. What defines posthuman bodies, according to Halberstam, is their extreme mediatization and the familiarity posthuman subjects have developed with unnatural and counter-cultural gender roles. Halberstam radicalizes the posthuman potential for the performance of multiple possibilities for constructing alternative bodies. These bio-techno bodies get de-materialized by bio-chemical and biotechnological interventions (Preciado, 2013a), or by media and digital platforms. But they also get re-grounded and re-materialized as enhanced or alternative embodied subjects. This double pull – towards de- and re-materialization, towards the virtual and the actual – is a constant process that designs our posthuman subjectivity. It is not a crisis but an energizing and affirmative practice.

For Halberstam, popular culture icon Lady Gaga embodies the force and potential of this ambiguity or double pull exemplifying the posthuman modes of styling and inhabiting the contemporary body: 'In a post-feminist age when young women both benefit from and deny simultaneously leaps that have been engineered by feminism, we should explore carefully the new idioms of glamour and femininity as they appear within the performance-scape of stars like Lady Gaga' (2018: 171). Halberstam names this shift 'Gaga Feminism' and argues for an affirmative approach to the intense mediation that marks contemporary popular culture. Confirming the postmodernist intuition about the productive force of the artificial, Halberstam credits popular culture and mediated performances with the enabling power to promote counter- and sub-cultural productions that challenge the norms and rules of gender propriety. Halberstam defines this force as a kind of queer anarchism reminiscent of cyberfeminism, resisting the pull of digital data culture, going off the grid, causing chaos.

Because chaos is not chaotic but rather generative, it stands for different ways of becoming other-than the normal human. It is a constant process of becoming that diverges from the humanist norm and repurposes it. 'Gaga Feminism' brings this convulsive creativity into the sex and gender system, instilling radical ambivalence and subversive play as the new normal. Androgynous and disruptive, like David Bowie and Grace Jones before, Lady Gaga challenges gender roles and redefines them as multiplicity and perfect artifice.

When it comes to human bodies, posthuman feminist politics operates creative stylizations of bodies. This occurs with reference both to popular culture icons like Lady Gaga and her little monsters as she affectionately calls them, and to the images of female entrepreneurs in their Armani corporate gear as we saw in the *Posthuman* exhibition in the Introduction. It also involves emergent masses of not-yet-branded women and LGBTQ+ people, who may be delayed by opposition to their struggles, but will never be deleted. The subjects of emancipation and mainstreaming and the subjects of transgressive becoming follow their respective lines of fight within posthuman feminism. The flair for the post-natural and even the artificial is no longer a postmodern provocation but is now a praxis. The dissonant motifs of multiple feminisms leap across technological mediation and incorporate non-human entities – be it algorithms or bio-genetics. They design elemental techno lives, bonded by affirmative ethics, endowed with sexualities, beauty and creativity (Davis and Turpin, 2015). They construct posthuman bodies that are naturally technological, artificially unnatural, computer-activated, genetically engineered, but environmentally grounded.

Critical De-naturalization: Feminist Technoscience Studies

While cyberfeminism was the radical expression of technobodies in art and popular culture, feminist technoscience studies was one of the main scientific precursors of posthuman perspectives on technobodies. Åsberg and Lykke describe the field admirably: 'It is a shared assumption of researchers within the fields of Science Technology Studies and feminist technoscience studies that "pure", "basic" science is as entangled in societal interests, and can be held as politically and ethically accountable, as the technological practices and interventions to which it may give rise. The compound word "technoscience" was coined to emphasize this unavoidable link' (2010: 299). Feminist technoscience scholars address the social effects of science and technology, especially upon the marginal and the excluded, while keeping in mind the ecofeminist ideal of sustainable interdependence.

A formidable force with a split soul – half scientific, half literary and speculative – feminist technoscience studies is often at odds with itself. In spite of its uncommonly diverse constitution, it has exercised enormous influence, yet without getting due acknowledgement for the originality of its ideas and methods. Feminist technoscience studies attempt to reconcile, in rigorous as well as creative ways, the many souls of feminist theory. They meet the experimental and empirical methodological requirements of the Life Sciences and match them with the social-constructivist methods of the feminist tradition. Yet, they are also prone to flights of the imagination and imaginary visions (Lykke, 2008). Recently, feminist technoscience scholars have emerged directly from women's, feminist, gender, queer and trans-studies, often working within different scientific fields.[4] They moved away from feminist theories *of* or *in* science, to address 'feminism *out of* science' (Roosth and Schrader, 2012).

Feminist technoscience studies are positioned in the midst of the double pull of re-materialization and de-materialization of bodies. The bulk of feminist studies of technoscience advocates the critical *de*-naturalization of bodies, biologies and matter itself. Unsurprisingly, this de-naturalized or post-naturalistic approach covers a diverse range of positions, some profoundly rationalist, others speculative and imaginative.

Most feminist technoscience studies scholars are social-constructivists who push the nature–culture continuum to its logical conclusion, namely the equation of biology with technology. Sarah Franklin (1997, 2007) makes this point clearly by presenting biology and technology as interchangeable units. This equation of biology with technology sets feminist technoscience studies in potential opposition to the strategic re-naturalization proposed by ecofeminism and feminist materialism, but in the posthuman context the two approaches often intersect and even converge. Both strategic re-naturalization and critical de-naturalization agree on the basic point that there is no uncontaminated matter nor naturally born humans; that technological mediation is our second nature; and that reproduction is a process of sexually differing speciation. Feminist technoscience studies thus challenge gender and other binary organizations.

Another crucial strand of feminist technoscience studies emerges from the Humanities. In her illuminating overview of feminist cultural studies of technoscience, McNeil (2008) traces several interdisciplinary routes that have shaped the field of cultural studies in the UK (Hall, 1996), with the aim of assessing the impact of new technologies on social identity formations and relations of power (Franklin et al., 1991; Stacey, 1997, 2010; McNeil, 2007). Feminist technoscience scholars broadened the horizon of study, looking at the different facets of contemporary popular culture. Moreover, they addressed 'low culture' formations of everyday cultural expression, like advertisements, cartoons, songs, pub life and street art. They thus produced sharp analyses of the political economy of globalized capital, and of global nature and global culture (Franklin et al., 2000). Feminist cultural studies of technoscience, with strong links to media, music and popular culture (McRobbie, 2004), have a huge following outside the academy, notably to 'science art activism', as Haraway calls it (2017: 31). Feminist cultural studies of technoscience cover a broader interdisciplinary spectrum and are more open to posthuman theoretical discussions than the mainstream Science and Technology Studies. As Smelik and Lykke put it: 'The relation between biology and culture is not harmonious but conflictual. Our figuration assumes a posthuman definition of the body: a body that is not one' (2008: xi).

As a research community, feminist technoscience studies are mostly intent on negotiating experimental margins of intervention within the bio-medical sciences, reproductive and information technologies and climate sciences. Posthuman feminist bodies are resilient biocultural creatures (Frost, 2016).

Combining Re-naturalization and De-naturalization

Posthuman feminism combines the strategic re-naturalization of ecofeminism with the critical de-naturalization of feminist technoscience studies, using technology as the vector while remaining mindful of the importance of the intersectional variables of class, race, ethnicity, age and able-bodiedness. It is also open to the older insights and visions of Indigenous epistemologies and alternative technologies. This produces a qualitative leap into transversal notions of mixed assemblages, hybrid perspectives and unprogrammed techno-evolutions. Practices of algorithmic cultures and their politics and economic consequences are approached as parallel phenomena.

Tiziana Terranova (2004), for instance, calls for a collective engagement in the project of devising and implementing new digital networks of solidarity, on the joint model of the new digital commons and the old social welfare, resulting in 'posthuman commonfare'. This is an affirmative and action-oriented approach, which can be expanded with input from the women, LGBTQ+ people, migrants and asylum seekers. Any feminist discussion of digital citizenship must foreground voices from outside of Europe and the Global North, redefining global international relations in terms of the new interactive relationship to the technological apparatus.

As I have already extensively discussed new-materialist ecofeminism in chapter 3, I will not repeat its principles further here but rather point out the convergences between ecofeminism and technoscience feminism. Both are highly situated and accountable knowledge production practices, working within the feminist tradition of radical immanence and politics of locations. They aim at redefining the parameters of feminist subjectivity. They both embrace non-human objects and actors, the former gravitating around organic or naturalized others, the latter engrossed with the technological apparatus. They both juggle and struggle with the critical tensions between biological essentialism and discursive constructivism. They become vocal advocates of alternative, non-biological, extended families and multi-species kinship arrangements. The materialist and ecofeminist emphasis on naturecultures and symbiosis already includes technological mediation within the multiple materialist ecologies that structure posthuman *zoe*/geo/techno-mediated bodies. Technology therefore is the constitutive factor of the critical de- and re-naturalizations enacted by posthuman feminists positioned across a broad spectrum of locations and disciplinary perspectives.

The point of the posthuman convergence is that the two dimensions of new-materialist ecofeminism and feminist technoscience studies grow inseparable from each other, where the former stresses non-human life as *zoe* and the latter focuses on the non-human as technology. These two communities have a common circulatory system (Haraway, 1997). They are spread across a spectrum that covers both re-naturalized and de-naturalized practices in different degrees and scales. Xenofeminist Helen Hester summarizes the relationship between the ecofeminist and the feminist technoscience studies perspectives by showing their respective relationship to bodies, reproduction and power. She argues that ecofeminists embrace an 'enchanting alienation, achieved via the subjection of the impregnated body to forces beyond its control', which are cosmic and unpredictable. This is a re-naturalized version of bodies, reproduction and alienation. A technoscience approach, on the other hand, offers 'a disenchanted alienation, achieved via devolving epistemic authority to medical experts' (Hester, 2018: 17): a de-naturalized form of alienation.

The common denominator between these otherwise antagonistic positions is, on the one hand, the new posthuman understanding of matter as vital, self-organized and mediated and, on the other, the transformative and subversive force of feminist politics itself.

Genealogy of Feminist Technoscience Studies

Historically, the field of feminist technoscience studies starts with reference to women's and LGBTQ+ people's bodies and progresses gradually towards other sexed bodies, including non-human ones. This span stretches across the full spectrum of animals, plants, water, monocellular organisms and bacteria while it also embraces the technological apparatus such as algorithms, networks, digital platforms and infrastructure.

Emerging from the 1970s feminist activism in the women's health movement, feminist technoscience studies enjoys a distinguished historical pedigree (Boston Women's Health Collective, 1970). It criticized the medical profession's neglectful and condescending relationship to women's physical, mental and reproductive health (Ehrenreich and English, 1978). Feminist technoscience focused on biology and the bio-sciences, literally putting Alice through the microscope (Birke, 1980, 1986). The women's health movement also strove to account for women's and especially lesbian women's experience as recipients of bio-medical expertise (McNeil and Roberts, 2011).[5] This means that medicine and biology were at the heart of feminist technoscience studies, with an emphasis on bodies, reproductive health and sexualities (Martin, 1992; Rapp, 2000). But feminist technoscience studies did not stop at reparative measures: they also actively questioned the ways in which bio-medical sciences produced 'normal' bodies – anatomical, physiological, genetic, hormonal, behavioural, neurological – thereby pathologizing many other kinds of bodies (Birke, 2000; McNeil and Roberts, 2011: 29).

The methodology was social-constructivist, with special focus on the misconstruction of women, LGBTQ+, disabled people and people of colour as deficient, diseased or abnormal (Hubbard et al., 1979; Birke, 1980). Central to the normalizing efforts of the bio-sciences is the normative force of the patriarchal sex/gender system and of compulsory heterosexuality. This means that the patriarchal axe of discrimination falls with violence on LGBTQ+ people and gender non-conforming bodies (Fausto-Sterling, 1992 [1985], 2000; Balsamo, 1996). Feminist technoscience studies disclosed the ways in which biological arguments were used to justify social inequalities, especially in relation to sexualized and racialized bodies.[6] The politics was in keeping with the equality ideals, which meant that great attention was paid to emancipatory policies and the professional careers of women in science (Fox Keller, 1984, 1985; Wyer et al., 2001; Schiebinger, 2008).[7]

All this paves the way for further theoretical developments which help build the posthuman perspective. Feminist technoscience studies intersected with feminist philosophers (Irigaray, 1985a; Tuana, 1989) and challenged science's claim to objectivity, universality and value-neutrality. They argued forcefully that the experimental medical sciences are biased in favour of white, European, male bodies.[8] New interpretations of scientific objectivity were offered by standpoint feminist theory (Harding, 1986, 1998; Hartsock, 1987) and the claims to specific feminist ways of doing science (Fox Keller, 1984; Longino, 1989).

The primacy of vision as a method of scrutiny and scientific verification, but also of domination, was questioned. Feminists have a long-standing quarrel with the hegemony of vision and the ubiquity of lenses and optical technologies, over all other modes of perception and cognition (Fox-Keller and Grontkowski, 1983; Jordanova, 1989). Feminist scholars were among the first to critique the objectifying power of a gaze that is structured by masculine phallic power (Irigaray 1985a [1974]) and heterosexual male desire (Mulvey, 1975). Throughout the 1980s and 1990s feminist cultural studies was the forum where the powers of vision were examined most rigorously, notably in art history and criticism (Pollock, 1988). Feminists in media studies were at the forefront of the analysis of this phenomenon (Franklin et al., 1991, 2000), with leading critics like McRobbie (2004, 2015) and McNeil (2007) illuminating the different aspects of the link between feminism and visual culture, also in the making of science.

These pioneering studies fuelled the growth of radical critiques of scientific reason (Haraway, 1990; Stengers, 1997, 2015). The intersections of science and technology studies with issues of race, colonialism and multiculturalism were addressed explicitly and early on in feminist technoscience studies (Tuana, 1989; Hill Collins, 1991; Haraway, 1992; Alcoff and Porter, 1993; Hammonds, 1994; Harding, 1998; Schiebinger, 1999). Through a strong empirical methodology, feminist technoscience produces a strong speculative angle (Roberts, 2018).

This led to more critical interdisciplinary questions about the necessity of feminist approaches to science, including alternative approaches to the practice of science (Longino, 1989; Rosser, 1989; Schiebinger, 1999) and to feminist science history (Martin, 1992; Duden, 1998).

The rapid growth of objects of study entailed a qualitative shift: the early claims on women's health unfolded upon a critique of the limitations of patriarchal science, thereby contributing to the rapid growth of feminist epistemologies. Similarly, the shift to non-human objects resulted in questioning both humanism and anthropocentrism. Epistemology drives the ethics that defines the politics. Trans and queer feminism bring the unnatural and the deviant to the centre of the critical enquiry, focusing on repurposing scientific methods to materialize alternative modes of embodiment. From there on, the collective feminist exit from the kingdom of Anthropos began to gather momentum and explicit references to the posthuman appear in feminist texts from the 1990s (Braidotti, 1994; Halberstam and Livingston, 1995; Balsamo, 1996; Hayles, 1999). The post-anthropocentric turn takes off in dialogue with ecofeminism. The objects of study of feminist technoscience studies start to stretch beyond human health, while also questioning the expanding role of technology.

The non-human thematic focus in feminist theory takes off by the turn of the millennium (Hird and Roberts, 2011; Grusin, 2017), and affects studies of reproductive technologies (Franklin et al., 2000; Fox Keller, 2002; Franklin, 2007); research on hormones (Roberts, 2007); on the role of digital systems in science (Suchman, 2000; Waldby, 2000; Lury et al., 2012) and on neural sciences (Wilson, 1998, 2004; Malabou, 2011, 2012). Karen Barad (2007) takes on the physics of the universe as a whole by engaging with the theories of physicist Niels Bohr; Vicky Kirby also refers to quantum anthropology (2011). Molecular biologist Deboleena Roy (2018), relying on Deleuze's micropolitics and micro physiologies of desire, pushes a non-deterministic practice of biology and calls for experimenting with virtual queer becoming.

Kim TallBear (2013) combines feminist science studies of the American DNA with feminist theory. She gives a distinctly Indigenous frame to the notion of technobodies and reinscribes them into a relational ontology. Approaching feminist new materialism, environmentalism and genetics from an Indigenous perspective and as a contribution to native people's self-determination, TallBear argues for 'Indigenous governance of science' (2015: 231). The quest for points of encounter between Western and Indigenous and native science is one of the key issues on the cutting-edge of contemporary feminist and critical posthuman perspectives (Cajete, 2004).[9]

De-naturalization Re-naturalized: Dolly the Sheep

Posthuman feminism, as an accelerating combination of feminist technoscience studies and materialist ecofeminism, brings the social-constructivist tradition to a paradoxical point of implosion. Sarah Franklin's work is emblematic of this approach to matter as biocultural entity that blurs the distinction between the new biologies, the technologies and dominant cultural codes 'like gender, sex and species' (2007: 3). She argues that there are no real natural, material, factual or biological facts that exist entirely independent of technologically mediated human action. This creates a 'transbiology', in her words 'a biology that is not only born and bred, or born and made, but made and born' (Franklin, 2006: 171).

Two parallel lines of enquiry emerge from this radical de-naturalization of biology. A political anatomy of bio-genetic capitalism on the one hand, and the queering of biology, the life sciences and kinship systems on the other. Both lines are relevant for the posthuman turn. The conversion of nature into techniques leans to an explosion of 'trans-hybridities' or transgenic organisms that undo traditional understandings of biology, nature and genealogical descent. In the broader frame of contemporary genetic capitalism, reproductive technologies are not primarily about reproduction, or even the desire for a child as such, but about capitalizing on the vitality of matter and about social redefinitions of kinship systems.

The political anatomy of bio-genetic capitalism is often presented through the case study of Dolly the sheep. Or rather, Dolly the living techno-artifact, produced by the scientific technique known as somatic cell nuclear transfer (SCNT) or the 'second creation' as it is called. This non-human technobody centres on a vast reproductive mechanism that has been thoroughly disassembled and rearranged. The genetic stem-cell material emerging from IVF spins off in a number of significant directions: genomic databanks, stem cell research, regenerative medicine, etc. These are huge transnational markets that capitalize on life as surplus (Cooper, 2008); it is capital in the age of the politics of life itself (Rose, 2007).

Dolly the sheep points to queering the possibility of genealogy and kinship. Dolly is a trans-entity, of mixed sex and deviant biological origins, with genetic material from unrelated organisms, mixed, sampled and re-sequenced. In its making, genealogy implodes into a series of sub-sets of technological practices or protocols. Designed and made, grown and built, rather than bred and born, Dolly is for Franklin 'trans-viable' as the prototype of 'queer ancestry' (2007: 29). Dolly is the cyborg embryo of the transbiology era, inaugurating a queer lineage.

From a posthuman perspective, Dolly as the emblem of denatured and modified biology gives new insight into the vitality of matter. Vitality refers to the regenerative potential of cells, right across human and non-human species, which is the target of bio-medical research, regenerative medicine and technologically assisted reproduction. In other words, Dolly's body is a mediated kind of vitality: both *zoe* and *techno*, and in flows of transition between them. As Preciado astutely put it: 'There is nothing to discover in nature, there is no hidden secret. We live in a punk hyper-modernity. It is no longer about discovering the hidden truth in nature; it is about the necessity of specifying the cultural, political and technological processes through which the body as artifact acquires natural status' (2013b: 270). In some ways, the posthuman predicament is about re-naturalizing the artificial. The artificial nature of what we used to call nature, predicated on the equation of biology with technology, reasserts the primacy of social codes over realistic and new-materialist understandings of matter.

IVF is a manner for bio-genetic capitalism to collect embryonic-derived genetic material, gather more bio-genetic resources and data, save them in transnational databases and organize reproduction technoscientifically. This is an imploded or exploded scientific universe, where families end up as the rearrangement of biodiversity databases, animal and human genome projects, global seed banks and bio-agricultural food practices. Such intense techno-mediation opens significant margins of intervention for critical feminists, from cyber-feminism to Lady Gaga, from queer reproduction to trans experiments.

Naturalizing Queerness, Queering Nature

Many feminist theorists, striving to overcome the oedipalized sexual binary system, have equated the posthuman with post-gender and have taken the leap in the direction of multiple trans sexualities. Although the posthuman is not automatically hyper-queer, queering the non-human is a distinct trend in posthuman feminism. But it is not the only one, as multiple sexualities are alive and well also within fast-evolving posthuman bodies. De-naturalization is the assumption that supports queer inhumanism, resonating in queer and trans science studies. Mindful of the fact that LGBTQ+ people have historically been placed on the side of the unnatural, the deviant and the abnormal, the distinctions between these categories need to be questioned. The same goes for the underlying assumptions, key terms and notions that are applied to LGBTQ+ people. Commenting on these 'improbable manners of being', Eileen Joy states 'the queer and the nonanthropomorphic have always been importantly entwined and that the queer is always pushing against the limits of not just the "merely" but also the "overdetermined" human' (2015: 223).

One of the axioms of queer theory is to leave behind the essentialism implicit in unitary definitions of feminist, lesbian and gay identities, instead stressing their socially constructed nature (Butler, 1990; Sedgwick, 1990; Halberstam, 1998). The aim of queer science studies is to strengthen the subject positions and the capacity for resistance and transformation on the part of women, sexual minorities, gender-nonconforming people, and other historically marginalized groups.

Refashioning human embodiment in post- and anti-natural ways is central to queer inhumanism (Chen and Luciano, 2015; Muñoz, 2015) and the 'somatechnics' direction of queer theory (Sullivan and Murray, 2009). Trans-feminism starts from the assumption that 'the new condition of the body blurs the traditional modern distinction between art, performance, media, design, and architecture' (Preciado, 2013b: 271), which leads to designing alternative genders and self-designed sexes. Pushing biology beyond its limits, as a form of bio-hacking, queer technoscience studies displaces the boundaries of sexuality, reproduction and mortality. Queering the non-human is now in full swing, in a series of variations that include rethinking sexual diversity based on animal and other organic systems (Giffney and Hird, 2008).

Contemporary queer science studies strengthen the intersections between science and queer feminisms, raising a broad range of questions about sex, race, gender, sexuality and other systems of difference. Adopting an intersectional approach, they interrogate practices of normalization and foundational aspects of sexualized and racialized queerness, including the ancestral proximity between queer humans and non-human entities (Grewal and Kaplan, 2001; Hird, 2006). They stress the inseparability of the natural and the artificial, the normal and the deviant. This entails a critical aspect: the analysis of the operations of power and privilege; but also a creative one, 'highlighting potentialities for uncertainty, subversion, transformation, and play' (Cipolla et al., 2017: 4). Posthuman trans feminism is a crucial layer in exploring the political potential of posthuman technobodies. It runs along two intersecting axes: first by pursuing de-naturalization of the human and then by re-naturalizing the unnatural. Because trans and non-gender-conforming people are equated with the deviant, they are positioned in an in-between world. Stryker (2015) refers to this liminal position as 'inhuman'.

Trans feminism brings the posthuman debate to a higher level of philosophical abstraction about the posthuman condition, opening up a wider field of possibilities, potential alliances and actual affinities. It is about other ways of living, loving and relating to reality at large, and it is thus an ethical project at heart.[10] The assumption, shared with queer theory, is the critique of the gender binary system and how it is operationalized not only in society but also in the making of science. The normative gender categories end up not only excluding but also pathologizing LGBTQ+ people in biomedicine, science and society, and casting them on the side of abnormality. Queer and trans scholarship contests the legitimacy and self-evidence granted to dominant categories of natural and normal, as opposed to unnatural and deviant sexuality and aims to undo their binary opposition (Fausto-Sterling, 2000; Butler, 2004; Edelman, 2004; Halberstam, 2005; Puar, 2007). This contests the naturalization of the categories of normal and deviant sexuality.

Contemporary queer science studies emphasize the intersectional aspects of sexualized and racialized queerness, and the proximity between queer humans and non-human entities (Grewal and Kaplan, 2001; Hird, 2006; Hayward and Weinstein, 2015). They stress the imbrication or dependence of natural and the artificial, and normativity and deviance.

Disability Studies

The extreme de-naturalization and the embrace of the deviant and the unnatural brings trans theory closer to the contemporary practice of disability studies, as artist Sue Austin brilliantly demonstrates with her freewheeling wheelchair under water. Disability studies have become an important forum to assess the normative assumptions about bodies and body–mind abilities (Rapp et al., 2001). They singled out 'ableism' as a normative scientific taxonomy that actively discriminates against morphologically different human bodies by applying a narrow definition of normal humanness, which is intrinsically racialized (Chen, 2015). This definition, applied in medicine and evolutionary theory as well as in public health, follows the humanist aesthetics of Da Vinci's Vitruvian ideal of the perfect male, white human body. Refusing the imposition of this cultural ideal of normality, posthuman disability studies pleads for the radical diversity of alternative corporeal models. As Stuart Murray put it: 'It is precisely here that humanism's profound fear of the body with disabilities turns into the potential appreciation of the varieties of embodiment that disability presents, both in terms of the human body itself and its interactions with technology' (2020: 12).

Disability advocacy plays a central role in liberal humanist definitions of human rights and the respect for the dignity of all people (Nussbaum, 2006), but gets a new angle in the posthuman convergence. The complexity of the current predicament pushes the political agenda beyond the advocacy of equal rights, recognition and respect. These claims get broadened in a feminist intersectional framework that contests the norms used to assess bodies (and minds) as being disabled to begin with (Shildrick, 2012).

Posthuman feminism recasts disability studies in the affirmative mode of 'otherwise enabled' bodies that defy the expected standards of normality (Braidotti and Roets, 2012; Shotwell, 2016). In this respect, disability challenges the received conception of what it means to be human while at the same time asserting disabled people's full humanity (Goodley et al., 2012, 2014). The point of disability studies is not to diagnose, cure, palliate or repair disability, but to appreciate the alternative modes of embodiment it expresses and to develop the otherwise embodied capabilities (Kafer, 2013; Goodley et al., 2018).

Contemporary disability studies are in some ways a celebration of anomaly, monstrosity and weirdness (Braidotti, 2002; Shildrick, 2002), not unlike Kathy Acker or Lady Gaga. Those studies aim to refashion the human by undoing the binary normal/abnormal and able/disabled. They stress the inseparability of the natural and the artificial, the normal and the deviant, in a critique of ableism that is also a celebration of the 'flexible morphologies' of posthuman disabled bodies (Enke, 2013: 244).

Posthuman disability scholarship intersects productively with trans and queer theories' critiques of dualism and queer inhumanism (Chen and Luciano, 2015; McCormack, 2018). In a mode that Murray (2020) defines as 'precarious posthumanism', disability studies stress the multi-layered interconnectedness that is engendered by the disabled or 'Crip queer' disability studies and subject positions. Nikki Sullivan brings queer feminist disability studies into a qualitative 'somatechnics' dimension, by examining the diagnostic category of 'Body Integrity Identity Disorder' (BIID) (Sullivan and Murray, 2009). Susan Stryker sums it up: 'If transgender looks back to the human with the goal of making it something else, somatechnics faces a posthuman future' (2015: 230). Murray labels this position as 'prostheticized posthumanism' (2020: 139).

Otherwise-abled bodies, like trans bodies, assert the point that posthuman bodies are to a large extent self-designed bodies or 'bio-hacked' entities. Otherwise-designed bodies – like Sue Austin's – have been claimed, enacted and visualized in the public sphere. Similarly, an array of alternative bodies and multiple gender systems have been proposed by the LGBTQ+ movements, as well as degrees of sexual indeterminacy or undifferentiation. These counter-systems are often modelled on the morphology and sexual systems of non-human species. Post-gender sexualities, 'trans bodies, trans selves' (Erickson-Scroth, 2014), have also been postulated with a post-anthropocentric inflexion.

Queer Kinship

The case for the critical de-naturalization of biology, pushed to the extreme, produces a posthuman theory of kinship, that is to say an anti-foundationalist, post-natural theory of transgressive, non-heteronormative, LGBTQ+ kinship and family systems. I already analysed in earlier chapters the ways in which patriarchy naturalized the social system that best suited its political priority, preserving the powers and entitlements of men. Once this naturalized hierarchy is exposed for the power game it is, it can be undone. The demise of any naturalistic reproductive order is accelerated by advanced technology and cognitive capitalism. Within the posthuman convergence, this exchange is mutual in the sense that technological assistance is naturalized in return, as technologically mediated reality becomes our second nature. Thus, reproductive technology becomes 'biologized' because it makes perfectly normal human beings.

For feminist technoscience scholars, IVF and reproductive technologies go beyond maternal desire, female bodies or the lived experience and the desires of women – defined as the embodied and embedded subjects that identify with that category. IVF is at once a bio-medical technique and a major apparatus for remaking life. By shifting the focus of research outside the household and the heterosexual contract, IVF introduces new kinds of biological relatives, which include 'a multiplication of maternities, divided into genetic and gestational branches, as well as new types of siblings, such as twins born years apart or donor siblings connected via the Internet' (Franklin, 2013: 313). Nature and artifice become interchangeable and the female body is subsumed into bio-engineering. Fertilization is not only between egg and sperm, but also between biology and technology. This is the twenty-first-century ethos of biological engineering that now defines the fields of genomics, synthetic biology and technologically mediated offspring. Queer kinship learns from Strathern's anthropological work on assisted human reproduction in non-Western social systems (1992) as an example of strategic re-naturalization that realigns messy hybrid components into a structure called parenthood. This allows for non-traditional means of impregnation such as conception through donor sperm or surrogacy (Mamo, 2007). Kinship is accordingly 'naturalized, denaturalized and renaturalized' (Franklin et al., 2000).

Sophie Lewis (2019) radicalizes the issues involved in the new reproductive technologies by subjecting cognitive capitalism to a queer revolution. She agrees that bio-capitalism is using IVF, but also commercial surrogacy, for purposes other than to honour women's alleged desire to have children. Pregnancy is just not a problem that capitalism is actually concerned about. What is a priority is the production of the *right* kind of parents and children, who conform to the dominant norms about being human. The application of this hegemonic template of reproduction engenders a mixture of soft eugenics and endemic racism. Technologically assisted reproduction is catering mostly to the demand for genetic descent, for genetically certified parenthood and it does so by outsourcing IVF and commercial surrogacy. We already encountered this in chapter 2, where I examined the role of technologically assisted reproduction – notably freezing embryos – in the neoliberal feminist agenda as a way of ensuring a happy balance between motherhood and professional success of well-off aspirational women.

Lewis looks closely at the social relations of (re)production. Procreation has become a profitable branch of the global bio-genetic market, which employs poorer sections of the population, 'wherever they are cheapest (or most convenient) to enrol', to do the dirty work of pregnancy. This means that reproduction and pregnancy nowadays are 'bound up with colonialism, white supremacy, capital, gender – but also resistance' (Lewis, 2019: 165). The political resistance is predicated on an accelerationist queer project that consists in embracing surrogacy as a tool of liberation, not only for the surrogates, but for society as a whole. The strategy aims to uncouple gestation from issues of personalized desire, identities predicated on gender binaries and the sanctity of the family. Reproduction is attached instead to a floating labour market, which in turn assumes that surrogacy is not alienation but underpaid labour. Angela Balzano (2020) defends the argument that surrogacy needs to be repositioned in terms of women's labour and self-determination. As a result, queer feminist politics supports the claim to better wages for surrogacy workers and their gestational labour.

The precedent for this argument is the heated discussion about prostitution as sex work that was at the heart of the 1980s 'sex wars' that divided the feminist community.[11] Lewis is aware that she is lifting a taboo by speaking so explicitly about money in relation to pregnancy, traditionally deemed to be an intimate experience involving sacralized body parts and cherished family relationships. The desecrating effect of trans-biology critiques demystifies the whole experience of gestation and birth. Lewis demands respect for the commodification of gestation, just as Paul Preciado (2013a, 2013b) did for the biohacking of gender identities, sexuality and the commercialization of sex work.

Another historical precedent for this argument is the Italian socialist feminist case for paid housework. It is revived today by Federici, who campaigns for wages for household work and the domestic services provided by wives and partners as well as staff. What does love have to do with it? In favour of queer poly-maternalism, as opposed to individual female maternal desire, Lewis proposes that 'uteruses can only ever be put to use by bodies other than those of which they are part' (2019: 160). She makes a strong case against 'repro-normativity' (p. 107). The woman's body is no longer the only site of reproduction in advanced capitalism and Lewis argues that a queer take on this technological process has great liberatory potential for LGBTQ+ people. The leading figuration is the embryo as cyborg, as the equation between biology and technology. The embryo as an extra-corporeal entity means that the maternal function is diversified and distributed within intense technological intervention. In a queer perspective, the key political agenda is to abolish gender.

In order to avoid falling into neoliberalism and colluding with the market economy and its profit-driven accelerations, Lewis argues against the consumption of reproductive bodies by the market. She adds a queer communist twist and calls for 'worker-owned surrogacy cooperatives' (2019: 33) communally run against neoliberal commercialization. These reproductive communes are modelled on sex workers' cooperatives and explicitly call for the abolition of the patriarchal family, the destruction of the gender system, queer communism and communal ownership of the babies produced through surrogacy. In support of her argument, Lewis refers explicitly to 1970s feminist science fiction and the tradition of cyber utopias, notably Shulamith Firestone's vision of a feminist socialist cyber utopia. That vision claims generative spaces for the non-human, the company of monsters, perverts and other (in)human entities, including extra-terrestrial ones.

Strategic Re-materialization of Technobodies

Reproductive bodies have become posthuman. Surveying the field in 1995, Susan Squier analysed the phenomenon of technologically invested reproduction through the following figurations: the extra-uterine foetus, the surrogate mother and the pregnant man. Each figuration points to different locations and practices of biotechnological intervention. Returning to the field a decade later, Squier (2004) analysed the same phenomenon through a different line-up: the cultured cell, the hybrid embryo, the engineered intra-uterine foetus, the child treated with human growth hormone, the process of organ transplantation, and the elderly person rejuvenated by hormone replacement therapy or other artificial means. These examples of what she calls 'liminal lives' allow Squier to assess in a materialist and affirmative manner the multiplying effects of contemporary technobodies upon the different stages of existence. They enable posthuman ways of living and dying.

Bio-hacking means self-designing one's embodiment. The contemporary techniques are in a continuum with earlier experiments in perfecting human bodies through fitness, dieting, plastic surgery, and the cosmetics and wellness industries, and have been practised for decades. They accelerate in the posthuman convergence and reach another level of intervention. Today, both gene-editing and gender-editing have become part of our vocabulary and our social as well as technological practices. They affect humans and animals, plants and just about all living matter, in a way that Shiva had presciently defined as 'bio-piracy' (1997). Piracy here refers both to the criminal practice of robbing vessels at sea and to the outlawed reproduction of another's work. Unauthorized reproduction, as Kathy Acker cleverly predicted, refers both to intellectual property and copyrights laws, and to biological reproduction. But they also open up the possibility of exploring new paths for the deployment of sexualities, desires and pleasures.

The complexities of posthuman reproductive bodies also give pause for critical reflection. I have grown weary of techno-utopias, even of the feminist kind and by now find even Firestone's (1970) cyber-socialist visions from the 1970s a little too hopeful (more details in chapter 7). Returning to the materialist roots of posthuman feminism, let us see how real-life bodies are positioned in the practice of technologically assisted reproduction today. It is indeed the case that the technologies that 1970s utopian feminists were hoping would prove subversive have become reality. But it is also true that they have not brought about a radical feminist revolution or full human liberation. They have rather been co-opted into neoliberal economics as a profitable economic enterprise in a transnational reproductive market. Moreover, the contemporary status of women still shows many of the discriminatory patterns that radical feminists like Firestone were objecting to. The success of individualistic neoliberal feminism has shattered the hopes of a final downfall of traditional feminine patterns of socialization, let alone solidarity across classes and intersectional categories of women.

More importantly still, the new reproductive technologies have not broken up or abolished the family, but rather strengthened it (McNeil, 2007; Cooper, 2008, 2009). The reasons are, on the one hand, the backlash against feminism by the conservative Christians and the neo-natalist and heteronormative political Right. But, on the other hand, the family structure received a second lease of life from feminist and LGBTQ+ people, who were keen to repossess and reinvent it. On the positive side, this tactic has destabilized the monopoly of the heterosexual family and empowered a range of LGBTQ+ alternatives. The added irony is that technologically assisted reproduction, which was introduced to help heterosexual couples construct traditional families, has ended up exploding any notions of naturalness and has undone the traditional family (Rapp, 2000).

On the more critical side, the legalization of gay marriage and spreading acceptance of gay families may simply be a way of strengthening, rather than subverting, what Cooper ironically calls 'family values' (2017). Privatization of services, the commercialization of reproductive technology and surrogacy have entered neoliberal economies. Individualized options of different delayed forms of embryo implantation or other modes of reproduction have replaced utopian dreams of a mass insurrection against pregnancy. Capitalism bends, but it does not break. Sexual radicals may have just contributed to introduce a pluralistic range of possible family arrangements. In contrast to these trends, Haraway stands out in contemporary feminism by calling for zero population growth, and the making of kin, not babies, because 'it matters how kin makes kin' (2016: 103).

Moreover, reproductive technologies have only marginally improved the family lives of middle-class women by liberating them from the burden of childrearing and by outsourcing the entire reproduction cycle to other women, specifically employed for this purpose. Not only did middle-class women not achieve full equality, but also their advancement took place to the detriment of the status of many working-class, Black and migrant women, who are now employed in households and in care work to replace the new professionals. This creates new labour, race and class relations between women. As Cooper and Waldby (2014) point out, reproductive technologies have a dramatic impact on the sexualized and racialized bodies that are subjected to gestational and clinical labour in advanced capitalism. The point is made in a historical perspective by Weinbaum (2019) in her recent analysis of the legacy of slavery in bio-capitalism and reproductive biopolitics. Indigenous and Black feminists have exposed the devastating effects of Western bio-medical technologies upon racialized women for a very long time (Davis, 1981; Hammonds, 1994; Lucashenko, 2002; TallBear, 2015). There is nothing de-materialized about the labour performed here.

Cooper comments critically on the role of reproductive technologies and the commercialization of outsourced forms of human fertility as hard embodied labour. Trans-biology is also *in vivo* biology, 'through either the production of experimental data or the transfer of tissues' (Cooper and Waldby, 2014: 7). Surrogacy, the provision and sale of body and reproductive tissues, and participation in clinical trials have proliferated at the lower ends of the post-Fordist bio-medical economy. Cognitive capitalism champions these practices alongside other forms of capitalization of the human body. The burgeoning egg markets in Eastern Europe, India and other parts of the world are embodied, physical labour, which position women as hard labourers and as primary tissue providers in the new stem cell industries. Cooper also makes it clear that women who participate in any one sector of this reproductive economy are likely to migrate to another, so that the boundaries between actual bio-medical, reproductive labour, on the one hand, and sexual and domestic labour, on the other, are extremely fluid. Thus, 'what embryoid capital demands is a self-regenerating, inexhaustible, quietly sacrificial source of reproductive labor – *a kind of global feminine*' (Cooper, 2008: 150, my emphasis).

The reproductive technobodies can be said to be successfully integrated into the bioeconomy of cognitive capitalism and its brutal labour relations. But that does not exhaust the picture of sexual radicalism and the experimental mode endures. It is manifested in the quest for new kinship systems and chosen families based on affinity and affectivity. As we shall see in the next chapter, experiments with new philosophies of love, and the erotic arts of existence, carry on successfully today. Sexual promiscuity, free love and polyamorous arrangements, which were pioneered by 1970s feminists, were reassessed critically in the 1990s due to the AIDS epidemic and HIV. Posthuman, all too human, sexuality lives its life independently of reproduction. The irrepressible sexual radicals continue to be optimistic about the ongoing experiments with what desiring bodies can do.

Placenta Politics

There are other posthuman feminist ways of strategically re-positioning the maternal, gestational, reproductive technobodies within the schizoid flows of contemporary capitalism. In an insightful essay, Rodante van der Waal (2018) posits the 'pregnant posthuman' as a figuration for alternative feminist gestational subjectivity. Defying the dyad of the maternal body versus embryo-foetus-baby, van der Waal relocates the pregnant posthumans as transversal and transitional subjects, who experience intuitively and intimately the shifting borders of otherness within themselves.

Pregnancy means change and becoming, in a movement of matter flowing trans-corporeally between different entities. The pregnant posthuman embodies complexity and ambiguity, hybrid origins, technological mediation and ethical accountability. Technically female (Colman, 2014), it has become the *global gestational feminine*, but still continues to primarily affect female bodies. In a visionary intervention on this techno-maternal-matter, the iconic song 'O Superman!' (1982),[12] performance artist Laurie Anderson voiced curiosity, dismay and longing: 'So, hold me, Mom, in your long arms./ Your petrochemical arms. Your military arms./ In your electronic arms'. This complex affectivity anticipates posthuman loves to come.

There is a significant contradiction at play here, dictated by the conditions of our historical context and thus materially embedded. Let me extrapolate from a posthuman feminist angle: what does it mean to take seriously the fact that some bodies – both human and non-human – are capable of giving birth, or producing the life of another? And to do so both with and without technological assistance? This productive dimension of trans-corporeal materialism stresses the indivisible unity of matter, as well as its dynamic ability to fold in external entities and simultaneously unfold outwards (Deleuze, 1993). Posthuman feminism strips the gender ideology away from the reproductive body, highlighting its bio-genetic capabilities, the physics of its organic stratum, and its vital potency. But also, its intimate interconnection with technology and bio-medical sciences.

The generative force of intersubjective gestationality and vital (re)-production is relatively under studied in both philosophy and feminism.[13] The posthuman predicament allows for a critical reconsideration of the materialist relationality of pregnancy and gestation, and how it connects to love and some sort of trust in the future. Materialist feminists like Diprose (2002) had already stressed the 'corporeal generosity' of maternity. However intimate, the pregnant condition is also impersonal as it points to something beyond the self that is not yet completely another either. Hird (2007) builds on Diprose's insights, arguing that the corporeal generosity of maternity constitutes a symbiotic relationship beyond liberal individualistic autonomy, within differential sexuate matter. Whereas trans-biology and technologically supported surrogacy displace the centrality of female flesh from the scene of reproduction, posthuman materialist feminism reinscribes it. But not in the same place, not on the same terms, and not for the same purpose. A posthuman maternal materialism positions gestationality as something else than the techno-mediated uterus. Yet, it is also other than the classical, sacred maternal feminine of the old gender system, because it is a more extended and often technologically mediated milieu that stretches well beyond the sexually dimorphic, heterosexual bodies. As Hird put it, placental gifting is a crucial vector of transfer of genetic information: 'The placenta is an organ that develops around the foetus. It is a portal through which mother, foetus (and many other organisms) gift. The mother's body gifts oxygen, nutrients, blood, DNA and RNA strands, proteins, viruses, bacteria and other living and nonliving matter' (2007: 10).

The maternal, gestational, placental, foetal sequence is a heterogeneous generative assemblage. I call it 'placenta politics' in a materialist posthuman feminist fashion (Braidotti, 2018). Drawing on the work of French feminists (Irigaray, 1985a [1974], 1985b [1977]; Rouch, 1987), let me propose the biotechnological entity of the placenta as a third party between the uterus or maternal body and the foetus. As such it raises key issues of relationality, immunity and auto-immunity, which are best served by a new-materialist philosophy of becoming and affirmative ethics. The foetus is potentially just another parasitic body, which Jean-Luc Nancy would call 'an intruder' (2000). But in gestational politics, read with posthuman feminist lenses, it is a 'good' parasite, in Serres' sense of the term (1982 [1980]). The foetus and its host organism have in fact the ability to stabilize their relationship, in immunological terms, and co-exist, nurturing each other. The placenta is the third party, the porous membrane, a sort of liquid inner biosphere, that both connects and separates the dyad host/foetus. It undoes the inside/outside divide and allows for permanent flux of exchanges between the different parties. It splits the reproductive subject from within, in a non-dialectical process of internal differentiations that does not negate or annihilate the other but actually produces otherness within. It is a case of trans-corporeality (Alaimo, 2010) at work across permeable and inextricably interlinked matter.

Placenta politics illustrates several key features of new post-maternalist gestational praxis. It affirms a non-aggressive biopolitics that rejects the dialectics of weaponized binary differences. In terms of the immunological debate, this means that the question is not whether the organism is capable of self-preservation by attacking and eliminating alien or intruding or diseased parts of itself, but rather that in cases of pregnancy, it actually does *not* attack them. Specifically, in pregnancy the organism does not usually expel the foetal other but rather hosts and nurtures it.

This point is relevant to the mainstream posthumanist discussion about the immunological paradox (Derrida, 1981; Esposito, 2002; Wolfe, 2010). The auto-immunological principle of injecting the pathogen in controlled doses into the body does not aim to destroy the entirety of the organism, but rather helps the immune system learn how to defend itself. The auto-immunological defence points to a cure, or at least some immunity, from the very sources responsible for the pathology. The encounter with the source of the disease triggers the infection, but also creates a first line of defence against it. The ethics of biopolitical immunity proposes not the exclusion, but the coercive incorporation and vicarious substitution of the vital/lethal other in a dialectical mode of encounter.

Although few of the biopolitical thinkers ever take the female body – or the feminist corpus – into consideration, placenta politics makes the same point, but through a different route and in a less aggressive manner. It illuminates the specific form of auto-immunity that is the maternal, gestational, placental, foetal sequence as a heterogeneous assemblage. Posthuman pregnant assemblages foreground the crucial idea that the immune system does not always attack what has been injected into and contained within the body.

The placenta is the operative factor of the immunological compatibility between the host and the foetus. It is formed by the extension of the maternal body's blood vessels into another tissue that both connects and separates the embryo from the maternal organism. It is ejected as an extra entity about thirty minutes after the birth has taken place. It is a cooperative trans-corporeal model of symbiotic growth. This is a far cry from the thanato-political discourses about the tactical expulsion of alien elements or the aggressive elimination of the alien other, which dominate contemporary biopolitical discussions. The paradigm of placenta politics expresses instead not only another immunological paradigm, but also the posthuman feminist politics of generative relationality and affirmative auto-immunity.

In the midst of the global COVID-19 pandemic, immunity is everybody's top concern. The public discourse about vaccines and immunity has already taken the form of a belligerent, xenophobic campaign about 'invisible enemies' and unwanted alien others. Auto-immunity has become the theatre of war. In contrast and as an alternative to this violence, the model of generative placenta politics points to a different practice of good parasites, which can be hosted and cultivated through the interdependence of multiple technobodies. Placenta politics is about affirmative ethical encounters: it is the original form of trans-corporeality and of collaborative auto-immunity. It points to the heterogeneous co-creation of hospitable and sustainable environments. It is a process of differential modulations by organisms that define themselves by mutual relations within a common matter.

This kind of corporeal hospitality points to pacifist cooperation and co-creation between organisms, in a specific relational frame that facilitates their coexistence, interaction and growth. Just like the environmentalist idea of 'syndemic' (see chapter 3), generative placenta politics stresses the notion of evolution through mutual cooperation. It is a powerful collaboration between separate yet related organisms, agents and living matter: generative, gestational, maternal, placental and foetal. It is a figuration of affirmative relationality and multiple becoming. Posthuman feminist technobodies in this respect can shed a new light on the shifting boundaries between life and death and explore their ethical and political implications in a manner that honours basic principles of solidarity, care and compassion.

Conclusion

In this chapter, I unravelled the implications of the posthuman theoretical framework for the feminist understandings of the body. Posthuman feminism reinscribes technobodies at the centre of the posthuman debate. The range of positions emerging from the feminist politics of posthuman bodies is wide and contradictory. I have shown that feminist technoscience studies push towards a critical de-naturalization, while ecofeminism and feminist materialism propose a strategic re-naturalization. A strategic re-naturalization of the materially embedded maternal, with its strengths and limitations, coexists with a critical de-naturalization of gestation via technologically assisted reproduction. These seemingly opposite positions are accommodated within the posthuman convergence, giving rise to different claims and political strategies. Some feminists may potentiate the specificity of embodiment, while others may want to move away from it and abolish conventional morphological boundaries. There is no need to position these differences as mutually exclusive. Nor is there anything particularly new about such a diversity of feminist positions, because feminism has always been a movement without leaders or dogmas. Let us experiment with multiple modes of reproduction and invent kinship and social structures attuned to these radical experiments. I have explored cyberfeminism of the 1980s and 1990s as one of those experiments in producing new kinds of posthuman bodies in much the way that Gaga feminism is today.

The different strategies of de- and re-naturalization show how feminist technoscience studies are a precursor to posthuman feminism. The political implications of feminist technoscience studies are as varied and contradictory as the methods and genres that express them. On the one hand, there is a constant equality-minded line that runs through this entire community, from the women's health movement to the queer and trans health movements of today. Correcting the capitalist, neo-colonial, heteronormative bias of science and technology remains a perennial concern, as the degrees and intimacy of technological mediation shape life and death on this planet. The claim to make science more inclusive, more women and LGBTQ+ friendly, less white and Eurocentric, rings across the generations with painful regularity.

On the other hand, the claims to equality carry difference within them: more inclusiveness challenges the false universalism of Western science as well as the parochial nature of its idea of 'Man'. The partiality of scientific accounts, and their persistent bias, make mockery of objectivity. Or rather, posthuman feminism demands redefinitions of objectivity in terms of alternative embodied and embedded perspectives.

Within the posthuman convergence, what used to be reproduction and pregnancy have split into diversified practices. They range from technological mediations from IVF to embryo implants to gene-editing to material outsourcing to classes of women specially employed for the purpose. The family arrangements and kinship systems have multiplied accordingly. The contemporary reproductive body is not one. The range of technologically mediated practices and socially differentiated modes of reproduction ranges from IVT technologies and surrogacy, to new multi-parenthood and multi-parent family laws.[14] These new kinship arrangements are the result of the pervasive impact of the apparatus of reproductive technologies and socio-economic practices, but also of the political efforts of feminists and LGBTQ+ people to love and reproduce differently. The explosion of the alleged linearity of the reproductive process introduces new actors, from external donors to internal gene-editing and gender-editing practices, all of them reliant on technological mediation. A posthuman feminist approach allows us to analyse and rethink this posthuman 'exploded maternal body' thoroughly and to situate 'feminicity' as a specific mode of affect (Colman, 2017) in an ethically accountable framework. The impact of the fast-progressing reproductive technologies upon the complex reproductive assemblage is best addressed within an affirmative relational ethics. This is another way of politicizing and queering the reproductive bodies.

The posthuman turn empowers feminists to think of reproduction as gestational power (*potentia*). Reproductive power pertains to the specific properties, compositions and capacities of material bodies. It is an elemental force at play across many species and organisms. The real challenge is not only about the gendered identities that patriarchal culture may stick to these elemental capacities. It is rather the ability to devise a relational ethics that does justice to the elemental complexity of its components. Posthuman feminism does produce an affirmative philosophy of love, in the alternative forms of posthuman pregnant thought, gestationality and trans-corporeal encounters. What is ultimately at stake is a sense of futurity and love for the world.

Chapter 6
Sexuality Beyond Gender: A Thousand Little Sexes

> Praise our desires to know and not to know.
> Praise all our progeny, the empty womb, the full.
> Praise the will to become, love's credo.
> Deryn Rees-Jones, *What It's Like To Be Alive*, 2016

The Moth Shaking Its Wings in Me

In this chapter, I will reframe sexuality within the posthuman convergence. In a new-materialist posthuman frame, sexuality and gender get delinked and the sex–gender distinction is relaxed to be replaced by more subtle vectors of analysis. Sexual difference is accordingly relocated away from the dialectical opposition of the two sexes, as a process of differing. Difference is recast as trans-individual complexity, or the principle of not-One. The emphasis on posthuman materialism opens multiple paths for the exploration of renewed powers of Eros and trans-corporeal relational practices.

The overall picture is a tumultuous emergence of sexuality as both gratuitous and generative. Fundamentally prone to pleasure, embodied subjects are sexed in a multiplicity of ways. In a posthuman feminist perspective, bodies are heterogeneous and relational desiring machines. Sexuality, as a trans-corporeal, enfleshed nexus, facilitates the pleasures and the dangers of the interconnections between humans and non-humans. Sexuality lives its multiple lives independently of the politics of reproduction and there is just no knowing what posthuman desiring bodies can do.

Sexuality – sexual politics and liberation – are perennial concerns in feminism and one of its highest expressions is in feminist arts and literature. Let me start with a posthuman approach to the work of a modernist writer like Virginia Woolf who captures the elemental erotic energy of living matter, not without pain, but with perception and elegance. Here she expresses the impact that her lover Vita Sackville-West has upon her:

> Vita was here: and when she went, I began to feel the quality of the evening – how it was spring coming; a silver light; mixing with the early lamps; the cabs all rushing through the streets; I had a tremendous sense of life beginning; mixed with that emotion, which is the essence of my feeling, but escapes description ... I felt the spring beginning and Vita's life so full and flush; and all the doors opening; and this is I believe the moth shaking its wings in me. (Woolf, 1980 [1930]: 16 February, 287)

In this passage Woolf depicts the *shimmering* materiality of the world. Not only does she write about the perpetual motion of the waves but also about the flickering lights and the flow of cabs on Oxford Street in London. Cosmic and technological phenomena together form a fluctuating continuum that defies partitions as well as bland linearity.

This intensity speeds up even further when desire enters the scene. When Vita intersects with Virginia's trajectory, something happens. Vita does not just get under Virginia's skin, but makes every cell in her body vibrate. Something basic and elementary: the air grows thinner, the water more crystalline, fires self-combust into existence and the earth shakes. Of course, it is erotic: the perfect shape of those legs, the statuesque proportions of that body, the flamboyant colours of that face. The space between, beneath and beyond them is fertile – incandescent and shimmering. Magnified through the lens of erotic desire, stretching beyond the whimsical tricks of Eros, that cruel god, Vita endures in a field of her own which is one of perpetual becoming. Virginia flies to her like a moth to the candle. There is a specific quality of light and energy around Vita, which is recorded in Woolf's writing with geometrical precision. Virginia and Vita simply cannot help but write to, of and through each other: it is a sort of mutual seduction into 'Life'.

Woolf's molecular sensibility illustrates that sexuality is elemental, geological, meteorological, cross-species. It organizes entire territories of becoming by including non-human elements, like the quality of the light and the curve of the wind. Woolf creates heterogeneous assemblages of life lived more intensely. The spatio-temporal, geographical, historical and environmental features are a vector for collective non-human and more-than-human encounters. Sexuality constitutes the transversal plane of immanence that goes beyond individual psychologies and circumstances. Something much more elemental, more raw, is at stake: desire draws its own affective landscapes.

Posthuman feminism reflects seriously on the carnal powers of the flesh and elemental force of Eros, but also on its marginalization in the biopolitical management of posthuman bodies as reproductive and desiring machines. Posthuman feminists raise strong objections against the 'erotophobia of Western culture, a fear of the erotic so strong that only one form of sexuality is overtly allowed; only in one position; and only in the context of certain legal, religious, and social sanctions' (Gaard, 1997: 118). This is in keeping with a long tradition of feminist sexual politics. Black feminist poet and writer Audre Lorde argued passionately for the generative powers of embodied sexual difference against a racist, patriarchal and anti-erotic society: 'When I speak of the erotic, then, I speak of it as an assertion of the lifeforce of women; of that creative energy empowered, the knowledge and use of which we are now reclaiming in our language, our history, our dancing, our loving, our work, our lives' (2007 [1984]: 55). Lorde's poetic and political genius expresses and explores the vital force at play in the eroticism of the flesh, its socialized and racialized folds and its staggering capacity for sharing joys and sorrows. She is one in a long line of Black phenomenal women (Angelou, 1978) that illuminate the feminist paths (Nash, 2018). Posthuman feminism builds on this affirmative tradition and reaches out towards a different philosophy of love that is relational, heterogeneous, process-oriented, transgressive and moving beneath and beyond fixed unitary identities and gender binaries. A posthuman Eros emerges in the multiple modulations of sexuate matter across species and different temporalities.

In this chapter, I explore how posthuman feminism illuminates the profound vitality and the unity of living matter by approaching sexuality as both human and non-human. Within the posthuman convergence of high technologies and high risks, sexuality is rendered as an elemental force, as the hub of multiple sexuate becoming. I will first figure out the implications of this materialist of sexuality as an elemental force, notably in the undoing of the sex–gender distinction. I will then show how theorists, activists and artists combine ecofeminism with technofeminism in an intersectional frame that cross-refers to radical genealogies and learns from Indigenous cosmologies. I will also trace a genealogy of transgression in lesbian, queer and trans sexualities. Throughout the chapter, I will give examples of posthuman art rendering sexuality as a diffuse kind of eroticism that brings out and resonates with the sexuate structure of living matter. There are thousands of molecular sexes everywhere, and most of them are not human.

Shimmering

Indigenous cosmologies are fundamental in at least two ways: firstly, they conceptualize profound intimacy and love between humans and their environments. Secondly, they foreground the elemental principles of multi-species and multi-layered interdependence and care. Each living entity expresses its specific perspective while reasserting the ontological relationality that binds them together. As Deborah Bird Rose put it: 'the ancestral power of life arises in relationship and encounter' (2017: G51). The country, as land of the ancestors and hence upholder of the law, living environment and constant companion, frames and implements these basic ethical principles. The land spells the rhythm of this mutual interdependence. The specific concept Australian Indigenous Yolngu people use to designate these qualities is *bir'yun*, or 'shimmering'.

Shimmering expresses the vitality and brilliance of the light, its dynamic dancing quality. It also reflects the degrees of intensity of the unity of all matter and the intermingled modulations shared across multiple species. Neither full nor void, neither static nor fluid, shimmering is a transitive state of perpetual motion without pre-determined destination. Shimmering includes cross-species and inter-scalar physical encounters and communal narratives; it is the expression of familiar landscapes and affects. It assumes shared desires not only to coexist with other species within a territory, but also to take care of them and draw pleasure and joy from such love. Shimmering manifests a deep enchantment with the world, an engagement with its perennial flows of activity. It signals the sexuate fibre of matter and acknowledges phenomena of attraction and seduction taking place in the non-human world. In pollination as in other forms of elemental lovemaking, for instance, animals, birds, trees and insects mobilize perfume, music, colours, decorative plumage and exceptional blossoms to attract the organisms whose bodies they want and need. Sexuate perpetuation of life enacts in all species the most staggering aesthetic displays. In this respect, artistic expression can be said to be a non-human, earth-bound activity (Deleuze and Guattari, 1987). It is a *zoe*-geo-related action that affirms the living entities' propensity to persevere in their existence through collaborative relational activities, their inbuilt capacity to experience pleasure and empowerment from such interactions. Shimmering is a poetic and an aesthetic of light and play that animates Australian aboriginal art, some of which is now part of the mainstream art world, for instance the works of Doreen Reid Nakamarra, Kathleen Petyarre, Dorothy Napangardi, Gunybi Ganambarr and Abie Loy Kemarre.[1]

As Malone et al. (2020) put it in their academic-artistic exploration of the concept, 'shimmering' refers to the play of natural light from the surface of the waves to the stars. But it also extends as a fundamental principle across all living matter: 'encompassing light, cell vibrations, molecular vibrations, and a potentiality' (2020: 130). In a continuum with ecofeminist ethics, feminist artists explore the vital materiality of the world through the concept of shimmering across a variety of media 'in bark paintings, videos and digital photographs, and contexts from fine art, domestic decoration, and intricate ceremonial body designs' (Malone et al., 2020: 131). These complex yet elemental artistic explorations of the multi-scalar surfaces of the visible express a passionate attachment to the unity of all living matter. There is a spiritual as well as an erotic quality to this relational bond, which defies the divisive dualistic partitions the Western mind has imposed on such matter. Immersion into multi-species life enhances the powers (*potentia*) that humans can generate and share, increasing their affirmative force.

Working with the concept of shimmering within a posthuman feminist frame, Fiona Hillary, for instance, explores the aesthetic qualities of bioluminescence in algae.[2] Through it she focuses on the shimmer of the biosphere as a whole. Hillary's combination of artistic experiments with theoretical reflection highlights the sensuality and self-organizing vitality of sexuate matter. She explores it as a research method in support of a trans-disciplinary approach across the Humanities, artistic practice and scientific research, in keeping with posthuman methodology. What underscores this approach is a relational ethics of care and solidarity, centred on the shared pursuit of affirmation as a collaborative praxis.

In their analysis of feminist and queer indigenous scholarship on sexuality and sexed bodies, Mack and Na'puti (2019) issue a powerful reminder of the need to connect it to the decolonization of analytical practices. Gendered violence against Black and Indigenous people is colonial and imperial violence. Processes of racialization can never be abstracted from those of sexualization and naturalization through the imposition of the Western gender system and its compulsory heterosexuality scheme. By cross-referring to the work of the organization VLVB (Violence on the Land, Violence on our Bodies: Building an Indigenous Response to Environmental Violence[3]), they draw attention to the intersections between sexual and social violence against Indigenous women, the devastation of Indigenous cultures through settler colonialism and the desecration and depletion of the land itself. Decolonial approaches to Black and Indigenous sexualities foreground communal bonds and a collective history rather than white liberal individual rights. They also connect reproductive and sexual freedom to the sovereignty of Indigenous nations and the need for self-determination. The land, the body, the selves and the communities fight for freedom together.

Mack and Na'puti analyse closely the work of artist and activists Konsmo and Pacheco, based on the key principle that 'everything connected to the land is connected to our bodies' (2019: 360). The artwork illustrating this principle is significantly entitled 'Our Bodies Are Not Terra Nullius'. It features the torso of a black woman holding her arms over her belly and a colonial ship just above them. Right under the enlaced arms, parallel to the ship, are images from the extractive industries and mining. And at the bottom, brown bodies and skulls buried in the earth. The message is clear: it is impossible to ever abstract discussions of Indigenous sexual symbolic systems and gendered identities from issues of violent dispossession and exploitation. Ecocide, femicide and genocide work in tandem in Black and Indigenous histories. And yet, the shimmering power of beauty and endurance of that culture and those traditions endure for the enlightenment of all.

Sexuality Is Not Gender

Sexuality is an elemental, complex force at play before, beneath and beyond the gender binary. The gender system, we recall, is the divide between anatomical sex (biological determinism) and social gender (social constructionism). This binary social mechanism captures and reduces the vital materialist force of sexuality. Sexuality comes before gender, because matter is sexuate. The choice of that term is pointed. Sexuate refers to the inbuilt capacity of living beings to be sexed and sexual and to reproduce sexually. Sexuate matter is sexual in an open-ended manner that undoes the binary gender system of the patriarchal symbolic order, which means that sexuality reaches to the very core of our being and its unconscious substrata. But that does not make it immutable and unchangeable outside the reaches of historical processes of change. On the contrary, precisely because it is a constitutive feature of living matter, sexuality alters, mutates and moves along the other vicissitudes of our respective lives. Being sexuate means to be differentiated and endowed with multiple sexual morphologies and virtual bodies of desire. The reason for this multiplicity is that sexuate matter is relational, which means it gets mutually specified and defined in the encounter with others.

A sexuate process of becoming is both an ethical and a political project, which requires collective subjects and collaborative assemblages to carry it out. Often associated with Irigaray's work (1993 [1984]) on the feminine symbolic and the ethics of sexual difference, sexuate matter has developed into a project to activate alternative, virtual ways of becoming women and LGBTQ+ people outside the gender system. It is a nomadic political project (Braidotti, 1994) that steers a line of flight between biological determinism and social constructivism, by presenting sexual differences as processes of differing. These virtual differences as multiple patterns of becoming are so infinitesimal and so interactive that they go on proliferating. This dynamic notion of pluri-dimensional sexuate matter features prominently in new-materialist feminism and is central to posthuman feminism.

Posthuman sexualities are as much *zoe*-geo-techno-mediated as the bodies they invest. They design complex modes of relation with a vast array of non-human and impersonal elements: animal, geological, meteorological, technological, etc. They therefore mobilize and dramatize the untapped potentialities of sexuate organisms.

I have argued in the first part of this book that the gender system has historically evolved in Western modernity as a major tool of governance, population growth, reproduction and demographic management. Gender upholds dominant ideas of what constitutes the desirable form for the reproductive and childrearing human within the social unit of the family. The system is indexed on compulsory heterosexuality and predicated on reproductive sex within a fiscally recognizable family unit, which is expected to fulfil the demographic and emotional needs of capitalism's future generations. That unit is based on the exploitation of women's productive and reproductive labour, the male ownership of children and the exclusion of LGBTQ+ people from both private and public institutions. It is important to realize, however, that the restrictive gender system does not exhaust the vitality of embodied and embedded sexuate material entities. As a primary site of constitution of identities, gender is best analysed as a historically specific apparatus for the management of life that connects the vital capacities of bodies to systems of power. Gender politics is a biopolitical apparatus of production of entire populations, communities and territories (Cooper, 2008; Repo, 2016). Writing from a trans-feminist perspective, Beatriz Preciado puts it clearly: 'Gender (femininity/masculinity) is not a concept, it is not an ideology, and it is not simple performance: it is a techno-political ecology' (2013b: 272).

Posthuman feminism pursues radical criticism of the gender system, but it starts from the assumption that sexuality is a force that is neither reducible to, nor is it constructed by, the gender system. Gender does not even begin to paint the full picture of contemporary sexualities as materialist and disruptive forces that experiment with new intensive philosophies and practices of love. This is the affirmative aspect of sexuality that Foucault labelled the erotic arts of existence, as opposed to 'an anatomo-politics of the human body' (1978: 139), which is a form of biopolitical management. That management entails the optimization of the exploitable qualities of human bodies for all aspects of socio-economic life. This practice is 'the biopolitics of the population' (Foucault, 1978: 139), including both the heavy apparatus of medical and psycho-pharmaceutical interventions and the new reproductive technologies.

In contemporary gender theories a reference to Foucault's biopolitics (Foucault 1977b, 1978, 2007a, 2007b) has become a buzzword (Lemke, 2011; Povinelli, 2017). Posthuman feminism is cautious and approaches Foucault as a materialist philosopher of life and power, rather than as a social-constructivist theorist of identities.[4] For all materialist feminists, including the posthumanists, power is not a linguistic construct, but a thickly material one. It relies on clinical structures, medical procedures, legal parameters, real embodied subjects, exploited labour and influx of capital. Power is a multi-layered, material real-life technology.

Gender politics – which Foucault studiously ignores – is an integral part of the biopolitical power of advanced capitalism, but also of the flows of intensity that construct contemporary desiring subjects. This means that Foucault's relevance for posthuman feminism needs to be assessed critically, starting from his objectionable habit of side-lining feminist analyses of biopolitics. Materialist feminists from the very start criticized his neglect of female bodies as sites of strict disciplining.[5] Their criticism focused notably on reproduction, sexual health and birth control, but also on patriarchal violence in general.[6] Recent materialist feminist scholars of biopolitics developed insightful analyses of the links between gender, biopolitics and neoliberalism, moving well beyond Foucault.[7] Their analyses also focused on the necropolitical aspects of this management of the living (Mbembe, 2003; Braidotti, 2006, 2013). Thus, gender and sexuality are inscribed across the multiple layers of the biopolitical, as markers both of the individual properties of bodies and the life and survival of the entire species. Sexuality intersects with gender as biopolitical governance on the one hand and the erotic arts of existence on the other.

Sexuality, however, is not the same as gender because living matter, both human and non-human, is sexuate. What precedes and exceeds the social coding of gender is the vital force of sexuate matter itself. As I argued in chapter 4, all living entities are variations within a common matter, which is relational and differential. This instals the principle of ontological difference defined as differing within a commonly shared matter.

Indigenous feminist scholars made this point before anyone else. For instance, Kim TallBear (2015) working within the ancient tradition of Indigenous nature–culture continuum, explores the overlap between constructions of 'nature' and 'sexuality'. She denounces the imposition of the Western gender paradigm onto Indigenous cultures. She signals the contrast between the European traditions of viewing the body and sexual difference as binary-driven and exclusively explained by social conditions, and compares it to non-Western traditions. The latter postulate a nature–culture continuum that colonial science dismissed as animistic and pre-scientific. Challenging the equation between queer sexuality and the unnatural, TallBear adds an ecological take on Indigenous queer theory. This means she rejects both the Western politics of nature and the naturalization of Eurocentric heterosexual sexuality as dominant scientific and social models.

The approach that colonialism rejects as 'animism' needs to be reappraised. It argues that all entities are similar and equally human, in that they have a soul, but differ radically in terms of their bodily configurations (Descola, 2013). Indigenous philosophies tend to have a more cosmic understanding of sexuality and the body, which features positive relationships between human and non-human persons, including the land and water. A complex range of non-hierarchical interactions is envisaged, for instance between humans and animals, which includes collaboration, but also hunting and eating one another. The absence of a hierarchical order across species and elements allows feminist Indigenous environmental and sexuality studies to develop a more democratic approach to both research and policy making. Rauna Kuokkanen (2007, 2015, 2017) argues for the need to put an end to the epistemological marginalization of Indigenous knowledge systems. She calls for decolonizing the discussion on gender, sexuality and materialism and to construct knowledges across cultures and fields of expertise. Kuokkanen argues strongly against the sanctioned epistemic ignorance of contemporary scholarship, a great deal of feminist theory included. A better epistemic relational balance needs to be established.

Indigenous scholar Joanna Barker (2017) is also critical of gender dualism and the colonial projection of Western definitions and practices of sexuality upon Indigenous people, which forces heteronormative archetypes onto a retrospective vision of authentic Indigeneity. These colonial sexing and gendering regimes support both racial capitalism and the enslavement of Indigenous nations for the sake of the imperial project. The inscription of Eurocentric models of gender, sexuality, kinship and society delete or render irrelevant the historical and cultural differences between Western and Indigenous nations. It is challenging to remedy this epistemic violence without falling into the trap of neo-colonial reappropriation, or arrogantly assuming the intrinsic superiority of Western knowledge and methodology (Tuhiwai Smith, 1999). Thus, Barker points out that often Indigenous genders, sexualities and feminisms are used as illustrations of counter-arguments in feminist theory. One of these alternative visions is precisely the holistic naturalism of Indigenous knowledge systems. By extension, the rejection of the sex–gender distinction lies at the core of Indigenous cosmologies. Barker argues that biology-based arguments play a crucial role in Indigenous perspectives about heredity and lineage, status, labour and responsibilities, including reproduction. She joins the call for epistemological accountability on the part of Western feminists to resist the reduction of these complex systems to mere illustrations of feminist and LGBTQ+ theories about sexual liberation and equality. The call is twofold: firstly, to criticize the dominant position of Western feminist and LGBTQ+ experts in the critique of patriarchal sexism and misogyny, and, secondly, to dig up the historical evidence of the same kind of patriarchal violence, sexism and homophobia within Indigenous communities, revealing the intersecting histories of gender and colonialism. I think that respect for complexity and heterogeneity and a commitment to the respective politics of immanence or location on the part of different subjects of knowledge are key values. Practices of situated and accountable, materially embodied and embedded perspectives are effective ways to continue to construct collaborative relations.

Beyond the Sex–Gender Distinction

Posthuman feminism renders the sex–gender distinction obsolete, or at least less relevant than generally assumed (Gatens, 1983, 1991; Chanter, 1995). Because gender is a grid that captures and codes sexuate matter (Scott, 1986), it can be helpful as a tool to analyse the structures it contributes to create. But it is neither necessary nor sufficient as a category to explain or contain the complexity of living matter, especially sexuality as a transformative force. Gender as a tool of governance reinstates the distinction between nature (sex) and culture (gender), which does not work if you start from the assumption of sexuate differential matter as a vital continuum.

Posthuman feminism relies on contemporary materialist theories of autopoietic and sympoietic matter rather than on the social-constructivist theory of gender roles, which reduces gender to a representation, a linguistic structure, a cultural construct or a performance (Butler, 1990). It is not gender (social codes) that constructs sex (the body), but it is rather the case that sexuality is a human and non-human force always at work through the multiple organic and inorganic ecologies – hormonal, environmental, psychic and social – that co-produce bodies. They are not separate and distinct, but relational and co-implicated. There is one matter, intelligent, self-organizing and already sexuate, thereby spelling the primacy of sexuality over the patriarchal gender system (Lloyd, 2009).

The sex–gender distinction was not always canonical in American feminism. Historically, major Anglo-American feminists of the second wave did not engage with gender as a concept, but worked with multiple political references and used different terms, like sexual politics and patriarchy.[8] Nor does the concept play a major role in the Continental tradition of feminist corporeal materialism.[9] This tradition provides a more dynamic understanding of sexual difference as materially embedded, multi-scalar differing and molecular, virtual, processes of becoming.[10] Theories of sexual difference proposed by the materialist branch of poststructuralism and materialist feminism were marginalized (van der Tuin, 2015), mostly because the sex/gender distinction 'does not map neatly onto direct French equivalents' (Jones, 2011: 5).

The sexuate aspects of feminist materialism are resurfacing now (Stone, 2006, 2015; Jones, 2011), in relation to the generative matrix of matter, as the life-generating force that is disqualified in a metaphysical system of thought that privileges transcendence over immanence and mind over body. The transgressive force of sexual difference is a libidinal form of accelerationism that pushes the masculine/feminine dyad to the extreme. It makes the gender system implode by activating the sexuate matter that structures it. This transformation can be the source for a radical subversion of the gender system itself and achieves the same aims as gender abolitionism, but by different means. Beyond sex/gender, the sexuate force of autopoietic matter operates as negotiable, transversal and affective spaces of multiple becoming. It intersects the multiple differences among women in terms of other social variables, notably race, ethnicity, class, age and body abilities, igniting the infinite capacities that lay dormant within each woman and each LGBTQ+ subject.

In her molecular defence of non-essentialist difference, Luciana Parisi argues that the sex–gender distinction is not helpful, as sex is not the physical mark of gender, which in turn is not the cultural script of sex. Rather, the two are points in a parallel dimension that entails a continuous set of variations of bodies, challenging the dualism between the natural and the cultural and composing variations between them. This conception of sex diverges from the critical impasse between essentialism and constructivism and its negative principles of identity. It confirms the ideal of a shared human nature differently sexed without falling into dualisms. Posthuman feminism turns this into the possibility for multiply sexed variations, on a transversal scale of possible sexes and genders. It is a way of repudiating neutrality and idealized sameness, affirming difference without essentialism.

Nina Lykke (2010b) suggests the term 'post-constructionism' to designate the method that emerges once we discard the sex–gender distinction. A post-constructivist approach focuses on the interlinked flows of flesh and technology, materiality and discourse. These converging trends produce new ways of assessing the impact of feminist politics and policies. To move beyond the sex–gender distinction is not a way of discarding the progress made through the struggle for the de-naturalization of inequalities, but rather to signal both continuities and discontinuities with this tradition. The problem is that a notion of 'gender' – as sociality – as separated from 'sex' – as material embodiment – ends up confirming the anthropocentric indifference to vital matter and to sexual difference as process.

The challenge of the posthuman predicament consists precisely in accounting for both the living, embedded matter of bodies as pre-discursive phenomena, the role of culture, and the transversal, cross-species and trans-corporeal interrelations between them. Thus, paradoxically perhaps, the posthuman inaugurates a pan-sexual, elemental revolution.

The Principle of Not-One

While the sex/gender dyad is a binary social code of reduction, sexual difference is about a multiplicity of differences (Braidotti, 1994, 2011a). This means taking the vital power of matter as differing from itself, which is a far cry from a dualistic notion of sexual difference located between the binary masculine/feminine poles. Sexuality is made of relational variations before, beneath and beyond fixed identities. As such it is about differing across and within categories, producing alternative and in-between virtual sexes. It is a transversal force flowing across real and virtual dimensions of becoming, along multi-scalar flows of non-binary differences. Sexuality is the joyful tendency to replicate experiences that give pleasure and avoid those that cause pain, in so far as there is any choice on such matters. Sexuality within a vital notion of living matter enjoys transversal and vital powers of relationality. Sexuality as life force provides the organizing principle for carnal human affectivity and desire.

Sexual difference as the principle of not-One refers to the multiple and heterogeneous capacities and propensities for pleasure and self-preservation of living organisms. Sexuality in humans is polymorphous perversity in the sense that it is in itself playful and non-reproductive. This means that sexuality is an ontological force positioned before, beneath and beyond the social codes that entrap it in binary oppositions, compulsory heterosexuality and reproductive sex. Sexuality is the transversal force that extends to all variations beneath and beyond masculinity and femininity. It is an infinite process of becoming, across categories like sexes, genders, ethnicities, species, in a multi-scalar, post-binary way. We need to think about embedded and embodied entities in all their morphogenetic and topological virtualities and unprogrammed virtual sexualities.[11] The transversality of sexuality and the transsexual imaginary that reflects it means that sexual difference cannot be confused with genital dimorphism: it is rather a vital process of differing that runs across (in)dividuals, entities and species.

Posthuman feminism asserts the principle of sexual difference as not-One, that is, as multiplicity. It calls for a posthuman relational ethics at the in-depth structures of our subjectivity by acknowledging the ties that bind us to the multiple 'others' in a vital web of complex interrelations (Braidotti, 2002; MacCormack, 2012; Zylinska, 2014). This ethical relational principle breaks up the fantasy of unity, totality and autonomy of liberal individualism. This means it also rejects the oedipalized narratives of primordial loss, incommensurable lack and irreparable separation that Lacanian psychoanalytic theory formalized in a dualistic scheme of self–other antagonism.

On all these scores, the force of sexual difference is the force of multiplicity and movement. Sexuality activates the forces capable of mobilizing modes of becoming-other otherwise than the dominant logic of heteronormative patriarchy. Posthuman sexualities are experimental virtualities. Sexuate matter and multiple sexed bodies are the instantiation of virtual possibilities. This vital materialist notion of desire as a transversal life force points to a poly-sexuality that stretches way beyond the normative constructions of gender. It is multi-directional and dispersed, not linear; multiple, not binary; relational and interconnected, not dialectical; and in a constant flux, not fixed. It spells a molecular mode of becoming.

Differences – including sexual difference in the sense of differing – get dis-engaged from the binary dialectical scheme of opposition between two sexes, and get reformulated as a multiple, complex and heterogeneous set of variations within a common sexuate matter. This means that difference is not the interlude of negative opposition, but instead the modus operandi of vital, rhizomic or nomadic interconnections. Desire thrives in multiplicity, as the production of affirmative relations.

The exploration of virtual sexualities is one of the projects pursued by posthuman feminism, in a multi-dimensional and multi-scalar manner that has no pre-set targets. As a virtual force of becoming, sexual differing can generate myriad other possibilities and destabilize the bound identities that women and LGBTQ+ people are expected to coincide with. We simply do not know what sexed bodies can do. For instance, Shanghai-born new media artist Lu Yang specializes in experimental multimedia works in the tradition of cyberfeminism. She explores contemporary technoscience, especially neuroscience and sexuality, raising issues of mortality and ethical values. 'Uterus-man' (2013), a manga-like musical project, features an anime-style character who rides a 'pelvis chariot' and skateboards on a winged sanitary pad. Virtual sexes are important to posthuman feminist practices of sexuality.

There is a long-standing cultural association between multiplicity and the feminine. The feminine is the flowing, destabilizing force that manifests itself, for instance as oceanic feeling for Freud and cosmic jouissance for Lacan. This is the fluid, cosmic feminine that pulsates through Virginia Woolf's work, as the force that is capable of dissolving the boundaries of all categorical differences. The association of the feminine with fluidity also lies at the core of the feminist generations of French feminist writers who produced *écriture féminine*. They fell in love with and explored feminine jouissance as cosmic infinity[12] and elected water as the feminine element par excellence, as we saw also in the previous chapter.[13]

Posthuman feminism inherits this elemental materialism and accelerates it through diverse sexuate bodies accordingly. The feminine as multiplicity is the portal to infinite modes of becoming, and thus to the making of nth sexes. But it also imbues them with high degrees of technological mediation, and consequently de-materializes bodies and sexualities. As a result, in posthuman feminism the dissolution of boundaries and the emergence of trans-corporeal connections moves out of the feminine mystique and a cosmic infatuation with feminine jouissance. It settles into a more extended and dispersive – but not less pleasurable – economy of extensive rhizomatic technological networking. This is the spirit of Sue Austin dancing under water in her wheelchair, showing her utter delight in the freedom a watery environment affords to an otherwise-enabled human.

The feminine still stands for not-One-ness, multiplicity and complexity. In the posthuman convergence, however, the new-materialist turn is enabling a new take on this sexuate multiplicity. The posthuman feminine is overcoded as transversal multi-sexualities and multiple trans-femininities (Raha, 2017). Queer and trans sexualities move beyond binaries and claim unknown territories for being sexed otherwise (Stryker and Aizura, 2013). The erasure of the binary distinctions, far from undermining the possibility of political subjectivity, allows feminists to rethink and repurpose sexuality within the posthuman convergence. The mediated nature of sexuate matter de-essentializes the discussion and inserts more complexity in the contemporary experiments with alternative sexualities.

But these changes do not occur in a social vacuum. Relaxing the gender binary and undoing hierarchical sexual difference in favour of greater gender fluidity is also one of the features of advanced liberal economies. In other words, it has gone mainstream and lost some of its transgressive edge. The *Guardian*'s columnist Hinsliff (2019) commented on the fast-expanding category of 'queer' as meaning 'anything other than plain-vanilla 100% straight sex'. This is how the feminine gets dislodged from its female empirical reference to become a global sign of gender fluidity. For example, the demonstration against Trump in 2016 led by the 'pussy hat' movement claims pink as the feminist colour, but 'pink is now performing the double feat of being both the unabashedly female colour of fourth-wave feminism and the androgynous shade of modern gender fluidity' (Woods, 2017: 17).

Whereas in advanced capitalism these changes are predicated in terms of hyper-individualistic freedom of choice and gender mainstreaming, posthuman feminism pursues the sexual radical line in an inclusive manner. It assumes both a post-binary world and a constant interaction between re-materialized sexual practices affecting embodied subjects and de-materialized flows that decentre them. It supports experimental sexual relations and kinship arrangements. The speed and scale of mutation of sexuate mater, including human bodies, opens up a number of unprecedented scenarios for contemporary sexuality, which posthuman feminism is keen to explore in more transgressive and politically transformative directions.

Elemental Sexualities

We can find the inspiration for the imaginings and alternative scenarios of sexuality in art. A great deal of posthuman feminist art, especially media and installation art, is post-anthropocentric in that it does not feature anthropomorphic bodies and hence no recognizable or even detectable sexuality. Posthuman feminist artists emphasize human/non-human relations and interdependences with a strong environmental sensibility but also close attention to materials and materiality. This approach is a 'capsule aesthetics' of human to non-human interfaces. As Mondloch put it, they 'literally stage and enact scientific and technological interfaces in relation to the embodied phenomenal experience of human actors' (Mondloch, 2018: 16).

A significant example is the Icelandic feminist artist, singer and writer Björk, who has developed a neo-naturalistic style and has been experimenting with environmental feminist anti-racist themes for decades. Her 2019 performance show *Cornucopia* is a celebration of the earth that pursues her exploration of flora and fauna in the framework of Nordic saga and myths while joining forces with the climate change movement. Contemporary American artist Stephanie Sarley also practises an elemental variation of posthuman feminism by adding a new twist to the ancestral connection between sex and food. She notably explores visually the sexual qualities and erotic potential of fruit and flower.[14] Her vagina-like fruit and flower compositions are poetic as well as sexually explicit in an almost disarming manner. Fruit is her technological medium as much as the digital equipment she uses to film it.

In the multimedia artwork *The unsettling Eros of contact zones*, Tarsh Bates of the Australian collective Symbiotica gives a posthuman twist to the analysis of the conventional link food–sex. She focuses on the molecular aesthetics of the micro-organisms at work in baking bread.[15] Her preferred objects of display and study are the organisms that make organic artisanal white bread leaven: *Candida albicans* and *Saccharomyces cerevisiae*. They are actively embodied and activated in many of the foods we consume including the basics: cheese, bread, milk, hummus and beer. By foregrounding the cooperative bonds between human bodies and micro-organisms, Bates reiterates the primacy of symbiotic dependence.

Another example is the photographic and sculptural artistic practice of the Australian artists Honey Long and Prue Stent, who explore the intimate trans-corporeal relations between human – mostly female – bodies and elemental materials and environments. In their 'phygital' approach – a blend of the physical and the digital – they display images of bodies intermingled with the surface of the earth, the fluidity of water and waves, the mud and rocks. The human form is inextricable from the biosphere that supports it and the intimacy of that interdependence is loaded with sexuality, curiosity and pleasure.[16]

Berlin-based Margherita Pevere explores the sexuate nature of hydrofeminism, combining bio-art and research practices from the 'three cultures' of the Humanities, the Social and the Natural Sciences.[17] Starting from the assumption that bodies are liquid, that is to say open and porous, she investigates the specific relationality of this leaky materiality. The fluids in our molecular cells, the flow of mucus, sweat, urine that controls our bodies, connect each to an infinity of other bodies. Sexuality and hormonal contraception add the biotechnological dimension to the gestational environment of wombs and placentas.

Rachel Berwick is another contemporary artist who explores the ecosystem, through birds as the favourite vector.[18] Her sculptural installations investigate ideas of vulnerability and loss in the animal world, for instance the extinct Tasmanian Tiger; the Galápagos giant tortoise, Lonesome George; and Martha, the last passenger pigeon. Berwick employs materials such as amber, crystal, and glass to reference natural phenomena and create haunting reminders of what has been – or is nearly – lost.

A Genealogy of Transgression

There have been precursors to the alternative scenarios of sexuality: the feminist theories of lesbian, trans and queer sexualities. LGBTQ+ energy is everywhere in the history of modern feminism, cutting across the established political schools of feminist theory. In 1970 Rita Mae Brown produces, with the collective 'Radicalesbians', a foundational lesbian feminist manifesto by 'The Woman Identified Woman'. It argues that the real problem that has no name (pace Betty Friedan) is lesbianism, defined as women loving other women.[19] In 1973, Jill Johnston edited the iconic lesbian anthology *Lesbian Nation*, just as the very first anthology of radical feminism is published (Koedt and Levine, 1973), spelling out an unmistakably militant sex agenda.[20] The Redstockings' feminist classic *Feminist Revolution* (1975) confirms this vision (Gornick and Moran, 1971), which was consolidated in the first full study of lesbian sexuality (Stimpson and Person, 1980). Working within the tradition of Black radical feminism, Alice Walker coined the term 'womanist' in 1983 to define a woman-identified-woman, committed emotionally and politically to the freedom and wellbeing of other women, whether she has sex with them or not. In 1980 Adrienne Rich's seminal essay 'Compulsory heterosexuality and lesbian existence' lays the foundations for radical lesbian politics by positing the notion of woman-identified women as a political standpoint. It defines lesbian sexuality as a fluid model shared by all women on a broad spectrum.

Visionary Black poet Audre Lorde is an inexhaustible source of inspiration about the powers of the erotic (2007 [1984]). She defines sexuality as a life force that connects to the deepest sources of women's power: the political, creative and everyday aspects of their lives. She especially singles out lesbian desire as a creative and revolutionary force. For Lorde, there is a direct connection between the realization of one's desire, self-knowledge and political empowerment. The erotic dimension affects every aspect of one's life, notably work, professional achievement and social fulfilment. For Lorde, 'the erotic is the nurturer or nursemaid of all our deepest knowledge' (2007 [1984]: 57). It is relational and expresses the intrinsic human propensity for joy and the rejection of negative affects such as resignation, despair, self-effacement and depression. Lorde calls out to 'more women-identified women brave enough to risk sharing the erotic's electrical charge without having to look away, and without distorting the enormously powerful and creative nature of that exchange' (2007 [1984]: 59). Recognizing the power of the erotic is the source of the energy to pursue the feminist political project.

But not everybody agreed with this vision: for some feminists, lesbianism is a flight into, for others a flight away, from the feminine and the female body as such. It all depends on the locations and on the perspective. In opposition to this woman-centred approach, Monique Wittig (1980) posited the notion that a lesbian is not a woman but a third sex. Lesbian is not just any other but a diagonal; a way out of the masculine/feminine dyad imposed by what she calls 'the straight mind'. The option of wanting out was generated in the French women's movement in response to psychoanalytically inflected feminist theories that deliberately emphasized the feminine as the accelerationist opposition to patriarchal power. Redefining the feminine outside the phallocentric parameters and empowering it as a virtual alternative line of escape is the strategy adopted by women-identified women. Escaping from the entire framework by positing the lesbian as the line of flight out of the symbolic and social system of dichotomous sexual difference is the radical lesbian alternative. Wittig's suggestion intersected productively with Gayle Rubin's theory of the exchange of women within the patriarchal kinship system. It resulted in defining gender as the coercive imposition of binary socio-economic and reproductive roles between the sexes for the benefit of patriarchy. This combination of elements launches the tradition of lesbian gender abolitionism, which will prove inspirational for queer theory.[21]

The flight into womanhood and the feminine proposed by Rich, Lorde and Walker, and the flight out of it proposed by Wittig and Rubin, framed the debate on lesbian sexualities and identities within the radical feminist wing. They provided rich and diversified political options that allowed for a range of different positions and practices. They read like experiments with alternative ways of being sexed and of enacting virtual new sexualities. They were all located and situated, that is to say site- and culture-specific and not seeking for a hegemonic position, and thus they coexisted for a long time.

From a posthuman feminist perspective, it does not much matter whether sexuate female and LGBTQ+ bodies explore what they are capable of becoming, by accelerating into and through the feminine or by avoiding it altogether and starting from a different perspective.

While pursuing the struggle against patriarchal misogyny and violence against LGBTQ+ people, feminists may need to continue to agree to differ on whether to opt for the celebration of, as opposed to aversion to, femininity. These two approaches trace different but equally transformative trajectories across the reduction of human sexuality to a dualistic opposition of socially coercive gender roles. They both aim to re-assert sexuality as complexity and multiplicity before, beneath and beyond gender – i.e., sexual difference as on-going processes of differing. What matters is the political effort to bring about a qualitative change in the location, social status and value attributed to alternative sexualities. Through such transformations, sexuality itself is reasserted in an Eros-friendly manner as a de-territorializing force. It positions desiring subjects as transgressive agents of social and symbolic transformations. Sexual differing as a set of variations, or modulations, within a common matter is the practice for all living entities, non-humans included and goes to the core of their being. They are differentiated by qualitatively different degrees and capacity to act. Through a variety of strategies, posthuman feminism, queer and LGBTQ+ sexualities delink the feminine from the binary gender machine and turn it into a vector of multiple becomings. The feminine is the threshold to a thousand tiny sexes, multiple degrees of sexualization, racialization and becoming earth, or critical re-naturalization and becoming-machine, or strategic de-territorialization.

This positive, vital, material, molecular notion of sexuality as a polymorphous and complex visceral force is central to the multiple alternatives posthuman feminists have been exploring. There are a thousand different possibilities of sexes emerging from the current state of the human and entering into all sorts of assemblages. This is what I have called the feminist becoming-woman (Braidotti 1991, 1994), and later the 'virtual feminine' (Braidotti, 2002, 2006). On this point all vital materialist feminists concur (Grosz, 2002, 2011; MacCormack, 2008, 2012; Colebrook, 2014a, 2014b), as does the Deleuzian strand of queer theory (Nigianni and Storr, 2009; Guillaume and Hughes, 2011).

The crucial move is not to limit heterogeneous transversality to gender issues only, but to see it as a new-materialist reappraisal of the primacy of sexuality as a de-territorializing force. Sexuality is the virtual, trans-individual force in a perpetual process of becoming immanent, through collectively driven practices of actualization that exceed the programme of socially enforced gender. Sexual difference is virtual and intensive, qualitative as well as an ongoing mode of becoming.

Transversal Desires

Posthuman feminism repurposes and queers sexuality to the nth power. It invites us to think of differences as infinite and make their actualization into a political as well an ethical project. Sexuality being a vital, transversal force, shared by humans and non-humans, it follows that experimenting with intensity is an important aspect of the posthuman project: what are we capable of becoming? Multiple virtual sexes can be actualized, provided 'we' can compose an assemblage or transversal alliance that can carry out the project. The ultimate challenge for posthuman sexual politics is how to sustain socially, emotionally and carnally, the efforts of experimenting with virtual sexualities. Sexualities are forever in process, that is to say structurally unfinished and relationally open. The crucial thing here is not to mistake the virtual for the utopian or the fantastic, but to keep it grounded within embedded, embodied and affective modes of relation.

The diversity of transgressive, non-conforming and unprogrammed sexes is the crucial factor in feminist thought. Deleuze and Guattari write explicitly about 'one thousand tiny sexes' (1987: 213) and 'non-human trans-sexuality' (1987: 172) as the defining feature of posthumanist and post-anthropocentric sexuality. This is *zoe*-centred egalitarianism, liberated from the grip of negativity, because the ontological desire to connect and relate overrides all other ties. The emphasis on heterogeneous polysexual subject assemblages supports transfeminist and transsexual claims. As Mel Y. Chen put it: 'Much in the way that the idealized meaning *queer* signifies an adjectival modification or modulation, rather than a substantive core such as a noun. I wish to highlight a *prefixal* "trans-" not preliminarily limited to gender' (2013: 173).

Sexuality, returned to its transgressive carnal roots, raises the question of how to sustain the challenge and the burden of responsibility of relationality as the essence of our becoming. 'Desidero ergo sum' never rang truer than today, nor less obvious for posthuman subjects who experience their bodies as hubs of multi-directional desires and forces of encounter with multiple human and non-human actors. Sexuality is about multiplicity, complexity and affirmation. The vital materialist approach that positions sexual differing as an ontology of living systems is helpful to posthuman feminism because it rejects dualistic oppositions and gender binaries; it is post-anthropocentric in positioning sexuality as a non/in-human force at work in all living entities and not only in humans. It is a foundation that we all depart from to compose heterogeneous connections and multiple sexual systems.

The conceptual and political challenge consists in activating the multiplicity of plays, pleasures and yet unrealized potentials of bodies, while avoiding the essentialist trap of appealing to a 'genuine' female or LGBTQ+ people's 'nature'. Sexuate matter being relational it is differential and multi-faceted. A relational ontology implies a continuity between the natural and the socialized body. This means that social arrangements, codes and norms affect and modify the powers of embodied and embedded subjects and their awareness of themselves. Humans reflect that socialization in their structures. This reiterates the point that there is no pre-determined natural maleness or femaleness, no essence that functions independently of embodied sexuate entities' trans-corporeal relations, encounters and negotiations with social rules and infrastructures. Yet, no subject is reducible to just these rules and conventions: there is always the margin of virtual potential at the core of sexuality as an elemental force.

The thick interrelation between biological and socio-cultural processes cannot be reduced to a dichotomous sex–gender distinction or the *bios–polis* or *zoe–physis* divide, because what precedes and exceeds them is the vital force of sexuate matter itself. Posthuman feminism recasts politics into cross-species materiality and embodied and embedded relationality, while rejecting bio-centred human exceptionalism. It is a factual statement that bodies differ, but that difference is multiple and not binary, given that matter is sexuate and relational. This means that the outcome of the ongoing processes of transformation of the human cannot be played out in advance and pre-empted by foregone conclusions. What posthuman bodies may become is a project, not a given. Their posthuman future is a matter of negotiations with multiple forces that frame the pattern of their becoming as a transversal alliance. Posthuman feminism insists that, in this project, the voices, experiences and visions of embodied and embedded subjects who were not considered as fully human, play a central role in defining possible patterns of becoming posthuman.

The sexuate differences that constitute matter are, on the one hand, bound by *potestas* and thus reflect the social power and rules of contingent gender systems, and, on the other, they are open to the force of the virtual and work to activate *potentia*. In this respect, the process of sexual differing as the actualization of virtual sexualities does not demand a metaphysics of sexual difference at all. Difference is not taken as a problem to solve, or an obstacle to overcome, but rather as a fact and a factor of our situated, corporeal location (Braidotti, 1991; Grosz, 1994b; Colebrook, 2000). Sexuality provides the radical empirical grounding for the generation of multiple subject formations, pleasures, capacities and knowledge claims.

LGBTQ+ theories stress transversality of desire and the inextricable connection of the natural and the unnatural, and normativity and deviance in relation to human sexuality (Hird, 2006; Hayward and Weinstein, 2015). Queer theory is in some ways about how to be 'properly unnatural' (Barris, 2015) and to deviate from social expectations of heteronormativity. Queer scholarship challenges both the naturalization of heterosexuality and the gender binary that supports it.[22] It also criticizes the spurious naturalness attributed to monogamy and other patriarchal values (Willey, 2016). The queer animal and the trans and queer humans stand opposed to the patriarchal violence of compulsory heterosexuality. Strategically, this position ranges from strict social-constructivist arguments for the abolition of gender, to post-naturalist appeals to the naturalness of their differences. There is a productive encounter here between new-materialist notions of sexuality and ontological desire and contemporary trans feminist theories (Stryker and Aizura, 2013).

On the side of affirmative de-naturalization, we already saw in the previous chapter how 'somatechnics' theorists (Sullivan and Murray, 2009) embrace technological enhancement in order to refashion sexuality in post- and anti-natural ways. This approach accelerates the overcoming of biological limits, challenging not only (hetero)sexuality and reproduction, but also mortality (Giffney and Hird, 2008). In this quest for alternative sexualities, other non-human species are taken as models for new morphology and sexual systems of non-human species, in a radical form of post-anthropocentrism.

For instance, queer ecofeminists (Gaard, 1997; Mortimer-Sandliands and Erickson, 2010) argue for a sexuate continuum across multiple axes of discrimination and exclusion. Part of the same strategy consists in pointing out the homosexual and polysexual behaviour that has been recorded in a range of animals and insects. This natural diversity also involves procreative and sexual behaviour that can be classified as within, without and across genders. This kind of 'biological exuberance' (Bagemihl, 1999) exposes compulsory heterosexuality as both restrictive and scientifically partial.

Trans-feminism has also pursued this line, stressing the diversity of sexual behaviour in other species including sex-changes, transvestism in various insects and fish species. This cross-species resonance between modes of transsexuality results in a relation of 'trans-animality' (Hird, 2013: 159), which is often racialized as a double pejoration (Hayward and Weinstein, 2015).

The bizarre sexuality of bacteria is the focus of Luciana Parisi's project of blurring the boundaries between natural and unnatural sexualities (2004). We saw in chapter 4 that Parisi approaches life processes as webs of microbial relational assemblages. In a further step of her argument, she enquires what their implications are for our understanding of sexuality. Bridging the critical blockage between biological essentialism (re-materialization) and discursive constructivism (de-materialization), Parisi stresses the relation between the molecular dynamics of the organization of matter itself. She produces an innovative adaptation of a schizo-genesis of sexual difference as an organic variable of autopoiesis, that is to say as heterogeneous differing.

This emphasis on strategic and diversified re-materialization is a distinctive trait of posthuman feminist sexual politics (Stone, 1991; Braidotti, 1994; Turkle, 1995; Squires, 1996; Toffoletti, 2007). Posthuman feminism also has a vested interest in technologically mediated cyber sexualities (Wolmark, 1999), in electronic Eros (Springer, 1996), gendered cyborgs (Kirkup, 1999) and sexed technobodies (Balsamo, 1996). These are all situated along a continuum that stresses the non-linear coexistence of the biophysical, the biocultural and the biodigital, exposing their capacity to mutate and transform. Posthuman sexuality is a space of virtual becoming for n^{th} sexes, best rendered in terms of a transsexual imaginary. In the posthuman convergence, the technological apparatus is a de-territorializing force that functions transversally and respects no boundaries. Posthuman bodies are multi-directional, cross-species, in-between figures of interconnection, presenting a mixture of decorum and debauchery.

The Positivity of Desire

Sexuality is both a force of singular individuation and a transversal cross-species connection; it is gratuitous and excessive. It remains a constitutive force, an ontological grounding, a core feature and a virtual possibility that is always already present in living beings in conscious and unconscious ways. The ontological priority of sexuality as sexual differing positions difference as a self-transforming force: autopoiesis, sympoiesis, morphogenesis, becoming. Sexual difference is not binary, but rhizomatic (Braidotti, 1994). It triggers a multiplier effect that activates virtual and unprogrammed landscapes of relation and desire. Posthuman feminism explores the transformative potential of embodied entities both as living experiments and as political battlefields (Braidotti, 1994; Grosz, 1994b; Gatens, 1996; Olkowski, 1999).

Feminist psychoanalysts in the Lacanian (Irigaray, 1985a [1974]; Mitchell and Rose, 1985) and object-relation psychoanalytic traditions (Benjamin, 1988; Chodorow, 1988; Brennan, 1989; Flax, 1990) had already contributed to blurring the distinction between biology (sex) and society (gender). What drives the blurring of the boundaries is the energy that is constitutive of all humans, libidinal in its manifestations, but ontological in structure, namely desire. It would be regrettable if the emphasis on materialism resulted in dismissing the legacy of psychoanalysis, because it is one of the few viable philosophies of desire.

Psychoanalytic feminism is highly relevant to the posthuman predicament in that it de-naturalizes sexuality and undoes the distinction between the biological and the social. Or rather, it unifies them by highlighting the function of the imaginary and unconscious processes of identification. The imaginary is always already social, that is to say open to historical changes and contingent influences, while operating at the most intimate levels of one's self-understanding. Psychoanalysis has the last word here by reminding us that every subject is just work-in-progress, driven by desire as an ontological force without pre-established – that is to say natural or 'proper' – objects. The challenge that psychoanalysis throws perennially in our general direction consists in developing an adequate mode of understanding – a language and a system of representation – for the specificity of one's flows of desire.

The imaginary as vector of desire is not a tradeable repertoire of wilfully chosen performances. Nor is it the immutable black box of metaphysical essences. To see it as the 'free' expression of the chosen identities by liberal individuals is a misleading simplification. Desire is rather the materially embodied and embedded construction and transposition of material, memories, perceptions, intuitions, onto real-life conditions. Desire flows and cuts across categories, space and time coordinates, norms and conventions. Fluid, sexuate processes of becoming replace the dichotomous sex–gender distinction. Desire as the ontological force encompasses sexuality but cannot be reduced to it, which means that the propensity of all matter perseveres and expands in its existence. Desire to endure is built into the autopoietic force of matter itself.

Posthuman feminism disentangles sexuality from the dialectics of negativity, which tends to define desire as that which one is missing. Especially Lacanian psychoanalysis perpetuates a psychic form of Hegelian negativity by defining desire as lack: missing what you don't yet have. Feminist new materialism, however, defines desire as overflowing plenitude: giving what you did not even suspect you had in you.[23] Desire is not lack but plenitude; not negative dialectics, but generous excess. Desire as lack and negativity has been colonized by possessive individualism, that prioritizes locating the acquisition of commodities as the ultimate object of capitalist desire. Posthuman feminism is, on the contrary, allied with a gratuitous, neo-stoic debunking of egotism and self-interest. Hasana Sharp (2019) put it beautifully when she praised Spinoza's generous ethics as 'a strategy for antihatred' (Sharp, 2011: 159). This produces not only diametrically opposed political theories of what counts as the radical political gesture, but also dramatically different philosophies of love.

In the view that I propose here, sexuality refers to the scale, range and degree of relational challenges and pleasures living entities can co-produce. It expresses the profound joy that 'we' – living entities – derive from the sheer fact of being alive together. Joy or affirmation as an ethical affect is directly proportional to the ability of any organism to embrace and activate relationality as the fundamental value and persevere in and through its existence. This includes also encounters with and processes of transformation of pain and loss. Posthuman feminism emphasizes in an affirmative vein the positivity of desire as the generative force of relational subjects, which pulls them towards flows of encounters, interactions and affectivity. At the beginning there is always already a relation to an affective, interactive entity endowed with intelligent flesh and an embodied mind: ontological relationality and a generative notion of complexity.

Taking a more transversal approach to this generous love of the world, posthuman feminist politics aspires to in-depth transformation. Through practical forms of collaborative praxis, it hopes to lead to a more inclusive form of sociality. This radical political strategy consists in transversal accelerations that undo the dualistic oppositions and activate the potential for becoming. Moving beyond the dialectics of devalorized – sexualized, racialized and naturalized – differences, posthuman feminism grounds the political in the collective construction of alternative sexed identities beyond Western humanism and anthropocentrism. Because of its speed and scale of movement, there are radical possibilities of monstrous and deviant virtual re-embodiments and experiments with unprecedented sexualities, subject formations and social practices. One of the challenges facing posthuman feminism is how to find adequate forms of representation for the vitality and unconventionality of contemporary sexualities.

Desire as positivity and relationality is experienced as affect. It flows as the force that aims at setting up and supporting a maximum of relations, and draws pleasure from the fulfilment of this constitutive relationality. Desire as a transversal ontological force is set in a frame of affirmation; it enacts multiple flows, a crossing of boundaries, and an overflowing into a plenitude of affects where life is asserted to its highest degree. It is the ontological drive to become all that one's embodied and embedded relational selves are capable of enduring in an affirmative ethical frame. There is no pre-set object for the fulfilment of desire, as psychoanalysis in its great wisdom taught us already last century.

In this respect, desire is about intransitive becomings. Sexuality is indeed a transversal process of becoming, punctuated by affects. It flows its own paths, its own temporality, leaning on the chosen objects, but also bypassing them constantly. Enacting desire entails the production of new relations with these untimely, heterogeneous and unfamiliar objects. Such an assemblage requires the effort to synchronize the bound and limited self with the speed and multiplicity of sexuality as *zoe*/geo/techno-mediated relations, as positive, material vitality. Sexuate matter thus defined is a splendid complexity. It is in fact cosmic, or rather, 'chaosmic' (Guattari, 1995).

Life in an enchanted vital materialist perspective, driven by desire defined as a relational and affirmative ontological force, is an immensely seductive force. But posthuman feminism is not arguing for a romance with life itself. It is rather the case that desire is always social and contextualized and that it works in tandem with the project of affirmative ethics. Desire is always the desire to express its affirmative force and to make things happen. It is a surplus value, an over-the-top addition that is both superfluous and indispensable. A gift in some ways, but one that is disengaged from the political economy of exchanges regulated by lack and negativity.

It is inebriating to be freed from the limitations of a narrow liberal individualism that is indexed on narcissism and paranoia. It is humbling in that it displaces the presumptuous centrality of the anthropocentric subject, be it an author, writer or thinker. That singular entity is in fact a complex multiplicity, a vehicle of becoming, a vector for the actualization of *potentia*, that is to say a multiplier of virtual possibilities. Sexuality is *Eros*, as the fundamental power of desires, the most basic of which is to persevere in our existence. Human essence consists in the enjoyment of the freedom to express multiple powers and pleasures that the mind–body continuum is capable of. Posthuman feminism defines sexuality as a force before, beyond and beneath gender, propelling an Eros of becoming.

Ethics of Eros

Posthuman feminist experiments with contemporary sexuality ultimately face an ethical challenge. The challenge is how to construct a relational bond beyond the naturalistic paradigm, its hierarchical exclusions and its libidinal investment in negative differences and desire as lack. Stressing this dimension, feminist theory in the posthuman convergence embraces its historical responsibility to assess the ethical effects of this crucial mutation for affectivity, sexuality and desire.

As an example of posthuman ethics, Melbourne-based artist Patricia Piccinini explores the new patterns of love, desire and care emerging from the new relationship of humans to non-humans. She starts from the animal others but also includes technologically mediated hybrids. She jokingly describes her work as 'animal-pomorphic'. It's not about attributing human characteristics to animals as much as recognizing our shared 'animalness'. Empathy and care are qualities Piccinini finds in animals, monsters, as well as humans. The cross-species connection makes her critical of the exclusionary aspects of Western humanism, while sharing its compassionate values.

Piccinini reflects especially upon the transgenic creatures produced by contemporary technoscience and its manipulations of living matter. Technically, they are 'chimeras' but she tends to use 'creature', and loves them as beings endowed with a soul and intelligence. The hybrid creatures of Piccinini's 'media-naturecultures' world defeat the commercialized economy of bio-genetic patents to establish their own modes of relation, interrogating the very boundaries they contribute to dissolve. In Piccinini's work, transgenic couples refuse to occupy the stations that technoscience has prearranged for them. These transgenic lovers and other social hybrids express mutual support and delight in their intimacy.

Piccinini makes two political interventions: one against the stigma of pejoration socially attributed to monstrous, non-human and hybrid others. They are associated with moral and sexual abnormality, deviancy, criminality, abjection and aesthetic ugliness. They share these traits with the dehumanized 'others' of 'Man', the sexualized, racialized and naturalized others. The specific horror evoked by transgenic creatures expresses not only radical otherness, or degeneracy, as much as the permanent threat of a process of mutation – or of in-between-ness. Under Piccinini's caring hand, these creatures embody a power of endurance, at a time when many third millennium humans are incubating serious doubts about their own resilience.

The second visual displacement Piccinini operates concerns the monstrous feminine in relation to love, sexuality and reproduction. Her work privileges mother and child pairings, or larger family and social groupings, arranged in Renaissance-style visual compositions of Madonna and Child and Pietà imagery. In some ways this approach re-humanizes the non-human others, while displacing the centrality of anthropocentric arrogance. Not only do her transgenic creatures return our gaze, they look back at us and thus undo the voyeuristic consumption of their otherness. They also look into us, with eyes full of curiosity, compassion and longing. Piccinini's gaze transcends the binary divide between us and them by introducing a trans-species form of care, a posthuman relational ethics enacting what Mondloch describes as 'unbecoming human' (2018: 65). Piccinini tells us that posthuman love and universal care is at work here. Young-Bruehl and Bethelard (2000) opt for the notion of 'cherishment' to underline the affective element of relationships. The term designates both the expectation to be loved and the capacity to take care of the emotional needs of another. Deployed in psychoanalysis as well as in real life, it has etymological roots in the Latin *caritas* as a form of benevolence, a presumption of mutual good will, that sustains affirmative relations.

The message of this transgenic and cross-species intimacy is that it is crucial to nurture a culture of affirmation and joy and become loving posthuman subjects. Against the contemporary forms of nihilism and techno-accelerationism, a sensual philosophy of immanence should foreground affirmation and care. What if those hybrid others, far from being relics of a distant genetic past, were pointing the way instead to our evolutionary future?

Conclusion

Posthuman sexuality is a line of flight. As advanced capitalism evolves into a system that capitalizes on the potency, the vital, generative power of matter, sexuality remains the joker in the pack. Partly stultified by the constant repackaging into a reductive and antiquated gender system, sexuality re-emerges constantly as a point of resistance and reinvention. Irrepressible, generative on a cosmic scale, the force of desire is always sexuate before, beneath and beyond gender and breaks all moulds. It reconnects us to our ontological grounding, the fundamental joy of persevering in one's existence and increasing our relational abilities to encounter others. A multiplicity of others, of the human, more-than-human and non-human kind, this relational bond makes sexuality into a transversal connector that is accountable to and for these others. It is an ontological source of empowerment for women and LGBTQ+ people.

Eros needs to enter the posthuman equation. Desire is molecular becoming; it is never a given. Like an ongoing project from the past, it is a forward-moving horizon that lies constantly ahead towards which one moves. Between the no longer and the not yet, desire traces the possible patterns of becoming. Sexualities beyond gender trace the transformative paths of feminist politics. They point to virtual possibilities that escape, challenge and de-territorialize the accommodating policies of gender mainstreaming. Posthuman feminism offers vantage points and modes of political intervention suitable for the complexities of today. Against the platitudes of sex as conspicuous consumption and the violence of socio-economic exploitation, posthuman feminists today rethink sexuality beyond genders as a way to become posthuman otherwise.

Desire is the ontological force that activates all living matter – humans included – to go on. Inexhaustible and irrepressible, the sexuate structure of living matter delights in self-perpetuation. Pitching multiple sexualities beyond social mechanisms of capture, discipline and punishment, is one of the ways to channel this force towards the invention of new ways of living and loving together. Defending the virtual force of sexuality and its ability to generate a thousand little sexes is a project of consequence. It raises as its social counterpart the necessity of devising adequate social rules and institutions, discourses, narratives and images worthy of such multiplicity and heterogeneity. Sexualities before, beneath and beyond gender require new scripts for their fluidity. Legal, political, ethical, social, spiritual and epistemological scripts need to be redrafted.

Language and representation enter the scene again. Posthuman sexualities need material and symbolic structures, framed by shareable narratives. Posthuman feminists tell different stories, also about what kind of subjects of desire we can become. The creative imagination in the arts and literature is crucial for the task of forging alternative social imaginaries that support posthuman feminist visions. And this is exactly what Virginia did for Vita, by turning her into Orlando, the trans-historical figure who lives forever. Orlando is the trans-lover that transits in between sexes and genders, depending on who they fall in love with. This raises the haunting question that Elizabeth Young-Bruehl (2003) asked: where do you fall, when you fall in love? I think you fall into the spacetime of the world – a sort of breathlessness of desire as higher degrees of intensity and a speeding up of relational possibilities. If falling in love is a fall at all, it is a fall into the elemental force of the world, out of trite and predictable repetitions, into productive accelerations. Desire is a heightening of sensorial perception, an overflowing within specific geometries of relational forces.

Posthuman Eros is the stuff of the world.

Chapter 7
Wanting Out!

I'm not a girl. I'm a genius.

Joanna Russ, *The Female Man*

An imaginative and creative writing style driven by the diverse life experiences of feminist and LGBTQ+ subjects, is a distinct feature of feminist scholarship. Posthuman feminism, both critical and creative, is apt to combine apocalyptic visions of extinction with euphoric scenarios of escape to new extra-planetary homes. In addition to theoretical insights and social criticism, it has perfected a fantastic streak that runs through its rich and varied genealogies. This feminist genre stretches from the deliberate use of imaginative and even provocative figurations as modes of knowledge production in feminist research, to fully-fledged utopian genres of speculative literature, cyber-punk and science fiction. Often conveyed through poetic, fictionalized and imaginative styles, it has produced an extraordinary *corpus* that ranges from poetry to graphic novels, from satires and comic relief to revolutionary manifestos, pamphlets and utopias, rock operas, horror movies and fantasy series. These radical feminist voices manifest the desire for alternative worlds and for a sort of anthropological exodus from the dominant configurations of the human. They want out of the damaged state of this planet under the rule of Man/Anthropos. Delinking the sexualized, racialized and naturalized others from this regime, feminists rely on technologies and their own imagination to provide generative visions of alternative posthuman worlds outside their planetary homes.

This speculative genre rests on a combination of critical reason and the radical imagination, theoretical sophistication and visionary dreams. The spectacular expressions of these 'collective imaginings' (Gatens and Lloyd, 1999) call for talents other than analytical reason. It means that the skills of writers, poets, artists, musicians and activists are enlisted as an integral part of the feminist agenda. Speculative feminism is a posthuman form of activism of the imagination and a way of styling the political will for change beyond humanism and anthropocentrism.

This political and poetic project is crucial for posthuman feminism, that speculates and works towards alternative views on embodiment, sexuality, gender and reproduction, new family and social kinship structures and affective bonds. Feminist posthumanists eschew the political messianism that plagues so much political theory of previous and contemporary generations, by adopting a materialist approach that acknowledges social injustices and the possibility of transforming them. It is less redemptive than pragmatic, and secular in reappraising the affective factors that support the feminist political projects, starting from the pain of exclusion. The speculative fictions invent alternative forms of posthuman sexuality, a myriad of post-patriarchal genders not only across cultures and ethnicities, but also across species, and even planets and galaxies. Speculative texts are dystopian readings and stringent critiques of the injustices of the present. They point to multiple ways of becoming-posthuman. In this chapter, I will explore the different aspects of the speculative soul of posthuman feminism, both in theoretical and in fictional texts.

Feminist Figurations in Scholarship

Posthuman scholarship is marked by an upbeat and weird mood, rich in neologisms and provocative combinations of non-human and post-natural objects and references. Imaginative and speculative motifs and terminology are at play in mainstream feminist theory, even when it adopts conventional academic writing styles. If cartographies are the navigational tools that enable us to develop adequate understandings of our material life conditions and the complexities of the present, figurations are the projective anticipations of what can be done about them. They apply and operationalize into action the epistemic insights of feminist theory, like conceptual personae, or 'thinking aids', that help us work through complex issues. Figurations are theoretical fictions at work to dismantle the posture of scientific objectivity, academic hierarchies and lethal binary oppositions. They gesture towards worlds where being different-from is not an indictment and thinking differently-from does not necessarily mean being worth less than the standard norm set by Man/Anthropos.

In my work I have deployed several figurations: from 'the feminist philosopher' (1991), through 'nomadic subjects' (1994, 2011a) and 'the posthuman' (2013, 2019). These critical figurations target respectively the following power formations: the misogynist and exclusionary structures of patriarchal philosophy and the Humanities in general (1991); the controlling patterns of enforced and encouraged mobility of advanced capitalism (1994, 2011b); the invasive nature of contemporary technologies in an increasingly polarized world (2013); and the consequences for the production of knowledge today (2019). The figurations that organize these critical accounts are materially embedded and embodied signposts of crucial knots of knowledge and power, anticipating emergent meta-patterns of resistance and of dissonant and creative becoming. Figurations point to materialist understanding of literature and the arts as reflecting and respecting the complexity of the differential, materially embedded subject positions they represent and account for. All the more so as these subjects are anomalous, hybrid and 'weird'.

The feminist speculative genre in social and cultural theory has produced some spectacular figurations. Donna Haraway, for instance, is one of the great fabulators of the feminist tradition. She defines figurations as 'condensed maps of contestable worlds' (1997: 11). Her fantastic fabulations about 'the promises of monsters' (1992) draw inspiration from unacademic and hybrid cultural genres, such as science fiction, fantasy, horror and cyber punk. They provide fitting illustrations of the changes and transformations that are taking place in our posthuman present and lucid depiction of contemporary power.

Throughout her influential corpus, Haraway proposes a 'menagerie of figurations' (2000: 135) that mark different phases of her thinking. The iconic cyborg (1985) is a figure of hybrid interconnection that grounds technology into its earthly environment and conversely introduces mediation at the core of the natural world. The broader category of the companion species (2003) extends to many animals: dogs, cats, chickens, etc. It also signals a more complex relational and affective way to approach these *zoe*-related connections. Another key figuration, Oncomouse (1997), the first patented animal in the world, a transgenic organism created for the purposes of research and profit, circulates between the laboratories and the marketplace, the research benches and the legal sector. In a distinctly post-secular manner, Haraway devises a symbolic kinship system and spiritual connection with the transgenic, hybrid, mutant animals. They become sacred figures, victims and scapegoats that sacrifice themselves in order to find the cure for breast cancer and thus save the lives of many human women. Oncomouse is a non-human mammal rescuing human mammals.

Haraway is cautious about the posthuman and, as Hester put it, somehow overlooks its 'potential utility' for her own project (2019: 70). It is a figuration capable of igniting alternative visions and narratives. Dismantling the pretence at objectivity and distance, she renders the academic, scholar and thinker through the image of the 'modest witness' (1997). Witnessing, like listening, requires careful and unobtrusive observation, accountability, open-ended dialogue that suspends judgement. It signals a relational, but non-normative location for posthuman thinkers bent on producing collaboratively knowledge born of the experience of marginalization. This experience nurtures the desire to run away and construct alternative worlds.

Another illuminating example of posthuman feminist figurations as scholarly method is provided by Anna Tsing (2015). She constructs an ecofeminist technoscience project through the genre of the ethnographic essay, which she combines with multiple other sources of intellectual inspiration and scientific competence. This approach is enhanced by Tsing's considerable talents as a writer; her graceful storytelling combines with empirical scientific observations, to produce a very different kind of academic text. The result blends into an elegant piece of narrative that reads as part travel journey, part fieldwork notes, and part sheer imaginative creation. Practising a sort of conceptual minimalism, Tsing at times writes scientific accounts that resemble *haiku*, the Japanese nature poetry tradition. Humble in tone, but sophisticated in lexical simplicity and syntactical precision, her texts embody in their very structure deep respect for the environment and the subject-matters of the posthuman convergence. One of Tsing's preferred figurations is a non-anthropomorphic object of study: the matsutake mushroom. The collaborative resistance shown by the mushrooms against environmental disturbances – as shown by their ability to grow in ruined landscapes, devastated areas and even inside nuclear reactors – is both a feature of their vital materialism and a living response to human destructiveness.

Writing academic research in this speculative and figurative mode is risky business in the neoliberal university system, considering the quantified requirements of objectivity and neutrality that scientific research imposes on its practitioners. In her analysis of feminist experimental writing styles, Nina Lykke (2010a, 2014) praises their courage and imagination, especially in feminist technoscience studies. She foregrounds the special role that cultural and literary studies of technoscience have played in constructing posthuman theory (Bryld and Lykke, 2000). One of the features of that branch of feminist scholarship is that they can more easily adopt non-human objects of enquiry. Moreover, Lykke recommends more freedom in adopting a post-constructivist method and pushes transversality into full transdisciplinarity (2018). She presents this methodological change as a way to honour the agency of matter and the heterogeneous assemblages of posthuman subjects. Displaying genuine literary talent, Lykke defends a wonder-based approach to scientific research and writing. She develops 'a speculatively fabulating/poeticizing approach' that expresses both deep affectivity, technological mediation and environmental care (2019: 20). Beyond utilitarianism and profit-making, posthuman feminist scholarship is brought back to a profound gratuitousness and a fundamental obligation of care. Lykke (2019) has also developed this lyrical vein in inspirational accounts of the experience of queer death, loss, mourning and widowhood (Radomska et al., 2020).

The materialist feminist of locations granted great epistemic authority to the lived experience of the writing/speaking 'I', while challenging its unitary nature. This was a way for feminism to challenge the spurious objectivity of a scientific system that uncritically embraced the Enlightenment idea of universality and neutrality. This posture is what Haraway critiques as 'the god trick' (1988). A theoretical style is therefore not merely decorative, but quite central to a feminist thinker's conceptual and political project. Thinking creatively through figurations seeks for a balance of sorts: it means adopting a relational, empathic style, while remaining scientifically credible. Because posthuman feminism and critical theory require workable figurations, style is an essential tool that operationalizes the feminist philosophers' conceptual persona. Figurations dramatize the specific cartographic line they pursue in their quest for alternative modes of knowledge production. Thinking is about creativity and enlivenment. It is less a matter of representing others, or speaking on their behalf, than about joining in the collective construction of affirmative ways of knowing. This is crucial to the posthuman feminist project of turning thought into an instrument of creation of the new.

Affect, which is such a crucial component of a materialist feminist understanding of the subject as a heterogeneous, sexuate assemblage, plays a central role in the composition of narrative styles and the choice of figurations. Affects are relational, collective and respond to and correspond with their social surroundings and historical context. Posthuman feminists never fail to foreground this affective dimension, which resonates with the turbulence of the posthuman convergence.

The feminist style of posthuman figurations favours a cognitive brand of empathy, combining the power of understanding with the capacity for compassion and the force to endure. As we will see in the next section, it also cultivates longing and care for a multitude of intergalactic and extra-terrestrial homes and all sorts of non-human entities. Posthuman feminism dares to dream, even and especially among the ruins of our damaged planet, yearning for ways out (Tsing et al., 2017).

The Feminist Speculative Genre

Posthuman feminism contributes to the project of liberating humans and non-humans of the earth by conjuring up alternative worlds. This is the glorious feminist tradition of radical imagination and visions, fantasy, utopianism and other forms of escape from planet Earth into intergalactical futures. This subversive feminist line is posthuman in both spirit and aspiration as it offers far-reaching political transformations that encompass all of humanity. Beyond analyses and revendications on a planetary scale, posthuman feminism is driven by the ironic conviction that life on the Moon or Mars *has* to be better than daily existence under terrestrial patriarchy. As Isabel Waidner put it: 'We require a starship to whisk us away. (Nothing but a starship will do.) (A rocket to the moon will do)' (2019: 75).

The radical political imagination has a long history in feminism. Joan Kelly labelled this mix of critique and creativity as 'the double-edged vision of feminist theory' (1979). Audre Lorde (1973) linked the project of political liberation of women, African-Americans, decolonial and Indigenous people, to a reorientation of the collective imagination towards a poetics of rage, erotic energy and love. Affects are central to it. Carolyn Merchant, recognizing as early as 1980 the link between the exploitation of women and that of the natural environment, called for a leap of our moral imagination to develop a renewed sense of relationship to non-human entities. By 1987, Charlotte Bunch is writing about feminist theory in action as 'passionate politics', while Henrietta Moore wrote about 'a passion for difference' (1994).

Wanting social justice and aspiring to a better world are deep desires. They are not just words on paper, but materially embedded projections of other ways of becoming human, in their complex, messy materiality. They mobilize passions that call forth possible futures. This gesture involves not only a deep concern for what we already have, but also post-secular trust in what is to come. If you believe in justice, dignity and freedom, you are a believer.

Oppositional consciousness – the motor of feminist activism – is infused with empowering creativity in order to collectively produce not only immediate strategies and policies, but also broader visions for humanity and new ways of interacting. The challenge of developing new scenarios is constant in transformative movements like feminism and it calls for multiple skills, on top of sharp analytical reason. Faith in the powers of the imagination goes a long way in feminism and it established a creative tradition of counternarratives. It includes multiple and non-linear temporalities and a strong commitment to futurity.

This speculative genre stretches back to Mary Shelley's (daughter of feminist Mary Wollstonecraft) monstrous progeny, Frankenstein, the original hybrid of Western modernity. Monstrous anomalous entities embody ontological impropriety. Their appearance is a provocation that upsets the status quo and evokes anxiety, or rather a mixture of fascination and loathing. Their metamorphic powers are immense: they act as mirrors to reflect our sense of inadequacy or inner monstrosity (Braidotti, 2002). As Diane Arbus (1972) knew well: monsters and freaks embody a trauma that has already happened, that some were even born with. Because they have gone through the disaster and survived, they are existential aristocracy. They are now beyond some fundamental threshold of mutation, beyond the fears that torment us in the posthuman convergence. Their resilience grants them a cathartic function in relation to those – especially humans – who are still fearfully anticipating a fatal blow.

The affective and political alliance of women, monsters, goddesses, cyborgs, LGBTQ+ and other anomalies is reflected in a rich feminist literature of love for monsters (Kristeva, 1980; Haraway, 1992; Stacey, 1997; Braidotti, 2002). The monstrous, abject, non-human and more-than-human others have been generative sites of identification and invocation for feminist, queer and trans theories (Stryker, 1994, 2015). Revisited in today's world by Jeanette Winterson, 'Frankisssstein' becomes a posthuman icon who proudly affirms 'I am liminal, cusping, in between, emerging, undecided, transitional, experimental, a start-up (or is it an upstart?) in my own life' (2019: 29).

Since the 1970s, the science fiction horror genre has grown into a popular posthuman feminist genre. Feminist cultural and literary theorists commented on the unnatural alliance between the marginalized others and the extra-terrestrials (Barr, 1987, 1993; Creed, 1993; Lykke and Braidotti, 1996). The sexualized others (women and LGBTQ+); the racialized others (postcolonial, Black, Jewish, Indigenous subjects); the naturalized 'others' (the non-humans, animals, insects, plants, trees, viruses and bacteria); and the extra-terrestrials (Martians, rogue robots and insurgent replicants) – all are allied with full respect for their differences and perspectives. As LeFanu pointed out (1988), the alliances show this affective bond between various brands of monstrous or alien others, joining forces in their struggle against a common colonizer. It is an alliance of embodied and re-materialized posthuman subjects. Far closer to *zoe*/geo/technobodies than *bios* in the materiality of bodies that are vulnerable and deviant, posthuman feminists have shown a propensity to go as far as possible into subverting the sovereignty of Man.

The speculative literary genre features visionary feminist writers like Ursula Le Guin, *The Left Hand of Darkness* (1969); Marge Piercy's feminist visions in *Woman on the Edge of Time* (1976) and *Body of Glass* (1991). Just how socially grounded and realistic this speculative genre can be is illustrated by Margaret Atwood's dystopian text *The Handmaid's Tale* (1985). A multi-media phenomenon, it reads today almost like a prophecy of things to come a few decades later. Within the rich and varied tradition of Black feminisms, Afrofuturism and Black science fiction, superb feminist writers like Octavia Butler (*Kindred*, 1979; *Dawn*, 1987), and in the new generations, Nora K. Jemisin, look back – or rather 'Black' – to the past, in order to anticipate better futures.[1] They offer redemptive visions of futures that break from the legacy of pain, trauma and ancestral wounds. Black posthumanism meets technoscience and media culture head-on, envisaging 'non-apocalyptic possibilities for the future as well as the past and present' (Lillvis, 2017: 85).

This trans-species, trans-sex and trans-racial alliance manifests a chain of solidarity between the sexualized, racialized and naturalized 'others' of white, urbanized, heteronormative 'Man'. Transversality, however, does not mean sameness. It is indeed the case that there are substantial differences in the ways in which patriarchy deals with each category marked by the sign of negative difference. But the marginalized others do share in a political economy of brutal discrimination, social injustice and symbolic disqualification. They often inhabit this planet, its societies and symbolic orders, as an alien, unsafe and dangerous place.

The transversal alliance enacts a radical quest for planetary and even intergalactic ways out. This genre has a distinct posthuman flair for transgressive and transversal relations in moving out of the patriarchal world order. The feminist speculative genre expresses passionate resistance to oedipal power relations, celebrating what I have labelled 'the society of undutiful daughters' (Braidotti, 2012: ix). They are the rebellious, non-conforming women and LGBTQ+ people who have gone on record as saying 'I would prefer not to', that is to say, *not* to comply with 'your' laws and customs (Deleuze, 1998). Their civil disobedience extracts them from the social contract, so that they can run with wolves (Pinkola Estés, 1992) and strike dissonant but lively intergenerational notes (Evaristo, 2019). The alliance of the outsiders produces a powerful heterogeneous assemblage: women + LGBTQ+ people + Blacks + Indigenous + animals + extra-terrestrials – all fighting against the hegemony of 'Man'.

Nowadays this tradition has gathered momentum and a significant alliance between LGBTQ+ theorists and the speculative genre is one of the motors of fast-growing posthuman and inhuman feminisms. Queer theorists, ever alert to the opportunity of exiting the sexual binary system, have equated the posthuman with post-gender (Giffney and Hird, 2008). They propose an explicit alliance between extra-terrestrial monsters and freaks, social aliens and queer political subjects (Halberstam and Livingston, 1995; Halberstam, 2012). Alternative sexualities and multiple gender systems are speculatively projected into intergalactic multi-verses, often modelled on the sexual systems of non-human species including insects (Braidotti, 1994, 2002; Grosz, 1995). As we saw in the previous chapter, post-gender sexualities have been postulated in a radical form of post-anthropocentric reflection on the extinction of the current form of human embodiment. Halberstam is inspired by and attracted to post-cyborgian ecological entities (2011), while Mel Chen (2012) explores the humanity–animality nexus through race and queer theories. Disability studies also explores alternative bodily configurations (Murray and Sullivan, 2009)

The speculative tradition of feminist science fiction and gothic literary genres is emblematic of this genre, which nowadays has taken a 'zoo-poetic' turn (Ulstein, 2021) and a 'geo-poetic' planetary one (Last, 2017). With deviancy as an attractor, monstrosity expresses less anxiety about the status of the human and rather a distinct sense of relief at the collapse of the normative frameworks that used to define it. Mindful of the force of sexuality as generating a transformative potential that erodes the majoritarian pull of the binary gender system, multiple visions of sexualities beyond gender feed feminist posthuman speculations about possible futures. They engender alternative worlds, hybrid cross-species fertilizations and virtual sexed technobodies. They honour the *zoe*/geo/techno-mediated perspectives of the posthuman convergence and enlist the resources of the imagination for radical transformative aims.

As Gry Ulstein (2019) argues, the genre of speculative narrative is also the voice of the Anthropocene anxiety of today. The 'new weird', as opposed to the more classical genres of science fiction or fantasy horror, displays a new sensibility in welcoming the alien and the monstrous as sites of affirmation and becoming (Noys and Murphy, 2016). It also echoes the 'new human' in literature and culture (Rosendahl Thomsen, 2013). This alliance is partly strategic in that it allows shared critiques of binary power relations. But, more importantly, it is an experiment with alternative ways of designing the humans in their relation to others. It distorts their self-representations the better to reveal the inner workings of their relational political economy. This calculated form of 'anamorphic projection' (Ulstein, 2021: 2), not unlike the classical metamorphic mirror function of monsters, is ethical and political at heart. The paradoxical productivity of weird narratives and relations allows us to assess the risks of the aftermath of these encounters and mutation: how to envisage 'what comes *after* the weirding of reality, besides existential dread?' (Ulstein, 2019: 130). This approach points to a materialist understanding of literature and the arts as reflecting and respecting the complexity of the differential, materially embedded positions they reflect. All the more so, as these subjects are anomalous, hybrid and weird, because they are what comes after the end of our world.

Feminist Techno-utopianism

Utopian visions are political anticipatory projections of more equitable, pleasurable and sustainable futures. The utopian vein runs high and mighty in posthuman feminism across a variety of writing genres. A visionary activist edge was expressed for instance by Ti-Grace Atkinson (1974) in *Amazon Odyssey*, a feminist theory book that doubles up as an urban guerrilla training manual. Valerie Solanas is another proponent of armed rebellion against patriarchy and author of the *SCUM*

Manifesto (1968). This iconic text combines the slightly delirious 'queering out' genre with level-headed biopolitical analysis of the management of life and death under patriarchy. Shulamith Firestone's 1970s classic *The Dialectic of Sex* is one of the main feminist techno-utopias of the twentieth century, inspired by and dedicated to Beauvoir. The original feminist accelerationist, Firestone built on a socialist view of the contradictions of capitalism to argue the case for a radical feminist revolution. She broke from the technophobic attitudes of her generation – which she saw as an abdication of historical responsibility – but also advocated a new feminist humanity built on the cyber-socialist utopia of complete automation.

Although I did mention in chapter 5 that I have grown slightly weary of this kind of utopianism, Firestone's fictional work is so important for the utopian genre that it is worth discussing. Firestone shared in two fundamental Marxist beliefs. The first is that capitalism prevents the fulfilment of humanity's full potential and consequently 'Man' as the representative of a truly universal humanity, can only come historically into his own through a socialist revolution. The second is that the status of women is the most accurate indicator of the level of historical evolution of any society. Sharing Beauvoir's conviction that the oppression of women is rooted in biology and reproduction, Firestone defines women's liberation as first and foremost a liberation from compulsory biological reproduction.

It follows that a feminist revolution has to put an end to natural procreation through the full-scale introduction of technologically assisted reproduction and communal childrearing in a socialist system. Famously claiming that pregnancy is barbaric, Firestone announced that the future of pregnancy is prosthetic. To defend artificial wombs in an age when most feminists defended female organicism, took a lot of courage. This radical position was also very productive for the movement in support of birth control and the anticonception pill (Franklin, 2010). In a surprising ecological twist, Firestone argues that the postrevolutionary feminist society will be not only class-less and sex-egalitarian, gender-neutral and anti-racist, but also ecologically sustainable. In this regard Firestone combines the two defining features of posthuman thought, namely the feminist critique of humanism and a post-anthropocentric approach to technology as well as to ecology and animal rights. What starts as a humanist argument about historical materialism and emancipation from natural bondage ends up as a posthumanist proposal. If nature is unjust, use the technology to change nature, as the Xenofeminists were to argue almost half a century later (Laboria Cubonics, 2018).

The Dialectic of Sex is a passionate feminist manifesto and not an academic treatise. It is rich in sweeping proclamations, but poor in arguments and concrete policy-making details. If the content of Firestone's techno-politics is radical cyberfeminism *avant la lettre*, the tone of her work is prophetic and visionary in keeping with the speculative tradition of feminist and queer utopias. It is an insurgent call to arms that provides a general framework for feminist activism. It will take almost thirty years for this accelerationist, posthumanist, pro-technology, but also radical ecological message to become reality. Although the techno-scientific control of fertility and reproduction started in the 1980s, it proved quite controversial.[2]

Feminist techno-utopianism is a critical commentary on the present; it takes patriarchal violence seriously and retaliates in kind. It joins forces with radical feminism in focusing on violent sexual politics as a system that imposes coercive heterosexuality and a reproductive heterosexual family structure (Millett, 1970; Greer, 1971). Radical feminists stress the alienation, marginalization and suffering of women and especially lesbians within it. They define patriarchy as a system that encourages and condones male violence against women and lesbians at all levels, physical, sexual, emotional and social. Sexual violence is analysed not as an individual psychological trait, but rather as a political economy structured by the widespread use of pornography and the trafficking of women in prostitution and sex work. These are the structural components of a system run by vested power interests, 'by which all men keep all women in a state of fear', as Susan Brownmiller (1975) eloquently put it. Patriarchal culture is rape culture. Utopian feminists' rejection of that culture is matched by their passionate embrace of a revolutionary – and mostly technology and Internet-backed – radical imagination. They activate an oppositional consciousness towards empowering creative alternatives to the objectionable present and embrace technology as a vehicle of human liberation.

Afrofuturism and Black Posthumanism

Afrofuturism mobilizes the counter-memories of racism, enslavement and dispossession to produce empowering counter-visions of black futurities (Eshun, 2003). The Afrofuturist intellectual and political tradition weaves themes from Black history, culture, thought and lived experiences in artistic, literary, cultural and musical productions. Often surreal, always visionary, the genre of Afrofuturism, featuring classic writers like O. Butler and Jemisin, has become a popular contemporary fantasy culture, best exemplified by the film *Black Panther* (2018) and the series *Watchmen* (2019).

Black posthumanists delink the racialized others from the hierarchical order that defines them as ontologically disqualified and socially excluded. They focus on the specific perspectives of the disenfranchised: the descendants of slavery, historical traumas and histories of dispossession have a different take on the climate crisis. After all, as the narrator in N.K. Jemisin put it (2017: 6), 'An apocalypse is a relative thing, isn't it?'. How to turn that exclusionary and inhumane humanism into an inclusive form of 'planetary humanism', as Gilroy suggests (2000), remains a top priority.

Compared to the urgency of anti-racist mobilization and the deletion of the Black cultural heritage, indulging in futurological visions may seem 'an unethical dereliction of duty' (Eshun, 2003: 288). But Afrofuturism manages to strike a balance between social critique of the present and total loss of faith in the future. It repurposes the negative differences, which are the roots of the exclusion and pain, into sources of knowledge and action. I see this as collective praxis that aims at redefining negative differences positively and reworking them into cognitive, affective and relational sources for the elaboration of alternatives. This praxis aims at coproducing affirmative ethics, in a non-hierarchical and intersectional plane of encounter. As Mann argues in his analysis of Octavia Butler's work (2018), the relationship between Afro-pessimism, which prioritizes blackness as an ontological impossibility, and Afrofuturism, which emphasizes the generative capacities to overturn that negative historical past by imagining better and often fantastic futures, is not mutually exclusive.

Afrofuturism is an affirmative response to Afro-pessimism and Black nihilism in two ways (Warren, 2015, 2017). The first is to value and appraise the cultural capital of Blackness, especially literature, art and music – from jazz to psychedelic hip hop, from Sun-Ra to Janelle Monáe's time-travelling musical narratives (Eshun, 2003). The second is to mix it with techno-materials and thus activate and affirm Black consciousness as the site of virtual becoming. That transformative move disconnects Blackness from negative dialectics and posits it as an empowering force on its own terms. Afrofuturism assumes a collective ability to reverse the negative terms of existing oppositions and a determination to undo Black alienation and reification so as to bring about a missing people of empowered Black subjects. N.K. Jemisin describes Afrofuturist fiction as the 'fight for the respect that everyone else is given without question' (2015: 1). The wounded and dispossessed put their imagination to work to make better worlds, elsewhere, starting from the assumption that this world is over and done with. This location provides the prophetic force of Black feminist posthuman visions of posthuman futures.

Afrofuturism puts alienation to creative uses. It extracts the disqualified Black body from the negative repetition of the pain and discrimination of the colonial past. It makes it occupy 'a place in history where the body of the African diaspora is more reminiscent of the strangeness of alien abduction, rather than signification of a self-determinant people' (Amaro, 2018: 17). The continuity of Black identity across space and time, and its ability to overturn a negative history into a positive future and thus create productive temporal discontinuities, is central to the speculative fictions of Afrofuturism.

The radical imagination of Afrofuturists and their restorative visions of other possible worlds visualizes a philosophy of extraterrestrial liberation. They set the framework for other histories to be written, splitting the dialectical oppositions that have kept blackness and progress, race and technology pitched against each other (Irani et al., 2012; Benjamin, 2019; Chun, 2021). It is time to take the time and the freedom to dream different dreams.

Wary of the facile optimism of capitalist market economies and mindful of the exclusion of Black peoples, and women especially, from the modernist horizons of hope, posthuman Black theory and Afrofuturism are marked by an affirmative ethical core. It is expressed in the quest for alternative views of Black humanity and alternative temporal frames for Black empowerment, drawing strength and inspiration from a past marked by oppression and pain. The authority and transformative energy that are missing from a traumatic past and the harsh conditions of the present can be borrowed from the future, defined as a site of empowerment to come. The virtual future is constructed in the present as a collective praxis based on Black women's and people's experience and of their ability to extract knowledge from that experiential location of suffering. They thereby relocate the wounded past to flourishing future scenarios. The key point of the ethics of becoming is to extend subjectivity to all entities, including the non-humans. In her *Broken Earth Trilogy* (Jemisin, 2015, 2016, 2017), N.K. Jemisin points out that 'when we say "the world has ended", it's usually a lie, because *the planet* is just fine'. The tradition of Black spirituality is important to the transformative and redemptive aspects of Afrofuturism. It has gained visibility in the public performances of contemporary stars like Beyoncé through the explicit references to African cosmological systems of death and rebirth through water and fire. This post-secular affect, or 'yearning', as bell hooks called it (1990), breathes generously through Afrofuturistic visions.

In a more critical posthuman vein, Alexander Weheliye (2014) works with Wynter's philosophy towards different ontologies of the human after the end of the humanist and liberal conception of 'Man'. He develops a relational mode of subject formation based on multiplicity and complexity. This subject is capable of multiple interactions with human and non-human others and thus intersects with the critical feminist posthuman agenda. The multiplicity is temporal as well as spatial and it mobilizes the non-linear force of a nomadic or rhizomic consciousness of becoming to overcome the alienation of pejorative difference, or disqualification. By defamiliarizing the painfully familiar experience of enslavement, through literature, music and the arts, Afrofuturism takes distance from the suffering. It also refuses to make a commodified spectacle out of it (Moten, 2003). Weheliye quotes Hortense Spillers' 1987 term 'pornotroping' to indicate 'the enactment of black suffering for a shocked and titillated audience' (2014: 90). Avoiding the repetition of that violence while exposing it remains a perennial challenge for the sexualized, racialized and naturalized others, who are constantly 'othered' in the gaze of their oppressors.

These are the flawed, imperfect creatures of Nnedi Okorafor – women, mothers and girls caught in cycles of structural racial political violence and the systemic destruction of their environment. Grounded in African traditions, as well as African-American ones, they work towards optimistic visions of the future.

Utopian techno-visions as the expression of the political imagination are also a form of love for the future. As Lillvis (2017) argues, posthuman futures in the Black feminist imagination are fuelled by the experience of liminality, based on the historical event of colonialism and enslavement. Inspired by bell hooks' classic text on postmodern Blackness (1990), Lillvis argues that, just as the postmodern condition spread for whites a deep sense of loss, alienation and despair that Black folks have always experienced, the posthuman convergence brings some disturbing news. The climate change crisis and the Anthropocene era are traumatic events for mainstream subjects of the developed world, who are suddenly confronted with their own vulnerability and the limits of the Western model of economic growth. For colonized, Indigenous and Black people, the 'end of the world' has already happened through violent colonialism, dispossession and enslavement. Lillvis argues for a way out of binary repetitions: 'The posthuman marks a solidarity between disenchanted liberal subjects and those who were always-already disenchanted' (2017: 41). The Black and Indigenous knowledge capital therefore is a global lesson in survival and endurance. This transformative and affirmative conviction forms the core of Afrofuturist imaginings.

Black posthumanism merges social theory with Black feminist politics to describe alternative modes of empowering the subjectivities of Black women, without positing a purely historical origin for their identity. Cultural essentialism – the claim to authenticity – is avoided, while historical specificity is highlighted as a source of transformative empowerment. Stressing the ability to become-other, 'posthumanist readings of contemporary Black women's historical narratives reveal that individual agency and collective authority develop not from historical specificity but, rather, from temporal liminality' (Lillvis, 2017: 4). The counter-memory and the aesthetics of Afrofuturism play for time. As queer Afrofuturist Nalo Hopkinson famously put it (2003), resting on the cumulated wisdom of millennia of African culture, black speculative writers are ready to take their chances with the twenty-first century. They labour to undo the negative hold of past traumas and unleash the desire for the future as a driver of possible transformations. Black and decolonial futurities is what colonial racialized capitalism has stolen and mutilated and yet, the radical Black political imagination projects otherworldly visions of equitable alternative futures.

This occurs alternatively through different vehicles of time travel. It runs through serious investigations of Black history and culture, but also through mythical re-readings of ancient, lost Black and pre-colonial Indigenous civilizations. This is the case for instance in the work of Karen Lord (2013), which stresses the importance of remembering your ancestors, while dreaming of your descendants and learning to be a good elder, but at the same time forcefully demonstrating that there is no way to go but forward: there is only the future. It is both a dystopian rendition of the present that brings out its horror and pain, and a utopian vision of black liberation. It mobilizes the resources of fantasy for the sake of atoning modes of liberation and the overcoming of suffering by imagining possible new worlds.

In this transformative trajectory, the technological apparatus that is complicit with the colonial project of Western modernity, is hacked to offer productive and quite subversive alternatives. Ramon Amaro stresses the force of the virtual to give technology a speculative relational twist by which 'the alienness of terrestrial belonging is re-scripted, re-coded and re-organized into alternative narratives of being and becoming' (2018: 17). Afrofuturism turns utopianism and science fiction into an operational programme aimed at new forms of self-representation within Black diasporic experience. These constructive flights of the political imagination disrupt the linearity of *Chronos*, through zigzagging patterns of becoming or virtual regenerations. This assumes a continuity and resonance of past/present/future. But it also asserts the disruptive power of Black feminist interventions and their ability to occupy multiple time zones at once. This upsets the linearity of teleological narratives of humanistic progress and interrupts the apocalyptic anxiety about the future generated in mainstream white culture.

Afrofuturist visions not only defy and defeat the Eurocentric whiteness of speculative fiction and future imaginings, but also stress the role of technologies in producing social practices and social imaginaries that confirm that particular regime. They consequently foreground the need for a rigorous analysis of the importance of racialized and racist discourses in the celebration of science and technology as liberatory tools for human and for their posthuman futures (Benjamin, 2019).

The power to dream alternative dreams expresses inner freedom, the transformative powers of the radical imagination and an unbridled sense of liberation from the material and symbolic burdens of oppression. It manifests disloyalty to patriarchal civilization and its sexualized and racialized hierarchies. This longing to get out rests on dis-identification of the marginalized others from the dominant vision of the human. The strategy of dis-identification was revisited productively by postcolonial theory as a critique of entrenched entitlements.[3] Spivak defined it as 'unlearning our privilege as our loss' (1990: 9). Black feminist theory turned this strategic technique into a form of civil and political dissent. It sounds as a generative call to action beyond the parameters of the here and now.

Posthuman Blackness resonates with posthuman feminism in that it pursues the critique of humanism and its liberal Eurocentric limitations. Posthuman solidarity rests on the notion of shared yearning and imaginings among liminal heterogeneous subjects. It offers ways of connecting those who were considered less than human, those who reject patriarchal, racist and heteronormative systems and those who aspire to different worlds. Re-combining their imaginative resources and cultural archives, posthuman feminism mobilizes them against the sinister perpetuation of patriarchal violence, imperial racism and environmental devastation.

Intergalactic Feminism

Some sceptics may think feminist longings to get out of this world are slightly excessive. Those fantasy scenarios may even appear frivolous and self-indulgent, considering the seriousness of the problems this planet is facing. But the point is that our contemporary world, caught in the convulsive tensions of the posthuman convergence, is no less unhinged and out of bounds. The paradoxes and contradictions of the co-occurrence of advanced technologies and environmental disasters often make contemporary earthly reality surpass even science fiction narratives. Such a fractured social system is forced to think about its possible futures.

The violent, irrational character of contemporary capital lies partly in its irrepressible desire to break boundaries, disrupt and crash through. The term 'delirium' (Cooper, 2008) is quite appropriate to describe cognitive capitalism's incursions into life itself. Delirious accelerationism designates the biotechnological drive to control and reinvent living forms beyond the terms set by the naturalized order of Western colonialist modernity. An exalted, grandiose imaginary characterizes the contemporary technological race, with its global telecommunication networks, space exploration and the regeneration of life beyond this planet and beyond our species. The developments of space biology and space biotech production raise the question whether the natural offspring of *homo post-sapiens* will be the space-travelling techno-devices. If so, 'the continued survival of our species will depend on the acceptance of Gaia by the cyborgs', as master transhumanist Lovelock poignantly suggests (2019: 106). May they show clemency!

The blueprint for new patriarchal cyborg species is a disclosure of possible futures. Advanced capitalism banks on the future and manipulates it by all possible means. Capitalizing on life imposes an obligation to design futurities, be it in the form of finding alternative sources of wealth, raw materials and labour, or through technologically enhanced reproduction. Corporate futurist designs rely on mathematical modelling, for instance of climate change, forecast of rates of COVID-19 infections, but also stock exchange trading flows in the futurities markets. They match speculative fiction in their exalted embrace of ever-expanding universes. As Eshun (2018) shrewdly points out, predicting the future is big business. Capitalism is quite adept at its own versions of science fiction-like scenarios in order to carefully calculate its chances to perpetuate the predatory greed that fuels it. Science fiction in the posthuman convergence has turned into a technique of corporate socio-economic governance.

Feminists of all denominations, being grounded and accountable, shudder at the neo-colonial undertones of these disembodied and disembedded scenarios of techno-capitalist futuristic bonanzas (Hayles, 1999; Braidotti, 2002; Vint, 2007). In particular, feminist scholars involved in neoliberal universities are quite aware of the extent to which the unfettered expansions of late capitalism and the delirious edges of contemporary science will impact on the funding for academic research and on government policies. This is a hard time for the Humanities, though they would seem to be more necessary than ever to bring insight, background, solace and critical acumen to a world in need. May the feminist Posthumanities come to the rescue (Åsberg et al., 2011; Åsberg, 2018; Åsberg and Braidotti, 2018; Braidotti, 2019).

For instance, space exploration is by now a business proposition marketing a sort of 'privatized futurism' (Shaw, 2021). Commercial companies today account for 80 per cent of the $424 billion global space industry in areas such as IT, tourism, manufacturing, biotech and pharmaceuticals (Jolly, 2021). Contemporary billionaires are setting up their space companies: Richard Branson created 'Virgin Galactic Hyperloop One'; Jeff Bezos' outfit is 'Blue Origin' working on Moon landing designs; Elon Musk Space X's plan focuses on a glass-domed colony on Mars. Their discourse is an apocalyptic form of transhumanism integrated into neoliberal economics: overpopulation and lack of resources on earth make space settlement imperative. Jody Byrd nails it: 'there is a certain ghastly revelling in the not-quite-dead-yet-but soon-to-be amnesias that drift now into political critiques' (2011: 225). She labels this morbid mood 'zombie capitalism' as the last stage of colonial and imperialist fantasies of total conquest. Oblivious to the environmentalist criticism that they show utter disregard for Planet Earth, and to the racism of their positions, corporate transhumanists equivocate by promising that space access will generate yet-unknown benefits for the world. Reality is surpassing science fiction by the hour when it comes to colonizing the future.

Expressing his distinctive contempt for environmental politics and his enthusiastic support for extraction economies of all kinds, in April 2020 – in the midst of the COVID-19 pandemic – then-president Trump signed an executive order encouraging American companies to mine resources from the moon and asteroids (Milman, 2020). This order makes clear that the United States does not view outer space as a 'global commons', and opens the way for commercial exploitation of the moon without any sort of international treaty.[4] It also allows proposed partnerships between the federal government and the private sector to mine the moon for resources, including water and certain minerals.[5] This law is one of the few aspects of Trump's legacy that the incoming Joe Biden's administration announced they would honour. This is not without precedents, because the United States had never signed a 1979 agreement known as the Moon Treaty, which stipulates that any activities in outer space should conform to international law. Moreover, the US government authorizes, should the opportunity arise, additional mining of Mars and 'other celestial bodies'. The development of space geo-engineering and astro-biology brings the equation of the biological and the technological to a delirious apotheosis (Cooper, 2008). According to Jodi Byrd, these measures transpose the colonialist doctrine of Manifest Destiny to outer space: 'The United States sits on the precipice, where empire either is now manifested in a deterritorialized sovereignty, or is on the verge of apocalyptic environmental collapse' (2011: 3). Or both at once – I would argue – in the worst possible resolution of the posthuman convergence into parallel black holes of mutually assured destruction.

Commenting on these extraordinary advances, iconic astronaut Samantha Cristoforetti acknowledges that the interplanetary dimension is here to stay and issues a double warning. In a deeply post-anthropocentric mode, she reminds us that the human species is temporary and transient: 'we could be gone and the earth would just keep on moving ... there's nothing permanent or inevitable about us' (2020). Cristoforetti believes the human species must become multi-planetary to survive unpredictable, but not impossible disasters, such as asteroid collisions or pandemics. These high risks alone justify the necessity of space travel.

Things are progressing quickly in this respect. Human settlements currently being planned for the Moon station will include men and women to ensure the continuity of the species. The NASA astronauts, with their badges of the Vitruvian Man dutifully sewn onto their suits, are not likely to do anything out of the blue. They are more likely to carry out their mission and probably perpetuate some of the Earthlings' heteronormative, profit-minded, Eurocentric habits. Pressing competition from the Chinese and the Russians is turning space settlement into a bestselling show. It is also the most concerted colonization effort since 500 years ago when European colonial expansion began.

Women are not new to outer space. The first female astronaut, the legendary Valentina Tereshkova of the USSR, flew out there in 1963. Although until 1978 NASA (established in 1958) only selected white men as astronauts, and the European Space Agency (ESA established in 1975) selected the first female astronaut – Claudie Haigneré – as late as 2001, things are picking up. In February 2021 the ESA announced a new drive to hire women and people with disabilities for missions to the Moon and eventually even to Mars.[6] Commenting on this intergalactic gender equality initiative, Cristoforetti struck an affirmative intergenerational feminist note and welcomed the twenty-six new positions that will be reserved for a batch of astronauts with a difference. The analogy between women and disabled may not be welcome in all quarters, but in a savvy insight into the surprising twists of the posthuman condition, Cristoforetti added: 'when it comes to space travel, we are all disabled' (Reuters, 2021). Indeed, in zero-gravity conditions, all bodies float as freely as Sue Austin does in underwater surroundings.

The scale and speed of these developments in real-life events shows that the posthuman convergence is already happening here and now, as a historical feature of our times and not a distant possibility. It also demonstrates the prescience and deep ethical motivations of the speculative genre of feminist and LGBTQ+ writings that are too often dismissed as escapist and out of this world.

In a rather sobering analysis of what he calls 'the global scramble for the world's last resources', Klare (2012: 1) comments on the new frontiers of global mining in an age of environmental depletion. The 'gold rush' in the Arctic region and deep-offshore gas and oil supplies in other parts of the globe, including rare earth minerals required for advanced electronics and electric cars, constitute a new 'land grab'. The fact that governments are directly involved in the commercial enterprise of mining raw material in demanding places, and purchasing arable land mostly in Africa, is an indirect acknowledgement of the environmental crisis. Such panic-buying shows awareness that the standard supplies of minerals are nearing exhaustion and new sources are needed. But it is also a discourse about the future, because this race for the remainder of the earth's resources expresses a grim determination to pursue the industrial age against all odds. Warning signs of dramatic climate change, unsustainable economies and socio-economic injustices are deliberately ignored in favour of a ruthless quest for new frontiers, on the margins, or the depths of the earth or on other planets. Extractive capitalism banks on its future expansion, situates it in outer space, but also in former colonial possessions on earth and declares them essential to its survival. If this scenario looks familiar, it is because it is a blatant repetition of imperial expansion. In their eagerness for the future, this system is destructive of the present. It also offers grim prospects for the Indigenous population, who will be the most affected by this irrational refusal to renounce extractive economic 'growth'. All living entities will ultimately be affected by the self-destructive nature of this neo-colonial capitalist economic order.

A cruel sacrificial logic of letting many earthly populations – human and non-human – die is at work in these new economies. Many are dehumanized to the sub-status of disposable bodies exposed to practices of exploitation, expulsion and extinction and the planetary escalation of warfare and security systems. But so are many non-human dwellers of this planet, triggering irreversible effects on the earth's sustainability.

The posthuman convergence is a powerful signal that it is time to change in deep, structural ways. Ignoring this warning begs the question what will be the status of all the other earthlings, who no longer support extractive economies, but are not yet cosmonauts and may not wish to become cyborgs. Are 'we' – the sexualized, racialized, naturalized others of 'Man' – earthbound by definition? Are we part of the remains that will be discarded? Does that make 'us' into disposable models of an antiquated body version, of no consequence to the project of multi-planetary neo-colonialism, destined at best to be the caretakers of a damaged and depleted planet?

Posthuman feminist scholars continue to display great ethical insights, courage and striking levels of prescience and creativity in dealing with these challenges. Commenting on the transhumanist project of space colonization, legal theorist Emily Jones, for instance, proposes a posthuman feminist approach to Mars (2018b). Supporting Keina Yoshida's call for a Constitution for Mars (2018), Jones warns against leaving the project of settling on Mars to the new techno-billionaire 'founding fathers'. They may follow the same, masculine, humanist blueprint of domination as they did on earth. Jones argues that posthuman feminist theory is the frame through which these challenges can be met. If intergalactic feminism is to happen, it must follow the long intergenerational tradition of critical feminism and combine speculative perspectives with a firm commitment to social justice and the abolition of poverty, oppression, sexism, racism and systemic inequalities.

As I am putting the finishing touches to this book, the Perseverance Rover space mission on Mars is in full swing. Astonishing images of the red planet are relayed back to earth, by smart technological devices that are self-organizing to function in their new habitat. And it just so happens that the head engineer for this historical mission, and the face of NASA, is a woman: Indian-American Swati Mohan. Those who used to be excluded are changing fast, but as Helen Lewis shrewdly put it: 'Misogyny mutates. Sexism and feminism are like bacteria and antibiotics; the latter forces the former to evolve' (2020: 320). And, I would add, their joined effect is to build up the collective political immunity of the entire community. But that political mutation requires active intervention. Unless feminist mobilizations keep on occurring, the project of space exploration may well be intergalactic, but will turn out just as patriarchal as what we've seen before. And life on Mars will be no less of a saddening bore.[7]

Epilogue: 'Get a Life!'

> We will go forward in a different mode of humanity, or not at all.
> Plumwood 2007: 1

Posthuman Feminism has foregrounded the politics of hope and ethics of affirmation through posthuman feminist activism and knowledge production practices. As such the book answers the question: where is the transformative force of feminism today? It lies in the enduring importance of critique and creativity. And in the quest to bring about alternative formations of subjectivity, other ways of becoming human and posthuman, for anybody. The aspiration to such freedom emerges from the lived experience of multiply embodied subjects who are marked negatively as the 'others' of 'Man/Anthropos'. All of these others are embodied and embedded, sexualized, racialized and naturalized in dichotomous systems and hierarchies, but not reducible to those systems alone. They are capable of exceeding the negative templates of power and to become anybody. This empowering political praxis is activated by an affirmative ethics that enfolds the positivity of difference. It expresses deep trust in their collective ability to constitute alternative human subjects and communities.

As the world looks for ways to rebuild its society and economies after or with the COVID-19 pandemic, new visions, social scenarios and unprecedented measures are called for.

The social context is marked not only by growing socio-economic inequalities but also by the resurgence of sexism and misogyny, homo- and trans-phobia, racism, Islamophobia and anti-Semitism. A populist wave is currently denying both climate change and the existence of the pandemic itself, let alone the need for global vaccination. These are violent and exhausting times on a planet that is undergoing its own human-made mutations.

In such a context, asking people to both endure the present and dream up possible new futures is asking a lot. How can posthuman feminism show solidarity and help to stimulate the collective imagination to produce new visions and blueprints? The sparkle of inspiration is never too far off. The imagination is a force, a faculty, a power (*potentia*) that can only be ignited and sustained collectively. The collective imaginings of posthuman feminism are projected transpositions that construct possible futures and, in so doing, make for a more bearable present. They express trust in and desire for better times, for communities, joys and pleasures to come. This anticipatory gesture sustains the political determination to persevere, to endure and go on constructing affirmative relations and options for the future. The future is what we are already in the process of becoming.

Posthuman feminism is a general ecology of alternative ways of becoming subjects and evolving within the contradictory forces of the posthuman convergence. It is an effective navigational tool that develops its own conceptual and methodological toolbox and applies it to the multi-scalar challenges confronting us today. It proposes an affirmative relational ethics, based on a pacifist ontology that predicates generosity and care in cross-species relationality. It is a political praxis that supports feminist commons and community-based experiments with what 'we' are capable of becoming. And I describe this we as 'we who are in *this* together but are not one and the same'. Posthuman feminism creates connections without amalgamations, stressing diversity while asserting that we are in this posthuman convergence together. It thus proposes a relational ethics that assumes one cares enough to minimize the fractures and seek for generative alliances.

Posthuman feminism is a radical force. It is a force for affirmative radicalism in an age of political exhaustion. It embraces the complexity of the current conjuncture, the better to resist, recode and transform them. The aspirations that fuel this innovative force are those that feminists have always upheld and defended: justice, respect, solidarity and affirmative transformations. They need to be applied to multiple, intersectional axes of differences, stretching across sexes, genders, classes, ethnicities and racialized locations, but also across non-human species and even other planets. They make feminism into an inexhaustible social movement. The virtual force of posthuman feminism is what makes it transformative in a generative manner. It continues to operate in the quest for alternative ways of becoming human, as heterogeneous processes of composing a missing people. These are communities to be actualized through praxis and shared affirmative values. The feminist subject mutates into multiple assemblages of people, of anybodies, rejecting structural injustices but also affirming relational ethics and love for the world. The subjects who trust in the collective ability to make a difference are a life-shaping force forever biding its time.

This is what needs to be kept first and foremost in mind: that feminism is the desire for freedom, a deep, visceral longing for overcoming conditions that are not bearable, unfair, not sustainable. Posthuman feminist theory cannot be satisfied just with accounting for the indignities and injustices of the present, though such an account is necessary as a critical cartography. The point of the cartographies is to record not only what we are ceasing to be but also what we are becoming. They point to affirmative alternatives. Because critical theory without alternative visions is a sterile exercise in negativity, feminists, like all freedom fighters, have to trust their dreams and to imagine a generative future. The feminist tradition to which posthuman feminism belongs is an ongoing event, which opens possibilities and creates fractures. It is not a historical precedent that can or should be replicated, but a virtual past of half-accomplishments and semi-successes, that call for renewed collective instantiation. The energy of feminism is an affirmative force infused with anticipatory and visionary powers, which need to be actualized and expressed by each new generation in its own way. The only good feminists are the undutiful daughters and children of formidable intellectual foremothers or generators. This transgenerational memory is an anticipatory act that expresses an intense and at times almost absurd love of the world and trust in its potentials. It is a gesture of confidence in what we are capable of becoming; we who are not one and not the same but are in this posthuman convergence together.

In the context of the posthuman convergence, public debates are strident and often aggressive. It seems that differences get weaponized and opinions run amok, resulting in polarizations, swift judgements and ever hastier dismissals of the others' points of view. The speed of Internet and online trolling increase the vitriolic epistemic violence of our times. Affirmative ethics is about the power to say no in the mode of 'I would prefer not to'. That can be expressed and enacted without aggression, injecting antidotes against the toxic negativity of the present. Affirmative ethics is geared to the composition of planes of encounter across different positions and potentially conflictual differences. Affirmation is a praxis that needs to be constructed by avoiding binary polarizations and suspending judgement. A respect for complexity needs to be developed, stressing the inevitable fact that contradictions are part of any worthy political and intellectual project. That the truth is not clear cut and is not a matter of 'either/or' but rather of 'and ... and'. Affirmative ethics, as we know by now, is about relational interconnections, pacifism, non-violence and generosity. We need to keep an open mind and an open heart to reach across the rich and complex itineraries of the feminist movements.

Posthuman feminism urges us to organize social and academic communities that reflect and enhance an ethically empowering notion of the emergent posthuman subjects of knowledge, especially the 'missing peoples'. Transversal interconnections across the categories, cultures and species, and in research, across disciplines and methodological traditions, is the way to implement an affirmative ethical praxis that aims to cultivate and compose a new collective subject. This subject is an assemblage – 'we' – that is a mix of humans and non-humans, *zoe*/geo/techno-bound, computational networks and earthlings, linked in a vital interconnection that is smart and self-organizing, but not chaotic. Let us call it, for lack of a better word, 'life'.

Death is an essential part of it. So many lives today are the object of biopower's thanato-politics, or new ways of dying, for example the refugees dying on the edges of Fortress Europe. We are all vulnerable to viruses and other illnesses, to the effects of climate change and other devastations. And many of these exposed lives are not human. Fortunately, humans are not the centre of creation. This is the insight of posthuman feminist thought as a secular, materialist eco-philosophy of becoming. Life is a generative force beneath, below and beyond what we humans have made of it. It is an inexhaustible generative force that potentially can transmute lives into sites of resistance – all lives, also the non-human.

The many interlocking tragedies that have occurred during the COVID-19 emergency magnify the disproportionate impact of environmental degradation and climate change upon the socially disempowered and marginalized, who are not part of the economies of growth, progress and profit. It thus amplifies recognition of the connections between racism, economic and social exclusion, violence and the continuing effects of environmental racism. Especially important are the vulnerable urban and rural communities that are exposed to contaminated environmental conditions, such as polluted water supplies, toxic grounds and air, as well as reduced health services and general impoverishment.

In that way, even a crisis like COVID-19 contains an affirmative nucleus, in that it manifests the rhizomatic entanglements and connections between viruses, climate change, racism and poverty, affecting specific groups of people. A chain reaction is triggered that is central to the effects of the pandemic. These complex entanglements drive home an important and positive truth of the inextricability of social and environmental factors. A 'global syndemic' (Adamson and Hartman, 2020) allows us to see the shared social, biological and historical drivers of our societies. As such, the pandemic is capable of triggering unplanned transformative changes in the ways we live and work together. Confronted by such injustices, and the mirroring pandemics of the virus and of racism and xenophobia, contemporary feminist scholars need to work towards a posthuman ethics of accountability, transversal and cross-species justice. Posthuman feminist scholars should learn the lessons and the neglected wisdom of ancient Indigenous epistemologies and acquire a new sense of community purpose. In this book I have argued that this requires a post-anthropocentric shift, as well as the recognition of mutuality and multi-species interdependence. A feminist new-materialist vision of subjectivity highlights the mutual capacity to affect and be affected by others, thereby stressing the need for collaborative bonds to

Epilogue

address the challenges we face. This call for collaboration neither denies nor belittles the differences of locations, entitlements and resources among different groups. It just aims at building collective responsibility for them.

This praxis of forging communal solutions through the confrontation of uncomfortable truths is central to the ethics of affirmation that I see as an integral part of posthuman feminism. Accepting our shared exposure to ways of living and dying together, amidst environmental and public health human-led disasters, is the starting point to assess what binds us together as an academic community. This is a task for posthuman feminism, operating in a world in pain that reiterates the never-ending nature of the different processes of becoming-human. What the world needs now is materially grounded but differential forms of solidarity and ethical relationality that encompass inclusive ways of caring across a transversal, multi-species spectrum encompassing the entire planet. If we are to change, we need to help one other in seeking sustainable patterns of dis-identification from the familiar. Only such a dis-identification with the dominant definition of the human can nurture new paths of becoming. Changes on this scale can only be enacted together, collectively. Because 'we' – who are not one and the same – are in *this* troubled world, in this painful moment, *together*. And the 'we' here includes the non-human.

Posthuman feminism is non-denominational when it comes to feminist theoretical allegiances. I do not much care what your pet theory is, who your master thinker is, or which feminist philosopher you would rather emulate and step into the shoes of. All that matters now is how much critique and creativity, energy and passion feminist critical thinkers are willing to put into the task of coping with and atoning for, a suffering and wounded world.

The task of posthuman feminism is to activate modes of collaborative interconnectedness, mutual interdependence, care and infinite compassion that may enhance our collective ability to pull through this. The most effective way to get this done is to stay grounded, act local but think global, cultivate affirmation and solidarity, never forget what you owe to infinite others. Keep the transformative rhythm going and the multiple counter-memories of feminist and LGBTQ+ resistance coming. These are the worst of times, these are the best of times. Our task as feminists is to stay grounded, connected and active. Do the most affirmative thing you can do and give it the best you have – for yourself and for the love of the world. Get *a* Life!

Notes

Introduction: Feminism by Any Other Name

1 This is a legendary quote that has become part of popular culture. The source is attributed to: Steinem, Gloria. 1973. The verbal karate of Florynce R. Kennedy, Esq. *Ms. Magazine*, March.

Chapter 1: Feminism Is Not (Only) a Humanism

1 There are many different terms to describe the same phenomenon: Deleuze and Guattari use the terms 'the Majority subject' or the Molar centre of being (1987). Irigaray calls it 'the Same', or the hyper-inflated, falsely universal 'He' (1985b [1977]; 1993 [1984]). Hill Collins calls to account the white and Eurocentric bias of this particular subject of humanistic knowledge (1991). Sylvia Wynter calls it 'Man1' (2015).
2 The story of Odysseus' encounter with Polyphemus and the Cyclops can be found in book 9 of Homer's *Odyssey*.
3 It is significant to remember that Beauvoir herself experienced discrimination in that she was not allowed into the elite 'Grandes Écoles' of the French education system, though she was allowed to attend the Sorbonne university.
4 The first Greenham Common Women's Peace and anti-nuclear Camp in the UK began in September 1981.
5 In the early 1970s several fascist dictatorships still existed in

Europe, notably Spain (1936–74), Portugal (1933–74) and Greece (1967–74).
6 Source: European Commission. 2018. *The Gender Pay Gap in the European Union*, https://ec.europa.eu/info/sites/info/files/aid_development_cooperation_fundamental_rights/equalpayday-eu-factsheets-2018_en.pdf
7 Source: ILO. 2019. Global Wage Report: How Big Is the Gender Gap in Your Country?, *ILO.org*, https://www.ilo.org/global/about-the-ilo/multimedia/maps-and-charts/enhanced/WCMS_650829/lang--en/index.htm
8 Laurie Anderson, *Home of the Brave*, 1986.
9 The subindex Power of the Gender Equality Index 2017 of the European Institute for Gender Equality gets a score of 48.5 per cent, which is the lowest score of all domains. https://eige.europa.eu/sites/default/files/documents/mh051704enn.pdf. The Global Gender Gap Index of the World Economic Forum has a gender disparity gap of 77.1 per cent worldwide. http://www3.weforum.org/docs/WEF_GGGR_2018.pdf
10 Source: EIGE. 2017. Gender Equality Index 2017: Power indicators in EU-28: Data table, *eige.europa.eu*, https://eige.europa.eu/gender-equality-index/2015/domain/power
11 Statistics on the exact rate of female ownership of wealth and assets are widely divergent. The 10 per cent figure was suggested by Oxfam in 2019.
12 With thanks to Premesh Lalu for our ongoing dialogues.

Chapter 2: The Critical Edge of Posthuman Feminism

1 This is changing nowadays in mainstream liberal feminism, however. For instance, international organizations like CEDAW (Convention on the Elimination of All Forms of Discrimination Against Women), are currently proposing a recommendation on women and climate change.
2 https://sheeo.world/about-us/credo/
3 https://www.girlboss.com/
4 https://www.theceomagazine.com/business/finance/the-rise-of-the-fempreneur/
5 https://www.investopedia.com/terms/m/mompreneur.asp
6 With thanks to Djurdja Trajkovic.
7 With thanks to Emily Jones.
8 Rottenberg signals that several Silicon Valley firms cover 'the cost of egg freezing as part of their employees' benefits package' (2018: 97).
9 This digital database is produced by the reduction of a human corpse into thousands of tiny slices.

10 For critical overviews of feminism and postmodernism, see hooks (1990), Nicholson (1990), Braidotti (1991, 2010), Butler and Scott (1992), Johnson (1998), Grewal and Kaplan (2001) and Gamble (2004).

Chapter 3: Decentring Anthropos: Ecofeminism Revisited

1 For an excellent introduction, see Disch and Hawkesworth (2016).
2 But, for a counter-example, see the eco-socialist journal *Climate & Capitalism*: http://climateandcapitalism.com. The life and work of Rosa Luxemburg are also relevant to the discussion between Marxism and environmental destruction.
3 For a feminist take on object-oriented ontology, see Behar (2016).
4 See Ursula Biemann, at https://www.geobodies.org/
5 In projects like 'Geography and the Politics of Mobility', 'The Maghreb Connection' and 'Sahara Chronicle'.
6 See 'Black Sea Files'.
7 See 'Forest Law'.
8 See 'Deep Weather' and 'Subatlantic'.
9 Founded by Nelson Mandela in 2007, The Elders are an independent group of global leaders working together for peace, justice and human rights. https://www.theelders.org/
10 Robinson sponsored the Climate Reframe action, with the input of researchers, campaigners and activists in the climate community, with Aisha Younis and Suzanne Dhaliwal. https://climatereframe.co.uk/ClimateReframe_Download_LR.pdf
11 The project is situated at Doc Society in London, and was funded by the Joseph Rowntree Charitable Trust and the Solberg Foundation. https://climatereframe.co.uk/ClimateReframe_Download_LR.pdf
12 http://landbodydefense.org/

Chapter 4: New Materialism and Carnal Empiricism

1 The continental philosophical tradition of (new) materialism includes, for example, Deleuze (1983), Patton (1993, 2016), Ansell Pearson (1999, 2018), DeLanda (2002, 2016), Patton and Protevi (2003), Daigle (2011), van der Tuin (2011), Vardoulakis (2011) and Ansell Pearson and Protevi (2016). For crossover to other philosophical traditions, see Mullarkey (2006) and Williams (2016).
2 For an analysis of Deleuze's position on the non/in/post-human,

see Braidotti (2013, 2019), Roffe and Stark (2015), Bignall et al. (2016) and Daigle and McDonald (2021).
3 See also the feminist qualitative neuro-research of Wilson (1998, 2004), Stafford (2007), Churchland (2011) and Malabou (2011).
4 The feminist art of the 1960s, 1970s and 1980s, for example Mary Kelly, Judy Chicago, Karen Finley, Eva Hesse, Lucy Lippard, Martha Rosler, Barbara Kruger, explores and expands the tradition of feminist bodily materialism. It does as much as theory to illuminate the concept.
5 For feminist overviews, see Nicholson (1990), Braidotti (1991), Butler and Scott (1992) and Grewal and Kaplan (2001).
6 I am taking George Eliot as an emancipated figure here. The author completed the translation before adopting her pen name, living in Berlin with George Lewes. Flood and Irvine (2019) write: 'If a publisher had taken it up, it would have been the first translation of *The Ethics* into English. But Lewes fell out with publisher Henry Bohn over £25, and the work fell by the wayside while Evans moved on to fiction and her nom de plume with the publication of *Scenes from Clerical Life* in 1857 and *Adam Bede* in 1859. The translation lay forgotten for decades until a few hundred copies were printed for an academic audience in 1980 by the University of Salzburg. Marking what would have been the 200th anniversary of Eliot's birth on Friday (November 22), publisher Princeton University Press has announced it will release a new edition in February 2020'.
7 For the turn to Spinoza in the circles around Louis Althusser, see Matheron (1969), Deleuze (1988a [1970]; 1990 [1968]); Guattari (1995, 2000); Serres (1995, 2008). See also Deleuze and Guattari (1987, 1994); Negri (1991 [1981]); Balibar (1994). As early as 1977 Macherey commented on this change of paradigm, but was not translated into English till 2011. Recent scholarship focusses on the implications of Spinozist materialism for scientific theories such as realism (DeLanda, 2002, 2006, 2016), especially in the Humanities (Citton and Lordon, 2008; Braidotti, 2006, 2019).
8 The English-speaking feminist Spinozist genealogy continues today (James, 2000, 2009; Lord, 2011) and is particularly strong still in Australia with Genevieve Lloyd (1994, 1996); Moira Gatens on Spinoza (1996, 2000) and George Eliot (2009, 2011), and the important *Collective Imaginings* volume (Gatens and Lloyd, 1999). Deleuzian new-materialist Australian scholars include Grosz (1994a, 1994b, 2011, 2017), Armstrong (2009), Colebrook (2000, 2004), MacCormack (2008), Vardoulakis (2011), Colman (2017) and Hicky-Moody (2016).
9 For a detailed comparison of Margulis and Deleuze's respective definitions of life, see Ansell Pearson (1997a, 1997b, 1999), Protevi (2013) and Damasio (2003). For an original elaboration of the connections between Guattari and Margulis, see Parisi (2004).

Notes to pp. 126–58

10 For Deleuze's relationship to Lucretius, see Deleuze (1961, 1966, 1990 [1968]). For Deleuze's stoicism, see Deleuze (1990 [1969]; 1994); Ansell Pearson (2014) and Johnson (2020).

Chapter 5: Technobodies: Gene- and Gender-editing

1 http://www.youtube.com/watch?v=IPh533ht5AU
2 A significant precedent of women engaging with technology is Ada Lovelace's work on maths and computer programming from the nineteenth century.
3 President Trump often referred to his political female opponents as 'nasty women', who then took it up as a badge of honour.
4 See, for instance, the special issues of the following feminist journals: *Hypatia*, 27/3 (2012); *differences*, 23/3 (2012), 25/1 (2014) and 30 (2019) and *The European Journal of Women's Studies*, 17/4 (2010).
5 This resulted, historically, in a significant range of applied empirical studies: of cancer survivors and activists (Singleton and Michael, 1993; Stacey, 1997; Cartwright, 2000), psychiatric patients including those suffering from anorexia (Gremillion, 2003; Orr, 2005), cosmetic surgery consumers (Davis, 1995; Fraser, 2003) including in genital areas (Braun, 2005). There is ample scholarship on women taking hormone replacement therapy (Martin, 1992; Roberts, 2007), but since the 1990s the focus has been on the new reproductive and genetic technologies (Stanworth, 1987; Franklin, 1997; Rapp, 2000; Thompson, 2005; Franklin and Roberts, 2006; McNeil, 2007). It is quite simply a staggering list of achievements that contributed to the setting up of the field of feminist technoscience studies.
6 See also Bleier (1984), Fausto-Sterling (1992 [1985]), Hubbard et al. (1982), Lowe and Hubbard (1983) and Jacobus et al. (1990). Brain and neural sciences were also high on the critical agenda (Schiebinger, 1989; Wilson, 1998).
7 Noteworthy is the gender equality project: *Gendered Innovations in Science, Health and Medicine, Engineering and the Environment*, directed by Londa Schiebinger, with the support of the European Commission and the US National Science Foundation. With thanks to Ineke Klinge.
8 For example, although the Human Genome Project was completed in 2003, after a 13-year effort, genetic material of African descent only makes up 2 per cent of the total (Munshi, 2020). For an Indigenous critique of genomics, see TallBear (2007, 2013).
9 For an incisive discussion of feminist postcolonial technoscience, see Pollock and Subramaniam (2016).

10 With thanks to Mijke van der Drift.
11 The 'sex wars' divided the anti-pornography campaigners from the 'feminists against censorship' front. The pro-pornography lesbians, LGBTQ+ (Rubin, 1984) and trans activists (Califia, 1988) confronted the opponents (Dworkin, 1981, 1987; MacKinnon, 1989). The conflict escalated at the 1982 Barnard College Conference on 'Pleasure and Danger' (Vance, 1984).
12 In the album 'Big science', Warner Brothers, 1982.
13 For enlightening insights, see Young (1984, 2004), Weiss (1999), Diprose (2002), Schott (2010) and Stone (2019).
14 http://www.familyandlaw.eu/tijdschrift/fenr/2019/07/FENR-D-18-00009

Chapter 6: Sexuality Beyond Gender: A Thousand Little Sexes

1 https://artradarjournal.com/2017/11/21/shimmering-country-aboriginal-australian-artists-at-the-met-in-new-york/
2 https://www.fionahillary.com/reverberating-futures
3 http://landbodydefense.org/
4 As Deleuze recommends in his illuminating study (1988b [1987]; 1992 [1990]). For a significant parallel reading of Deleuze and Foucault, see Morar et al. (2016).
5 For general discussions of Foucault and feminism, see Diamond and Quinby (1988); Braidotti (1991); Butler (1990); McNay (1992); Ramazanoglu (1993); Grosz (1994b); Hekman (1996); Taylor and Vintges (2004).
6 See Bartky (1988), Braidotti (1991), Sawicki (1991), Bordo (1999), Oksala (2012) and Stoller (1995).
7 For instance, Haraway (1990, 1997); Cooper (2008); Jones (2010); Braidotti (2013); Cooper and Waldby (2014); Lemm and Vatter (2014); Brown (2015); Repo (2016); Povinelli (2016).
8 See for instance Ti-Grace Atkinson (1974), Kate Millett (1970), Shulamith Firestone (1970), Valerie Solanas (1968), Betty Friedan (1963) and Adrienne Rich (1976).
9 See Irigaray (1985a [1974], 1985b [1977]); Cixous (1975, 1986, 1987); Cixous and Clément (1975); Wittig (1992); Gatens (1991); Grosz (1994b); Braidotti (1994).
10 Early receptions of Irigaray's work on sexual difference honoured this dimension of her work (Braidotti, 1991; Grosz, 1989; Whitford et al., 1994; Gatens, 1996), which were then sidelined. Recent scholarship on Irigaray's work also stresses her materialist sexuate aspects (Stone, 2006; Jones, 2011; Hill, 2016).
11 This is known in Deleuze's scholarship as 'the incorporeal' or 'bodies without organs' (BWO).

12 Luce Irigaray's liquid lover (1991 [1980]); Hélène Cixous on the cosmic lesbian feminine (1987); Clarice Lispector on elemental cross-species feminine passion (1978); Marguérite Duras (1984) and Jeanne Hyvrard (1976).
13 Woolf *The Waves* (1931); Alaimo (2010); Neimanis (2017).
14 https://www.vice.com/en/article/nzq8qd/sticky-fingers-meet-the-oakland-artist-using-fruit-to-explore-female-sexuality
15 https://tarshbates.com/portfolio/t-he-unsettling-eros-of-contact-zones-2015/
16 https://www.honeyandprue.com/about
17 https://www.margheritapevere.com/. With thanks to Marietta Rodomska.
18 https://www.rachelberwick.com/
19 See also Mae Brown (1973).
20 *Lesbian Nation* presents seminal essays like Anne Koedt's 'The myth of vaginal orgasm', Celestine Ware's 'Black feminism' and Mary Daly's 'The spiritual dimension of women's liberation'.
21 The term 'queer theory' was coined by Teresa de Lauretis in 1991 in a special issue of the journal *differences*.
22 See Fausto-Sterling (2000); Butler (2004); Halberstam (2005); Puar (2007); Edelman (2004).
23 This is in keeping with the Spinozist materialism revisited with Deleuze. For a comparison of these two approaches, see Lacan (1998) and Deleuze and Guattari (1977). For feminist introductions to Lacan, see Mitchell (1974); Mitchell and Rose (1985); Brennan (1989); Grosz (1991) and Braidotti (1991). On Deleuze and the unconscious, see Kersake (2007).

Chapter 7: Wanting Out!

1 Jemisin was the first African-American writer to win the prestigious Hugo Award for best fantasy and science fiction in 2016 and two consecutive years after that, for her *Inheritance* trilogy.
2 Feminist opposition to reproductive technologies continued through the 1980s. See Corea (1985); Klein (1989); Arditti et al. (1984); Steinberg and Spallone (1988).
3 Defamiliarization originally refers to the artistic technique of disrupting an audience's expectation of theatre, art or music representation in order to enhance their perception. This was a central strategy in twentieth-century art and theory, from Bertolt Brecht to Dada, postmodernism, punk music and science fiction, culture jamming and trolling.
4 https://trumpwhitehouse.archives.gov/wp-content/uploads/2020/12/National-Space-Policy.pdf
5 With thanks to Emily Jones.

6 In April 2021, NASA announced that the new ARTEMIS lunar landing project (contracted to Elon Musk's SpaceX Company) will send the first woman and first person of colour to the Moon. https://www.nasa.gov/specials/artemis/
7 With a nod to David Bowie.

References

Acker, Kathy. 1990. *In Memoriam to Identity*. New York: Pantheon Books.
Acker, Kathy. 1991. *Hannibal Lecter, My Father*. New York: Semiotext(e) Books.
Acker, Kathy. 1995. The end of the word of white men. In: Judith Halberstam and Ira Livingston (eds.) *Posthuman Bodies*. Bloomington, IN: Indiana University Press.
Acker, Kathy. 1997. *Bodies of Work*. London: Serpent's Tail.
Adams, Carol. 1990. *The Sexual Politics of Meat: A Feminist-Vegetarian Critical Theory*. New York: Continuum.
Adams, Carol. 2018 [1994]. *Neither Beast Nor Man*. London: Bloomsbury Academic.
Adams, Carol and Josephine Donovan (eds.). 1995. *Animals and Women*. Durham, NC: Duke University Press.
Adams, Carol and Lori Gruen (eds.). 2014. *Feminist Intersections with Other Animals and the Earth*. London: Bloomsbury Academic.
Adamson, Joni and Steven Hartman. 2020. From ecology to syndemic: Accounting for the synergy of epidemics. *Bifrost Online*, 8 June. https://bifrostonline.org/joni-adamson-and-steven-hartman/
Adichie, Chimamanda Ngozi. 2014. *We Should All Be Feminists*. London: Fourth Estate.
Ahmed, Sarah. 2004. *The Cultural Politics of Emotion*. Edinburgh: Edinburgh University Press.
Ahmed, Sarah. 2010. *The Promise of Happiness*. Durham, NC: Duke University Press.
Al-Ali, Nadje and Nicola Pratt. 2009. *What Kind of Liberation? Women and the Occupation in Iraq*. Berkeley, CA: University of California Press.

Alaimo, Stacy. 2008. Trans-corporeal feminisms and the ethical space of nature. In: Stacy Alaimo and Susan Hekman (eds.) *Material Feminisms*. Bloomington, IN: Indiana University Press, pp. 237–64.

Alaimo, Stacy. 2010. *Bodily Natures*. Bloomington, IN: Indiana University Press.

Alaimo, Stacy. 2013. Jellyfish science, jellyfish aesthetics: Posthuman reconfigurations of the sensible. In: Janine MacLeod, Cecilia Chen and Astrida Neimanis (eds.) *Thinking with Water*. Montreal: McGill-Queens University Press.

Alaimo, Stacy. 2014. Thinking as the stuff of the world. *O-Zone: A Journal of Object Oriented Studies*, 1.

Alaimo, Stacy. 2016. *Exposed*. Minneapolis, MN: University of Minnesota Press.

Alaimo, Stacy. 2017. Your shell on acid: material immersion, Anthropocene dissolves. In: Richard Grusin (ed.) *Anthropocene Feminism*. Minneapolis, MN: University of Minnesota Press.

Alaimo, Stacy. 2018. Material feminism in the Anthropocene. In: Cecilia Åsberg and Rosi Braidotti (eds.) *A Feminist Companion to the Posthumanities*. Cham: Springer International.

Alaimo, Stacy and Susan Hekman (eds.). 2008. *Material Feminisms*. Bloomington, IN: Indiana University Press.

Alcoff, Linda. 2006. *Visible Identities*. Oxford: Oxford University Press.

Alcoff, Linda. 2015. *The Future of Whiteness*. Cambridge: Polity Press.

Alcoff, Linda and Elizabeth Porter (eds.). 1993. *Feminist Epistemologies*. London and New York: Routledge.

Allen, Irma Kinga. 2020. Thinking with a feminist political ecology of air-and-breathing-bodies. *Body and Society*, 26/2, 79–105.

Amaro, Ramon. 2018. Afrofuturism. In: Rosi Braidotti and Maria Hlavajova (eds.) *Posthuman Glossary*. London: Bloomsbury Academic.

Anderson, Ben. 2009. Affective atmospheres. *Emotion, Space and Society*, 2/2, 77–81.

Ang, Ien. 2019. Museum and cultural diversity: A persistent challenge. In: Kirsten Drotner, Vince Dziekan, Ross Parry and Kim Christian Schroder (eds.) *The Routledge Handbook of Museums, Media and Communication*. London and New York: Routledge.

Angelou, Maya. 1978. 'Phenomenal woman' and 'Still, I rise'. In: *And Still I Rise*. New York: Random House.

Ansell Pearson, Keith. 1997a. *Viroid Life*. London and New York: Routledge.

Ansell Pearson, Keith. 1997b. Viroid life: On machines, technics and evolution. In: Keith Ansell Pearson (ed.) *Deleuze and Philosophy*. London and New York: Routledge.

Ansell Pearson, Keith. 1999. *Germinal Life*. London and New York: Routledge.

Ansell Pearson, Keith. 2014. Affirmative naturalism: Deleuze and

Epicureanism. *Cosmos and History: The Journal of Natural and Social Philosophy*, 10/2, 121–37.

Ansell Pearson, Keith. 2018. *Bergson: Thinking Beyond the Human Condition*. London: Bloomsbury Academic.

Ansell Pearson, Keith and John Protevi. 2016. Naturalism in the Continental tradition. In: Kelly James Clark (ed.) *Blackwell Companion to Naturalism*. Oxford: John Wiley & Sons.

Anzaldúa, Gloria. 1987. *Borderlands/La Frontera: The New Mestiza*. San Francisco, CA: Aunt Lute.

Arbus, Diane. 1972. *Diane Arbus*. New York: Millerton.

Arditti, Rita, Renate Klein and Shelley Minden (eds.). 1984. *Test Tube Women*. London: Pandora.

Armstrong, Aurelia. 2009. Autonomy and the relational individual. Spinoza and feminism. In: Moira Gatens (ed.) *Feminist Interpretations of Benedict Spinoza*. University Park, PA: University of Pennsylvania Press.

Armstrong, Nancy and Warren Montag. 2009. The future of the human: An introduction. *differences*, 20/2–3, 1–8.

Åsberg, Cecilia. 2013. The timely ethics of posthumanist gender studies. *Feministische Studien*, 1, 7–12.

Åsberg, Cecilia. 2018. Feminist posthumanities in the Anthropocene: Forays into the postnatural. *Journal of Posthuman Studies: Philosophy, Technology, Media*, 1/2, 185–204.

Åsberg, Cecilia and Rosi Braidotti. (eds.). 2018. *A Feminist Companion to the Posthumanities*. Cham: Springer International.

Åsberg, Cecilia and Nina Lykke. 2010. Feminist technoscience studies. *European Journal of Women's Studies*, 17/4, 299–305.

Åsberg, Cecilia, Redi Koobak and Ericka Johnson. 2011. Beyond the humanist imagination. *NORA: Nordic Journal of Feminist and Gender Research*, 19/4, 218–230.

Atkinson, Ti-Grace. 1974. *Amazon Odyssey*. New York: Links.

Atwood, Margaret. 1985. *The Handmaid's Tale*. Toronto: Seal Books.

Bagemihl, Bruce. 1999. *Biological Exuberance*. New York: Saint Martin's Press.

Baker, Mona and Bolette Blaagaard (eds.). 2016. *Citizen Media and Public Spaces*. London: Routledge.

Balibar, Etienne. 1994. *Spinoza and Politics*. London: Verso Books.

Balsamo, Anne. 1996. *Technologies of the Gendered Body*. Durham, NC: Duke University Press.

Balzano, Angela. 2020. A biology commodification and women self-determination: Beyond the surrogacy ban. *Italian Sociological Review*, 10/3, 655–77.

Banerji, Debashish and Makarand R. Paranjape (eds.). 2016. *Critical Posthumanism and Planetary Futures*. Cham: Springer International.

Barad, Karen. 2003. Posthumanist performativity: Toward an understanding of how matter comes to matter. *Signs*, 28/3, 801–31.

Barad, Karen. 2007. *Meeting the Universe Half Way*. Durham, NC: Duke University Press.

Barker, Joanna (ed.). 2017. *Critically Sovereign*. Durham, NC: Duke University Press.

Barr, Marleen. 1987. *Alien to Femininity: Speculative Fiction and Feminist Theory*. New York: Greenwood.

Barr, Marlene. 1993. *Lost in Space: Probing Feminist Science Fiction and Beyond*. Chapel Hill, NC: University of North Carolina Press.

Barratt, Virginia, 2016. https://vnsmatrix.net/the-artists

Barrett, Estelle and Barbara Bolt (eds.). 2013. *Carnal Knowledge: Towards a 'New Materialism' Through the Arts*. London: I.B. Tauris.

Barris, Jeremy. 2015. *Sometimes Always True*. New York: Fordham University Press.

Bartky, Sandra Lee. 1988. Foucault, femininity and the modernisation of patriarchal power. In: Irene Diamond and Lee Quinby (eds.) *Feminism & Foucault*. Boston, MA: Northeastern University Press.

Baudrillard, Jean. 1988. *The Ecstasy of Communication*. New York: Semiotext(e).

Beauvoir, Simone de. 1973 [1949]. *The Second Sex*. New York: Bantam Books.

Bechdel, Alison. 2007. *Fun Home*. Boston, MA: Houghton Mifflin Company.

Behar, Katherine (ed.). 2016. *Object-Oriented Feminism*. Minneapolis, MN: University of Minnesota Press.

Benjamin, Jessica. 1988. *The Bonds of Love*. New York: Pantheon Books.

Benjamin, Ruha. 2019. *Race after Technology*. Cambridge: Polity Press.

Bennett, Jane. 2010. *Vibrant Matter*. Durham, NC: Duke University Press.

Benterrak, Krim, Stephen Muecke and Paddy Roe. 1983. *Reading the Country: Introduction to Nomadology*. Melbourne: re.press.

Berlant, Lauren. 2011. *Cruel Optimism*. Durham, NC: Duke University Press.

Bernstein, Elizabeth. 2012. Carceral politics as gender justice? The 'traffic in women' and neoliberal circuits of crime, sex, and rights. *Theory and Society*, 41/3, 233–59.

Bertotti, Sara, Gina Heathcote, Emily Jones and Sheri Labenski. 2020. *The Law of War and Peace: A Gender Analysis (Volume 1)*. London: Zed Books.

Bhabha, Homi. 1994. *The Location of Culture*. London and New York: Routledge.

Bhattacharyya, Gargi. 2018. *Rethinking Racial Capitalism*. London: Rowman and Littlefield.

Bignall, Simone. 2010. *Postcolonial Agency: Critique and Constructivism*. Edinburgh: Edinburgh University Press.

Bignall, Simone and Paul Patton (eds.). 2010. *Deleuze and the Postcolonial*. Edinburgh: Edinburgh University Press.

Bignall, Simone and Daryle Rigney. 2019. Indigeneity, posthumanism and nomad thought: Transforming colonial ecologies. In: Rosi Braidotti and Simone Bignall (eds.) *Posthuman Ecologies*. London: Rowman & Littlefield.

Bignall, Simone, Steve Hemming and Daryle Rigney. 2016. Three ecosophies for the Anthropocene: Environmental governance, continental posthumanism and indigenous expressivism. *Deleuze Studies*, 10/4, 455–78.

Bikini Kill. 1991. The Riot Grrrl Manifesto. *BIKINI KILL ZINE*, 2. https://www.historyisaweapon.com/defcon1/riotgrrrlmanifesto.html

Birke, Lynda. 1980. *Alice Through the Microscope*. London: Virago.

Birke, Lynda. 1986. *Women, Feminism and Biology: The Feminist Challenge*. Hemel Hempstead: Harvester Wheatsheaf.

Birke, Lynda. 2000. *Feminism and the Biological Body*. Edinburgh: Edinburgh University Press.

Birke, Lynda and Tora Holmberg. 2018. Intersections: The animal question meets feminist theory. In: Cecilia Åsberg and Rosi Braidotti (eds.) *A Feminist Companion to the Posthumanities*. Cham: Springer International.

Birke, Lynda, Mette Bryld and Nina Lykke. 2004. Animal performances: An exploration of intersections between feminist science studies and studies of human/animal relationships. *Feminist Theory*, 2/5, 167–83.

Bleier, Ruth. 1984. *Science and Gender*. New York: Pergamon Press.

Bobel, Chris, Inga T. Winkler, Breanne Fahs, Katie Ann Hasson, Elizabeth Arveda Kissling and Tomi-Ann Roberts (eds.). 2020. *The Palgrave Handbook of Critical Menstruation Studies*. London: Palgrave Macmillan.

Bonta, Mark and John Protevi. 2004. *Deleuze and Geophilosophy: A Guide and Glossary*. Edinburgh: Edinburgh University Press.

Bordo, Susan. 1987. *The Flight to Objectivity*. Albany, NY: SUNY Press.

Bordo, Susan. 1993. *Unbearable Weight: Feminism, Western Culture and the Body*. Berkeley, CA: University of California Press.

Bordo, Sandra. 1999. *Feminism, Foucault and the Politics of the Body*. London and New York: Routledge.

Boston Women's Health Collective. 1970. *Our Bodies Ourselves*. Boston, MA: New England Press.

Bostrom, Nick. 2014. *Superintelligence: Paths, Dangers, Strategies*. Oxford: Oxford University Press.

Bozalek, Vivienne, Rosi Braidotti, Tamara Shefer and Michalinos Zembylas (eds.). 2018. *Socially Just Pedagogies: Posthumanist, Feminist and Materialist Perspectives in Higher Education*. London: Bloomsbury Academic.

Brah, Avtar. 1996. *Cartographies of Diaspora: Contesting Identities*. New York and London: Routledge.

Braidotti, Rosi. 1991. *Patterns of Dissonance*. Cambridge: Polity Press/ New York: Routledge.
Braidotti, Rosi. 1994. *Nomadic Subjects: Embodiment and Sexual Difference in Contemporary Feminist Theory*. New York: Columbia University Press.
Braidotti. Rosi. 1996. Cyberfeminism with a difference. *New Formations*, 29, 9–25.
Braidotti, Rosi. 2002. *Metamorphoses: Towards a Materialist Theory of Becoming*. Cambridge: Polity Press.
Braidotti, Rosi. 2006. *Transpositions: On Nomadic Ethics*. Cambridge: Polity Press.
Braidotti, Rosi. 2008. In spite of the times: The postsecular turn in feminism. *Theory, Culture and Society*, 25/6, 1–24.
Braidotti, Rosi. 2010. *The History of Continental Philosophy*. Volume 7. *After Poststructuralism: Transitions and Transformations*. Chicago, IL: Chicago University Press.
Braidotti, Rosi. 2011a. *Nomadic Subjects: Embodiment and Sexual Difference in Contemporary Feminist Theory*, 2nd edn. New York: Columbia University Press.
Braidotti, Rosi. 2011b. *Nomadic Theory*. New York: Columbia University Press.
Braidotti, Rosi. 2012. The society of undutiful daughters. In: Henriette Gunkel, Chrysanthi Nigianni and Fanny Söderbäck (eds.) *Undutiful Daughters: New Directions in Feminist Thought and Practice*. London: Palgrave Macmillan.
Braidotti, Rosi. 2013. *The Posthuman*. Cambridge: Polity Press.
Braidotti, Rosi. 2018. A theoretical framework for the critical posthumanities. *Theory, Culture & Society*, 36/6, 31–61.
Braidotti, Rosi. 2019. *Posthuman Knowledge*. Cambridge: Polity Press.
Braidotti, Rosi and Simone Bignall (eds.). 2019. *Posthuman Ecologies*. New York: Rowman and Littlefield.
Braidotti, Rosi and Maria Hlavajova (eds.). 2018. *Posthuman Glossary*. London: Bloomsbury Academic.
Braidotti, Rosi and Griet Roets. 2012. Nomadology and subjectivity: Deleuze, Guattari and Critical Disability Studies. In: Dan Goodley, Bill Hughes and Lennard Davis (eds.) *Disability and Social Theory: New Developments and Directions*. New York: Palgrave Macmillan, pp. 161–78.
Braidotti, Rosi, Ewa Charkiewicz, Sabine Hausler and Saskia Wieringa. 1994. *Women, the Environment and Sustainable Development: Towards a Theoretical Synthesis*. London: Zed Books.
Braun, Virginia. 2005. In search of (better) sexual pleasure: Female genital 'cosmetic' surgery. *Sexualities*, 8/4, 407–24.
Brennan, Teresa (ed.). 1989. *Between Feminism and Psychoanalysis*. London: Routledge.

References

Brown, Wendy. 2006. *Regulating Aversion*. Princeton, NJ: Princeton University Press.
Brown, Wendy. 2015. *Undoing the Demos: Neoliberalism's Stealth Revolution*. New York: Zone Books.
Brownmiller, Susan. 1975. *Against Our Will: Men, Women and Rape*. New York: Simon & Schuster.
Bryld, Mette and Nina Lykke. 2000. *Cosmodolphins: Feminist Cultural Studies of Technologies, Animals and the Sacred*. London: Zed Books.
Buikema, Rosemarie, Nina Lykke and Gabriele Griffin (eds.). 2011. *Theories and Methodologies in Postgraduate Feminist Research: Researching Differently*. London and New York: Routledge.
Bukatman, Scott. 1993. *Terminal Identity: The Virtual Subject in Postmodern Science Fiction*. Durham, NC: Duke University Press.
Bunch, Charlotte. 1987. *Passionate Politics: Feminist Theory in Action*. New York: St. Martin's Press.
Burns, Lorna and Birgit Kaiser (eds.). 2012. *Postcolonial Literatures and Deleuze: Colonial Pasts, Differential Futures*. London: Palgrave Macmillan.
Butler, Judith. 1990. *Gender Trouble*. London and New York: Routledge.
Butler, Judith. 1997. *Excitable Speech*. New York and London: Routledge.
Butler, Judith. 2004. *Undoing Gender*. London and New York: Routledge.
Butler, Judith and Joan W. Scott. 1992. *Feminists Theorize the Political*. New York: Routledge.
Butler, Octavia. 1979. *Kindred*. New York: Doubleday.
Butler, Octavia. 1987. *Dawn*. New York: Little Brown & Company.
Byrd, Jodi. 2011. *The Transit of Empire. Indigenous Critiques of Colonialism*. Minneapolis, MN: University of Minnesota Press.
Cadigan, Pat. 1991. *Synners*. London: HarperCollins.
Cajete, Gregory. 2004. *Native Science*. Santa Fe, NM: Clear Light Publishers.
Califia, Pat. 1988. *Macho Sluts*. Boston, MA: Alyson Books.
Carby, Hazel. 1982. White woman listen! Black feminism and the boundaries of sisterhood. In: University of Birmingham Centre for Contemporary Cultural Studies (ed.) *The Empire Strikes Back*. London: Hutchinson.
Carson, Rachel. 1962. *Silent Spring*. New York: Houghton Mifflin.
Cartwright, Laura. 2000. Community and the public body in breast cancer media. In: Janine Marchessault and Kim Sawchuk (eds.) *Wild Science: Reading Feminism, Medicine and the Media*. London and New York: Routledge, pp. 120–38.
Césaire, Aimé. 2000 [1955]. *Discours sur le colonialisme*. Paris: Présence Africaine.

Chakrabarty, Dipesh. 2009. The climate of history: Four theses. *Critical Enquiry*, 35, 197–222.
Chanter, Tina. 1995. *Ethics of Eros*. London and New York: Routledge.
Chemaly, Soraya. 2019. How women and minorities are claiming their right to rage. *The Guardian*, 11 May.
Chen, Mel Y. 2012. *Animacies: Biopolitics, Racial Mattering, and Queer Affect*. Durham, NC: Duke University Press.
Chen, Mel Y. 2013. Animals without genitals: Race and transubstantiation. In: Susan Stryker and Aren Z. Aizura (eds.) *The Transgender Studies Reader 2*. New York and London: Routledge
Chen, Mel Y. 2015. Unpacking intoxication, racializing disability. *Medical Humanities*, 41, 25–9.
Chen, Mel Y. 2020. Feminisms in the air. *Signs*, Autumn. http://signsjournal.org/covid/chen/
Chen, Mel Y. and Dana Luciano (eds.) 2015. Queer inhumanisms. *GLQ: A Journal of Lesbian and Gay Studies*, 21/2–3.
Chodorow, Nancy. 1988. *The Reproduction of Mothering*. Berkeley, CA: University of California Press.
Chow, Rey. 2010. Postcolonial visibilities: Questions inspired by Deleuze's method. In: Simone Bignall and Paul Patton (eds.) *Deleuze and the Postcolonial*. Edinburgh: Edinburgh University Press.
Chun, Wendy. 2021. *Discriminating Data*. Cambridge, MA: MIT Press.
Churchland, Patricia. 2011. *Braintrust: What Neuroscience Tells Us About Morality*. Princeton, NJ: Princeton University Press.
Cielemęcka, Olga and Cecilia Åsberg. 2019. Toxic embodiment and feminist environmental humanities. *Environmental Humanities*, 11, 101–7.
Cipolla, Cyd, Kristina Gupta, David A. Rubin and Angela Willey (eds.). 2017. *Queer Feminist Science Studies: A Reader*. Seattle, WA: University of Washington Press.
Citton, Yves and Frédéric Lordon. 2008. *Spinoza et les sciences sociales: de la puissance de la multitude à l'économie politique des affects*. Paris: Éditions Amsterdam.
Cixous, Hélène. 1975. Le rire de la Meduse. *L'Arc*, 61, 39–54.
Cixous, Hélène. 1986. *Entre l'Écriture*. Paris: des femmes.
Cixous, Hélène. 1987. *Le Livre de Promethea*. Paris: Gallimard.
Cixous, Hélène and Catherine Clément. 1975. *La Jeune Née*. Paris: U.G.E.
Clark, Nigel. 2008. Aboriginal cosmopolitanism. *International Journal of Urban and Regional Research*, 32/3, 737–44.
Clark, Nigel. 2016. Politics of strata. *Theory, Culture & Society*, 34/2–3, 211–31.
Clarke, Andy. 1997. *Being There: Putting Brain, Body and World Together Again*. Cambridge, MA: MIT Press.

Clarke, Andy. 2008. *Supersizing the Mind: Embodiment, Action and Cognitive Extension*. Oxford: Oxford University Press.

Clarke, Andy and David Chalmers. 1998. The extended mind. *Analysis*, 58/1, 7–19.

Clarke, Bruce. 2008. *Posthuman Metamorphosis*. New York: Fordham University Press.

Clarke, Bruce. 2020. *Gaian Systems*. Minneapolis, MN: University of Minnesota Press.

Cloud, Dana L. 2004. 'To veil the threat of terror': Afghan women and the 'clash of civilizations' in the imagery of the US war on terrorism. *Quarterly Journal of Speech*, 90/3, 285–306.

Clough, Patricia Ticineto with Jean Halley. 2007. *The Affective Turn: Theorizing the Social*. Durham, NC: Duke University Press.

Code, Lorraine. 2006. *Ecological Thinking: The Politics of Epistemic Location*. Oxford: Oxford University Press.

Cohen, Jeffrey Jerome and Lowell Duckert (eds.). 2018. *Elemental Ecocriticism*. Minneapolis, MN: University of Minnesota Press.

Cohn, Simon and Rebecca Lynch (eds.). 2018. *Posthumanism and Public Health*. London and New York: Routledge.

Colebrook, Claire. 2000. Is sexual difference a problem? In: Ian Buchanan and Claire Colebrook (eds.) *Deleuze and Feminist Theory*. Edinburgh: Edinburgh University Press.

Colebrook, Claire. 2004. Postmodernism is a humanism: Deleuze and equivocity. *Women: A Cultural Review*, 15/3, 283–307.

Colebrook, Claire. 2014a. *Death of the Posthuman*. Ann Arbor, MI: Open Humanities Press/University of Michigan Press.

Colebrook, Claire. 2014b. *Sex After Life*. Ann Arbor, MI: Open Humanities Press/University of Michigan Press.

Colman, Felicity. 2014. Digital feminicity: Predication and measurement, materialist informatics and images. *Artnodes*, 14. https://doi.org/10.7238/a.v0i14.2408

Colman, Felicity. 2017. Affectology: On desiring an affect of one's own. In: Marie-Luise Angerer (ed.) *Ecology of Affect: Intensive Milieus and Contingent Encounters*. Lüneburg: Meson Press.

Combahee River Collective. 1979. The Combahee River Collective Statement. In: Zillah Eisenstein (ed.) *Capitalist Patriarchy and the Case for Socialist Feminism*. New York: Monthly Review Press.

Coole, Diana and Samantha Frost. 2010. *New Materialisms: Ontology, Agency, and Politics*. Durham, NC: Duke University Press.

Cooper, Melinda. 2008. *Life as Surplus: Biotechnology & Capitalism in the Neoliberal Era*. Seattle, WA: University of Washington Press.

Cooper, Melinda. 2009. The silent scream: Agamben, Deleuze and the politics of the unborn. In: Rosi Braidotti, Claire Colebrook and Patrick Hanafin (eds.) *Deleuze and Law: Forensic Futures*. London: Palgrave Macmillan, pp. 142–62.

Cooper, Melinda, 2017. *Family Values*. Cambridge, MA: Zone Books/ MIT Press.
Cooper, Melinda and Catherine Waldby. 2014. *Clinical Labor*. Durham, NC: Duke University Press.
Corea, Gina. 1985. *The Mother Machine*. New York: Harper and Row.
Coward, Rosalind and John Ellis. 2016 [1977]. *Language and Materialism*. London and New York: Routledge.
Creed, Barbara. 1993. *The Monstrous-Feminine: Film, Feminism, Psychoanalysis*. New York and London: Routledge.
Crenshaw, Kimberle. 1991. Mapping the margins: Intersectionality, identity politics, and violence against women of color. *Stanford Law Review*, 43/6, 1241–99.
Crenshaw, Kimberle, Neil Gotanda, Gary Peller and Thomas Kendall (eds.). 1995. *Critical Race Theory*. New York: The New Press.
Cristoforetti, Samantha. 2020. *Diary of an Apprentice Astronaut*. Harmondsworth: Penguin.
Crosby, Alfred W. 1986. *Ecological Imperialism*. Cambridge: Cambridge University Press.
Cudworth, Erika and Stephen Hobden. 2017. *The Emancipatory Project of Posthumanism*. London and New York: Routledge.
Cusset, François. 2008. *French Theory*. Minneapolis, MN: University of Minnesota Press.
D'Amico, Debby. 2000 [1971]. To my white working class sisters. In: Barbara A. Crow (ed.) *Radical Feminism: A Documentary Reader*. New York: New York University Press.
D'Eaubonne, Françoise. 1974. *Le feminisme ou la mort*. Paris: Horay.
D'Ignazio, Catherine and Lauren Klein. 2020. *Data Feminism*. Cambridge, MA: MIT Press
Daigle, Christine. 2011. Nietzsche's notion of embodied self: Proto-phenomenology at work? *Nietzsche Studien Gesamtregister Bände 1–20*, 40/1, 226–43.
Daigle, Christine and Terrance H. McDonald 2021. *From Deleuze and Guattari to Posthumanisms*. London: Bloomsbury Academic.
Damasio, Antonio. 2003. *Looking for Spinoza*. Orlando, FL: Harcourt.
Danowski, Déborah and Eduardo Viveiros de Castro. 2017. *The Ends of the World*. Cambridge: Polity Press.
Davies, Tony. 1997. *Humanism*. London and New York: Routledge.
Davis, Angela. 1981. *Women, Race, & Class*. New York: Vintage Books.
Davis, Heather and Etienne Turpin. 2015. *Art in the Anthropocene*. London: Open Humanities Press.
Davis, Kathy. 1995. *Reshaping the Female Body: The Dilemma of Cosmetic Surgery*. London and New York: Routledge.
Dawkins, Richard. 1989. *The Selfish Gene*. Oxford: Oxford University Press.
De Fontenay, Elisabeth. 2001 [1981]. *Diderot ou le Matérialisme Enchanté*. Paris: Grasset.

de Lauretis, Teresa. 1991. Queer theory. Lesbian and gay sexualities: An introduction. *differences*, 3/2, iii–xviii.
De Sutter, Laurent. 2018. *Narcocapitalism*. Cambridge: Polity.
de Waal, Frans. 1996. *Good Natured*. Cambridge, MA: Harvard University Press.
Deitch, Jeffrey. 1992. *Post Human*. Athens, Greece: Cantz Deste Foundation for Contemporary Art.
DeLanda, Manuel. 2002. *Intensive Science and Virtual Philosophy*. London: Bloomsbury Academic.
DeLanda, Manuel. 2006. *A New Philosophy of Society: Assemblage Theory and Social Complexity*. London: Bloomsbury Academic.
DeLanda, Manuel. 2016. *Assemblage Theory*. Edinburgh. Edinburgh University Press.
Deleuze, Gilles. 1961. Lucrèce et le naturalisme. *Études philosophiques*, 1, 19–29.
Deleuze, Gilles. 1966. Renverser le platonisme (Les simulacres). *Revue de Métaphysique et de Morale*, 71, 426–38.
Deleuze, Gilles. 1983. *Nietzsche and Philosophy*. New York: Columbia University Press.
Deleuze, Gilles. 1988a [1970]. *Spinoza: Practical Philosophy*. San Francisco, CA: City Lights Books.
Deleuze. Gilles. 1988b [1987]. *Foucault*. Minneapolis, MN: University of Minnesota Press.
Deleuze, Gilles. 1990 [1968]. *Expressionism in Philosophy: Spinoza*. New York: Zone Books.
Deleuze, Gilles. 1990 [1969]. *The Logic of Sense*. New York: Columbia University Press.
Deleuze, Gilles. 1992 [1990]. Postscript on the societies of control. *October*, 59, 3–7.
Deleuze, Gilles. 1993. *The Fold: Leibniz and the Baroque*. Minneapolis, MN: University of Minnesota Press.
Deleuze, Gilles. 1994. *Difference and Repetition*. London: Athlone Press.
Deleuze, Gilles. 1998. *Essays Critical and Clinical*. London: Verso Books.
Deleuze, Gilles. 2003. *Pure Immanence: Essays on a Life*. New York: Zone Books.
Deleuze, Gilles and Felix Guattari. 1977. *Anti-Oedipus*. New York: Viking Press.
Deleuze, Gilles and Felix Guattari. 1987. *A Thousand Plateaus: Capitalism and Schizophrenia*. Minneapolis, MN: University of Minnesota Press.
Deleuze, Gilles and Felix Guattari. 1994. *What is Philosophy?* New York: Columbia University Press.
Della Costa, Mariarosa and Selma James. 1972. *The Power of Women and the Subversion of the Community*. London: Butler and Tanner.

Dement, Linda. 2017. Cyberfeminist bedsheet. *Artlink*, 1 December. https://www.artlink.com.au/articles/4647/cyberfeminist-bedsheet/

Denike, Margaret. 2008. The human rights of others: Sovereignty, legitimacy, and 'just causes' for the 'war on terror'. *Hypatia*, 23, 95–121.

Derrida, Jacques, 1981. *Dissemination*. London: Athlone Press.

Derrida, Jacques. 1984. No apocalypse, not now. *Diacritics*, 14/2, 20–31.

Derrida, Jacques. 2002. The animal that therefore I am (more to follow). *Critical Inquiry*, 28/2, 369–418.

Derrida, Jacques. 2006. Is there a philosophical language? In: Lasse Thomassen (ed.) *The Derrida-Habermas Reader*. Edinburgh: Edinburgh University Press.

Descola, Philippe. 2009. Human natures. *Social Anthropology*, 17/2, 145–57.

Descola, Philippe. 2013. *Beyond Nature and Culture*. Chicago, IL: University of Chicago Press.

Diamond, Irene and Lee Quinby (eds.). 1988. *Feminism & Foucault*. Boston, MA: Northeastern University Press.

Diprose, Rosalind. 2002. *Corporeal Generosity*. Albany, NY: SUNY Press.

Disch, Lisa and Mary Hawkesworth (eds.). 2016. *Oxford Handbook of Feminist Theory*. Oxford: Oxford University Press.

Dolphijn, Rick and Iris van der Tuin. 2012. *New Materialism: Interviews & Cartographies*. Ann Arbor, MI: Open Humanities Press.

Donovan, Josephine. 1990. Animal rights and feminist theory. *Signs*, 15/2, 350–75.

Donovan, Josephine and Carol J. Adams (eds.). 1996. *Beyond Animal Rights: A Feminist Caring Ethic for the Treatment of Animals*. New York: Continuum.

Donovan, Josephine and Carol J. Adams (eds.). 2007. *The Feminist Care Tradition in Animal Ethics*. New York: Columbia University Press.

Duden, Barbara. 1998. *Woman Beneath the Skin*. Harvard, MA: Harvard University Press.

Duffy, Simon. 2010. French and Italian Spinozism. In: Rosi Braidotti (ed.) *After Post-Structuralism*. Vol 7 of Alan Schrift (ed.) *The History of Continental Philosophy*. Chicago, IL: University of Chicago Press.

Duras, Marguérite. 1984. *L'Amant*. Paris: Editions de Minuit.

Duyvendak, Jan Willem. 1996. The depoliticization of the Dutch gay identity, or why Dutch gays aren't queer. In: Steven Seidman (ed.) *Queer Theory/Sociology*. Cambridge: Blackwell.

Dworkin, Andrea. 1981. *Pornography: Men Possessing Women*. New York: G.P. Putnam's Sons.

Dworkin, Andrea. 1987. *Intercourse*. New York: Free Press.

Edelman, Lee. 2004. *No Future: Queer Theory and the Death Drive*. Durham, NC: Duke University Press.
Ehrenreich, Barbara. 2009. *Smile or Die: How Positive Thinking Fooled America and the World*. London: Granta.
Ehrenreich, Barbara and Dierdre English. 1978. *For Her Own Good: 150 Years of the Experts' Advice to Women*. New York: Anchor Press.
Ehrenreich, Barbara and Arlie Russell Hochschild. 2002. *Global Woman: Nannies, Maids and Sex Workers in the New Economy*. New York: Metropolitan Books.
Eisenstein, Hester. 2005. A dangerous liaison? Feminism and corporate globalization. *Science & Society*, 69/3, 487–518.
Eisenstein, Hester. 2009. *Feminism Seduced: How Global Elites Use Women's Labor and Ideas to Exploit the World*. Boulder, CO: Paradigm Publishers.
Eisenstein, Zillah. 1998. *Global Obscenities: Patriarchy, Capitalism and the Lure of Cyberfantasy*. New York: New York University Press.
Elshtain, Jean Bethke. 1981. *Public Man, Private Woman*. Princeton, NJ: Princeton University Press.
Elton, C.S. 2000 [1958]. *The Ecology of Invasions by Animals and Plants*. Chicago, IL: Chicago University Press.
Engle, Karen. 2019. Feminist governance and international law: From liberal to carceral feminism. In: Janet Halley, Prabha Kotiswaran, Rachel Rebouché and Hila Shamir (eds.) *Governance Feminism: Notes for the Field 3*. Minneapolis, MN: University of Minnesota Press.
Enke, Finn. A. 2013. The education of little cis. Cisgender and the discipline of opposing. In: Susan Stryker and Aren Z. Aizura (eds.) *The Transgender Studies Reader 2*. New York and London: Routledge
Enloe, Cynthia. 2020. Femininity and the paradox of trust building in patriarchies during COVID-19. *Signs*, Autumn. http://signsjournal.org/covid/enloe/
Erickson-Scroth, Laura. 2014. *Trans Bodies, Trans Selves: A Resource for the Transgender Community*. Oxford: Oxford University Press.
Eshun, Kodwo. 2003. Further considerations of Afrofuturism. *The New Centennial Review*, 3/2, 287–302.
Eshun, Kodwo. 2018. *More Brilliant than the Sun: Adventures in Sonic Fiction*, 2nd edn. London: Verso.
Esposito, Roberto. 2002. *Immunitas: The Protection and Negation of Life*. Cambridge: Polity Press.
Esposito, Roberto. 2008. *Bios: Biopolitics and Philosophy*. Minneapolis, MN: University of Minnesota Press.
Essed, Philomena. 1991. *Understanding Everyday Racism*. London: Sage.
Evaristo, Bernardine. 2019. *Girl, Woman, Other*. London: Hamish Hamilton.

Fanon, Frantz. 1963 [1961]. *The Wretched of the Earth*. London: Penguin.
Farris, Sara. 2017. *In the Name of Women's Rights. The Rise of Femonationalism*. Durham, NC: Duke University Press.
Fausto-Sterling, Anne. 1992 [1985]. *Myths of Gender: Biological Theories about Women and Men*. New York: Basic Books.
Fausto-Sterling, Anne. 2000. *Sexing the Body: Gender Politics and Construction of Sexuality*. New York: Basic Books.
Federici, Silvia. 2004. *Caliban and the Witch: Women, the Body and Primitive Accumulation*. Brooklyn, NY: Autonomedia.
Federici, Silvia. 2014. Foreword. In: Maria Mies, *Patriarchy and Accumulation on a World Scale*. London: Zed Books.
Ferguson, Michaele. 2005. 'W' stands for women: Feminism and security rhetoric in the post-9/11 Bush Administration. *Gender and Politics*, 1, 9–38.
Ferrando, Francesca. 2013. Posthumanism, transhumanism, antihumanism, metahumanism, and new materialisms: Differences and relations. *Existenz: An International Journal in Philosophy, Religion, Politics and the Arts*, 8/2, 26–32.
Ferrando, Francesca. 2018. Transhumanism/Posthumanism. In: Rosi Braidotti and Maria Hlavajova (eds.) *Posthuman Glossary*. London: Bloomsbury Academic.
Finlayson, Lorna. 2019. Travelling in the wrong direction. *London Review of Books*, 41/13.
Firestone, Shulamith. 1970. *The Dialectic of Sex*. New York: Bantam Books.
Flax, Jane. 1990. *Thinking Fragments*. Berkeley, CA: University of California Press.
Flood, Alison and Lindesay Irvine. 2019. George Eliot's translation of Spinoza sheds new light on her fiction. *The Guardian*, 22 November.
Foucault, Michel. 1970. *The Order of Things: An Archaeology of Human Sciences*. New York: Pantheon Books.
Foucault, Michel. 1977a. Preface. In: Gilles Deleuze and Felix Guattari, *Anti-Oedipus*. New York: Viking Press.
Foucault, Michel. 1977b. *Discipline and Punish*. New York: Pantheon Books.
Foucault, Michel. 1978. *The Will to Knowledge: The History of Sexuality: 1*. London: Penguin Books.
Foucault, Michel. 2007a. *The Birth of Biopolitics: Lectures at the Collège de France 1978–79*. London: Palgrave.
Foucault, Michel. 2007b. *Security, Territory, Population: Lectures at the Collège de France (1977–1978)*. New York: Palgrave.
Fox Keller, Evelyn. 1984. *A Feeling for the Organism*. New York: Henry Holt.
Fox Keller, Evelyn. 1985. *Reflections on Gender and Science*. New Haven, CT: Yale University Press.

Fox Keller, Evelyn. 2002. *Making Sense of Life*. Cambridge, MA: Harvard University Press.
Fox Keller, Evelyn and Christine R. Grontkowski. 1983. The mind's eye. In: Sandra Harding and Merrill B. Hintikka (eds.) *Discovering Reality*. New York: Springer, pp. 207–24.
Fraiman, Susan. 2012. Pussy panic versus liking animals: Tracking gender in animal studies. *Critical Inquiry*, 39/1, 89–115.
Franklin, Sarah. 1997. *Embodied Progress: A Cultural Account of Assisted Conception*. London and New York: Routledge.
Franklin, Sarah. 2006. The cyborg embryo: Our path to transbiology. *Theory, Culture & Society*, 23/7–8, 167–87.
Franklin, Sarah. 2007. *Dolly Mixtures*. Durham, NC: Duke University Press.
Franklin, Sarah. 2010. Revisiting reprotech: Firestone and the question of technology. In: Mandy Merck and Stella Sanford (eds.) *Further Adventures of the Dialectic of Sex*. London: Palgrave Macmillan.
Franklin, Sarah. 2013. *Biological Relatives*. Durham, NC: Duke University Press.
Franklin, Sarah and Celia Roberts. 2006. *Born and Made: An Ethnography of Preimplantation Genetic Diagnosis*. Princeton, NJ: Princeton University Press.
Franklin, Sarah, Celia Lury and Jackie Stacey (eds.). 1991. *Off-Centre: Feminism and Cultural Studies*. London: HarperCollins.
Franklin, Sarah, Celia Lury and Jackie Stacey. 2000. *Global Nature, Global Culture*. London: Sage.
Fraser, Mariam, Sarah Kember and Celia Lury (eds.). 2006. *Inventive Life: Approaches to the New Vitalism*. London: Sage.
Fraser, Nancy. 2009. Feminism, capitalism and the cunning of history. *New Left Review*, 56, March–April, 97–117.
Fraser, Nancy. 2013. *Fortunes of Feminism*. London: Verso Books.
Fraser, Nancy. 2016. Expropriation and exploitation in racialized capitalism: A reply to Michael Dawson. *Critical Historical Studies*, 3/1: 160–78.
Fraser, Suzanne. 2003. *Cosmetic Surgery, Gender and Culture*. London: Palgrave.
Frawley, Jodi and Iain McCalman (eds.). 2014. *Rethinking Invasion Ecologies from the Environmental Humanities*. London and New York: Routledge.
Freire, Paulo. 2005 [1970]. *Pedagogy of the Oppressed*. London: Continuum.
Freud, Sigmund. 1927. *The Future of an Illusion*. Standard Edition, vol. 21. London: Hogarth Press.
Freud, Sigmund. 2001 [1913]. *Totem and Taboo*. London and New York: Routledge.
Friedan, Betty. 1963. *The Feminine Mystique*. New York: W.W. Norton.

Frost, Samantha. 2016. *Biocultural Creatures*. Durham, NC: Duke University Press.
Fuller, Matthew. 2005. *Media Ecologies: Materialist Energies in Art and Technoculture*. Cambridge, MA: MIT Press.
Fuller, Matthew. 2008. *Software Studies: A Lexicon*. Cambridge, MA: MIT Press.
Fuller, Matthew. 2017. *How to Be a Geek: Essays on the Culture of Software*. Cambridge: Polity Press.
Fuller, Matthew. 2018. *How to Sleep: The Art, Biology and Culture of Unconsciousness*. London: Bloomsbury Academic.
Funk, Nanette. 2013. Contra Fraser on feminism and neoliberalism. *Hypatia*, 28/1, 179–96.
Gaard, Greta. 1993. *Ecofeminism: Women, Animals, Nature*. Philadelphia, PA: Temple University Press.
Gaard, Greta. 1997. Toward a queer ecofeminism. *Hypatia*, 12/1, 114–37.
Gaard, Greta. 2011. Ecofeminism revisited: Rejecting essentialism and re-placing species in a material feminist environmentalism. *Feminist Formations*, 23/2, 26–53.
Gaard, Greta. 2020. Preface. In: Douglas A. Vakoch, *Transecology: Transgender Perspectives on Environment and Nature*. New York and London: Routledge.
Gabrys, Jennifer. 2011. *Digital Rubbish: A Natural History of Electronics*. Ann Arbor, MI: University of Michigan Press.
Gabrys, Jennifer. 2016. *Program Earth: Environmental Sensing Technology and the Making of a Computational Planet*. Minneapolis, MN: University of Minnesota Press.
Gabrys, Jennifer. 2020. Smart forests and data practices: From the Internet of trees to planetary governance. *Big Data and Society*, January–June, 1–10.
Gamble, Sarah (ed.). 2004. *The Routledge Companion to Feminism and Postfeminism*. London and New York: Routledge.
Gatens, Moira. 1983. A critique of the sex/gender distinction. In: Judith Allen and Paul Patton (eds.) *Beyond Marxism: Interventions after Marx*. Sydney: Leichhardt.
Gatens, Moira. 1991. A critique of the sex/gender distinction. In: Sneja Gunew (ed.) *A Reader in Feminist Knowledge*. London and New York: Routledge.
Gatens, Moira. 1996. *Imaginary Bodies*. London and New York: Routledge.
Gatens, Moira, 2000. Feminism as password. The 'possible' with Spinoza and Deleuze. *Hypatia*, 15/2, 59–75.
Gatens, Moira (ed.). 2009. *Feminist Interpretations of Benedict Spinoza*. University Park, PA: Pennsylvania State University Press.
Gatens, Moira, 2011. *Spinoza's Hard Path to Freedom*. Amsterdam: van Gorcum.

Gatens, Moira and Genevieve Lloyd. 1999. *Collective Imaginings: Spinoza, Past and Present*. London and New York: Routledge.
Gay, Roxane. 2014a. *The Bad Feminist*. New York: HarperPerennial.
Gay, Roxane. 2014b. Emma Watson? Jennifer Lawrence? These aren't the feminists you're looking for. *The Guardian*, 10 October. https://www.theguardian.com/commentisfree/2014/oct/10/-sp-jennifer-lawrence-emma-watson-feminists-celebrity
Gay, Roxane. 2014c. Beyoncé's control of her own image belies the bell hooks 'slave' critique. *The Guardian*, 12 May. https://www.theguardian.com/commentisfree/2014/may/12/beyonce-bell-hooks-slave-terrrorist
Geerts, Evelien. 2019. Re-vitalizing the American feminist-philosophical classroom: Transformative academic experimentations with diffractive pedagogies. In: Carol A. Taylor and Anouchka Bayley (eds.) *Posthumanism and Higher Education*. London: Palgrave Macmillan.
Geerts, Evelien and Delphi Carstens. 2019. Ethical onto-epistemology. *Philosophy Today*, 63/4, 915–25.
Genosko, Gary. 2018. Four elements. In: Rosi Braidotti and Maria Hlavajova (eds.) *Posthuman Glossary*. London: Bloomsbury Academic.
George, Susan. 1976. *How the Other Half Dies: The Real Reasons for World Hunger*. London: Penguin.
George, Susan. 1988. *A Fate Worse than Debt*. London: Penguin Books.
George, Susan. 2015. *Shadow Sovereigns*. Cambridge: Polity Press.
Gessen, Masha. 2014. *The Passion of Pussy Riot*. London: Granta.
Gibson, William. 1984. *Neuromancer*. New York: Ace Books.
Gibson, Katherine, Deborah Bird Rose and Ruth Fincher (eds.). 2015. *Manifesto for Living in the Anthropocene*. Brooklyn, NY: Punctum Books.
Giffney, Noreen and Myra J. Hird. 2008. *Queering the Non/Human*. Aldershot: Ashgate.
Gilligan, Carol. 1983. *In a Different Voice*. Cambridge, MA: Harvard University Press.
Gilroy, Paul. 2000. *Against Race: Imaging Political Culture beyond the Colour Line*. Cambridge, MA: Harvard University Press.
Gilroy, Paul. 2004. *After Empire: Melancholia or Convivial Culture?* London: Routledge.
Gilroy, Paul. 2016. Not yet humanism or the non-Jewish Jew becomes the non-humanistic humanist. In: Rosi Braidotti and Paul Gilroy (eds.) *Conflicting Humanities*. London: Bloomsbury.
Glissant, Edouard. 1997. *Poetics of Relation*. Ann Arbor, MI: University of Michigan Press.
Goodley, Dan, Bill Hughes and Lennard Davis (eds.). 2012. *Disability and Social Theory: New Developments and Directions*. London: Palgrave Macmillan.

Goodley, Dan, Rebecca Lawthorn and Katherine Runswick. 2014. Posthuman disability studies. *Subjectivity*, 7/4, 341–61.
Goodley, Dan, Rebecca Lawthorn, Kirsty Liddiard and Katherine Runswick. 2018. Posthuman disability and dishuman studies. In: Rosi Braidotti and Maria Hlavajova (eds.) *Posthuman Glossary*. London: Bloomsbury Academic, pp. 342–5.
Gornick, Vivian and Barbara Moran. 1971. *The Case for Women's Liberation*. New York: Basic Books.
Gottfried, Heidi. 2007. Changing the subject: Labour regulations and gender (in)equality. In: Ilse Lenz, Charlotte Ullrich and Barbara Fersch (eds.) *Gender Orders Unbound?* Farmington Hills, MI: Barbara Budrich.
Gouges, de Olympe. 1791. *Declaration of the Rights of Woman and the Citizen*. https://www.bl.uk/collection-items/the-declaration-of-the-rights-of-woman-and-the-citizen
Gray, John. 2002. *Straw Dogs*. London: Granta Books.
Greenpeace. 2019. *Feeding the Problem: The Dangerous Intensification of Animal Farming in Europe*. https://www.greenpeace.org/eu-unit/issues/nature-food/1803/feeding-problem-dangerous-intensification-animal-farming/
Greer, Germaine. 1971. *The Female Eunuch*. New York: McGraw-Hill.
Gremillion, Helen. 2003. *Feeding Anorexia: Gender and Power at a Treatment Center*. Durham, NC: Duke University Press.
Grewal, Inderpal and Caren Kaplan (eds.) 2001. *Scattered Hegemonies: Postmodernity and Transnational Feminist Practices*. Minneapolis, MN: University of Minnesota Press.
Griffin, Susan. 1978. *Woman and Nature: The Roaring Inside Her*. New York: Harper Colophon Books.
Grimshaw, Jean. 1986. *Philosophy and Feminist Thinking*. Minneapolis, MN: University of Minnesota Press.
Grosz, Elizabeth. 1989. *Sexual Subversions*. Sydney: Allen and Unwin.
Grosz, Elizabeth. 1991. *Jacques Lacan: A Feminist Introduction*. London and New York: Routledge.
Grosz, Elizabeth. 1994a. A thousand tiny sexes: Feminism and rhizomatics. In: Constantin V. Boundas and Dorothea Olkowski (eds.) *Gilles Deleuze and the Theatre of Philosophy*. London and New York: Routledge.
Grosz, Elizabeth. 1994b. *Volatile Bodies: Towards a Corporeal Feminism*. Bloomington, IN: Indiana University Press.
Grosz, Elizabeth. 1995. *Sexy Bodies: The Strange Carnalities of Feminism*. London and New York: Routledge.
Grosz, Elizabeth. 2002. A politics of imperceptibility: A response to 'anti-racism, multiculturalism and the ethics of identification'. *Philosophy and Social Criticism*, 28/4, 463–72.
Grosz, Elizabeth. 2004. *The Nick of Time*. Durham, NC: Duke University Press.

Grosz, Elizabeth. 2011. *Becoming Undone*. Durham, NC: Duke University Press.
Grosz, Elizabeth. 2017. *The Incorporeal: Ontology, Ethics and the Limits of Materialism*. New York: Columbia University Press.
Grove, Richard. 1995. *Green Imperialism*. Cambridge: Cambridge University Press.
Gruber, David. 2019. There is no brain: Rethinking neuroscience through a nomadic ontology. *Body & Society*, 25/2, 56–87.
Gruen, Lori. 1994. Toward an ecofeminist moral epistemology. In: Karen J. Warren (ed.) *Ecological Feminism*. London and New York: Routledge.
Gruen, Lori. 2015. *Entangled Empathy*. New York: Lantern Books.
Grusin, Richard. 2017. *Anthropocene Feminism*. Minneapolis, MN: University of Minnesota Press.
Grytsenko, Oksana. 2020. The stranded babies of Kyiv and the women who give birth for money. *The Guardian*, 15 June.
Guattari, Felix. 1995. *Chaosmosis: An Ethico-Aesthetic Paradigm*. Sydney: Power Press.
Guattari, Felix. 2000. *The Three Ecologies*. London: Athlone Press.
Guillaume, Laura and Joe Hughes (eds.). 2011. *Deleuze and the Body*. Edinburgh: Edinburgh University Press.
Halberstam, Judith. 1998. Between butches. In: Sally R. Munt and Cherry Smyth (eds.) *Butch/Femme: Inside Lesbian Gender*. London: Cassell.
Halberstam, Jack. 2005. *In a Queer Time and Place*. New York: New York University Press.
Halberstam, Jack. 2011. *The Queer Art of Failure*. Durham, NC: Duke University Press.
Halberstam, Jack. 2012. *Gaga Feminism: Sex, Gender and the End of Normal*. Boston, MA: Beacon Press.
Halberstam, Jack. 2018. Gaga feminism. In: Rosi Braidotti and Maria Hlavajova (eds.) *Posthuman Glossary*. London: Bloomsbury Academic.
Halberstam, Judith and Ira Livingston (eds.). 1995. *Posthuman Bodies*. Bloomington, IN: Indiana University Press.
Hall, Stuart. 1996. What is Black in Black popular culture? In: David Morley and Kuan-Hsing Chen (eds.) *Stuart Hall: Critical Dialogues in Cultural Studies*. London and New York: Routledge.
Halley, Janet, Prabha Kotiswaran, Rachel Rebouché and Hila Shamir (eds.). 2019. *Governance Feminism: An Introduction*. Minneapolis, MN: University of Minesota Press.
Hamad, Hannah and Anthea Taylor. 2015. Introduction: feminism and contemporary celebrity culture. *Celebrity Studies*, 6/1, 124–7.
Hammonds, Evelynn. 1994. Black (w)holes and the geometry of black female sexuality. In: Jacqueline Bobo, Cynthia Hudley and Claudine Michel (eds.) *The Black Studies Reader*. London and New York: Routledge.

Hammonds, Evelynn. 2020. A moment or a movement? The Pandemic, political upheaval and racial reckoning. *Signs*, Autumn. http://signsjournal.org/covid/hammonds/

Haraway, Donna. 1985. A manifesto for cyborgs: Science, technology, and socialist feminism in the 1980s. *Socialist Review*, 5/2, 65–108.

Haraway, Donna. 1988. Situated knowledges: The science question in feminism as a site of discourse on the privilege of partial perspective. *Feminist Studies*, 14/3, 575–99.

Haraway, Donna. 1990. *Simians, Cyborgs and Women*. London: Free Association Press.

Haraway, Donna. 1992. The promises of monsters: A regenerative politics for inappropriate/d others. In: Lawrence Grossberg, Cary Nelson and Paula Treichler (eds.) *Cultural Studies*. London and New York: Routledge.

Haraway, Donna. 1997. *Modest_Witness@Second_Millennium. FemaleMan©_Meets_Oncomouse*. London and New York: Routledge.

Haraway, Donna. 2000. *How Like a Leaf. An Interview with Thyrza Nichols Goodeve*. New York and London: Routledge.

Haraway, Donna. 2003. *The Companion Species Manifesto: Dogs, People and Significant Otherness*. Chicago, IL: Prickly Paradigm Press.

Haraway, Donna. 2006. When we have never been human, what is to be done? *Theory, Culture & Society*, 23/7–8, 135–58.

Haraway, Donna. 2016. *Staying with the Trouble: Making Kin in the Chthulucene*. Durham, NC: Duke University Press.

Haraway, Donna. 2017. Symbiogenesis, sympoiesis, and art science activisms for staying with the trouble. In: Anna Tsing, Heather Swanson, Elaine Gan and Nils Bubandt (eds.) *Art of Living on a Damaged Planet*. Minneapolis, MN: University of Minnesota Press.

Harcourt, Wendy. 2016. *Palgrave Handbook of Gender and Development*. London: Palgrave Macmillan.

Harding, Sandra. 1986. *The Science Question in Feminism*. Ithaca, NY: Cornell University Press.

Harding, Sandra. 1991. *Whose Science? Whose Knowledge?* Milton Keynes: Open University Press.

Harding, Sandra. 1993. *The 'Racial' Economy of Science*. Bloomington, IN: Indiana University Press.

Harding, Sandra. 1998. *Is Science Multicultural? Postcolonialisms, Feminisms, and Epistemologies*. Bloomington, IN: Indiana University Press.

Harding, Susan. 2001. *The Book of Jerry Falwell*. Princeton, NJ: Princeton University Press.

Harman, Graham. 2009. *Prince of Networks: Bruno Latour and Metaphysics*. Melbourne: re.press.

References

Harris, Angela. 1990. Race and essentialism in feminist legal theory. *Stanford Law Review*, 42, 581–93.
Hartsock, Nancy. 1987. The feminist standpoint: Developing the ground for a specifically feminist historical materialism. In: Sandra Harding (ed.) *Feminism and Methodology*. London: Open University Press.
Harvey, David. 2006. *Spaces of Global Capitalism*. London: Verso Books.
Hassan, Ihab. 1977. Prometheus as performer: Toward a posthuman culture? Performance in postmodern culture. *The Georgia Review*, 31/4, 830–50.
Hayles, Katherine. 1999. *How We Became Posthuman: Virtual Bodies in Cybernetics, Literature and Informatics*. Chicago, IL: University of Chicago Press.
Hayward, Eva. 2008. More lessons from a starfish: Prefixial flesh and transspeciated selves. *Women's Studies Quarterly*, 36/3–4, 64–85.
Hayward, Eva. 2012. Sensational jellyfish: Aquarium affects and the matter of immersion. *differences*, 23/3, 161–96.
Hayward, Eva and Jamie Weinstein. 2015. Introduction: Transanimalities in the age of trans* life. *TSQ: Transgender Studies Quarterly*, 2/2, 195–208.
Hekman, Susan (ed.). 1996. *Re-Reading the Canon: Feminist Interpretations of Michel Foucault*. University Park, PA: Penn State Press.
Hester, Helen. 2018. *Xenofeminism*. Cambridge: Polity Press.
Hester, Helen. 2019. Sapience+Care. Reason and responsibility in posthuman politics. *Angelaki*, 24, 67–80.
Hicky-Moody, Anna. 2016. *Arts, Pedagogy and Cultural Resistance*. New York: Rowman and Littlefield.
Hill, Rebecca. 2016. The multiple readings of Irigaray's concept of sexual difference. *Philosophy Compass*, 11/7, 390–401.
Hill Collins, Patricia. 1991. *Black Feminist Thought: Knowledge, Consciousness, and the Politics of Empowerment*. London and New York: Routledge.
Hinsliff, Gaby. 2019. The pansexual revolution: How sexual fluidity became mainstream. *The Guardian*, 14 February.
Hird, Myra J. 2006. Animal transex. *Australian Feminist Studies*, 21/49, 35–50.
Hird, Myra J. 2007. The corporeal generosity of maternity. *Body &Society*, 13/1, 1–20.
Hird, Myra J. 2009. *The Origins of Sociable Life: Evolution after Science Studies*. New York: Palgrave Macmillan.
Hird, Myra J. 2013. Animal transex. In: Susan Stryker and Aren Z. Aizura (eds.) *The Transgender Studies Reader 2*. New York and London: Routledge.
Hird, Myra J. and Celia Roberts (eds.). 2011. Feminism theorises the nonhuman. *Feminist Theory*, 12/2, 109–17.

Holmberg, Tora. 2011. Unfamiliar biological futurities: Animals in techno-science. *Humanimalia*, 2/2, 60–6.
hooks, bell. 1981. *Ain't I a Woman*. Boston, MA: South End Press.
hooks, bell. 1990. Postmodern blackness. In: *Yearning: Race, Gender and Cultural Politics*. Toronto: Between the Lines.
hooks, bell. 1992. *Black Looks*. Boston, MA: South End Press.
hooks, bell. 2000. *Feminism is for Everybody*. London: Pluto Press.
hooks, bell. 2016. *Moving Beyond Pain*. Brea College: bell hooks Institute.
Hopkinson, Nalo. 2003. *The Chaos*. New York: Warner Books.
Horl, Erich (ed.). 2017. *General Ecology*. London: Bloomsbury Academic.
Howie, Gillian. 2010. *Between Feminism and Materialism*. London: Palgrave Macmillan.
Hu, Tung-Hui. 2015. *A Prehistory of the Cloud*. Cambridge, MA: MIT Press.
Hubbard, Ruth, Mary Sue Henifin and Barbara Fried (eds.). 1979. *Women Look at Biology Looking at Women*. Cambridge, MA: Schenkman.
Hubbard, Ruth, Mary Sue Henifin and Barbara Fried (eds.). 1982. *Biological Woman: The Convenient Myth*. Cambridge, MA: Schenkman.
Huffer, Lynne. 2016. Foucault's fossils: Life itself and the return to nature in feminist philosophy. In: Hasana Sharp and Chloe Taylor (eds.) *Feminist Philosophies of Life*. Montreal: McGill-Queen's University Press.
Huggan, Graham. 2004. 'Greening' postcolonialism: Ecocritical perspectives. *Modern Fiction Studies*, 50/3, 701–33.
Huggan, Graham and Helen Tiffin. 2007. Green postcolonialism. *interventions*, 9/1, 1–11.
Huggan, Graham and Helen Tiffin (eds.). 2010. *Postcolonial Ecocriticism*. London and New York: Routledge.
Huggins. Jackie. 2001. The gift of identity. *ATSIC News*, February, 44.
Hunt, Krista. 2006. Embedded feminism and the war on terror. In: Krista Hunt and Kim Rygiel (eds.) *(En)Gendering the War on Terror: War Stories and Camouflaged Politics*. Aldershot: Ashgate.
Hyvrard, Jeanne. 1976. *Mère la Mort*. Paris: Editions de Minuit.
Ingold, Tim. 2000. *The Perception of the Environment*. London and New York: Routledge.
Irani, Lily, Janet Vertesi, Paul Dourish and Philip Kavita. 2012. Postcolonial computing: A tactical survey. *Science, Technology, & Human Values*, 37/1, 3–29.
Irigaray, Luce. 1985a [1974]. *Speculum of the Other Woman*. Ithaca, NY: Cornell University Press.
Irigaray, Luce. 1985b [1977]. *This Sex Which Is Not One*. Ithaca, NY: Cornell University Press.

Irigaray, Luce. 1991 [1980]. *Marine Lover.* New York: Columbia University Press.

Irigaray, Luce. 1993 [1984]. *An Ethics of Sexual Difference.* Ithaca, NY: Cornell University Press.

Irigaray, Luce. 1994 [1987]. Equal to Whom? In: Naomi Schor and Elizabeth Weed (eds.) *The Essential Difference.* Bloomington, IN: Indiana University Press.

Irigaray, Luce. 1999 [1983]. *The Forgetting of Air in Martin Heidegger.* Austin, TX: University of Texas Press.

Jackson, Mark (ed.). 2018. *Coloniality, Ontology and the Question of the Posthuman.* London and New York: Routledge.

Jackson, Mark and Maria Fannin. 2011. Letting geography fall where it may – Aerographies address the elemental. *Environment and Planning D: Society and Space,* 29/3, 435–44.

Jackson, Sue, Lee Godden and Katie O'Bryan. 2020. Indigenous water rights and water law reforms in Australia. *Environmental and Planning Law Journal,* 37/6, 655–78.

Jackson, Zakiyyah Imam. 2020. *Becoming Human.* New York: New York University Press.

Jacobus, Mary, Evelyn Fox Keller and Sally Shuttleworth (eds.). 1990. *Body/Politics: Women and the Discourses of Science.* New York: Routledge

Jaggar, Alison. 1983. *Feminist Politics and Human Nature.* Lanham, MD: Rowman & Littlefield.

Jaggar, Alison and Iris M. Young (eds.). 1998. *The Blackwell Companion to Feminist Philosophy.* Oxford: Blackwell.

James, Susan. 2000. The power of Spinoza: Feminist conjunctions. *Hypatia,* 15/2, 40–58.

James, Susan. 2009. Law and sovereignty in Spinoza's politics. In: Moira Gatens (ed.) *Feminist Interpretations of Benedict Spinoza.* University Park, PA: University of Pennsylvania Press.

Jemisin, Nora Keita. 2015. *The Fifth Season.* London: Orbit Books.

Jemisin, Nora Keita. 2016. *The Obelisk Gate.* London: Orbit Books.

Jemisin, Nora Keita. 2017. *The Stone Sky.* London: Orbit Books.

Jenkins, Barbara. 2017. *Eros and Economy: Jung, Deleuze, Sexual Difference.* New York: Routledge.

Johnson, Barbara. 1998. *The Feminist Difference: Literature, Psychoanalysis, Race and Gender.* Cambridge, MA: Harvard University Press.

Johnson, Jill. 1973. *Lesbian Nation: The Feminist Solution.* New York: Simon and Schuster.

Johnson, Ryan J. 2020. *Deleuze, A Stoic.* Edinburgh: Edinburgh University Press.

Jolly, Jasper. 2021. US billionaires vie to make space the next business frontier. *The Guardian,* 6 February.

Jones, Donna V. 2010. *The Racial Discourses of Life Philosophy*. New York: Columbia University Press.
Jones, Emily. 2018a. A posthuman-xenofeminist analysis of the discourse on autonomous weapons systems and other killing machines. *Australian Feminist Law Journal*, 44/1, 93–118.
Jones, Emily. 2018b. A posthuman feminist approach to Mars. *INTLAWGRRLS. Voices on International Law, Policy, Practice*, 17 October.
Jones, Emily. 2019. Feminist technologies and post-capitalism: Defining and reflecting upon xenofeminism. *Feminist Review*, 123/1, 126–34.
Jones, Rachel. 2011. *Irigaray: Towards a Sexuate Philosophy*. Cambridge: Polity Press.
Jordanova, Ludmilla. 1989. *Sexual Visions: Images of Gender in Science and Medicine between the Eighteenth and Twentieth Centuries*. Hemel Hempstead: Harvester Wheatsheaf.
Joy, Eileen. 2015. Improbable manners of being. *GLQ: A Journal of Lesbian and Gay Studies*, 21/2–3, 221–4.
Judt, Tony, 2005. *Post War: A History of Europe Since 1945*. New York: Penguin Press.
Kafer, Alison. 2013. *Feminist, Queer, Crip*. Bloomington, IN: Indiana University Press.
Kagan, Jerome. 2009. *The Three Cultures: The Natural Sciences, Social Sciences and the Humanities in the Twenty-first Century*. Cambridge: Cambridge University Press.
Kelly, Joan. 1979. The doubled vision of feminist theory: A postscript to the 'Women and Power' conference. *Feminist Studies*, 5/1, 216–27.
Kersake, Christian. 2007. *Deleuze and the Unconscious*. London: Continuum.
King, Katie. 2011. *Networked Reenactments: Stories Transdisciplinary Knowledges Tell*. Durham, NC: Duke University Press.
King, Ynestra. 1989. The ecology of feminism and the feminism of ecology. In: Judith Plant (ed.) *Healing the Wounds: The Promises of Ecofeminism*. Philadelphia, PA: New Society Publishers.
Kirby, Vicki. 2008. Natural convers(at)ions: Or, what if culture was really nature all along? In: Stacy Alaimo and Susan Hekman (eds.) *Material Feminisms*. Bloomington, IN: Indiana University Press.
Kirby, Vicki. 2011. *Quantum Anthropologies: Life at Large*. Durham, NC: Duke University Press.
Kirksey, Eben. 2015. *Emergent Ecologies*. Durham, NC: Duke University Press.
Kirkup, Gill (ed.). 1999. *The Gendered Cyborg*. London and New York: Routledge.
Klare, Michael T. 2012. *The Race for What's Left*. New York: Picador.
Klein, Naomi. 2019. *On Fire: The Burning Case for a Green New Deal*. London: Allen Lane.

Klein, Renate. 1989. *Infertility*. London: Virago.
Koedt, Anne and Ellen Levine (eds.). 1973. *Radical Feminism: The Book*. New York: Times Books.
Kolbert, Elizabeth. 2014. *The Sixth Extinction*. New York: Henry Holt.
Konsmo, Erin Marie and Kaheah Pacheco. 2016. *Violence on the Land, Violence on our Bodies: Building an Indigenous Response to Environmental Violence*. Toronto, Canada: Land Body Defense. http://landbodydefense.org/uploads/files/VLVBReportToolkit2016.pdf
Koyama, Emi. 2001. *The Transfeminist Manifesto*. https://eminism.org/readings/pdf-rdg/tfmanifesto.pdf
Kristeva, Julia. 1980. *Pouvoirs de l'horreur*. Paris: Editions du Seuil.
Kroker, Arthur. 2014. *Exits to the Posthuman Future*. Cambridge: Polity.
Kroker, Arthur and Marilouise Kroker. 1987. *Body Invaders: Panic Sex in America*. New York: St. Martin's Press.
Kruger, Barbara. 1983. *We Won't Play Nature to Your Culture*. London: Institute of Contemporary Arts.
Kuokkanen, Rauna. 2007. *Reshaping the University. Responsibility, Indigenous Epistemes and the Logic of the Gift*. Vancouver: University of British Columbia Press.
Kuokkanen, Rauna. 2015. Decolonizing feminism in the North. *NORA: Nordic Journal of Feminist and Gender Research*, 23/4, 275–81.
Kuokkanen, Rauna. 2017. Indigenous epistemes. In: Imre Szeman, Sarah Blacker and Justin Sully (eds.) *A Companion to Critical and Cultural Theory*. London: John Wiley & Sons.
Kuokkanen, Rauna. 2019. At the intersection of Arctic indigenous governance and extractive industries: A survey of three cases. *The Extractive Industries and Society*, 6, 15–21.
Kurzweil, Ray. 2006. *The Singularity is Near*. New York: Penguin Putnam.
Laboria Cubonics. 2018. *The Xenofeminist Manifesto: A Politics for Alienation*. https://www.laboriacuboniks.net/
Lacan, Jacques. 1998. Seminar XX. *Encore: On Feminine Sexuality: The Limits of Love and Knowledge*. New York: W.W. Norton.
Last, Angela. 2017. We are the world? Anthropocene cultural production between geopoetics and geopolitics. *Theory, Culture & Society*, 34/2–3, 147–68.
Lazzarato, Maurizio. 2012. *The Making of the Indebted Man: An Essay on the Neoliberal Condition*. Los Angeles, CA: Semiotext(e).
Le Guin, Ursula. 1969. *The Left Hand of Darkness*. New York: Ace Books.
LeFanu, Sarah. 1988. *In the Chinks of the World Machine: Feminism and Science Fiction*. London: The Women's Press.
Lemke, Thomas. 2011. *Biopolitics: An Advanced Introduction* (trans. Eric Frederick Trump). New York: New York University Press.

Lemm, Vanessa and Miguel Vatter (eds.). 2014. *The Government of Life: Foucault, Biopolitics and Neoliberalism*. New York: Fordham University Press.

Lenz Taguchi, Hillevi. 2018. The fabrication of a new materialisms researcher subjectivity. In: Cecilia Åsberg and Rosi Braidotti (eds.) *A Feminist Companion to the Posthumanities*. Cham: Springer International.

Lewis, Helen. 2020. *Difficult Women: A History of Feminism in 11 Fights*. London: Jonathan Cape.

Lewis, Sophie. 2019. *Full Surrogacy Now: Feminism Against the Family*. London: Verso.

Lillvis, Kristen. 2017. *Posthuman Blackness and the Black Female Imagination*. Athens, GA: The University of Georgia Press.

Lispector, Clarice. 1978. *La Passion Selon G.H*. Paris: des femmes.

Livingston, Julie and Jasbir K. Puar 2011. Interspecies. *Social Text*, 29/1, 3–14.

Lloyd, Genevieve. 1984. *The Man of Reason: Male and Female in Western Philosophy*. London: Methuen.

Lloyd, Genevieve. 1994. *Part of Nature: Self-knowledge in Spinoza's Ethics*. Ithaca, NY: Cornell University Press.

Lloyd, Genevieve. 1996. *Spinoza and the Ethics*. London and New York: Routledge.

Lloyd, Genevieve. 2009. Dominance and difference: A Spinozist alternative to the distinction between 'sex' and 'gender'. In: Moira Gatens (ed.) *Feminist Interpretations of Benedict Spinoza*. University Park, PA: Pennsylvania State University Press.

Longino, Helen. 1989. Can there be a feminist science? In: Nancy Tuana (ed.) *Feminism and Science*. Bloomington, IN: Indiana University Press.

Lord, Beth. 2011. 'Disempowered by nature': Spinoza on the political capabilities of women. *British Journal for the History of Philosophy*, 19/6, 1085–106.

Lord, Karen. 2013. *The Best of All Possible Worlds*. London: Quercus.

Lorde, Audre. 1973. Who said it was simple. *The Collected Poems of Audre Lorde*. New York: W.W. Norton.

Lorde, Audre. 2007 [1984]. *Sister Outsider*. Berkeley, CA: Crossing Press

Lorraine, Tamsin. 1999. *Irigaray & Deleuze: Experiments in Visceral Philosophy*. Ithaca, NY: Cornell University Press.

Louverture, Toussaint. 2011. *Lettres à la France. Idées pour la Libération du peuple noir d'Haiti (1794–1798)*. Bruyères-le-Chatel: Nouvelle Cité.

Lovelock, James. 2019. *Novacene. The Coming Age of Hyperintelligence*. London: Allen Lane.

Lovelock, James and Lynn Margulis. 1974. Atmospheric homeostasis by and for the biosphere: The Gaia hypothesis. *Tellus*, 26/1–2, 2–10.

Lowe, Marion and Ruth Hubbard (eds.). 1983. *Woman's Nature: Rationalizations of Inequality*. New York: Pergamon Press.
Lucashenko, Melissa. 2002. Many prisons. *Hecate*, 28/1, 130–44.
Lugones, Maria. 2007. Heterosexualism and the colonial modern gender system. *Hypatia*, 22/1, 186–209.
Lugones, Maria. 2010. Towards a decolonial feminism. *Hypatia*, 25/4, 742–59.
Lury, Celia, Luciana Parisi and Tiziana Terranova (eds.). 2012. Topologies of culture. *Theory, Culture & Society*, 29/4–5.
Lykke, Nina. 2008. Feminist cultural studies of technoscience. In: Anneke Smelik and Nina Lykke (eds.) *Bits of Life: Feminism at the Intersections of Media, Bioscience and Technology*. Seattle, WA: University of Washington Press.
Lykke, Nina. 2010a. *Feminist Studies: A Guide to Intersectional Theory, Methodology and Writing*. London and New York: Routledge.
Lykke, Nina. 2010b. The timeliness of post-constructionism. *NORA: Nordic Journal of Feminist and Gender Research*, 18/2, 131–6.
Lykke, Nina (ed.). 2014. *Writing Academic Texts Differently*. London and New York: Routledge.
Lykke, Nina. 2018. Passionately posthuman: From feminist disidentifications to postdisciplinary posthumanities. In: Cecilia Åsberg and Rosi Braidotti (eds.) *A Feminist Companion to the Posthumanities*. Cham: Springer International.
Lykke, Nina. 2019. Co-becoming with diatoms: Between posthuman mourning and wonder in algae research. *Catalyst: Feminism, Theory, Technoscience*, 5/2, 1–25.
Lykke, Nina and Rosi Braidotti. 1996. *Between Monsters, Goddesses and Cyborgs*. London: Zed Books.
Lyotard, Jean-François. 1984 [1979]. *The Postmodern Condition*. Minneapolis, MN: University of Minnesota Press.
Lyotard, Jean-François. 1989 [1988]. *The Inhuman: Reflections on Time*. Oxford: Blackwell.
Maathai, Wangari. 2010. *Replenishing the Earth: Spiritual Values for Healing Ourselves and the World*. New York: Doubleday.
MacCormack, Patricia. 2008. *Cinesexuality*. London: Ashgate.
MacCormack, Patricia. 2010. Becoming vulva: Flesh, fold, infinity. *New Formations*, 68, 93–107.
MacCormack, Patricia. 2012. *Posthuman Ethics*. London: Ashgate.
MacCormack, Patricia. 2014. *The Animal Catalyst*. London: Bloomsbury.
McCormack, Donna. 2018. Queer disability, postcolonial feminism and the monsters of evolution. In: Cecilia Åsberg and Rosi Braidotti (eds.) *A Feminist Companion to the Posthumanities*. Cham: Springer International.
MacKinnon, Catherine. 1989. *Towards a Feminist Theory of the State*. Cambridge, MA: Harvard University Press.

MacKinnon, Catharine. 2007. *Are Women Human?* Cambridge, MA: Belknap Press of Harvard University Press.
McKittrick, Katherine (ed.). 2015. *Sylvia Wynter: On Being Human as Praxis*. Durham, NC: Duke University Press.
McNay, Lois. 1992. *Foucault and Feminism*. Cambridge: Polity Press.
McNeil, Maureen. 2007. *Feminist Cultural Studies of Science and Technology*. London and New York: Routledge.
McNeil, Maureen. 2008. The making of feminist cultural studies of technoscience. In: Anneke Smelik and Nina Lykke (eds.) *Bits of Life: Feminism at the Intersections of Media, Bioscience and Technology*. Seattle, WA: University of Washington Press.
McNeil, Maureen and Celia Roberts. 2011. Feminist science and technology studies. In: Rosemarie Buikema, Gabriele Griffin and Nina Lykke (eds.) *Theories and Methodologies in Postgraduate Feminist Research: Researching Differently*. London and New York: Routledge.
MacPherson, Crawford B. 1962. *The Theory of Possessive Individualism*. Oxford: Oxford University Press.
McRobbie, Angela. 2004. Post-feminism and popular culture. *Feminist Media Studies*, 4/3, 255–64.
McRobbie, Angela. 2015. Notes on the perfect: Competitive femininity in neoliberal times. *Australian Feminist Studies*, 30/83, 3–20.
Macherey, Pierre. 2011 [1977]. *Hegel or Spinoza*. Minneapolis, MN: University of Minnesota Press.
Mack, Ashley Noel and Tiara R. Na'puti. 2019. 'Our bodies are not *terra nullius*': Building a decolonial feminist resistance to gendered violence. *Women's Studies in Communication*, 42/3, 347–70.
Mae Brown, Rita. 1973. *Rubyfruit Jungle*. Plainfield, VT: Daughters.
Mahdawi, Arwa. 2020. After the sleep economy, what's next to be monetised? Breathing? *The Guardian*, 15 January.
Mahmood, S. 2005. *Politics of Piety: The Islamic Revival and the Feminist Subject*. Princeton, NJ: Princeton University Press.
Malabou, Catherine. 2011. *Changing Difference*. Cambridge: Polity Press.
Malabou, Catherine. 2012. *The Ontology of the Accident: An Essay on Destructive Plasticity*. Cambridge: Polity Press.
Malm, Andreas. 2016. *Fossil Capital*. London: Verso Books.
Malone, Karen, Marianne Logan, Lisa Siegel, Julie Regalado and Bronwen Wade-Leeuwen. 2020. Shimmering with Deborah Rose: Posthuman theory-making with feminist ecophilosophers and social ecologists. *Australian Journal of Environmental Education*, 36/2, 129–45.
Mamo, Laura. 2007. *Queering Reproduction*. Durham, NC: Duke University Press.
Mandela, Nelson. 1994. *A Long Walk to Freedom*. Randburg, SA: Macdonald Purnell.

Mann, Justin Louis. 2018. Pessimistic futurism: Survival and reproduction in Octavia Butler's Dawn. *Feminist Theory*, 19/1, 61–76.
Margulis, Lynn and Dorion Sagan. 1995. *What Is Life?* Berkeley, CA: University of California Press.
Margulis, Lynn and Dorion Sagan. 1997. *Slanted Truths*. New York: Copernicus.
Marks, John. 1998. *Gilles Deleuze: Vitalism and Multiplicity*. London: Pluto Press.
Martin, Emily 1992. *The Woman in the Body: A Cultural Analysis of Reproduction*. Milton Keynes: Open University Press.
Massumi, Brian. 2002. *Parables for the Virtual: Movement, Affect, Sensation*. Durham, NC: Duke University Press.
Matheron, Alexandre. 1969. *Individu et communauté chez Spinoza*. Paris: Les Editions de Minuit.
Maturana, Humberto and Francisco Varela. 1972. *Autopoesis and Cognition: The Realization of the Living*. Dordrecht: Reidel Publishing.
Mbembe, Achille. 2003. Necropolitics. *Public Culture*, 15/1, 11–40.
Mbembe, Achille. 2021. The universal right to breathe. *Critical Inquiry*, 47, S58–62.
Mepschen, Paul and Jan-Willem Duyvendak. 2012. European sexual nationalisms: The culturalization of citizenship and the sexual politics of belonging and exclusion. *Perspectives on Europe*, 42/1, 70–6.
Merchant, Carolyn. 1980. *The Death of Nature: Women, Ecology, and the Scientific Revolution*. San Francisco, CA: Harper.
Merry, Sally E. 2016. *The Seduction of Quantification*. Chicago, IL: University of Chicago Press.
Mertens, Mahlu and Gry Ulstein. 2020. Decolonizing the Cli-Fi corpus. *Collateral. Online Journal for Cross-Cultural Close Reading*, 26.
Meyer, Birgit. 2012. Material religion: How things matter. In: Dick Houtman and Birgit Meyer (eds.) *Things: Religion and the Question of Materiality*. New York: Fordham University Press.
Mezzadra, Sandro and Brett Neilson. 2013. *Border as Method*. Durham, NC: Duke University Press.
Midgley, Mary. 1996. *Utopias, Dolphins and Computers: Problems of Philosophical Plumbing*. London and New York: Routledge.
Mies, Maria. 2014 [1986]. *Patriarchy and Accumulation on a World Scale*. London: Zed Books.
Mies, Maria and Vandana Shiva. 1993. *Ecofeminism*. London: Zed Books.
Millett, Kate. 1970. *Sexual Politics*. New York: Doubleday.
Milman, Oliver. 2020. Trump order encourages US to mine the moon. *The Guardian*, 8 April.
Minsky, Marvin. 1985. *The Society of Mind*. New York: Simon and Schuster.

Miss M. 1996. An interview with Sadie Plant and Linda Dement. http://future-nonstop.org/c/bb37122bc11c3dd0787d5205d9debc41
Mitchell, Juliet. 1966. Women: The longest revolution. *New Left Review*, 40, 11–37.
Mitchell, Juliet. 1973. *Women's Estate*. New York: Vintage Books.
Mitchell, Juliet. 1974. *Psychoanalysis and Feminism*. New York: Pantheon Books.
Mitchell, Juliet and Jacqueline Rose. 1985. *Feminine Sexuality*. New York: W.W. Norton.
Mohanty, Chandra. 1991. Under Western eyes: Feminist scholarship and colonial discourses. In: Chandra Mohanty, Ann Russo and Lourdes Torres (eds.) *Third World Women and the Politics of Feminism*. Bloomington, IN: Indiana University Press.
Mondloch, Kate. 2018. *A Capsule Aesthetics: Feminist Materialisms in Media Art*. Minneapolis, MN: University of Minnesota Press.
Moore, Henrietta. 1994. *A Passion for Difference*. Cambridge: Polity Press.
Moraga, Cherríe and Gloria Anzaldua (eds.). 1981. *This Bridge Called My Back: Writing by Radical Women on Color*. Watertown, MA: Persephone Press.
Morar, Nicolae, Thomas Nail and Daniel W. Smith. 2016. *Between Deleuze and Foucault*. Edinburgh: Edinburgh University Press.
More, Max. 2013. The philosophy of transhumanism. In: Max More and Natasha Vita-More (eds.) *The Transhumanist Reader*. London: Wiley-Blackwell.
Moreton-Robinson, Aileen. 2003. I still call Australia home: Indigenous belongings and place in a white postcolonizing society. In: Sarah Ahmed, Claudia Castada, Anne-Marie Fortier and Mimi Sheller (eds.) *Uprootings/Regroundings: Questions of Home and Migration*. London: Bloomsbury Academic, pp. 23–40.
Moreton-Robinson, Aileen. 2009. Introduction: Critical indigenous theory. *Cultural Studies Review*, 15/2, 11–12.
Morgan, Robin (ed.). 1970. *Sisterhood is Powerful*. New York: Penguin Random House.
Morris, Meaghan and Paul Patton. 1979. *Michel Foucault: Power, Truth, Strategy. Working Papers 2*. Sydney: Feral Publications.
Morrissey, Philip and Chris Healy (eds.). 2018. *Reading the Country: 30 Years On*. Sydney: University of Technology Sydney.
Mortimer-Sandilands, Catriona and Bruce Erickson (eds.). 2010. *Queer Ecologies: Sex, Nature, Politics, Desire*. Bloomington, IN: Indiana University Press.
Moten, Fred. 2003. *In the Break: The Aesthetics of the Black Radical Tradition*. Minneapolis, MN: University of Minnesota Press.
Moulier-Boutang, Yann. 2012. *Cognitive Capitalism*. Cambridge: Polity.
Mullarkey, J. 2006. *Post-Continental Philosophy: An Outline*. London and New York: Continuum.

References

Mulvey, Laura. 1975. Visual pleasure and narrative cinema. *Screen*, 16/3, 6–18.

Muñoz, José Esteban. 1999. *Disidentifications: Queers of Color and the Performance of Politics*. Minneapolis, MN: University of Minnesota Press.

Muñoz, José Esteban. 2015. Theorising queer inhumanism: The sense of brownness. *GLQ: A Journal of Lesbian and Gay Studies*, 21/2–3, 209–10.

Munshi, Neil. 2020. How unlocking the secrets of African DNA could change the world. *The Financial Times*, 5 March.

Murray, Stuart. 2020. *Disability and the Posthuman*. Liverpool: Liverpool University Press.

Nancy, Jean-Luc. 2000. *L'Intrus [The Intruder]*. Paris: Editions Galilée.

Narayan, Uma. 1989. Project of feminist epistemology: Perspectives from a nonwestern feminist. In: Alison M. Jaggar and Susan Bordo (eds.) *Gender/Body/Knowledge: Feminist Reconstructions of Being and Knowing*. New Brunswick, NJ: Rutgers University Press.

Nash, Jennifer. 2018. Black sexualities. *Feminist Theory*, 19/1, 61–76.

Negri, Antonio. 1991 [1981]. *The Savage Anomaly: The Power of Spinoza's Metaphysics and Politics*. Minneapolis, MN: University of Minnesota Press.

Neimanis, Astrida. 2015. Review of *Ecofeminism: Feminist Intersections with Other Animals and the Earth*, edited by Carol J. Adams and Lori Gruen. *The Goose*, 14/1, article 20, https://scholars.wlu.ca/thegoose/vol14/iss1/20

Neimanis, Astrida. 2017. *Bodies of Water: Posthuman Feminist Phenomenology*. London: Bloomsbury.

Neimanis, Astrida. 2018. Posthuman phenomenologies for planetary bodies of water. In: Cecilia Åsberg and Rosi Braidotti (eds.) *A Feminist Companion to the Posthumanities*. Cham: Springer International.

Neimanis, Astrida, Cecilia Åsberg and Johan Hedrén. 2015. Four problems, four directions for environmental humanities: Toward critical posthumanities for the Anthropocene. *Ethics & the Environment*, 20/1, 67–97.

Nicholson, Linda (ed.). 1990. *Feminism/Postmodernism*. London and New York: Routledge.

Nigianni, Chrysanthi and Merl Storr (eds.). 2009. *Deleuze and Queer Theory*. Edinburgh: Edinburgh University Press.

Nixon, Rob. 2011. *Slow Violence: Environmentalism of the Poor*. Cambridge, MA: Harvard University Press.

Noys, Benjamin and Timothy Murphy. 2016. Introduction: Old and new weird. *Genre*, 49/2, 117–34.

Nussbaum, Marta. 2006. *Frontiers of Justice: Disability, Nationality, Species Membership*. Cambridge, MA: Harvard University Press.

Oksala, Johanna. 2012. *Foucault, Politics and Violence*. Evanston, IL: Northwestern University Press.

Okorafor, Nnedi. 2010. *Who Fears Death*. New York: DAW Books.
Old Boys Network (eds.). 1998. *First Cyberfeminist International: Old Boys Network Reader 1*, Documentation of September 1997 conference held as part of Hybrid Workspace at Documenta X, Kassel.
Olkowski, Dorothea. 1999. *Gilles Deleuze and the Ruin of Representation*. Irvine, CA: University of California Press.
Orr, Jackie. 2005. *Panic Diaries: A Genealogy of Panic Disorder*. Durham, NC: Duke University Press.
Ortner, Sherry B. 1974. Is female to male as nature is to culture? In: M.Z. Rosaldo and L. Lamphere (eds.) *Woman, Culture, and Society*. Stanford, CA: Stanford University Press, pp. 68–87.
Otto, Dianne and Gina Heathcote. 2014. Rethinking peacekeeping, gender equality and collective security: An introduction. In: Gina Heathcote and Dianne Otto (eds.) *Rethinking Peacekeeping, Gender Equality and Collective Security*. London: Palgrave Macmillan.
Parikka, Jussi. 2015a. *A Geology of Media*. Minneapolis, MN: University of Minnesota Press.
Parikka, Jussi. 2015b. *The Anthrobscene*. Minneapolis, MN: University of Minnesota Press.
Parisi, Luciana. 2004. *Abstract Sex: Philosophy, Bio-Technology, and the Mutation of Desire*. London: Continuum Press.
Parr, Adrian. 2013. *The Wrath of Capital: Neoliberalism and Climate Change Politics*. New York: Columbia University Press.
Pateman, Carole. 1988. *The Sexual Contract*. Cambridge: Polity Press.
Patton, Paul (ed.). 1993. *Nietzsche, Feminism and Political Theory*. London and New York: Routledge.
Patton, Paul. 2016. Deleuze and naturalism. *International Journal of Philosophical Studies*, 24/3, 348–64.
Patton, Paul. 2000. *Deleuze and the Political*. London and New York: Routledge.
Patton, Paul and John Protevi (eds.). 2003. *Between Deleuze and Derrida*. London: Continuum.
Pert, Petina L., Rosemary Hill, Catherine J. Robinson, Diane Jarvis and Jocelyn Davies. 2020. Is investment in Indigenous land and sea management going to the right places to provide multiple co-benefits? *Australasian Journal of Environmental Management*, 27/3, 249–74.
Perugini, Nicola and Neve Gordon. 2015. *The Human Right to Dominate*. Oxford: Oxford University Press.
Peters, John Durham. 2015. *The Marvelous Clouds: Towards a Philosophy of Elemental Media*. Chicago, IL: University of Chicago Press.
Peterson, Elin. 2007. The invisible carers: Framing domestic work(ers) in gender equality policies in Spain. *European Journal of Women's Studies*, 14/3, 265–80.
Piercy, Marge. 1976. *Woman on the Edge of Time*. New York: Alfred A. Knopf.

Piercy, Marge. 1991. *Body of Glass*. New York: Penguin Books.
Pinkola Estés, Clarissa. 1992. *Women Who Run with the Wolves: Myths and Stories of the Wild Woman Archetype*. New York: Ballantine Books.
Pitts-Taylor, Victoria. 2016. *Mattering: Feminism, Science and New Materialism*. New York: New York University Press.
Plant, Sadie. 1997. *Zeroes and Ones: Digital Women and the New Technoculture*. London: Fourth Estate.
Plant, Sadie. 2000. *Writing on Drugs*. New York: Farrar, Straus and Giroux.
Plate, Liedeke. 2019. Dancing at the museum: Parataxis and the politics of proximity in Beyoncé and Jay-Z's 'APESHIT'. *Stedelijk Studies*, 8.
Plumwood, Val. 1993. *Feminism and the Mastery of Nature*. London and New York: Routledge.
Plumwood, Val. 1994. The ecopolitics debate and the politics of nature. In: Karen Warren (ed.) *Ecological Feminism*. London and New York: Routledge.
Plumwood, Val. 2002. *Environmental Culture*. London and New York: Routledge.
Plumwood, Val. 2007. A review of Deborah Bird Rose's *Reports from a Wild Country*. *Australian Humanities Review*, 42, 1–4.
Pollock, Griselda. 1988. *Vision and Difference*. London and New York: Routledge.
Pollock, Anne and Banu Subramaniam. 2016. Feminist postcolonial technosciences. *Science, Technology and Human Values*, 4/6, 951–66.
Pope Francis. 2015. Encyclical Letter *Laudato si': On Care for our Common Home*. Rome: The Vatican Press.
Povinelli, Elizabeth. 2016. *Geontologies: A Requiem to Late Liberalism*. Durham, NC: Duke University Press.
Povinelli, Elizabeth. 2017. The three figures of geontology. In: Richard Grusin (ed.) *Anthropocene Feminism*. Minneapolis, MN: University of Minnesota Press.
Preciado, Paul. 2013a. *Testo Junkie*. London: The Feminist Press.
Preciado, Beatriz. 2013b. The pharmaco-pornographic regime: sex, gender, and subjectivity in the age of punk capitalism. In: Susan Stryker and Aren Z. Aizura (eds.) *The Transgender Studies Reader 2*. New York and London: Routledge.
Protevi, John. 2009. *Political Affect*. Minneapolis, MN: University of Minnesota Press.
Protevi, John. 2013. *Life, War, Earth*. Minneapolis, MN: University of Minnesota Press.
Protevi, John. 2018. Geo-hydro-solar-bio-techno-politics. In: Rosi Braidotti and Maria Hlavajova (eds.) *Posthuman Glossary*. London: Bloomsbury Academic, pp. 175–8.
Puar, Jasbir. 2007. *Terrorist Assemblages*. Durham, NC: Duke University Press.

Puig de la Bellacasa, Maria. 2017. *Matters of Care: Speculative Ethics in More than Human Worlds*. Minneapolis, MN: University of Minnesota Press.

Rabinow, Paul. 2003. *Anthropos Today*. Princeton, NJ: Princeton University Press.

Radicalesbians. 1971. The woman-identified woman. In: Anne Koedt (ed.) *Notes from the Third Year*. New York: Pamphlet.

Radomska, Marietta, Tara Mehrabi and Nina Lykke (eds.). 2020. Queer death studies. *Australian Feminist Studies*, 35/104.

Raha, Nat. 2017. Transfeminine brokenness: Radical transfeminism. *South Atlantic Quarterly*, 116/3, 632–46.

Rajan, Kaushik Sunder. 2006. *Biocapital: The Constitution of Postgenomic Life*. Durham, NC: Duke University Press.

Ramazanoglu, Caroline (ed.). 1993. *Up Against Foucault: Explorations of Some Tensions Between Foucault and Feminism*. London and New York: Routledge.

Rapp, Rayna. 2000. *Testing Women, Testing the Fetus*. London and New York: Routledge.

Rapp, Rayna, Deborah Heath and Karen-Sue Taussig. 2001. Genealogical dis-ease: Where hereditary abnormality, biomedical explanation, and family responsibility meet. In: Sarah Franklin and Susan McKinnon (eds.) *Relative Values: Reconfiguring Kinship Studies*. Durham, NC: Duke University Press, pp. 384–409.

Redfield, Marc. 2016. *Theory at Yale: The Strange Case of Deconstruction in America*. New York: Fordham University Press.

Redstockings. 1975. *Feminist Revolution*. New York: Redstockings inc.

Rees-Jones, Deryn. 2016. *What It's Like To Be Alive*. Bridgend: Seren Books.

Reich, Robert. 2021. When America's richest men pay $0 income tax, this is wealth supremacy. *The Guardian*, 10 June.

Repo, Jemima, 2016. *The Biopolitics of Gender*. Oxford: Oxford University Press.

Reuters. 2021. Europe launches recruitment drive for female and disabled astronauts. *The Guardian*, 17 February.

Rich, Adrienne. 1976. *Of Woman Born: Motherhood as Experience and Institution*. New York: W.W. Norton.

Rich, Adrienne. 1978. *Disloyal to Civilization*. New York: W.W. Norton.

Rich, Adrienne. 1980. Compulsory heterosexuality and lesbian existence. *Signs*, 5/4, 631–60.

Rich, Adrienne. 1981. *A Wild Patience Has Taken Me This Far*. New York: W.W. Norton.

Rich, Adrienne. 1984. Notes toward a politics of location. In: *Blood, Bread and Poetry*. New York: W.W. Norton.

Rich, Adrienne. 2001. *Arts of the Possible: Essays and Conversations*. New York: W.W. Norton.

Rijneveld, Marieke Lucas. 2020. *The Discomfort of Evening.* London: Faber & Faber.
Ringrose, Jessica, Karie Warfield and Shiva Zarabadi. 2019. *Feminist Posthumanisms, New Materialisms and Education.* London and New York: Routledge.
Roberts, Celia. 2007. *Messengers of Sex: Hormones, Biomedicine and Feminism.* Cambridge: Cambridge University Press.
Roberts, Celia. 2008. Fluid ecologies: Changing hormonal systems of embodied difference. In: Anneke Smelik and Nina Lykke (eds.) *Bits of Life: Feminism at the Intersections of Media, Bioscience and Technology.* Seattle, WA: University of Washington Press.
Roberts, Celia. 2018. Practising ambivalence: The feminist politics of engaging with technoscience. In: Cecilia Åsberg and Rosi Braidotti (eds.) *A Feminist Companion to the Posthumanities.* Cham: Springer International.
Rodríguez Castro, Mayra A. 2020. *Audre Lorde: Dream of Europe. Selected Seminars and Interviews 1984–1992.* Chicago, IL: Kenning Editions.
Roffe, Jon and Hannah Stark. 2015. *Deleuze and the Non-Human.* London: Palgrave Macmillan.
Rooney, Sally. 2018. *Normal People.* London: Faber & Faber.
Roosth, Sophia and Astrid Schrader (eds.). 2012. Feminist theory out of science. *differences*, 23/3.
Rose, Deborah Bird. 2004. *Reports from a Wild Country.* Sydney: University of New South Wales Press.
Rose, Deborah Bird. 2015. The ecological humanities. In: Katherine Gibson, Deborah Bird Rose and Ruth Fincher (eds.) *Manifesto for Living in the Anthropocene.* Brooklyn, NY: Punctum Books, pp. 1–6.
Rose, Deborah Bird. 2017. Shimmer: When all you love is being trashed. In: Anna Tsing, Heather Swanson, Elaine Gan and Nils Bubandt (eds.) *Arts of Living on a Damaged Planet.* Minneapolis, MN: University of Minnesota Press.
Rose, Deborah Bird, Thom van Dooren, Matthew Chrulew, Stuart Cooke, Matthew Kearnes and Emily O'Gorman. 2012. Thinking through the environment, unsettling the humanities. *Environmental Humanities*, 1/1, 1–5.
Rose, Hilary. 2001. Nine decades, nine women, ten Nobel prizes: Gender politics on the apex of science. In: Mary Wyer, Mary Barbercheck, Donna Giesman, Hatice Örün Ötzürk and Marta Wayne (eds.) *Women, Science and Technology: A Reader in Feminist Science Studies.* London and New York: Routledge.
Rose, Nicholas. 2007. *The Politics of Life Itself: Biomedicine, Power and Subjectivity in the Twentieth-first Century.* Princeton, NJ: Princeton University Press.
Rosendahl Thomsen, Mads. 2013. *The New Human in Literature:*

Posthuman Visions of Changes in Body, Mind, and Society after 1900. London: Bloomsbury Academic.
Rosser, Sue. 1989. Re-visioning clinical research: Gender and the ethics of experimental design. *Hypatia*, 4/2, 125–39.
Rottenberg, Catherine. 2018. *The Rise of Neoliberal Feminism*. Oxford: Oxford University Press.
Rouch, Hélène. 1987. Le placenta comme tiers. *Langages*, 21/85: 71–9.
Rovelli, Carlo. 2014. *Seven Brief Lessons on Physics*. London: Penguin Random House.
Rowbotham, Sheila. 1973. *Woman's Consciousness, Man's World*. London: Penguin Books.
Roy, Deboleena. 2018. *Molecular Feminism*. Seattle, WA: University of Washington Press.
Rubin, Gayle. 1975. Traffic in women: Notes on the political economy of sex. In: Rayna Reiter (ed.) *Toward an Anthropology of Women*. New York: Monthly Review Press.
Rubin, Gayle. 1984. Thinking sex: Notes for a radical theory of the politics of sexuality. In: Carole Vance (ed.) *Pleasure and Danger*. New York: Routledge & Kegan Paul.
Russ, Joanna. 1975. *The Female Man*. New York: Bantam Books.
Russell, Bertrand. 1961. *Has Man a Future?* London: George Allen & Unwin.
Said, Edward. 2004. *Humanism and Democratic Criticism*. New York: Columbia University Press.
Saldanha, Arun and Jason Michael Adams (eds.). 2013. *Deleuze and Race*. Edinburgh: Edinburgh University Press.
Sands, Danielle. 2019. *Animal Writing: Storytelling, Selfhood and the Limits of Empathy*. Edinburgh: Edinburgh University Press.
Sartre, Jean-Paul. 1963. Introduction. In: Frantz Fanon, *The Wretched of the Earth*. New York: Grove Press.
Sassen, Saskia. 1994. *Cities in a World Economy*. Thousand Oaks, CA: Pine Forge Press.
Sassen, Saskia. (ed.). 2002. *Global Networks, Linked Cities*. London and New York: Routledge.
Sassen, Saskia. 2005. The global city: Introducing a concept. *Brown Journal of World Affairs*, 11/2, 27–43.
Sassen, Saskia. 2014. *Expulsions: Brutality and Complexity in the Global Economy*. Cambridge, MA: Harvard University Press.
Sawicki, Jana. 1991. *Disciplining Foucault*. London and New York: Routledge.
Schiebinger, Londa. 1989. *The Mind Has No Sex?* Cambridge, MA: Harvard University Press.
Schiebinger, Londa. 1999. *Has Feminism Changed Science?* Cambridge, MA: Harvard University Press.
Schiebinger, Londa. 2008. *Gendered Innovations in Science and Engineering*. Stanford, CA: Stanford University Press.

Schott, Robin May. 2010. *Birth, Death, and Femininity: Philosophies of Embodiment*. Bloomington, IN: Indiana University Press.

Schrader, Astrid. 2012. The time of slime: Anthropocentrism in harmful algal research. *Environmental Philosophy*, 9/1, 71–94.

Schwab, Klaus. 2015. The fourth industrial revolution. *Foreign Affairs*, 12 December.

Scott, Joan W. 1986. Gender: A useful category of historical analysis. *American Historical Review*, 91/5, 1053–75.

Scott, Joan W. 2007. *The Politics of the Veil*. Princeton, NJ: Princeton University Press.

Sedgwick, Eve. 1990. *Epistemology of the Closet*. Berkley, CA: University of California Press.

Segal, Lynne. 2017. *Radical Happiness: Moments of Collective Joy*. London: Verso.

Serres, Michel. 1982 [1980]. *The Parasite*. Baltimore, MD: Johns Hopkins University Press.

Serres, Michel. 1995. *The Natural Contract*. Ann Arbor, MI: University of Michigan Press.

Serres, Michel. 2008. *The Five Senses*. London: Continuum.

Serres, Michel. 2016. Au fond, je suis devenu philosophe à cause d'Hiroshima. France Culture Radio, 10 March. https://www.franceculture.fr/philosophie/michel-serres-au-fond-je-suis-devenu-philosophe-cause-d-hiroshima

Sharp, Hasana. 2011. *Spinoza and the Politics of Renaturalization*. Chicago, IL: University of Chicago Press.

Sharp, Hasana. 2019. Generosity and freedom in Spinoza's ethics. In: Jack Stetter and Charles Ramond (eds.) *Spinoza in Twenty-first Century American and French Philosophy*. New York: Bloomsbury Academic.

Sharp, Hasana and Chloe Taylor (eds.). 2016. *Feminist Philosophies of Life*. Montreal: McGill-Queen's University Press.

Shaw, Matt. 2021. Billionaire capitalists are designing humanity's future. Don't let them. *The Guardian*, 15 February.

Shildrick, Margrit. 1997. *Leaky Bodies and Boundaries*. London and New York: Routledge.

Shildrick, Margrit. 2002. *Embodying the Monster*. London: Sage.

Shildrick, Margrit. 2012. *Dangerous Discourses of Disability, Subjectivity and Sexuality*. London: Palgrave Macmillan.

Shiva, Vandana. 1988. *Staying Alive*. New Dehli: Kali for Women.

Shiva, Vandana. 1997. *Biopiracy: The Plunder of Nature and Knowledge*. Boston, MA: South End Press.

Shiva, Vandana. 2012. *Making Peace with the Earth*. London: Pluto Press.

Shotwell, Alexis. 2016. *Against Purity: Living Ethically in Compromised Times*. Minneapolis, MN: University of Minnesota Press.

Silva, D. Ferreira da. 2007. *Toward a Global Idea of Race*. Minneapolis, MN: University of Minnesota Press.

Singer, Peter. 1975. *Animal Liberationism*. New York: Avon Books.
Singleton, Vicky and Mike Michael. 1993. Actor-networks and ambivalence: General practitioners in the UK cervical screening programme. *Social Studies of Science*, 23/2, 227–64.
Smelik, Anneke and Nina Lykke (eds.). 2008. *Bits of Life: Feminism at the Intersections of Media, Bioscience and Technology*. Seattle, WA: University of Washington Press.
Smith, Barbara. 1978. Towards a Black feminist criticism. *The Radical Teacher*, 7, 20–7.
Smith, Barbara. 1998. *The Truth That Never Hurts: Writings on Race, Gender, and Freedom*. New Brunswick, NJ: Rutgers University Press.
Smith-Rosenberg, Carol. 1975. The female world of love and ritual: Relations between women in nineteenth-century America. *Signs*, 1/1, 1–29.
Sobchack, Vivian. 2004. *Carnal Thoughts*. Berkeley, CA: University of California Press.
Solanas, Valerie. 1968. *SCUM Manifesto*. New York: Olympia Press.
Solnit, Rebecca. 2014. *Men Explain Things to Me*. New York: Haymarket Books.
Solnit, Rebecca. 2017. *The Mother of All Questions*. London: Granta Books.
Somerville, Margaret. 2020 *Riverlands of the Anthropocene: Walking Our Waterways as Places of Becoming*. London and New York: Routledge.
Soper, Kate. 1986. *Humanism and Anti-Humanism*. LaSalle, IL: Open Court Press.
Spicer, Andre. 2019. 'Self-care': How a radical feminist idea was stripped of politics for the mass market. *The Guardian*, 21 August.
Spillers, Hortense. 1987. Mama's baby, Papa's maybe: An American grammar book. *Diacritics*, 17/2, 64–81.
Spivak, Gayatri Chakravorty. 1985. Can the subaltern speak? *Wedge*, 7/8, 120–30.
Spivak, Gayatri Chakravorty. 1987. *In Other Worlds*. New York: Methuen.
Spivak, Gayatri Chakravorty. 1989. Feminism and deconstruction, again. In: Teresa Brennan (ed.) *Between Feminism and Psychoanalysis*. London and New York: Routledge.
Spivak, Gayatri Chakravorty. 1990. *The Postcolonial Critic*. London and New York: Routledge.
Spivak, Gayatri Chakravorty. 1999. *A Critique of Postcolonial Reason: Toward a History of the Vanishing Present*. Cambridge, MA: Harvard University Press.
Springer, Claudia. 1996. *Electronic Eros: Bodies and Desire in the Postindustrial Age*. Austin, TX: University of Texas Press.
Squier, Susan. 1995. Reproducing the posthuman body: Ectogenetic fetus, surrogate mother, pregnant man. In: Judith Halberstam and

Ira Livingston (eds.) *Posthuman Bodies*. Bloomington, IN: Indiana University Press, pp. 113–34.

Squier, Susan Merrill. 2004. *Liminal Lives: Imagining the Human at the Frontiers of Biomedicine*. Durham, NC: Duke University Press.

Squier, Susan Merrill. 2018. *Epigenetic Landscapes: Drawings as Metaphor*. Durham, NC: Duke University Press.

Squires, Judith. 1996. Fabulous feminist futures and the lure of cyberculture. In: Jon Dovey (ed.) *Fractal Dreams*. London: Lawrence & Wishart.

Srnicek, Nick. 2016. *Platform Capitalism*. Cambridge: Polity.

St. Pierre, Elizabeth A., Alecia Y. Jackson and Lisa A. Mazzei. 2016. New empiricisms and new materialisms: Conditions for new inquiry. *Cultural Studies*, 16/2, 99–110.

Stacey, Jackie. 1997. *Teratologies: A Cultural Study of Cancer*. London and New York: Routledge.

Stacey, Jackie. 2000. The global within: Consuming nature, embodying health. In: Sarah Franklin, Celia Lury and Jackie Stacey, *Global Nature, Global Culture*. London and New York: Routledge.

Stacey, Jackie. 2010. *The Cinematic Life of the Gene*. Durham, NC: Duke University Press.

Stafford, Barbara. 2007. *Echo Objects: The Cognitive Work of Images*. Chicago, IL: University of Chicago Press.

Stanworth, Michelle (ed.). 1987. *Reproductive Technologies: Gender, Motherhood and Medicine*. Cambridge: Polity Press.

Starhawk. 1979. *The Spiral Dance*. San Francisco, CA: HarperCollins.

Stark, Hannah. 2017. *Feminist Theory After Deleuze*. Edinburgh: Edinburgh University Press.

Stein, Gertrude. 2008 [1923]. If I told him: A full portrait of Picasso. In: *Selections: Gertrude Stein*. Berkeley, CA: University of California Press.

Steinberg, Deborah and Patricia Spallone (eds.). 1988. *Made to Order: The Myth of Reproductive and Genetic Progress*. London: Pergamon.

Stengers, Isabelle. 1997. *Power and Invention: Situating Science*. Minneapolis, MN: University of Minnesota Press.

Stengers, Isabelle. 2011. *Cosmopolitics II*. Minneapolis, MN: University of Minnesota Press.

Stengers, Isabelle. 2015. *In Catastrophic Times: Resisting the Coming Barbarism*. London: Open Humanities Press.

Sterling, Bruce. 1992. *The Hacker Crackdown: Law and Disorder on the Electronic Frontier*. New York: Bantam Books.

Sterling, Bruce. 2012. *The Manifesto of Speculative Posthumanism*. Available at http://www.wired.com/2014/02/manifesto-speculative-posthumanism/

Stimpson, Catharine. 2016. The nomadic humanities. *Los Angeles Review of Books*, 12 July.

Stimpson, Catharine and Ethel Spector Person (eds.). 1980. *Women, Sex and Sexuality*. Chicago, IL: University of Chicago Press.
Stoller, Ann. 1995. *Race and the Education of Desire*. Durham, NC: Duke University Press.
Stoller, Ann. 2002. *Carnal Knowledge and Imperial Power*. Berkeley, CA: University of California Press.
Stone, Alison. 2006. *Luce Irigaray. The Philosophy of Sexual Difference*. Cambridge: Cambridge University Press.
Stone, Alison. 2015. Irigaray's ecological phenomenology: Towards an elemental materialism. *Journal of the British Society for Phenomenology*, 46/2, 117–31.
Stone, Alison. 2019. *Being Born: Birth and Philosophy*. Oxford: Oxford University Press.
Stone, Allucquère Rosanne. 1991. Will the real body please stand up? In: Michael Benedikt (ed.) *Cyberspace: First Steps*. Cambridge, MA: MIT Press.
Stone, Allucquère Rosanne. 1995. *The War of Desire and Technology at the Close of the Mechanical Age*. Cambridge, MA: MIT Press.
Strathern, Marilyn. 1992. *Reproducing the Future*. Manchester: Manchester University Press.
Stryker, Susan. 1994. My words to Victor Frankenstein above the village of Chamounix: Performing transgender rage. *GLQ. A Journal of Gay and Lesbian Studies*, 1/3, 237–54.
Stryker, Susan. 2015. Transing the queer (in)human. *GLQ: A Journal of Lesbian and Gay Studies*, 21/2–3, 227–30.
Stryker, Susan. 2020. Foreword. In: Douglas A. Vakoch (ed.) *Transecology: Transgender Perspectives on Environment and Nature*. New York and London: Routledge.
Stryker, Susan and Aren Z. Aizura (eds.). 2013. *The Transgender Studies Reader 2*. London and New York: Routledge.
Sturgeon, Noel. 1997. *Ecofeminist Natures*. London and New York: Routledge.
Suchman, Lucy. 2000. Embodied practices of engineering work. *Mind, Culture and Activity*, 7, 4–18.
Sullivan, Nikki and Samantha Murray. 2009. *Somatechnics: Queering the Technologisation of Bodies*. New York: Ashgate.
Sundberg, Juanita. 2013. Decolonizing posthumanist geographies. *Cultural Geography*, 21/1, 33–47.
TallBear, Kim. 2007. Narratives of race and indigeneity in the Genographic Project. *Journal of Law, Medicine and Ethics*, 35/3, 412–24.
TallBear, Kim. 2013. *Native American DNA: Tribal Belonging and the False Promise of Genetic Science*. Minneapolis, MN: University of Minnesota Press.
TallBear, Kim. 2015. An Indigenous reflection on working beyond the

human/not human. *GLQ: A Journal of Lesbian and Gay Studies*, 21/2–3, 230–5.
Taylor, Dianna and Karen Vintges (eds.). 2004. *Feminism and the Final Foucault*. Urbana, IL: University of Illinois Press.
Taylor, Dorceta E. 2016. *The Rise of the American Conservation Movement*. Durham, NC: Duke University Press.
Terranova, Tiziana. 2004. *Network Culture*. London: Pluto Press.
The Care Collective. 2020. *The Care Manifesto*. London: Verso Books.
Thompson, Charis. 2005. *Making Parents: The Ontological Choreography of Reproductive Technologies*. Cambridge, MA: MIT Press.
Thunberg, Greta. 2019. *No One is Too Small to Make a Difference*. London: Penguin Books.
Todd, Zoe. 2015. Indigenizing the Anthropocene. In: Heather Davis and Etienne Turpin (eds.) *Art in the Anthropocene: Encounters among Aesthetics, Politics, Environments and Epistemologies*. London: Open Humanities Press, pp. 241–54.
Todd, Zoe. 2016. An indigenous feminist's take on the ontological turn: 'Ontology' is just another word for colonialism. *Journal of Historical Sociology*, 29/1, 4–22.
Toffoletti, Kim. 2007. *Cyborgs and Barbie Dolls: Feminism, Popular Culture and the Posthuman Body*. New Brunswick, NJ: Rutgers University Press.
Tofighian, Omid. 2020. Introducing Manus Prison theory: knowing border violence. *Globalizations*, 17/7, 1138–56.
Tronto, Joan. 1995. Care as a basis for radical political judgments. *Hypatia*, 10/2, 141–9.
Tsing, Anna. 2015. *The Mushroom at the End of the World*. Princton, NJ: Princeton University Press.
Tsing, Anna, Heather Swanson, Elaine Gan and Nils Bubandt (eds.). 2017. *Arts of Living on a Damaged Planet*. Minneapolis, MN: University of Minnesota Press.
Tuana, Nancy (ed.). 1989. *Feminism and Science*. Bloomington, IN: Indiana University Press.
Tuana, Nancy. 1992. *Woman and the History of Philosophy*. New York: Paragon Press.
Tuana, Nancy. 2008. Viscous porosity: Witnessing Katrina. In: Stacy Alaimo and Susan Hekman (eds.) *Material Feminisms*. Bloomington, IN: Indiana University Press, pp. 188–213.
Tuana, Nancy. 2019. *Climate Apartheid. The Forgetting of Race in the Anthropocene*. University Park, PA: Penn State University Press.
Tuhiwai Smith, Linda. 1999. *Decolonizing Methodologies: Research and Indigenous Peoples*. London: Zed Books.
Turkle, Sherry. 1995. *Life on the Screen: Identity in the Age of the Internet*. New York: Simon and Schuster.
Ulmer, Jasmine B. 2017. Posthumanism as research methodology:

Inquiry in the Anthropocene. *International Journal of Qualitative Studies in Education*, 30/9, 832–48.

Ulstein, Gry. 2019. 'Through the eyes of Area X': (Dis)locating ecological hope via new weird spatiality. In: Julius Greve and Florian Zappe (eds.) *Spaces and Fictions of the Weird and the Fantastic: Ecologies, Geographies, Oddities.* London: Palgrave Macmillan, pp. 129–47.

Ulstein, Gry. 2021. 'Just a surface': Anamorphic perspective and nonhuman narration in Jeff VanderMeer's *The Strange Bird*. In: Yvonne Liebermann et al. (eds.) *Nonhuman Agency in the 21st-Century Novel*. London: Palgrave Macmillan.

van der Tuin, Iris. 2011. A different starting point, a different metaphysics: Reading Bergson and Barad diffractively. *Hypatia*, 26/1, 22–42.

van der Tuin, Iris. 2015. *Generational Feminism*. New York: Lexington Books.

van der Tuin, Iris and Rick Dolphijn. 2010. The transversality of new materialism. *Women: A Cultural Review*, 21/2, 153–71.

van der Waal, Rodante. 2018. The pregnant posthuman. In: Rosi Braidotti and Maria Hlavajova (eds.) *Posthuman Glossary*. London: Bloomsbury Academic.

van Dooren, Thom, Eben Kirksey and Ursula Münster. 2016. Multispecies studies: Cultivating arts of attentiveness. *Environmental Humanities*, 8/1, 1–23.

Vance, Carole. 1984. *Power and Danger: Exploring Female Sexuality*. London: Routledge & Kegan Paul.

Vardoulakis, Dimitris. 2011. *Spinoza Now*. Minneapolis, MN: University of Minnesota Press.

Vint, Sherryl. 2007. *Bodies of Tomorrow: Technology, Subjectivity, Science/Fiction*. Toronto: University of Toronto Press.

Viveiros de Castro, Eduardo. 1998. Cosmological deixis and Amerindian perspectivism. *Journal of the Royal Anthropological Institute*, 4/3, 469–88.

Viveiros de Castro, Eduardo. 2014. *Cannibal Metaphysics*. Minneapolis, MN: Univocal Publishing.

Viveiros de Castro, Eduardo. 2015. *The Relative Native: Essays on Indigenous Conceptual Worlds*. Chicago, IL: HAU Press.

VNS Matrix. 1991. *The Cyberfeminist Manifesto for the Twenty-first Century*. https://vnsmatrix.net/projects/the-cyberfeminist-manifesto-for-the-21st-century

VNS Matrix. 1994. *Bitch Mutant Manifesto*. https://vnsmatrix.net/projects/bitch-mutant-manifesto

Waidner, Isabel. 2019. *We Are Made of Diamond Stuff*. Manchester: Dostoyevsky Wannabe.

Waldby, Catherine. 2000. *The Visible Human Project: Informatic Bodies and Posthuman Medicine*. London and New York: Routledge.

Walker, Alice. 1983. *In Search of Our Mother's Gardens*. New York: Harcourt Brace Jovanovich.
Ware, Vron. 1992. *Beyond the Pale: White Women, Racism and History*. London: Verso.
Warren, Calvin L. 2015. Black nihilism and the politics of hope. *CR: The New Centennial Review*, 15/1, 215–48.
Warren, Calvin L. 2017. Onticide: Afro-pessimism, Gay Nigger #1, and surplus violence. *GLQ: A Journal of Lesbian and Gay Studies*, 23/3, 391–418.
Warren, Karen J. (ed.). 1994. *Ecological Feminism*. London and New York: Routledge.
Weheliye, Alexander. 2014. *Habeas Viscus*. Durham, NC: Duke University Press.
Weil, Kari. 2010. A report on the animal turn. *differences*, 21(2), 1–23.
Weinbaum, Alys Eve. 2019. *The Afterlife of Reproductive Slavery*. Durham, NC: Duke University Press.
Weiss, Gail. 1999. *Body Images: Embodiment and Intercorporeality*. London and New York: Routledge.
Wekker, Gloria. 2016. *White Innocence*. Durham, NC: Duke University Press.
Westcott, Sarah. 2016. The Great Pacific Garbage patch. In: *Slant Light*. Liverpool: Liverpool University Press.
Whitford, Margaret, Naomi Schor and Carolyne Burke (eds.). 1994. *Engaging with Irigaray*. New York: Columbia University Press.
Whyte, Kyle P. 2013. On the role of traditional ecological knowledge as a collaborative concept: A philosophical study. *Ecological Processes*, 2/7.
Whyte, Kyle P. 2016. Is it colonial déjà vu? Indigenous peoples and climate injustice. In: Joni Adamson, Michael Davis and Hsinya Huang (eds.) *Humanities for the Environment: Integrating Knowledges, Forging New Constellations of Practice*. Abingdon-on-Thames: Earthscan Publications, pp. 88–104.
Whyte, Kyle P. 2017. Indigenous climate change studies: Indigenizing futures, decolonizing the Anthropocene. *English Language Notes*, 55/1–2, 153–62.
Wilding, Faith and the Critical Art Ensemble. 1998. Notes on the political condition of cyberfeminism. *Art Journal*, 57/2, 46–59.
Willey, Angela. 2016. Biopossibility: A queer feminist materialist science studies manifesto, with special reference to the question of monogamous behavior. *Signs*, 41/3, 553–77.
Williams, James. 2016. *A Process Philosophy of Signs*. Edinburgh: Edinburgh University Press.
Willis, Ellen. 2000 [1970]. Women and the Left. In: Barbara A. Crow (ed.) *Radical Feminism: A Documentary Reader*. New York: New York University Press.
Wills, David. 2016. *Inanimation*. Minneapolis, MN: University of Minnesota Press.

Wilson, Elizabeth. 1998. *Neural Geographies: Feminism and the Microstructure of Cognition.* New York: Routledge.

Wilson, Elizabeth. 2004. *Psychosomatic: Feminism and the Neurological Body.* Durham, NC: Duke University Press.

Winnubst, Shannon. 2018. Decolonial critique. In: Rosi Braidotti and Maria Hlavajova (eds.) *Posthuman Glossary.* London: Bloomsbury Academic.

Winterson, Jeanette. 2019. *Frankisssstein.* London: Jonathan Cape.

Wittig, Monique. 1980. La pensée straight. *Questions Féministes*, 7, 45–53.

Wittig, Monique. 1992. *The Straight Mind.* Boston, MA: Beacon.

Wolfe, Cary. 2010. *What is Posthumanism?* Minneapolis, MN: University of Minnesota Press.

Wolmark, Jenny (ed.). 1999. *Cybersexualities: A Reader on Feminist Theory, Cyborgs and Cyberspace.* Edinburgh: Edinburgh University Press.

Woods, Hannah R. 2017. Fantasy and the collective millennial psyche. *New Statesman*, 19–25 May, 16–17.

Woolf, Virginia. 1931. *The Waves.* London: Hogarth Press.

Woolf, Virginia. 1980 [1930]. *The Diary of Virginia Woolf, Volume 3 (1925–1930).* New York and London: Harvest.

Wyer, Mary, Mary Barbercheck, Donna Giesman, Hatice Orün Oztürk and Marta Wayne (eds.). 2001. *Women, Science and Technology.* London and New York: Routledge.

Wynter, Sylvia. 2003. Unsettling the coloniality of being/power/truth/freedom: Towards the human, after Man, its over-representation. An argument. *The New Centennial Review*, 3/3, 257–337.

Wynter, Sylvia. 2015. Unparalleled catastrophe for our species? In: Katherine McKittrick (ed.). *Sylvia Wynter: On Being Human as Praxis.* Durham, NC: Duke University Press.

Yoshida, Keina. 2018. A constitution for Mars. *INTLAWGRRLS. Voices on International Law, Policy, Practice*, 4 October. https://ilg2.org/2018/10/04/a-constitution-for-mars-a-call-for-founding-feminists/

Young, Chris. 2021. Why bitcoin mining consumes more electricity than entire countries. *Interesting Engineering*, 11 February. https://interestingengineering.com/why-bitcoin-mining-consumes-more-electricity-than-entire-countries

Young, Iris Marion. 1984. Pregnant embodiment: Subjectivity and alienation. *The Journal of Medicine and Philosophy*, 9/1, 45–62.

Young, Iris Marion. 2004. *On Female Body Experience: Throwing Like a Girl and Other Essays.* Oxford: Oxford University Press.

Young, Robert. 1990. *White Mythologies. Writing History and the West.* London and New York: Routledge.

Young, Robert. 1995. *Colonial Desire.* London and New York: Routledge.

Young-Bruehl, Elizabeth. 2003. *Where Do We Fall When We Fall in Love?* New York: Other Press.
Young-Bruehl, Elizabeth and Faith Bethelard. 2000. *Cherishment: A Psychology of the Heart.* New York: The Free Press.
Yusoff, Kathryn. 2018. *A Billion Black Anthropocenes or None.* London: Verso Books.
Zuboff, Shoshana. 2019. *The Age of Surveillance Capitalism.* Oxford: Blackwell.
Zylinska, Joanna. 2014. *Minimal Ethics for the Anthropocene.* Ann Arbor, MI: University of Michigan Press.

Index

ableism 162, 163
Aborigines, *see* Indigenous people/culture
academic feminism 12, 27, 87
academics, female 53
  see also writing, feminist
acceleration 97–102, 112, 136–7, 144
accelerationism 148, 189, 208, 229
  epistemic acceleration 112
accountability 116, 226
Acker, Kathy 41, 146–7, 168
activism, animal rights 83
activism, feminist 152, 155, 222
Adams, Carol 80, 81
Adamson, Joni and Hartman, Steven 103
Adichie, Chimamanda Ngozi 2
affect
  and desire 205, 206
  and literary and creative writing 216, 217

affirmation/affirmation ethics 9, 122, 221, 236–42
  and sexuality 205, 206, 208
  see also joy
Afrofuturism 224–9
Afro-pessimism 224
agriculture 85, 99
Ahmed, Sarah 148
Alaimo, Stacy 68, 89–90, 100, 107, 127, 135, 136
alienation 89, 154, 223, 225
alliances/assemblages, heterogeneous 79, 104, 113, 136–8, 179, 219, 220
  see also transversality
Althusser, Louis 120
Alyokhina, Maria 148
Amaro, Ramon 228
Anderson, Laurie 26, 171
androcentrism 31
Anglo-American feminism 108, 110, 188
animals 80–4, 195
  animal rights 81, 84, 98

see also non-humans; zoe-geo-techno-mediated relations
animism 186
Anthropocene 3–4, 129, 221, 227
 and ecofeminism 90, 93, 95
anthropocentrism 38, 44, 65, 133, 190
 and human exceptionalism 10–11, 68–104
 and ecofeminism 77–8, 82–3, 84
 and post-anthropocentrism 61, 138, 201
anthropomorphism 65, 136, 138–9
Anthropos 20, 75, 91–7, 221
 and ecofeminism 68–9, 74–7, 83–4
 see also 'Man'/'Man of Reason'
anti-naturalism 70, 100
anti-racism 36, 67, 132
 anti-racist feminism 21, 23
 anti-Semitism 48, 131
 'Black Lives Matter' movement 5, 33, 127
Anzaldúa, Gloria 35
Arbus, Diane 218
Ardern, Jacinda 26
art
 and materialism 195, 246n4
 and sexuality 181, 192, 194–5
 and technoscience 152, 195
artificiality 1–2, 77, 150, 159
Åsberg, Cecilia and Lykke, Nina 151
assemblages/heterogeneous alliances 79, 104, 113, 136–8, 179, 219, 220

astronauts, female 232
Atkinson, Ti-Grace 221
atmosphere 124, 127
Atwood, Margaret 219
Austin, Sue 140, 162, 192
Australia 91, 120, 246n8
auto-immunity 172, 173, 174
 see also biopolitics
autopoiesis 124–5, 142, 202

Bachelard, Gaston 110, 245n1
bacteria 122–3, 124–5, 135, 194–5, 202, 235
Balzano, Angela 166
Barad, Karen 94, 157
Barker, Joanna 187
Bates, Tarsh 194–5
Baudrillard, Jean 62
Beauvoir, Simone de 21, 72, 222, 243n3
becoming 37, 89, 174, 221
 and Afrofuturism 225–6, 228
 and gender 189, 192
 and materialism 113, 128, 135–6, 137
 and sexuality 183–4, 189, 192, 198, 205
 virtual ways of becoming 137, 157, 183, 202, 225, 238
belonging 115, 228
Berlant, Lauren 47
Berwick, Rachel 195
Beyoncé 2, 226
Bezos, Jeff 231
Bhandari, Bidya Devi 26
Bhattacharyya, Gargi 56, 76
Biemann, Ursula 97–8
Bignall, Simone 71, 95, 120
biocapital/biocapitalism 56, 57, 131–2
bio-colonialism 75, 84–5

Index

bio-genetic capitalism 158, 159, 165, 166–7, 207
bio-hacking 161, 163, 167
biology 152–3, 158–62, 164–6, 187–8, 201
  see also environment; reproduction/fertility; technobodies; technoscience
bioluminescence 182
bio-medicine 4, 60, 155, 159, 164, 169–70
  see also reproduction/fertility
'bio-piracy' 158, 167–8
biopolitics 37, 51–2, 185–6
  and environment 128, 131, 133
  and reproduction/fertility 169, 173–4
  see also auto-immunity
bio-racism 75
bios 71, 83, 126, 200, 219
biosciences 144
biosecurity 128
biosphere 124, 127, 195
biotechnology 52–4, 58–60, 149
biovalue 56
Birke, Lynda and Holmberg, Tora 134–7
Bitcoin 101–2
Björk 194
Black and Indigenous women 37, 51, 86, 100, 169, 226, 227
Black feminism 2, 34, 37, 179, 219, 227–9
'Black Lives Matter' movement 5, 33, 127
Black Panther film 224
Black posthumanism 219, 224–9
bodies 12, 112–13, 140–76
  and de-materialization 142, 144
  disabled bodies 162–4
  LGBTQ+ bodies 155, 164
  non-human bodies 112, 155
  normal bodies 155
  otherwise-designed bodies 163–4
  white, male, European bodies 156, 162, 247n8
  women's bodies 1–2, 155, 166
  see also embodiment; technobodies
bodily/carnal materialsm 112–16, 118, 126
brain, human 61, 113–15
Branson, Richard 231
breathing 107, 127
Brnabić, Ana 26, 48
Brown, Rita Mae 195–6
Brownmiller, Susan 223
Bunch, Charlotte 217
Burke, Tarana 33
Butler, Octavia 219
Byrd, Jodie 231–2

capitalism
  and colonialism 32, 230–4
  and environment 85, 233
  and Indigenous people 75, 233–4
  and mineral extraction 231, 233–4
  and neo-colonialism 57–8, 70, 175, 230, 231, 233–4
  and race issues 95–6, 227
  and space exploration 231, 232
  and commodification/

consumption/
consumerism 47, 56,
58
and COVID-19 4, 53
and dehumanization 56–7,
76, 111, 234
and environment 85, 231
and colonialism 85, 233
and Indigenous people/
culture 95, 100, 233–4
and materialism 130,
131–2, 138
and technoscience 57,
100
and feminism 10, 21,
43–67, 222
and cyberfeminism 145,
146–7
and liberal feminism 24,
26–30
and neoliberal feminism
44, 45–54
and neo-socialist
feminism 54–61
and posthuman feminism
6–8, 63, 65–7
and socialist feminism
32, 34, 60
and freedom 53, 193
and gender 28, 168, 185,
187
and Indigenous people/
culture 51
and colonialism 75,
233–4
and environment 95,
100, 233–4
and inequality 4, 28, 57–8,
95–6, 132, 227
and LGBTQ+ 40, 48, 49,
59
and materialism 60,
111–12, 123–4, 131–2,
138
and de-materialization
55, 59
and environment 130,
131–2, 138
and migration 52, 55, 57–8
and mineral extraction 55,
85, 129, 130, 132,
231, 233–4
and race issues 57–8, 95–6,
187, 227
and sexuality 184, 193,
204
and technoscience 10, 56,
57–60, 229–31, 234
cognitive capitalism
58–60, 66, 143, 165,
169–70
and environment 57, 100
and inequality 57–8, 175
and LGBTQ+ 40, 59
and reproduction/fertility
50–4, 158–9, 165,
166–7, 169–70, 175
and transnationality 128,
159, 168
see also accelerationism;
biocapital/
biocapitalism;
bio-genetic capitalism;
cognitive capitalism;
delirium; racial/
racialized capitalism;
surveillance capitalism;
territorialization;
zombie capitalism
carceral feminism 50
care ethics
and ecofeminism 79–80,
92–3, 98
and sexuality 182, 207–8
'Care Manifesto' 80
caring roles 72
Carson, Rachel 69
Cartesian theory 64, 119

cartographies
  and figurations 212, 238
  and locational politics 116, 118
celebrities, feminist 2, 46–7
CEOs, female 45–6
Césaire, Aimé 36
Chakrabarty, Dipesh 100
change, egalitarian 24, 26–8, 34
chaos 150
Chen, Mel Y. 135, 199, 220
cherishment 208
child care 52, 53
Chronos 228
citizenship 26, 73, 80
Clarke, Bruce 123, 125
class equality 169–70
  and humanism 25, 30–4, 37
  and neoliberal feminism 51, 52, 53
  white, middle-class women 25, 51, 52, 53, 169
classical humanist 18, 25, 61, 66–7
climate change 194, 227, 237
  and materialism 125, 127–8, 130–1, 233
  and race issues 85–6, 93, 98–9
Climate Reframe 99–100, 245n10
Clinton, Hillary 24, 49
Code, Lorraine 79
cognitive capitalism 4, 138
  and inequality 28, 132
  and neo-socialist feminism 55–6, 57, 58–60
  and technoscience 58–60, 66, 143, 165, 169–70
colonialism
  and capitalism 32, 230–4
  and environment 85, 233
  and Indigenous people 75, 233–4
  and mineral extraction 231, 233–4
  and race issues 95–6, 227
  and space exploration 231, 232
  and environment
    and capitalism 85, 233
    and climate change 84–6, 93, 98–9
    and Indigenous people/culture 85–6, 89–90, 91–7, 98–9
    and materialism 95, 130
  and gender issues 32, 182–3
  and humanism 20, 23, 35, 63
  and Indigenous people/culture 186–7, 217
    and capitalism 75, 233–4
    and environment 85–6, 89–90, 91–7, 98–9
    and materialism 95, 130, 132
    and nature-culture 71, 75–6, 186
    and oppression 91, 95
  and race issues 35, 91, 95–6, 182–3, 217
    and Afrofuturism 225, 227, 228
    capitalism 95–6, 227
  and violence 91, 182–3
  see also bio-colonialism; decolonialism; neo-colonialism; postcolonialism; race issues
Combahee River Collective 36
commercialization 58–9, 169

commodification 33, 56, 58, 85
commonfare 153
commons 153, 231, 237
community, collaborative 121–2, 123–4, 241
compassion 82, 216, 241
complexity
  and difference 177, 213, 221, 239
  and materialism 116, 121, 126, 132, 134, 193
  and sexuality 177, 188, 193, 198, 199, 206
  see also heterogeneity; multiplicity
consciousness, human 19, 61, 64, 72
conservation programmes 89
consumerism/consumption 47, 56, 58
continental philosophy 110, 245n1
contraception/birth control 195, 222
Coole, Diana and Frost, Samantha 108
Cooper, Melinda 60, 169, 169–70
Cornucopia show (Björk) 194
corporate feminism 45–6
COVID-19 4–5, 53, 79, 103–4, 127, 174, 240
cows 81
creativity 150
  see also figurations; imagination; speculative genre; writing
Cristoforetti, Samantha 232, 233
Critical Posthumanities 96
  see also Humanities; posthumanism; Posthumanities
Cubonics, Laboria 140
Cullors, Patrisse 33
cultural identity, national 48–50
cultural studies, feminist 129, 152, 156
cyberfeminism 63, 145–9, 175, 192, 222
Cyberfeminist Manifesto for the Twenty-first Century (VNX Matrix) 145
cyberpunk writers 62–3
  see also punk
cyborgs 202, 214, 220

Danowski, Déborah and Viveiros de Castro, Eduardo 64–5, 93, 133
data
  collection of 112
  production of 130
  statistical data 27–8
  storage of 138
Dawkins, Richard 78, 123
death 239
  see also necropolitics
d'Eaubonne, Françoise 69
decolonial feminism 34–5, 36–7, 67, 69–70
decolonialism 93, 95, 129, 182, 186–7, 217
dehumanization 8
  and capitalism 56–7, 76, 111, 234
  and LGBTQ+ 39, 75
  and nature-culture 71, 75
  and patriarchy 37, 71, 83, 97, 207–8
  and race issues 24, 37
Deitch, Jeffrey 1

Deleuze, Gilles 21, 95, 119, 123, 128, 141, 199
delirium 229
see also cognitive capitalism
de-materialization 192
  and bodies 142, 144
  and capitalism 55, 59
  and technoscience 59, 112, 149
Dement, Linda 145
democracy 80, 119
de-naturalization 72
  and posthuman feminism 143, 144, 175
  and re-naturalization 101, 153–4, 158–60, 175
  and technoscience 59, 136, 151–4, 162
    and biology 141, 158–60, 164, 201, 203
dependence, inter-species 135–6
Derrida, Jacques 22, 90
Descola, Philippe 91, 186
desire 178, 199–206, 208–10
  and affect 205, 206
  and affirmation/affirmation ethics 205, 206
  and individualism 204, 206
  and transversality 191, 199–203, 205
difference
  and complexity 177, 213, 221, 239
  and posthuman feminism 62, 67
  and sexuality 72, 146, 177, 198, 201, 203
    and multiplicity 190, 192
    and not One 190
differential materialism 67, 213, 221
digital feminism 148

digital waste 130
Diprose, Rosalind 171
disability/disability studies 162–4, 220, 232–3
dis-identification 39, 41, 142, 146, 228–9, 241, 249n3
diversity 162
  and ecofeminism 78, 81, 85, 87, 88
  and humanism 27, 35, 38–40
  and sexuality 199, 202
DNA 123, 124
Dolly the sheep 58, 158–60
Donovan, Josephine and Adams, Carol J. 79–80
dualism 92, 189
  and gender 187, 189
  and nature-culture 101, 134, 137, 187

earth 71, 75, 99, 102, 128
  as Gaia 86
  Indigenous cosmologies 94, 99–100, 125, 180
ecocriticism 84, 129
ecofeminism 11, 68–104
  and Anthropocene 90, 93, 95
  and anthropocentrism 77–8, 82–3, 84
  and Anthropos 68–9, 74–7, 83–4
  and care ethics 79–80, 92–3, 98
  and diversity 78, 81, 85, 87, 88
  and environment 69, 81–2, 83–4, 94, 98–9, 215
  and ethics 80, 81–2, 84, 98–9
  and hierarchies 70–4, 75, 78, 79, 81, 92, 94

and human exceptionalism 77–8, 82–3, 84
and interdependence 11, 76, 78, 80, 92, 94, 97
and intersectionality 77–9, 85–6, 91–2
and LGBTQ+ 73–4, 75, 87–8
and 'Man'/'Man of Reason' 80, 89
and materialism 94, 97–8, 143
and nature-culture 69, 71, 72–3, 74, 75–6
  and re-naturalization 101, 102, 103, 153, 175
and patriarchy 74, 76
and postcolonialism 32, 79, 84, 86, 93, 95
and posthuman convergence 80, 84, 91–2, 99, 101, 103, 154
and race issues
  and hierarchies 78, 79
  and Indigenous people/culture 69–70, 98, 99
  and relational ontology/rationality 94, 98
and reproduction/fertility 72–3, 95
and sexuality 78, 79, 181, 202
and social constructivism 76, 86, 88, 98
  and nature-culture 71, 72–3
and species-ism 69, 70
and spirituality 86–90, 103
and technoscience 175, 214–15
  and technofeminism 143, 153–4
and *zoe* 80–4, 97–9, 154
and territorialization 143
and transversality 77–9, 88, 103–4
and universalism 84, 98
ecological reason 77–80
ecology, *see* earth; environment
education for women 27
egg market 170
Ehrenreich, Barbara 47
Eisenstein, Zillah 58
Elders 99, 245n9
elemental feminist materialism 125–31, 138, 192, 194–5
Eliot, George 119, 246n6
embedded feminism 49
embeddedness 49, 110, 115, 137–8, 191
embodiment
  and materialism 110, 113–15, 117, 137–8
  and sexuality 191, 200–1
  and technoscience 140, 160–1, 163, 167
empathy 82, 83, 94, 207, 216
empiricism, carnal 112–16, 118
empowerment 176, 236
  and Afrofuturism 225–6, 227
  and liberal feminism 24, 45–6
  and sexuality 179, 181, 196, 209
endurance 207, 227
energy, human 178, 179, 203, 238
enhancement, human 22, 58, 61, 62, 64
Enlightenment 18, 35, 40, 41, 61, 71

Enloe, Cynthia 79
enslavement 76, 85, 226, 227
entrepreneurship 33, 51
environment 3, 85
  and biopolitics 128, 131, 133
  and capitalism 85, 231
    and Indigenous people/culture 95, 100, 233–4
    and materialism 130, 131–2, 138
    and technoscience 57, 100
  and colonialism
    and capitalism 85, 233
    and climate change 84–6, 93, 98–9
    decolonialism 93, 95, 129
    and Indigenous people/culture 85–6, 89–90, 91–7, 98–9
    and materialism 95, 130
  and ecofeminism 69, 81–2, 83–4, 94, 98–9, 215
  and ethics 81–2, 98–9, 240
  and feminism 44, 88
    and ecofeminism 81–2, 94, 98–9
    and neoliberal feminism 44, 46–7
    and posthuman feminism 65, 66, 83–4, 92, 101, 125–6, 194–5
  and gender 85–6, 99
  and Indigenous people/culture 85, 99
    and capitalism 95, 100, 233–4
    and materialism 129, 130
  and inequality 4–5, 8
  and literary and creative writing 215, 217
  and materialism 94, 112, 124–5, 127–31
    and capitalism 130, 131–2, 138
    and colonialism 95, 130
    and Indigenous people 129, 130
    and racism 127, 129, 130, 133–4
  and postcolonialism 84, 86
  and posthuman convergence 86, 88, 95, 99, 215, 227, 234
  and power 81, 130
  and racism 84–6, 99–100, 240
    and materialism 127, 129, 130, 133–4
  and technoscience 42, 57, 88, 89, 95, 101, 129–31, 234
    and capitalism 57, 100
  and transversality 89, 125–6
Environmental Humanities 86, 96, 135
environmental justice 80, 83, 86, 93, 104
environmental racism 84–6
equality *see* inequality
eroticism/Eros 179, 181, 196
  see also love/passion
Eshun, Kodwo 230
essentialism 160–1, 189, 227
ethics 13
  affirmation/affirmation ethics 9, 122, 205, 206, 208, 221, 236–42
    see also Spinoza
  care ethics 79–80, 92–3, 98, 182, 207–8
  compassion ethics 82
  and ecofeminism 79–80, 81–2, 84, 92–3, 98

Index

and environment 81–2, 98–9, 240
and indigeneity 75, 187
relational ethics 9, 67, 80, 84, 176, 191
and sexuality 182, 191, 205, 206, 207–8
and technoscience 176, 239
ethnography 96, 98, 136
Eurocentric humanism 17, 22, 34, 37, 64, 67
Eurocentrism 64, 74, 84, 95, 228
  and humanism 18–19
    Black feminist humanism 34–5, 36–7
    Eurocentric humanism 17, 22, 37
  and sexuality 186, 187–8
European humanism 18, 22, 25
  and Black, feminist humanism 34–5, 36–7
  and transhumanism 63, 64
European Union 26, 28, 81
evolution 18, 64, 122–3, 222
exceptionalism, human 22, 44, 200
  and anthropocentrism 10–11, 77–8
  and ecofeminism 77–8, 82–3, 84
  and materialism 111–12, 121, 125, 136, 139
  and transhumanism 65, 67
exclusion 116–17
exclusive humanism 78, 129
experience
  life/lived experience 3, 38, 51, 59, 236
  and materialism 115, 117

experimentation 221, 237
and sexuality 182, 185, 193, 199
and technoscience 142, 145, 151, 170, 175
exposure 136
expression, artistic/cultural 152, 178, 181, 212
extinction 93, 195
  Sixth Extinction 5, 57, 60, 112

family structure 167, 168–9, 176
Fanon, Frantz 20, 36
fantasy writing 221, 229
fascism 20, 21
Federici, Silvia 32, 76, 166
femininity 192, 193, 197–8
feminism 10, 12–13, 17–42, 43–67, 236–42
  and capitalism 10, 21, 43–67, 222
  and cyberfeminism 145, 146–7
  and liberal feminism 24, 26–30
  and neoliberal feminism 44, 45–54
  and neo-socialist feminism 54–61
  and posthuman feminism 6–8, 63, 65–7
  and socialist feminism 32, 34, 60
  definitions 3
  and environment 44, 88
  and ecofeminism 81–2, 94, 98–9
  and neoliberal feminism 44, 46–7
  and posthuman feminism 65, 66, 83–4, 92, 101, 125–6, 194–5

feminism (*cont.*)
  and gender 50–4, 97, 149, 150, 160–2, 220–1
  and 'Man'/'Man of Reason'
    and ecofeminism 80, 89
    and liberal feminism/neoliberal 25, 43–4
    and posthuman feminism 67, 211
    and socialist feminism/neo-socialist 34, 43–4
  non-humans
    and ecofeminism 75, 80–4, 154
    and posthuman feminism 62, 65–6, 67, 77
  and patriarchy
    and cyberfeminism 145, 146–8
    and ecofeminism 74, 76
    and liberal feminism 24, 25
    and neoliberal feminism 49, 53–4
    and socialist feminism 31, 32, 33–4
  and posthuman convergence 30, 41–2
    and ecofeminism 80, 84, 91–2, 99, 101, 103, 154
    and posthuman feminism 67, 141, 216, 237, 239
  and power 21, 76
    and liberal feminism 24, 26–8, 45–6
    and neoliberal feminism 45–6, 50
  and race issues 21, 27, 32
    anti-racist feminism 21, 23
    and Black posthumanism 219, 224–9
  and ecofeminism 69–70, 78, 79, 91, 98, 99
  and sexuality
    and ecofeminism 78, 79, 181, 202
    and feminist new-materialism 184, 185, 189, 198
    and posthuman feminism 184–5, 188, 192–3, 194, 197–8, 200
    and socialist feminism 31
  and technoscience
    and ecofeminism 80–4, 97–9, 143, 153–4, 175, 214–15
    and Gaga feminism 149, 150
    and posthuman feminism 66, 108, 141–5
    and technofeminism 87, 143, 153–4
  see also academic feminism; Anglo-American feminism; Black feminism; carceral feminism; corporate feminism; cyberfeminism; decolonial feminism; digital feminism; embedded feminism; feminist new-materialism; Gaga feminism; Indigenous feminism; intergalactic feminism; liberal feminism; neoliberal feminism; neo-socialist feminism; postcolonial feminism; posthuman feminism; socialist feminism; speculative feminism;

technofeminism;
transfeminism;
twentieth century feminism;
Xenofeminism
feminist Black humanism 34–8
feminist new-materialism 11, 97–8, 107–39, 171, 215–16
  and ecofeminism 94, 97–8
  and sexuality 184, 185, 189, 198
  and technoscience 12, 157
Feminist Revolution (Redstockings) 196
Ferrando, Francesca 63
figurations 212–16, 238
Firestone, Shulamith 222–3
flows 190, 192, 193, 195, 204, 205–6
  see also capitalism; territorialization
foetuses 172, 173
food 81, 194–5
forests 130–1
Foucault, Michel 22, 50, 128, 185
  see also biopolitics
Francis, Pope 86
Frankenstein 218
Franklin, Sarah 58, 90, 152, 158–60
Fraser, Nancy 32
Frawley, Jodi and McCalman, Iain 85
freedom
  and affirmation ethics 228, 238
  and capitalism 53, 193
  and materialism 113, 122, 133
  and sexuality 182, 196
  and technoscience 140, 192

'Freewheeling' artwork (Austin) 140, 162, 192
Freire, Paulo 117
French Universal Declaration 23
Freud, Sigmund 20, 73, 120
Friedan, Betty 24

Gaard, Greta 86, 87–8, 90
Gabrys, Jennifer 130–1
Gaga feminism 149–51, 175
Gaia 5, 86, 124–5
Garza, Alicia 33
Gay, Roxane 45–6
gender 12, 23–30, 177–210
  and becoming 189, 192
  and capitalism 28, 168, 185, 187
  and colonialism 32, 182–3
  and dualism 187, 189
  and environment 85–6, 99
  and femininity 192, 193, 197–8
  and feminism 50–4, 97, 149, 150, 160–2, 220–1
  and masculinity 17, 25–6, 31, 80
  and materialism 185, 188–9, 192–3
  and nature-culture 72–3, 99, 101, 186
  and race issues 85–6, 182–3, 187
  and sexuate matter 183–4, 186, 188–9
  and social constructivism 188, 189, 201
  and technoscience 140–76, 192
    and Gaga feminism 149, 150
    and reproduction/fertility 166, 184, 185, 190

gender (*cont.*)
   and space exploration 232–3, 234–5
   and transversality 189, 190–1
   and Western culture 186, 187–8
   see also sexuality
gender equality 23–30, 99, 168, 169, 232–3, 234–5
gender metrics and statistics 28, 51
gender pay gap 26, 244n7
gender politics 184–5
gender roles 28, 53, 188
   and nature-culture 72–3, 99, 101
   and technoscience 149, 150
gender studies 27
gender systems 150, 184–5, 201
   binary system 12, 39, 74, 87, 101, 183, 189
   and patriarchy 37, 155, 167, 172, 182, 188
   multiple system 164, 184, 220
gene-editing 167
genetic screening 56
genocide 92, 95, 100, 131, 183
Genosko, Gary 127
geo 12, 128–9, 138, 220
   see also zoe-geo-techno-mediated relations
geography/geopolitics 96
geology 129–30, 132
Georgieva, Kristalina 26
Gibson, Katherine 91
Gibson, William 62
'gilets jaunes' movement 33
Gilligan, Carol 79
Gilroy, Paul 36, 224

'Girls just wanna have fun' song 145–6
globalization 87, 152
Goop company 46
Gouges, Olympe de 23
greed, capitalist 34, 95
Green New Deal 85
Grimshaw, Jean 25
Grosz, Elizabeth 29
Gruber, David 114
Gruen, Lori 81
Guattari, Felix 21, 120, 123, 199

Haigneré, Claudie 232
Halberstam, Judith 41, 149–50, 220
happiness 47, 48, 52
Haraway, Donna 63, 213–14, 216
   capitalism 54, 56, 169
   ecofeminism 87, 88, 90
   materialism 124, 125
Harding, Sandra 25
Harris, Kamala 27
Hassan, Ihab 63
Hayles, Katherine 63, 64
Hayward, Eva 127, 135
health, women's 155–6, 157, 247n5
health services 47–8, 147, 155, 247n5
Hester, Helen 154
heterogeneity 116, 123, 187, 202
   assemblages/heterogeneous alliances 79, 104, 113, 136–8, 179, 219, 220
heterogenesis 115
heterosexuality 73–4, 87–8, 155–6, 184, 186, 201, 202
hierarchies
   sexualized and racialized

hierarchies 11, 70–4, 75, 78, 79, 92, 94
species hierarchies 81, 94
see also natural order
Hill Collins, Patricia 25
Hillary, Fiona 182
Hinsliff, Gaby 193
Hird, Myra J. 171–2
hooks, bell 2, 226, 227
hormones 128, 195
'housewifization' 32
Howie, Gillian 27
Huffer, Lynne 108
Human Genome Project 247n8
human life (*bios*) 71, 83, 126, 200, 219
human rights 6–7, 23–4, 41, 49, 84, 162
humanism 10, 17–42
  and colonialism 20, 23, 35, 63
  and diversity 27, 35, 38–40
  and emancipation 17, 26–9
  and Eurocentrism 17, 18–19, 22, 34–5, 36–7, 64, 67
  and human exceptionalism 65, 67
  and individualism 29–30, 61, 65
  and inequality 23–30, 38–42
    class equality 25, 30–4, 37
    race issues 21, 25, 34–8, 224
  and LGBTQ+ 23–4, 38–40
  and 'Man'/'Man of Reason' 18–20, 22, 25, 37
  and masculinity 17, 25–6, 31
  and patriarchy 21, 63

  and postcolonialism 4, 20, 32, 35, 49
  and technoscience 20–1, 42, 61, 62, 64–5
  and universalism 19, 23, 25, 34, 82
  see also classical humanist; Eurocentric humanism; European humanism; exclusive humanism; feminist Black humanism; Marxist humanism; neo-humanism; planetary humanism; socialist humanism; transhumanism
Humanities 27, 129, 152, 230
  see also Posthumanities, Critical Posthumanities, feminist Posthumanities
human/non-human relationships 62, 194, 207–8

imaginaries, sexual 191, 202, 203–4
imaginaries, social 67, 210, 228
imagination 216–21, 237
  political 144, 217, 227, 228
immanence 67, 102, 110, 116, 139, 179, 187, 208
immunology 172, 173–4
imperialism 19, 35, 46, 49, 84–5
  see also colonialism
Indigenous feminism 11, 91, 93, 98, 102, 186

Indigenous people/culture 157–8, 240
  and capitalism 51
    and colonialism 75, 233–4
    and environment 95, 100, 233–4
  and colonialism 186–7, 217
    and capitalism 75, 233–4
    and environment 85–6, 89–90, 91–7, 98–9
    and ecofeminism 69–70, 98, 99
  and environment 85, 99, 100
    and capitalism 95, 100, 233–4
    and colonialism 85–6, 89–90, 91–7, 98–9
    and materialism 129, 130
  and materialism 129, 130, 133–4
  and perspectivism 92, 93–4, 134
  and postcolonialism 86, 218
  and race issues 69–70, 98, 99, 134, 182–3
  and sexuality 180–3, 186–8
  and transhumanism 64, 65
  see also land/country
individualism 94, 121
  and feminism 65
    and liberal feminism 24, 29–30, 33
    and neoliberal feminism 45–6, 50, 51–2
    and humanism 29–30, 61, 65
    and sexuality 191, 204, 206
  and transhumanism 61, 65
inequality 3–5, 237
  and capitalism 4, 28, 57–8, 95–6, 132, 227
  and COVID-19 4, 103–4
  and environment 4–5, 8
  and feminism 8–9, 26–8, 32–3, 46–8
  and humanism 23–30, 38–42
    class equality 25, 30–4, 37
    race issues 21, 25, 34–8, 224
  and patriarchy 70–4, 75
  and sexualized and racialized hierarchies 70–4, 75
  and technoscience 57–8, 155–6, 165–6, 175
  and violence 37, 41
  see also class equality; gender equality; race issues; social and economic equality
inhumanism 17, 38–40, 160, 163
injustice, social 19, 54–5, 60
intercorporeality 135
intercultural collaboration 95
interdependence 194, 240, 241
  and ecofeminism 11, 76, 78, 80, 92, 94, 97
  and materialism 11, 118, 122, 123, 124, 125–6, 137
  and sexuality 180, 195
interdisciplinarity 118, 152, 157
intergalactic feminism 229–35
intergeneration 9, 220, 232, 234

Index

International Labour Organization 26
International Monetary Fund 26
international relations 153
intersectionality 144, 182–3
  and ecofeminism 77–9, 85–6, 91–2
  and materialism 125, 129, 131
  and sexuality 39, 161–2, 182
  and technoscience 42, 91–2, 144, 156–7, 161–2, 163
Irigaray, Luce 126, 183
IVF 159–60, 164, 165

Jaggar, Alison 25
Jemisin, Nora K. 219, 249n1
Johnston, Jill 196
Jones, Donna V. 131
Jones, Emily 49, 234
Joon-ho, Bong 56
joy 204–5, 208
  see also affirmation/affirmative ethics
Joy, Eileen 160
justice, environmental 80, 83, 86, 93, 104
justice, social 147, 217, 239, 240

Kennedy, Flo 1
kinship 159, 164–7, 168–9, 176, 214
Kirby, Vicki 109, 157
Klare, Michael T. 233
Koyama, Emi 39
Kroker, Arthur and Kroker, Marilouise 62
Kuokkanen, Rauna 51, 96, 186–7

labour, domestic 32, 52, 53, 166
labour, human 56, 130, 132
  and labour relations 53, 130, 169–70
  and technoscience 130, 169–70
  and reproductive technology 60, 165–6
labour/work, women's 32, 99, 169
Lacanian psychoanalytic theory 107, 109, 191, 203, 204
Lagarde, Christine 26, 46
land/country 133–4
  see also Indigenous people/culture
language 109–10, 209
Latour, Bruno 90
law, international 231
Le Guin, Ursula 219
LeFanu, Sarah 218–19
Leonardo da Vinci 18
Lesbian Nation anthology 196, 249n20
Lewis, Helen 147, 235
Lewis, Sophie 165, 166, 167
LGBTQ+ 135–6, 164–7, 220
  and capitalism/neoliberalism 40, 48, 49, 59
  and dehumanization 39, 75
  and ecofeminism 73–4, 75, 87–8
  and humanism 23–4, 38–40
  and inhumanism 17, 38–40, 160, 163
  and naturalization 73, 160–2
  and patriarchy/compulsory heterosexuality 73–4, 155–6, 184, 187, 201

LGBTQ+ (cont.)
  and sexuality 187, 192, 193, 195–7, 201
  lesbianism 87, 195–7, 223
  and technoscience 40, 88, 155, 157, 160–2, 164–7
  and capitalism 40, 59
  LGBTQ+ bodies 155, 164
LGBTQ+ rights 23–4
liberal democracies 28, 29
liberal feminism 6, 24, 26–30, 32–3, 45–6
liberalism, classical 45–6, 71
life force and sexuality 190, 191, 196
Life Sciences 27, 52, 108, 151, 158
Lillvis, Kristen 227
Linnaeus 75
Lloyd, Genevieve 25, 120, 121
locational politics 116–18, 138–9
Long, Honey 195
Lorde, Audre 38, 179, 196, 217
Louverture, Toussaint 23
Lovelock, James 124–5, 230
love/passion 179–80, 181, 182, 206–8, 210
  see also eroticism/Eros
Ludosky, Priscillia 33
Lugones, Maria 37
Lykke, Nina 151, 153, 189, 215
Lyotard, Jean-François 62

MacCormack, Patricia 83, 126, 191, 198
McClintock, Barbara 123
Mack, Ashley Noel and Na'puti, Tiara R. 182
MacKinnon, Catharine 25
McNeil, Maureen 152
Malone, Karen 181
Manifest Destiny doctrine 231–2
'Man'/'Man of Reason' 10, 222
  and feminism
  and ecofeminism 80, 89
  and liberal feminism/ neoliberal 25, 43–4
  and posthuman feminism 67, 211
  and socialist feminism/ neo-socialist 34, 43–4
  and humanism 18–20, 22, 25, 37
  and LGBTQ+ 39, 40
Margulis, Lynn 90, 122–3, 124–5, 127, 135
  see also symbiogenesis
Marin, Sanna 26
marriage 73, 168–9
Marxism 120, 222
Marxist humanism 21
masculinity 17, 25–6, 31, 80
material process ontology 112, 114, 121, 125, 133, 137
materialism 11, 107–39, 215–16
  and art 195, 246n4
  and becoming 113, 128, 135–6, 137
  and *bios* 126, 219
  and capitalism 60, 111–12, 123–4, 131–2, 138
  and de-materialization 55, 59
  and environment 130, 131–2, 138
  and collaborative community 121–2, 123–4

and colonialism 95, 130, 132
and embeddedness 110, 115, 137–8
and embodiment 110, 113–15, 117, 137–8
and environment 94, 112, 124–5, 127–31
  and capitalism 130, 131–2, 138
  and climate change 125, 127–8, 130–1, 233
  and colonialism 95, 130
  and Indigenous people 129, 130, 133–4
  and race issues 127, 129, 130, 133–4
and experience 115, 117
and feminism 60, 143
  and ecofeminism 94, 97–8, 143
  and new-materialist feminism 184, 185, 189, 198
  and posthuman feminism 107–8, 111–12, 125–6, 137, 144, 192, 194, 200
and freedom 113, 122, 133
and gender 185, 188–9, 192–3
and human exceptionalism 111–12, 121, 125, 136, 139
and Indigenous people/ culture 129, 130, 133–4
and interdependence 11, 118, 122, 123, 124, 125–6, 137
and intersectionality 125, 129, 131
and multiplicity 125, 132, 134
and nature-culture 120, 121, 129, 130, 134
and non-humans 110, 125, 126–7
and posthumanism 127, 135, 136
and poststructuralism 110, 117, 188
and power 111–12, 115–16, 117, 118, 130, 132, 138
and race issues 127, 129, 130, 131–4
and relational ontology 135, 137
and re-naturalization 119, 122, 136, 175
and sexuality 178
  and elemental feminist materialism 192, 194–5
  and new-materialist feminism 184, 185, 189, 198, 204
  and posthuman feminism 194, 200
  vital materialism 181, 183, 191, 199–200, 206
and technoscience 112, 126, 129, 130–1, 143, 172, 175
  feminist new-materialism 12, 157
  and transversality 111, 131–2, 138, 191
  vital materialism 111, 143
  and *zoe*-geo-techno-mediated relations 97–8, 125, 126–7, 138, 139, 219
and transversality 108–9, 111, 131–2, 138, 191

materialism (*cont.*)
  see also bodily/carnal materialism; de-materialization; differential materialism; elemental feminist materialism; feminist new-materialism; re-materialization; vital materialism
matter, symbiotic 122–5
#MeToo movement 5, 33
meat industry 81
media culture 149–51, 219
media studies 129–30, 156
medianatures 130, 207
medical science, experimental 156, 247n8
Merchant, Carolyn 217
Merkel, Angela 26
methods 38, 70, 76–7, 98, 110, 116–18, 130, 133, 138, 151, 155–6, 175, 182, 189, 214–15, 237–9
  see also post-constructivism; post-foundational qualitative enquiry methods; social constructivism; transdisciplinarity
Midgley, Mary 78
Mies, Maria 32, 76
migration 52, 55, 57–8
militarism, Western 49–50
mineral extraction 55, 85, 129, 130, 132, 231, 233–4
missing people 96, 225, 238, 239
Mitchell, Juliet 31
mobility, human 57–8
modernism 18–19, 143, 184
Mohan, Swati 235

Mohanty, Chandra Talpade 35
monsters 218–19, 220, 221
Moon 231, 232
Moore, Henrietta 217
motherhood 51, 87
multinaturalism 65, 133
multiplicity 88, 164, 226
  and materialism 125, 132, 134
  and sexuality 177, 183, 191, 198, 199–200, 206, 209
  and difference 190, 192
  not-One 126, 177, 190–3
  and sexuate matter 11, 191, 193, 197, 200–1, 206, 208–9
  see also complexity
mushrooms, matsutake 215
Musk, Elon 102, 231

Nancy, Jean-Luc 172
National Front, France 48
nationalism 48, 49, 75, 89
naturalization 39, 76
  and LGBTQ+ 73, 160–2
  and sexuality 182, 186, 201
  see also de-naturalization; re-naturalization
nature 65, 71, 75
nature-culture 70–6, 152
  and colonialism 71, 75–6, 186
  and dehumanization 71, 75
  and dualism 101, 134, 137, 187
  and ecofeminism 69, 74, 75–6
  and re-naturalization 101, 102, 103, 153, 175
  and gender/gender roles 72–3, 99, 101, 186

and Indigenous people/
    culture 71, 75, 76
  and materialism 120, 121,
    129, 130, 134
  and patriarchy 73–4, 76
  and posthuman feminism
    97, 108–9, 144
  and reproduction/fertility
    72–3, 152
  and social constructivism
    71, 72–3
necropolitics 133, 185
  see also death
negativity 89, 94, 104, 199,
    204, 224–5, 239
Neimanis, Astrida 86, 127,
    131
neo-colonialism 46, 187
  and capitalism 57–8, 70,
    175, 230, 231, 233–4
neo-humanism 38, 61, 62
neoliberal feminism 43–54,
    165, 168
  and class equality 51, 52,
    53
  and feminist solidarity 46,
    49
  and individualism 45–6,
    50, 51–2
  and patriarchy 49, 53–4
  and power 45–6, 50
  and United States 47, 49
  and wellness industry
    46–7, 52
neoliberalism 45–6, 48, 49,
    62, 85, 166
  see also capitalism
neo-socialist feminism 43–4,
    54–61
neural function 114–15
Nietzsche, Friedrich 20, 120
non-human rights 82–3
non-humans
  and bodies 112, 155

feminism
  and ecofeminism 75,
    80–4, 154
  and posthuman feminism
    62, 65–6, 67, 77
  human/non-human
    relationships 62, 194,
    207–8
  and literary and creative
    writing 215, 217
  and materialism 110, 125,
    126–7
  and sexuality 186, 199,
    207–8
  and technoscience 150,
    154, 157, 159, 167
  zoe 12, 71, 80–4, 125,
    126–7, 143, 154, 159
notions, common 119
not-One 190–3
  and multiplicity 126, 177

'O superman!' song
    (Anderson) 171
Odysseus 19–20
Oncomouse 214
Oneness 19, 92
ontology
  material process 112, 114,
    121, 125, 133, 137
  racialized 34, 36–7, 131,
    132
  relational 65, 157, 174,
    180, 200
  and ecofeminism 94, 98
  and materialism 135,
    137
oppression 13, 89, 116–17
  and colonialism 91, 95
  and patriarchy 30, 32, 34,
    228
  and race issues 132, 225,
    226
  of women 32, 72, 222

Ortner, Sherry B. 72
other/otherness 18–19, 23, 75, 207–8, 218
'Our Bodies Are Not Terra Nullius' artwork (Konsmo and Pacheco) 182–3
ownership, female 27, 244n11
Oxford school of transhumanism 64

Paltrow, Gwyneth 46, 47
Parasite (Joon-ho), film 56
parenthood 51, 165, 176
Parikka, Jussi 130
Parisi, Luciana 109, 189, 202
Parr, Adrian 56–7
passion 217
patriarchy 63, 90
  and dehumanization 37, 71, 83, 97, 207–8
  and feminism
    and cyberfeminism 145, 146–8
    and ecofeminism 74, 76
    and liberal feminism 24, 25
    and neoliberal feminism 49, 53–4
    and socialist feminism 31, 32, 33–4
  and gender systems 37, 155, 167, 172, 182, 188
  and humanism 21, 63
  and inequality 70–4, 75
  and kinship 164, 167
  and LGBTQ+ 73–4, 155–6, 184, 187, 201
  and literary and creative writing 219, 221–2
  and nature-culture 73–4, 76
  and oppression 30, 32, 34, 228
  and power 19, 197
  and race issues 187, 228–9
  and sexuality 187, 197, 201
    binary system 37, 155, 167, 172, 182, 188
    and heterosexuality 73–4, 155–6, 184, 201, 202
    and species supremacy/natural order 19, 70–4, 97
    and technoscience 155–6, 157, 164, 167, 235
    and utopianism 221–2, 223
    and women's health 155–6, 157
  see also capitalism; colonialism; race issues
Pelosi, Nancy 26–7
perspectivism 65, 98, 133
  and Indigenous people/culture 92, 93–4, 134
  see also materialism; relationality
Pevere, Margherita 195
Piccinini, Patricia 207–8
Piercy, Marge 219
Pietá imagery 103, 208
pink 193
placenta politics 170–4
planetary 8, 22, 25, 57, 67, 102–3, 125–8
  extra planetary 211–12, 219, 232–4
  planetary humanism 36, 224
Plumwood, Val 79, 80, 91, 92, 235
polis 71, 73–4
politicians, female 26
politics, gestational 170–4

Index

politics, left-wing 34, 54, 87, 89–90
politics, right-wing 48, 168
populism 48, 237
pollution 125, 240
polysexuality 191, 202
popular culture 149–51, 152
population growth 51, 169
positivity 203–6, 224–5, 236
Post Human exhibition 1, 150
post-anthropocentrism 61, 68–104, 138, 201
see also ecofeminism
postcolonial feminism 35, 49, 95
postcolonialism
  and ecofeminism 32, 79, 84, 86, 93, 95
  and environment 84, 86
  and humanism 4, 20, 32, 35, 49
  and Indigenous people/culture 86, 218
  and literary and creative writing 218, 229
post-constructivism 118, 137, 189–90, 215
post-foundational qualitative inquiry methods 118
posthuman convergence 3–8, 68, 112, 234
  and environment 86, 88, 95, 99, 215, 227, 234
  and feminism 30, 41–2
    and ecofeminism 80, 84, 91–2, 99, 101, 103, 154
    and posthuman feminism 67, 141, 216, 237, 239
  and literary and creative writing 215, 218, 230
  and power 43, 57, 132, 148
  and race issues 85, 86, 95, 132, 227
  and sexuality 180, 193
  and technoscience 143–4, 154, 162–3, 233, 234
posthuman feminism 9–14, 221–3, 237–9
  and capitalism 6–8, 63, 65–7
  and difference 62, 67
  and environment 65, 66, 83–4, 92, 101, 125–6, 194–5
  and 'Man'/'Man of Reason' 67, 211
  and materialism 107–8, 125–6, 137, 144, 192
  and sexuality 194, 200
  and nature-culture 97, 108–9, 144
    and de-naturalization 143, 144, 175
    and re-naturalization 77, 143, 144
  and non-humans 62, 65–6, 67, 77
  and posthuman convergence 67, 141, 216, 237, 239
  and posthuman feminist subjectivity 40, 90, 94, 131, 149
  and re-naturalization 77, 143, 144
  and sexuality 184–5, 188, 192–3, 197–8, 200
  and materialism 194, 200
  and technoscience 66, 108, 141–5
posthumanism 63–4, 83, 98
  Black posthumanism 219, 224–9
  critical feminist posthumanism 6–7, 65, 138, 145, 158

posthumanism (*cont.*)
  and materialism 127, 135, 136
  posthuman scholarship 7, 212–16
  and technoscience 163, 219
Posthumanities 96
  feminist Posthumanities 129, 230
postmodernism 62–3, 109, 150
post-naturalism 137, 152, 201
  see also de-naturalization
post-secularism 86–90
poststructuralism 25, 93, 100
  and materialism 108, 110, 117, 188
potentia 43, 81, 115, 138, 176, 182, 201
  see also embeddedness
potestas 43, 81, 115, 138, 201
poverty 33, 46, 99, 103
Povinelli, Elizabeth 128
power 4, 143, 221
  empowerment 176, 236
    and Afrofuturism 225–6, 227
    and liberal feminism 24, 45–6
  and sexuality 179, 181, 196, 209
  and environment 81, 130
  and feminism 21, 76
    and liberal feminism 24, 26–8, 45–6
    and neoliberal feminism 45–6, 50
  and materialism 111–12, 115–16, 117, 118, 130, 132, 138
  and patriarchy 19, 197
  and posthuman convergence 43, 57, 132, 148
  and *potentia* 43, 81, 115, 138, 176, 182, 201
  and *potestas* 43, 81, 115, 138, 201
  and race issues 76, 132
Power of the Gender Equality Index 244n7
praxis 95, 104, 205
  and affirmation ethics 103, 118, 182, 224, 237–8, 239, 241
  and race issues 224, 226
Preciado, Beatriz 184
Preciado, Paul 59, 159
pre-determination 200
pregnancy 170–4, 222
presidents/prime ministers, female 26–7
proletariat 31, 57, 130
prostitution 166–7, 223
psychoanalysis 107, 109, 191, 203–4, 205
punk 145–7, 148
  see also cyberpunk
Pussy Riot 148

queer theory 37, 160–1, 186, 197, 198, 201, 220, 249n21

race issues 5
  and capitalism 57–8, 95–6, 187, 227
  and colonialism 35, 91, 182–3, 217
    and Afrofuturism 225, 227, 228
    capitalism 95–6, 227
  and dehumanization 24, 37
  and environment 84–6, 99–100, 240

and climate change 85–6, 93, 98–9
and materialism 127, 129, 130, 133–4
and feminism 21, 27, 32
anti-racist feminism 21, 23
and Black posthumanism 219, 224–9
and ecofeminism 69–70, 78, 79, 91, 98, 99
and gender 85–6, 182–3, 187
and hierarchies 11, 70–4, 75, 78, 79, 92, 94
and humanism 21, 25, 34–8, 224
and Indigenous people/culture 69–70, 98, 99, 134, 182–3
and literary and creative writing 217, 219
and materialism 127, 129, 130, 131–4
and mineral extraction 85, 132
and oppression 132, 225, 226
and patriarchy 187, 228–9
and posthuman convergence 85, 86, 95, 132, 227
and power 76, 132
and praxis 224, 226
and resilience 86, 95, 133
and technoscience 130, 155–6, 169–70, 219, 228
and violence 37, 182–3
see also anti-racism; environmental racism
racialized ontology 34, 36–7, 131, 132

racial/racialized capitalism 57–8, 187, 227
rape culture 147, 223
rationality 50
  instrumental 86, 137
  scientific 20, 22, 35, 76, 78, 87
Rees-Jones, Deryn 177
regeneration 228, 229
relationality 144
  relational ethics 9, 67, 80, 84, 176, 191
  relational ontology 65, 157, 174, 180, 200
  and ecofeminism 94, 98
  and materialism 135, 137
  and sexuality 200–1, 205
relationships, human/non-human 194, 207–8
re-materialization 40, 112, 219
  and sexuality 193, 202
  and technoscience 142, 144, 149, 152, 167–70
re-naturalization ch 4, 11, 100, 107–39
  and de-naturalization 101, 153–4, 158–60, 175
  and feminism
    and ecofeminism 101, 102, 103, 153, 175
    and posthuman feminism 77, 143, 144
    and materialism 119, 122, 136, 175
    and nature-culture 101, 102, 103, 153, 175
    and Spinozism 119, 122
    and technoscience 141, 152, 153–4, 158–60, 165, 175
Repo, Jemima 50

reproduction/fertility
  and biopolitics 169, 173–4
  and capitalism 50–4, 158–9, 165, 169–70
  and ecofeminism 72–3, 95
  and family structure 167, 168–9, 176
  and gender 166, 184, 185, 190
  and IVF 159–60, 164, 165
  and nature-culture 72–3, 152
  and sexuality 152, 185, 190
  and technoscience 152, 170–4, 175
    and capitalism 165, 166–7
    and gender 166, 185, 190
    and human labour 60, 165–6
    and kinship 164–6, 176
    and reproductive technology 52–4, 158–60, 164–6, 167–8
    and utopianism 222, 223
resilience 86, 92, 95, 133
responsibility, sense of 24, 50, 69, 104, 241
rhizomic 123, 192, 203
Rich, Adrienne 43, 116, 196
Rijneveld, Marieke Lucas 81
Roberts, Celia 128
Robinson, Mary 99, 245n10
Rose, Deborah Bird 92–3, 133–4, 180
Rottenberg, Catherine 46, 53
Rovelli, Carlo 111, 121
Rowbotham, Sheila 31–2
Roy, Deboleena 157
Rubin, Gayle 72–3, 197
Russ, Joanna 211

Sackville-West, Vita 178–9, 210
Sandberg, Sheryl 45
Sander, Helke 31
Sarley, Stephanie 194
Schrader, Astrid 127
science *see* technoscience
Science, Technology, Engineering and Mathematics (STEM) 27
science fiction 218–19, 221, 228, 230, 231
  see also cyberpunk, speculative genre
scientism 78
selfish gene 123–4
Serres, Michel 21–2, 102
'sex wars' 166, 248n11
sex-gender distinction 177, 187, 188–90, 200
'sex-race-species' system of domination 77–8
sexuality 12, 38–40, 177–210
  and affirmation/affirmation ethics 205, 206, 208
  and art 181, 192, 194–5
  and becoming 183–4, 189, 192, 198, 205
  and capitalism 184, 193, 204
  and care ethics 182, 207–8
  and complexity 177, 188, 193, 198, 199, 206
  and decolonialism 182, 186–7
  and difference 72, 146, 177, 198, 201, 203
  and multiplicity 190, 192
  and diversity 199, 202
  and embodiment 191, 200–1
  and empowerment 179, 181, 196, 209

and eroticism 179, 181, 196
and ethics 182, 191, 205, 206, 207–8
and Eurocentrism 186, 187–8
and experimentation 182, 185, 193, 199
and femininity 192, 193, 197–8
and feminism
  and ecofeminism 78, 79, 181, 202
  and feminist new-materialism 184, 185, 189, 198
  and posthuman feminism 184–5, 188, 192–3, 194, 197–8, 200
  and socialist feminism 31
and flowing 190, 192, 193, 195, 204, 205–6
and freedom 182, 196
and heterosexuality 184, 186
  and patriarchy 73–4, 155–6, 184, 201, 202
and human/non-human relationships 194, 207–8
and Indigenous people/culture 180–3, 186–8
and individualism 191, 204, 206
and interdependence 180, 195
and intersectionality 39, 161–2, 182
and joy 204–5, 208
and LGBTQ+ 187, 192, 193, 195–7, 201
  and compulsory heterosexuality 73–4, 155–6, 184, 187, 201

and life force 190, 191, 196
and love/passion 179–80, 181, 182, 206–8, 210
and materialism 178
  and elemental feminist materialism 192, 194–5
  and new-materialist feminism 184, 185, 189, 198, 204
  and posthuman feminism 194, 200
  and re-materialization 193, 202
  vital materialism 181, 183, 191, 199–200, 206
and multiplicity 177, 183, 191, 198, 199–200, 206, 209, 220–1
  and difference 190, 192–3
  not-One 126, 177, 190–3
  and sexuate matter 11, 191, 193, 197, 200–1, 206, 208–9
and naturalization 182, 186, 201
and non-humans 186, 199, 207–8
and patriarchy 187, 197, 201
  binary system 37, 155, 167, 172, 182, 188
  and heterosexuality 73–4, 155–6, 184, 201, 202
and polysexuality 191, 202
and posthuman convergence 180, 193
and power
  empowerment 179, 181, 196, 209
  potentia 182, 201

sexuality (*cont.*)
　and relationality 200–1, 205
　and re-materialization 193, 202
　and reproduction/fertility 152, 185, 190
　and sexuate matter 200–1
　　and gender 183–4, 186, 188–9
　　and multiplicity 11, 191, 193, 197, 200–1, 206, 208–9
　　and vitality of matter 182, 184, 205, 206
　and social constructivism 184, 188, 189, 201
　and technoscience 192, 195, 202, 207–8
　and territorialization 198, 203, 209, 232
　and transversality 209
　　and desire 191, 199–203, 205
　　and gender 189, 190–1
　and virtuality 197, 198, 199, 200, 201, 203, 205, 209
　and Western culture 186, 187–8
　and *zoe*-geo-techno-mediated relations 184, 199, 206
　see also desire; gender; LGBTQ+
Sharp, Hasana 204
Shelley, Mary 218
shimmering 180–3
Shiva, Vandana 32, 58, 76, 85, 167
Singularity 61, 65
sleep economy 47
Smelik, Anneke and Lykke, Nina 153

social and economic equality 30, 32–3, 44, 54, 57, 237
social contract theory 71
social movements 21
social constructivism 11, 100–1, 133
　and ecofeminism 74, 76, 86, 88, 98
　and nature-culture 71, 72–3
　and sexuality 184, 188, 189, 201
　and technoscience 152, 155, 158
socialism 21, 30, 32
socialist feminism 6, 30–4, 60, 89–90
socialist humanism 30–4
socio-metrics 50, 51
Solanas, Valerie 221
solidarity, feminist 33, 46, 49, 153, 182
solidarity, post-human 229
somatechnics 160, 163, 201
space exploration 22, 229–35, 250n6
species hierarchies 81, 94
species supremacy/natural order 19, 70–4, 97
species-ism 69, 70, 77
spectacle 226
speculative feminism 212
speculative genre, feminist 13, 212, 213, 216–21, 233
Spinoza, Benedict de 11, 114, 118–22, 204
　critical Spinozism 121–2
spirituality 86–90, 103, 226
Spivak, Gayatri Chakravorty 35, 38, 229
Squier, Susan Merrill 124, 167

standpoint theory 116–17
Starhawk 87
Stein, Gertrude 17, 25
Stent, Prue 195
Sterling, Bruce 63
Stimpson, Catharine 118
Strathern, Marilyn 58–9, 165
Stryker, Susan 39, 88, 163
Subjective Factor (Sander), film 31
subjectivity 6, 80, 154, 193
suffering 41, 223, 226
Sullivan, Nikki 163
Sundberg, Juanita 96
surrogacy 53–4, 165–7, 169, 176
surveillance capitalism 55, 57
symbiogenesis 122–3
symbiosis 125, 135, 142, 195
syndemic 103, 174, 240

TallBear, Kim 134, 157–8, 186
technobodies *see* biology; bodies; technoscience
technofeminism 87, 88, 143, 153–4, 180
technoscience 3–4, 12, 62–3, 140–76, 238–9
  and art 152, 195
  and biology 144, 152–3, 164–6
  and de-naturalization 141, 158–60, 164, 201, 203
  and capitalism 10, 56, 57–60, 229–31, 234
    cognitive capitalism 58–60, 66, 143, 165, 169–70
  and environment 57, 100
  and inequality 57–8, 175
  and LGBTQ+ 40, 59
  and reproduction/fertility 50–4, 158–9, 165, 169–70, 175
  and COVID-19 4, 174
  and de-naturalization 59, 136, 151–4, 162
  and biology 141, 158–60, 164, 201, 203
  and embodiment 140, 160–1, 163, 167
  and environment 42, 88, 89, 95, 101, 129–31, 234
  and capitalism 57, 100
  and experimentation 142, 145, 151, 170, 175
  and feminism 52–4, 55
  and ecofeminism 80–4, 97–9, 143, 153–4, 175, 214–15
  and Gaga feminism 149, 150
  and posthuman feminism 66, 108, 141–5
  and technofeminism 87, 143, 153–4
  and freedom 140, 192
  and gender 140–76, 192
  and gender roles 149, 150
  and reproduction/fertility 166, 184, 185, 190
  and space exploration 232–3, 234–5
  and human labour 130, 169–70
  and reproductive technology 60, 165–6
  and humanism 20–1, 42, 61, 62, 64–5
  and inequality 40, 57–8, 155–6, 165–6, 175
  and intersectionality 42, 91–2, 144, 156–7, 161–2, 163

technoscience (*cont.*)
  and kinship 159, 164–7, 168–9, 176
  and LGBTQ+ 40, 88, 155, 157, 160–2, 164–7
  and capitalism 40, 59
  and materialism 112, 126, 129–31, 143, 172, 175
  and de-materialization 59, 112, 149
  feminist new-materialism 12, 157
  and transversality 111, 131–2, 138, 191
  vital materialism 111, 143
  and *zoe*-geo-techno-mediated relations 97–8, 125, 126–7, 138, 139, 219
  and non-humans 150, 154, 157, 159, 167
  and patriarchy 155–6, 157, 164, 167, 235
  and posthuman convergence 143–4, 154, 162–3, 233, 234
  and posthumanism 163, 219
  and race issues 130, 155–6, 169–70, 219, 228
  and re-materialization 142, 144, 149, 152, 167–70
  and re-naturalization 141, 152, 153–4, 158–60, 165, 175
  and reproduction/fertility 152, 170–4, 175
    and capitalism 50–4, 158–9, 165, 166–7, 169–70, 175
    and family structure 167, 168–9, 176
    and gender 166, 185, 190
    and human labour 60, 165–6
    and IVF 159–60, 164, 165
    and kinship 164–6, 176
    and utopianism 222, 223
  and sexuality 192, 195, 202–3, 207–8
  and space exploration 230–2, 234–5
  and territorialization 142, 143, 144, 147
  and transhumanism 61, 62, 64–5
  and transversality 111, 131–2, 138, 153, 191
  and utopianism 222, 223
  and virtuality 221, 228
  and vitality of matter 142, 143, 158, 159
  and women 155, 166, 169
technoscience studies, feminist 151–3, 156–7, 158–62, 175
techno-totalitarianism 148
temporality 100, 149, 206, 218, 225–6, 227
  virtual past 14, 238
Tereshkova, Valentina 232
Terra Nullius 91
Terranova, Tiziana 153
territorialization 232
  and sexuality 198, 203, 209, 232
  and technoscience 142, 143, 144, 147
  see also capitalism; earth; flows
Thunberg, Greta 46–7
Tometi, Opal 33
tools 3, 13, 212, 237
trans-corporeality 135–7, 171, 172, 174

transdisciplinarity 118, 130, 215
transfeminism 39, 59, 160–2, 184, 193, 199, 202
transgender 163
transgenic creatures 207–8, 214
transgression 195–8
transhumanism 44, 61–6, 133
transnationality
  and capitalism 128, 159, 168
  and environmental justice 80, 83, 86, 93, 104
transpositions 123, 237
transsexuality 191, 202
trans-species 80, 208, 219
transversality 9, 219
  and assemblages/ heterogeneous alliances 134–7, 153, 239
  and ecofeminism 77–9, 88, 103–4
  and environment 89, 125–6
  and materialism 108–9, 111, 131–2, 138, 191
  and sexuality 209
    and desire 191, 199–203, 205
    and gender 189, 190–1
  and technoscience 89, 111, 131–2, 138, 153, 191
Trump, Donald 231
Tsing, Anna 90, 135, 214–15
Tuana, Nancy 77, 86, 132, 134
twentieth century feminism 24–5
two/three cultures 108, 195

Ulstein, Gry 221
United States 47, 49, 120, 147, 231–2

universal rights *see* animals; human rights
universalism
  and ecofeminism 84, 98
  and humanism 19, 23, 25, 34, 82
utopianism 221–3, 227, 228

van der Tuin, Iris 66
van der Waal, Rodante 170
violence 229
  and colonialism 91, 182–3
  and inequality 37, 41
  and race issues 37, 182–3
  and women 99, 147, 182–3, 223
'Violence on the Land' (VLVB) project 100, 182
virtuality
  and sex/sexuality 197, 198, 199, 200, 201, 203, 205, 209
  and technoscience 221, 228
  virtual past 14, 238
  virtual possibilities 89, 95, 140, 191, 203, 206, 209
  virtual potential 3, 137
  virtual ways of becoming 137, 157, 183, 202, 225, 238
visibility/invisibility 50, 57
Visible Human Project 56, 244n9
vital materialism 191
  and re-naturalization 119, 136
  and sexuality 181, 183, 191, 199–200, 206
  and technoscience 111, 143
vitality of matter 56, 89, 111, 125, 126, 128, 137
  and sexuate matter 182, 184, 205, 206

vitality of matter (*cont.*)
  and technoscience 142, 143, 158, 159
Vitruvian Man 22, 39, 162, 232
Viveiros de Castro, Eduardo 65, 93, 94–5, 133
VNS Matrix 145, 148
von der Leyen, Ursula 26

Waidner, Isabel 217
Waldby, Catherine 56, 60, 169
Walker, Alice 196
war 20, 21, 22, 49, 174
Watchmen series 224
water 127–8, 192, 195
wealth, female 27, 50–1, 244n11
'wealth supremacists' 45
Weheliye, Alexander 226
Weinbaum, Alys Eve 169
weird, new 221
welfare services 47–8
well-being 33, 46–8, 79–80, 155
wellness industry 46–7, 52
Westcott, Sarah 68
Winfrey, Oprah 2
Winterson, Jeanette 218
Wittig, Monique 197
womanism 196
woman-nature 69, 75, 99
women
  Black and Indigenous women 37, 51, 86, 100, 169, 226, 227
  'nasty women' 147, 247n3
  non-conforming women 219–20
  oppression of 32, 72, 222
  pregnant women 170–4
  violence against 99, 147, 182–3, 223
  white, middle-class women 25, 51, 52, 53, 169
women's bodies 1–2, 155, 166
women's health 155–6, 157, 247n5
women's labour/work 32, 99, 169
women's rights 23–4
see also bodies; disability/disability studies; race issues; reproduction/fertility
women's health movement 155–6, 247n5
Woolf, Virginia 12, 27, 147, 178–9, 192, 210
World Inequality Report 30
World War II 20, 22
writing, feminist 211–12
writing, literary and creative
  and affect 216, 217
  and environment 215, 217
  and fantasy 221, 229
  and feminist speculative genre 13, 212, 213, 216–21, 233
  and monsters 218–19, 220, 221
  and non-humans 215, 217
  and patriarchy 219, 221–2
  and postcolonialism 218, 229
  and posthuman convergence 215, 218, 230
  and race issues 217, 219
  science fiction 218–19, 221, 228, 230, 231
  and *zoe*-geo-techno-mediated relations 219, 221
Wynter, Sylvia 35, 36–7

Xenofeminism 51, 148, 154, 223
xenophobia 48–9, 174

Yang, Lu 192
yearning 226, 229
Yolngu people 180
Young-Bruehl, Elizabeth 208, 210
Yusoff, Kathryn 127, 129, 132

zoe 12, 71, 80–4, 143, 159, 199
  and ecofeminism 80–4, 97–9, 154
  and materialism 125, 126–7
  see also immanence; life force and sexuality; non-humans
zoe-geo-techno-mediated relations 12, 97–8, 100–2, 126, 131
  and affirmative ethics 239
  and bodies 142, 143
  and ecofeminism 97–9, 154
  geo 12, 128–9, 138, 220
  and interdependence 97
  and literary and creative writing 219, 221
  and materialism 97–8, 125, 126–7, 138, 139, 219
  and sexuality 184, 199, 206